RESPOND

To the User of This Book

This book is self-contained, and one copy will provide you with sufficient material to carry out the many program suggestions it offers. It is suggested, however, that each youth group will find it helpful to purchase three or four copies so that several persons may use them in planning and presenting the programs.

The Editors

RESPOND

VOLUME 1

A RESOURCE BOOK
FOR YOUTH MINISTRY

KEITH L. IGNATIUS

JUDSON PRESS,® VALLEY FORGE

Respond, Volume 1

Copyright © 1971
Judson Press
Valley Forge, Pa. 19481

Sixth Printing, 1977

Bible quotations used in this volume are from:
The New English Bible. © The Delegates of the Oxford University Press and The Syndics of the Cambridge University Press 1961, 1970.

The New Testament in Modern English. Copyright © J. B. Phillips 1958. Used by permission of The Macmillan Company and Geoffrey Bles, Ltd.

The New Testament in Today's English Version. Copyright © American Bible Society 1966.

International Standard Book No. 0-8170-0542-0
Library of Congress Catalog Card No. 77-159050

The name JUDSON PRESS is registered as a trademark in the U.S. Patent Office.

Printed in the U.S.A.

Using This Book

Pick it up!
    Hold it!
        Love it!
    See it as a beautiful example of a youth ministry resource and then—

We Suggest You Do This!

Browse through the book to see what's hidden behind its innocent look. Note the various sections. Read a couple of the plans. Get a feel of what's here and what may have some possibilities for your group. Discover the sensation of gripping an extensive compilation of action and study resources, leadership helps and retreat models that have never been produced before. Realize, however, that —

It's Not the Gospel.

Respond is a book of suggestions. Don't be afraid to modify, tear out, change, or discard any of the material that is of no value to your group. (The editor will never know.) But don't throw away some stuff that you may use later — like twelve months from now.

Stay with It!

Browse through the book several times. Get to know it inside out. And when the moment comes that your group has an idea it wants to explore, but no resources, you can say, "Hey, I've got just the thing!" Flip to the appropriate page and surprise the "living daylights" out of them.

When Using the Suggested Articles:

1. *Read* through the session plans in order to get an idea of what the session is about.

2. *Reread* the objective or purpose. Restate it in your own words. Then ask: Does it fit the group? How should it be changed? What other appropriate experiences does it enable you to recall?

3. *Reread* the procedures. How do they fit the needs of your group — size, temperament, amount of session time, setting, room size, equipment, leadership, etc.?

4. *Recheck* the Pre-session Plans. Do you have enough time to get ready for the session? Necessary resources? Leadership?

5. If you've got the answer to all those questions, get on with it and have a successful experience.

ONE FINAL COMMENT

Respond took a lot of hard work by a lot of people to produce. Our reasons for doing the book are:
1. Hopefully, it will make your work in youth ministry a little easier;
2. it will make you smile
    more often
    and not worry so much
    about where you are in youth ministry;
3. and that will help your group and the gospel get together
    more often and more intimately.

Good luck,
Good reading, and
A Great Ministry!
    — From the people
      of *Respond*

Contents

Section 1
Resources for Study and Action

It's a Puzzlement—Problems at Home

by Gary W. Harris

IT'S A PUZZLEMENT

Empathize, if you can, with the King of Siam (from the motion picture "The King and I") as he exclaims, with hands thrown up in the air, "It's a puzzlement!" If adults find so many things "nearly so" or "nearly not," so many evidences of change (and I am sure they do), think of how teens feel about their world. No longer children, they are not yet on their own either. Life in the home is quite often anything but a bed of roses. Members of each age group feel as though they are bearing the brunt of all criticism of our rapidly changing world.

"When I was your age . . ." **"You were never my age . . ."** There is really a great deal of truth in the youth's alleged response to the parent who said, "When I was your age . . ." "You ain't never gonna be my age!" The adolescent world of the parent was totally different from the world known to today's adolescent. Yet, there is a common meeting ground, and it is discovered whenever the communication gap is bridged. When experiences are shared and values are considered, it is possible to walk together on that ground.

PURPOSE

This program is designed as an experience for youth and their parents in which they can scrutinize each other's worlds, examine each other's values, and understand each other's idiosyncrasies. Sounds like a big order? So? We can at least try. And in trying perhaps improve problems at home.

PREPLANNING

The following experiences are for the planning team to help them plan better.

It is important that a small group of people spend some time together in preparation for the program. In addition to the youth advisors, both youth and parents should be represented. Have a supply of magazines, scissors, paste, marking pens, newsprint, a large sheet of poster board (20" x 30" or 24" x 36"), pencils and paper.

Have each person find two pictures from the magazines which either suggest communication (or lack of it) between youth and adults, or depict a variance from or a rebellion against values held by the other generation.

Take time to allow each person to share at least one of the pictures he has chosen with those present. Be sure to consider the following areas:

1. What attracted you to this particular picture?

2. To what specific parent/teen problem does it refer?

3. Can you put yourself in the place of one of the persons in your picture? Explain.

4. Do you know of a situation like the one pictured? Talk about it.

You will discover that your discussion has suggested a number of problems which exist between teenagers and their parents. These problems and others should be listed on the newsprint. Brainstorm. Do not spend a large amount of time discussing the problems. This is to be done in the program session itself. You are talking about the problems primarily to convince each

Picture Collage

other that a perfect, harmonious parent/youth relationship cannot be assumed and that problems of communication do indeed exist.

Now, arrange all of the pictures in montage fashion on the poster board. When all have been pasted securely, someone should create a large jigsaw puzzle by outlining each piece with a marking pen and then cutting out the entire puzzle in preparation for use in the forthcoming session.

Film Interview

If possible, you ought to preview the film, "The Interview," suggested for use in the program. "The Interview" deals with the problems of communication. A rather straight, typical radio-TV announcer and Shorty Petterstein, a jazz musician he is interviewing, illustrate the ways we fail to give and receive meanings and messages. Although it lasts only five minutes, this animated color film is, in its own way, an unmistakeable commentary which will be extremely useful in this and other similar programs. ("The Interview" is available on a rental basis for $10 from Mass Media Ministries. See Resource Section for address.)

HAVE WORK FOR MEMBERS OF PLANNING GROUP

Send the youth home with a cassette or tape recorder to record sounds which typify their world (e.g., school bell, noisy halls, crowd at athletic event, dance, rock music, etc.). Give the adults a similar assignment. Their recording will include such sounds as a factory whistle or time clock, typewriters or computers in operation, expressway traffic, kitchen sounds, appropriate music, etc.

Life's Sounds

Pictures and/or slides should also be collected by youth and adults. Other appropriate posters and signs will be helpful, too. Youth may wish to secure incense and strobe candles as a way of demonstrating their generation's interest in involving all the senses.

PREPARING THE MEETING ROOM

Plan to have a room large enough for the youth to prepare and decorate one side and the parents the other. The pictures, posters, etc., should be arranged in an attractive fashion to provide the visual means of viewing each other's world. The cassettes or tape recorders should be set up and ready to play as the members arrive.

On the wall at one end of the room, arrange the puzzle pieces at random and number each piece. Arrange chairs in a large circle in the middle of the room or plan to sit on the floor.

PROGRAM SESSION

1. As members arrive, hand each one a piece of paper and a pencil. Ask them to experience the two worlds, listening, observing, sharing, etc. Inform them that they are to examine the puzzle pieces, number their paper to correspond with the number of pieces, write the first word that comes to mind as they view each piece, and then concentrate on the one which strikes them the most and write down some of their thoughts. (If your group is such that some parents and youth may not know each other you will want to provide name tags as well.)

2. Call the group together and show the film, "The Interview." A very brief introduction will help the viewers to "tune in" at the very beginning of the film. At the conclusion, allow for a short period of discussion in which you will want the viewers to merely identify those instances in which Shorty or the radio-TV announcer talked past each other. Try not to let the group get down in a discussion over specific details of the interview.

Interview

3. Using the initial experience and the film as background you will now want to turn to a discussion of a more specific nature. You might want to use the fishbowl approach. Have the youth occupy chairs in an inner circle with their parents in an outer, concentric circle. The parents observe as the youth speak about the pictures they have chosen from the puzzle. (See discussion questions in preplanning section.) When you feel there has been enough time for the teenagers to share their pictures, have them turn to the question, "What would you identify as the one or two greatest problems of parents today?" Then reverse the circles.

Fishbowl

4. The parents' first task is to react to what happened as the youth shared. You will want them to respond to such questions as: How did you feel about not being able to enter into the discussion with your teenagers?

What did you learn about the ways youth today view some of the same things you see as well? Were you able to detect differences in values from those you hold? What would you identify as the one or two greatest problems of youth today? The second task for the parents is

Difference Between Youth/Adults

to share some of the pictures they have chosen, although you may find that they will naturally share as they respond to the observations during the first half of this experience.

5. Now merge the two circles. Divide a sheet of newsprint in half and brainstorm the problems brought out in the discussion, listing the problems of the youth on one side and the problems of parents on the other. When the two lists have been drawn, ask the group to identify similar problems. List these on another piece of newsprint. Then, on another sheet, list those problems which appear to be irreconcilable.

6. Ask members of the group to team up in pairs — one youth and one adult. Have them spend no more than three to five minutes talking about one of these irreconcilable problems.

7. In these same pairs, instruct those present that they are now to share in a silent experience. One person will close his eyes (or wear a blind-fold). The other person will take him on a walk around the building for approximately ten minutes. In silence the person who is leading is to provide as many experiences as possible for the other. Use stairs. Go from dark rooms to lighted rooms. Encourage the person to touch things as you go. After ten minutes switch places. When the time is up, return to the meeting room but remain in pairs discussing your experience. When all have returned, call the entire group together to reflect on the experience. You may also want to handle this sharing in fishbowl fashion, first having those who were the first followers in the center circle. This exercise is sometimes called a

"trust walk," for it helps to explore this area of relationships. This exercise will be particularly meaningful for youth and their parents. It may have been impossible for the two to really talk with each other up to this point, but after sharing this kind of experience there should be a great deal to talk about in terms of trusting and caring for one another, relating to each other.

8. A variation on these last two steps would be to have a youth team up with his own parent. The dynamics in this relationship are even greater than those between different youth and parents. Although this is the hoped-for result of this program, you must decide whether to program this or allow it to happen on its own back in the home.

9. An effective way to begin concluding the session would be to share some refreshments and informal talk together. It might also be good to suggest that members of the group put together the pieces of the puzzle to form the whole: adults and teens in it together, struggling, experiencing, caring.

10. Group in a circle. Pray together the following prayer:
Our Father (whose title of Father implies a family relationship with us), hear us now as you've heard this evening.
Pray:
Help us . . . (each person verbally complete the sentence. Everyone will be speaking at the same time.)
We thank you . . .
We shall try . . .

A series of questions, feelings, and impressions about "why" youth are and "who" adults are.

Freak Out—Communicate with Dad!

YOUTH WONDER...

"Why do parents feel that youth have to accept what they say as always being right?"

"Do you really try to understand your young people — or just push your ideas on them?"
"Parents talk to us for hours but when you try to talk to them, they often turn their backs."

"Why do parents try to dictate to their children on matters of clothing, music, movies, etc.?"

"Why do things that are important to parents have to be important to their kids?"

"Why do we have to do things as a family?"

"Why do they always want to know where I am and what I am doing every moment?"

PARENTS ASK...

"It seems like the only time my child is happy is when he's getting his own way or stirring up trouble with the rest of the family."

"Why do kids get so upset about sharing some of their world with us? We'd like to know some of the things they do, places they go — not out of distrust, but out of curiosity and love."

"How can parents ask questions without incurring youth resentment?"

"What do you feel is the real source of disrespect for parents?"

"Why do our kids think we're so materialistic when they've a billion dollar record business, and a whole line of youth products?"

A PASTOR COMMENTS...

"After a youth/parent meeting I question if a generation gap really does exist or whether youth feel compelled to live out the headlines. After all, it is not very 'in' to have a good relationship with your parents.

"There is an obvious lack of respect for each other as communication equals. Rather than trying to communicate, each side is trying to win. They seem more interested in making 'scoring points' against each other than in scoring together."

MAKE SOME BUTTONS

"I often talk to people over 30!"
"Trust someone over/under 30 today!"
"My parents really like me . . . I like them."
"Freak out — communicate with Dad!"
"Listen, your children can teach you . . ."
"I listen a lot."

PURPOSE

This session is designed for a beginning at some parent-youth communications, but just a beginning. So don't expect too much unless you're willing to continue the talks in the privacy of your own home.

PRESESSION PLANNING

*Invitations to parents of youth.
*Simple meal, planned and prepared by youth. Served family style.
*Speaker for the after-meal discussion should be someone respected by youth and their parents

and capable of speaking on the subject of communication between youth and adults.

*Narrator for the quotes.

*Group of parents to prepare the closing worship.

PROCESS

During the meal youth become "parents" and parents become "youth." In other words, the youth pretend to be "adults/parents." They take the initiative in the conversations, etc. Adults/parents pretend to be youth. (It's a reversal of real life situation.) This will give the parents a chance to be "young" again and for youth to "grow up" a little.

At some point a narrator interrupts the table conversation. He reads one of the youth quotes from the opening of this section and invites the "pretend parents" to discuss it with their pretend youth. After 2-3 minutes he reads a parent quote and has the "pretend youth" discuss it with their "parents." This alternative process continues until discussion begins to become routine. The narrator concludes this aspect of the session by reading the pastor's quote and allows for full discussion.

After the meal retire to a comfortable room where the pretend roles are dropped. Spend 5-10 minutes talking about the experience. What kind of answers were "you" able to give in your pretend role? How did you feel about the experience? What one thing did you learn about the gap in adult-youth communications?

At this point, if it has been possible to arrange, have the group talk with your guest leader about communication and some of the ways for improving the "talk-lines" between youth and their parents.

Conclude with a brief worship experience that has been preplanned by the parents.

A plea to youth and their parents.

For Christ's Sake, Talk!

The "Generation/Communication Gap" is so much a part of the current sociological jargon that it can sound "far removed" from where you are at this moment. But it's there.

A church in Oregon found the problem to be more acute than they originally thought. Having instituted a "Coke n' Conversation" center every Tuesday and Thursday for high school students, the church found parents and families to be the number one topic of conversation and concern. There was a continual harangue about parents, restrictions, and lack of understanding regardless of the nature of the subject they had intended to discuss. Discussion of these topics became so intense that high schoolers were breaking down in tears at the frustration the "problem" caused them. A quick survey of some of the parents indicated a similar frustration and bitterness about the attitudes, lack of respect, demands, etc., of the youth generation. For the most part, the parents were initially not interested in involving themselves in any sort of "communication" activity. Some attitudes exactly paralleled some of those of the young people: "Why talk about it? It won't do any good!"

YOU CAN DO SOMETHING ABOUT IT.

This church did and almost won the communication battle.

PURPOSE

To create a new climate in the family by helping youth and parents come to a better understanding of each other.

SESSION PLANS

If at all possible, try to have a 2-3 hour block of time for this experience. It's advantageous to have an *equal number of parents and youth* (or just adults, if the purpose has been changed to help youth and adults understand each other).

PROCESS

1. GETTING STARTED

Divide into two groups, an all adult group and a youth group. Each group will meet separately to build a role play that represents their thinking about the opposite generation. The youth will create a play reflecting their primary impression of the adult world; the adults will do one of youth. (20-30 minutes)

A good moderator is important.

Merge to share impressions after the role plays have been presented. (15-20 minutes)

2. ASKING THE RIGHT QUESTIONS

Divide again. Each group will decide on the five most important questions they would like to ask the other group. (10-15 minutes)

3. ANSWERING

The groups come together. The groups asking the questions sit in a large circle. The answering group is inside of the circle. One question is asked. The inside group talks about it and then decides on the best possible group answer to it. This continues until all the questions are answered. There can be no talking from the outside group during this period.

Free-for-All: Let anything be said that needs to be said by either group.

Reverse: Reverse the procedure. The answering group now becomes the questioners. Conclude with a merged discussion.

4. POOLING LEARNINGS

Divide into teams of four — two adults, two youth in each. Compare notes on what has been learned about the communication gap. *What one thing did each person learn?*

Write it on the chalkboard. Share with total group.

What one Scripture passage best describes your experiences this evening? Share.

Who's Who in Your Family?
by Bill Shook

INTRODUCTION

Parents have been raising children for so long that it would seem there could not possibly be any more problems in child management. But somehow the job does not seem to be very simple. Youth and their parents never seem to be quite what the magazines, newspapers, and books say they should be.

A quick survey of the biblical literature certainly paints a very clear picture as to how the biblical writers envisioned the role of a parent and the response of a child. Paul writes with emphasis as he states his position.

"Children, it is your Christian duty to obey your parents, for this is the right thing to do. 'Honor your father and mother' is the first commandment that has a promise added: 'so that all may be well with you, and you may live a long time in the land.'

Parents, do not treat your children in such a way as to make them angry. Instead, raise them with Christian discipline and instruction" (Ephesians 6:1-4, TEV).

The passage implies that a parent and youth are placed in a relationship which has every possibility of growing and maturing. The components of a good relationship are mutual respect, good communication (talking and listening), mutual involvement, and mutual understanding. The quality of the relationship depends directly on the presence of these components. This is not to imply that there will never be a strained relationship between parent and youth. To assume this would be naive, if not foolish. But if we have

shared in a genuine, loving relationship, we are better able to handle the mistakes of anger, injustice, and shortsightedness.

This passage of Scripture also implies that a parent consider the rules that affect a child. This is an area that needs more consideration than will be given here. One person offered an insight into this issue by interpreting the purpose of a playpen. He states: "The playpen is not to keep the baby in, but rather to keep the world out." Within the playpen, the child has a world he can handle and negotiate without much difficulty. As the child grows his world expands, so he needs new rules which will help him negotiate his expanded world. The child needs some sort of structure that provides enough security so that he is able to develop his own conscience and to accept added responsibility for himself. Maturity and growth equip a child to negotiate more of the world on his own.

Parents are presented with a big problem of determining how much of the world their young person can negotiate. Parents make errors in this determination. But it is hoped that the relationship between the parent and the youth is wholesome enough so that candid and frank recognition of mistakes can take place.

The decision-making process in the family plays an important role in the cohesiveness of the family unit. A young person has to be a part of the decision-making process as it relates to issues concerning him. He will feel a part of the decision only insofar as he is a part of the process.

The important thing that a parent and youth have to remember is that they are in a relationship which both value very much. If there are obstacles preventing this relationship from being meaningful to both, then they should have the love and courage to find out what is wrong.

ADVANCE PREPARATION

Bibles, pencils, paper, and newsprint should be available.

Prepare a short presentation from the introduction.

SESSION

1. Present a short introduction to the issue to be considered.

2. Divide the group into subgroups of five. Have each subgroup work on the biblical passage (Ephesians 6:1-4). Ask them to come up with a written translation of the passage. Pay special attention to the words used for *obey* and *honor*. Bring the subgroups together for a sharing of the translations. (20-25 minutes)

3. Return to the subgroups of five. Have them work on these questions:

   a. How much direction do I really want from my parents?

   b. How adequate am I to deal with the issues of life I have to face?

   c. How much responsibility do I have in my relationship with my parents?

   d. What role do I want to play in the decision-making process in my family?

   e. Write a proposal to your parents about the kind of style for family living that you would like to have and that would be possible for the family to obtain. Share this for group feedback. Rewrite and share with your family. (15-20 minutes)

4. Worship
   Read the Scripture, Ephesians 6:1-4.
   Prayer:
   Lord, help us to remember that our parents are people too, and that they need us to say "I love you," as much as we need to hear it. Amen.

Mirrors

When you look in a mirror
What do you see —
A person alive
And happy and free?

Or is it a person
Afraid to show through —
Hiding in shame
From an outsider's view?

Perfection in actions
And deeds can't be bought —
It is something to strive for;
It has to be sought.

Do the best that you can
According to you.
If you know that you're right,
What else could you do?

Your life is a mirror.
Reflection of you.
People will see
What comes into view.

by Nancy Peterson, Senior
Shawnee Mission East High School
Prairie Village, Kansas

MIRRORS

This poem is printed backwards. To read, place in front of a mirror.

Nancy built a most unique display holder for her poem which was on display in her high school. She placed a mirror on a board. A second board was attached with a hinge. The poem, written backwards, was placed on the second board. When the board was raised the poem could be read.

You can try it. Place the poem in a busy church corridor where it can be read by both youth and adults. Leave a card for people to write their reactions. Have a "drop-in" box for the cards. You may wish to use the cards for:

1. GROUP DISCUSSION

Share the cards with the group. What kinds of things were being said? Were there any obvious trends? Are there any differences between the youth and adults reactions? What Scripture passages reflect the meaning of the poem?

2. NEWSLETTER

Publish some of the typical reactions to the poem in your church newsletter. Or publish your own paper for distribution to the church.

PLACE ON EASEL

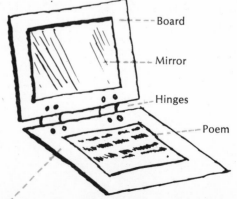

Board

Mirror

Hinges

Poem

Board (which must be raised to reflect the poem)

20

I Know I Can Come In. I'm Trying to Decide if I Want to Be a Part of Your Group.

by Robert Middleton, Jr.

ASSUMPTION

Many groups face the problem of having people there who do not feel they really belong. Perhaps they come because they have to, perhaps because they really do want to be included in the group. Whatever the reason, the members of the group need to be aware of each other and the feelings which they have toward one another.

PURPOSE

To help the members of the group understand each other a little better, and to understand the meaning of church or fellowship.

PROCESS

1. Sit in a circle.
2. Choose a topic of interest to the entire group.
3. Leader starts conversation with his ideas and/or memories.
4. Conversation moves around the circle spontaneously.

Leader should be on the lookout for the following:

1. Was conversation free and easy, or forced?
2. Did anyone try to dominate the discussion? If so, how?
3. Did the group make an effort to include everyone?
4. Did some withdraw voluntarily or were some forced out by others?
5. Were all ideas treated in the same manner, or were some given more preference?

Talk about the experience with the group. How do they feel when their actions, as pinpointed by these questions, are pointed out to them? Can they accept criticism? Are there some things which the group can do to help include all?

WORSHIP

Have a large sheet of newsprint on an easel set up so that all members of the group can see it. Have crayons, felt-tip markers, tempera paints, etc., available.

Invite the members of the group to go up and express their feelings with color.

Talk about what is on the newsprint. What does this say about your group?

What one Scripture passage best suits the mood and feeling of your group at this moment? Share.

Play "Within You — Without You" by the Beatles. (It is helpful to supply the words.)

Without talking say goodbye to each other.

Groups That Clique
by Mason Brown

PURPOSE

To deal with the feelings that individuals have about their place in your group. To explore what a Christian group ought to be.

> Groups "click"
> when people find their
> niche in the clique!

THE APPROACH

The activities presented will call the group into an honest evaluation of its group's life. There will be no observers. Everyone is asked to participate. Honest evaluation will otherwise not occur. *This group and my place in it* is the theme. It is hoped that a setting will be provided in which the members will feel free to share their real feelings toward the group. It is also hoped that this sharing will lead to creative changes in the feelings of the group toward each other; that "he who was once 'out' is now 'in' and he who was withdrawn is now accepted."

GETTING STARTED

Form small groups of threes as people arrive. They are to spend time (1) catching up on the local news (five minutes) and (2) discussing the following statements (which should be posted on large sheets of paper around the room):

I like to be part of a group when . . .

I am uncomfortable in a group when . . .

When I have a *real* choice I like to attend, or not attend, meetings when I know (choose one of the following)

1. what topic is to be dealt with.

2. who will be present.

3. methods of presentation to be used.

4. what's happening after the program.

In the same small groups examine these Scriptures in terms of how they relate to your group.

Mark 9:33-35

1 Corinthians 1:10-13

Colossians 3:12-17

KEEP GOING

Some of the ice has been broken. People are beginning to say "how it is" about the group. Keep going by breaking up the small groups and handing each person a sheet of paper and pencil. Post on the wall the following assignment:

INFLUENCE

The following statements deal with you and the members of your group. Answer each question. When you have finished, go to the people you have listed and share your answers. Indicate why you put their names where you did.

1. The two people who can cause me to change my opinion the easiest are _____ and _____.

2. The two people who will listen to me the most are _____ and _____.

3. The two people who can keep our group from going in circles are _____ and _____.

4. The two people I can most easily influence are _____ and _____.

5. The two people I can least easily influence are _____ and _____.

ENTER IGNORANCE!

When the group has started moving about the room to share, have "Mr. Ignorance" enter unobtrusively. (By prearrangement this is a group member who is to come into the group when things have already started.) His task is to find out what's going on and try to get involved. He cannot ask the leader for help. The group must bring him on board. Do not stop or alter the meeting for him. *A little later he will talk about his experience.*

GROUPS THAT CLIQUE

Form in small groups of three or four. Spend about five minutes talking about the previous experience. Was it fun? Embarrassing? What did they learn about themselves?

For the concluding part to this experience have the group form a circle. Join hands. Ask for three volunteers to drop out of the circle and leave the room.

Assignment:

The group is to quickly decide which of the three people they will let back into the circle. The three people are returned to the room and told they are to get back into the circle. They do it individually. Spend a few minutes with each person. Don't permit too much roughness.

POOLING LEARNINGS

Sit in a large circle. Place the three volunteers in the middle to talk about their feelings during the experience. What did they feel like? Were they happy to get in? How did it feel to be rejected? The outside group remains silent.

Now add *Mr. Ignorance* to the circle. Have him explain what happened to him and how he felt upon entering the room.

Permit the total group to share their experiences in a kind of free-for-all discussion. Then on newsprint or chalkboard list some of the things learned in this session by the members. Was the objective accomplished? If not, what should have been done differently? What would have increased the meaning of the program?

Some ideas to think about. Cliques are not all bad. They evidence the fact that some people have meaningful friends in this group. Outside forces are at work which affect the church. Social class, school loyalties, relatives, dating patterns all have an influence on the nature of a group. It is true that we should have a oneness in Jesus Christ, but it is also true that there are forces that attack that oneness. Most of us are uncomfortable in groups where all the others present are strangers to us. We feel much better in a group that contains at least one close friend with whom we can feel free to be ourselves. If you are the "best friend" of someone who is new or on the fringes of your group, how much attention you give to that person may be very important until he makes other friends in the group.

WORSHIP SUGGESTIONS

Listen to a recording of "Where Is Love?" and "Consider Yourself at Home!" from *Oliver*. Think about the meaning of the words. It would be helpful if the words could be passed out to be looked at while the recording is playing. Are there other popular songs which speak to your group and its needs? Read 1 John 1:1-4. A group grows when inactive youth are reactivated, when new youth are involved. These experiences bring us joy. To express the mood the following music is suggested: "Blest Be the Tie That Binds," "What the World Needs Now Is Love," "We Are One in the Spirit," and "I Bind My Heart This Tide." A closing prayer should lift up the concerns which came out of the evening.

PRESESSION ARRANGEMENTS

1. Questions printed and posted for "Getting Started." Bibles available.

2. Influence questionnaire printed. Pencil and paper for each person.

3. *Mr. Ignorance* obtained beforehand.

4. Music decided on for the worship.

> The people who walked in darkness have seen a great light.
>
> Environment makes the mood and moods make people persons.

Black Light
by Robert Beaumont

INTRODUCTION

This experience is designed to help you see and sense what is around you. It is an experiment in creative seeing. The experience has two parts. Each is designed to cause you to experience a certain kind of feeling or mood.

It's fun.

It's stimulating.

It's experiential education.

So let's try it.

The success of this thing depends on two key elements. One is *spontaneity:* let it be a happening that will allow each participant to feel and do what comes to him. Another element is *involvement:* make sure many people get into the planning and assembling of the components so that it becomes "their thing." This experience isn't something one person can do alone. The leader should be an enabler and resource person.

GETTING READY

Two rooms are needed. Remove as much of the furniture as is possible. Designate one room as *The Negative Pad.* Try to create the following stimuli in this room:

* *a harsh flashing light* (a floodlight with a flasher button)
* *gravel* on the floor (if shoes are worn) or *burlap* under bare feet
* *strong pungent odor* (place a garbage can in the center of the room. Strew paper and cans around.)
* *object of violence* (hang on walls: gun, machete, heavy chain, hangman's noose, cross, etc.)
* flash *slides* on the wall
* do whatever else is needed so this room will reflect the evil, harshness, and despair of life

The Positive Pad is just the opposite. It is a happy room.

* bright colored *scarves* and *streamers*
* assorted *balloons* and stuffed *animals*
* *color wheel* (a Christmas one will do)
* *posters*
* *bouncy music*
* a *black light show* (if you can get the equipment)

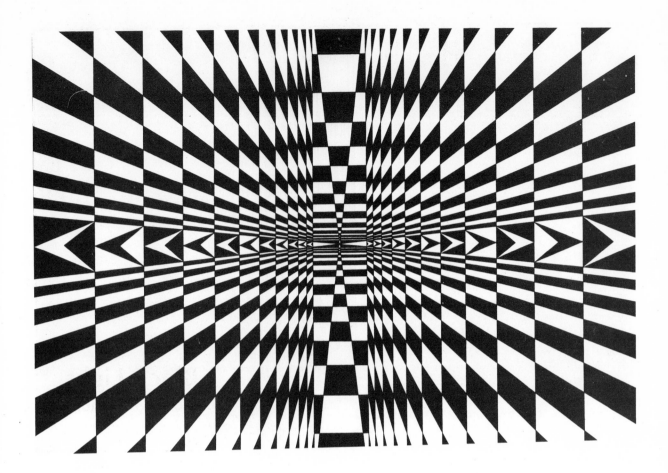

DOING IT

Explain to the group they are to be conscious of what is around them as they progress from one room to the other. Let them do whatever they feel led to do.

Spend about ten minutes in the *Negative Room*. Have some magazines and glue. The group could make collages of what the room is saying to them. No talking.

Move, as a group, into the *Positive Room*. At the end of ten minutes turn the light on and ask everyone to find a comfortable place.

DISCUSS

What are your feelings right now?

What do you remember most about the Negative Room?

What do you remember most about the Positive Room?

Would it have made a difference which room you went into first?

What does this experience say about life? About where you live, eat, study, worship?

If you had to stay in the *Negative Room* all the time, how would you feel?

REFLECTION

Compare your experience with the following Scriptures. What do they say?

"The people who walked in darkness have seen a great light. . . . Thou hast increased their joy and given them great gladness" (Isaiah 9:2-3, NEB).

Read one of the following:

Isaiah 60:1-7
Luke 24:1-9
Revelation 15:2-4
Play "The Nicene Creed" from the album *Rejoice.*°

Sing "Allelu" by Ray Repp from *Hymns for Now.*°

Get together in a group, hum and sing the chorus to "Amen" from *Hymns for Now.*

° Listed in Resource Section.

Will the real "ME" please stand up
    and who will the "I" be that stands:
    ME—as I really am?
    ME—as I'd like to be?
    ME—as others see and think I am?
Which One?
and which one is the "REAL" ME?

Will the Real Me Please Stand Up?
by Janet DeOrnellas

This is the story of masks. Your masks. The masks you wear when you want to be what you are not or when you are not what you want to be.

Read it again, if it didn't make sense the first time through. Then look up.

This is the story of masks and what we would like you to do with them. "Take them off. All off. We'd like you and your group to begin doing that, to begin taking off the masks (both youth and adults) and see miracles of God that lie behind them. That's what we'd like to do — to get the "real" you ready to stand in case the question should ever come.

INTRODUCTION

Mask is both a verb and noun. Most of us wear a "mask" at some time or other. We "mask" when we try to protect our inner feelings and thoughts. The fear of being rejected is so strong that most of us are afraid to be really "me." So we project a "new" me, a "different" me, and hide the real one. For example:

"Men are courageous. I am a male. Therefore, I am not afraid. Deep inside, however, I am badly scared. But the mask I wear gives no evidence of my fear — or at least I'm hoping it doesn't."

"Girls are not mechanical. My boyfriend's car will not start. I could fix it but . . ."

So we play the game of "masks." We act and live the way we think others are thinking we should. If I think you like a witty, mischievous person, that's what I'll become in order to be a friend — and the game goes on.

Masks cover anything and everything we want

to hide. But do they? Did you know that there are really three of you — three of me. There is: (1) myself as I really am (with all my tensions, hopes, and joys); (2) myself as I'd like to be (my dream world); and (3) myself as you see me (which is a combination of 1 and 2 and everything that you are). Number 2 is the "mask wearing" part. We get an idea of what we would like to be or should be in a given situation and act it out. Sometimes we really become the part we acted out. Other times it's nothing but a game. "We laugh when we really want to cry."

Those of us who take seriously the Scripture, "and you will know the truth, and the truth will make you free" (John 8:32), should work at relating openly with one another. Certainly the church should attempt to provide an atmosphere of honesty and acceptance.

PURPOSE

To stimulate your group to look honestly at the masks people wear and to discuss ways in which they can become more open with each other.

PROCESS

1. INTRODUCTORY ACTIVITY

As members arrive, have them begin making individual masks out of paper bags. Have available a supply of crayons, colored chalk, tempera paint, construction paper, glue, felt-tip markers, and scissors. Continue until all have arrived and have a mask. (When preparing for this session, place several large mirrors and many small ones around the room.)

2. INVOLVEMENT

Instruct everyone to put on his mask and begin moving about the room talking to one person at a time. After greeting an individual, say to him:

"What your mask says about you is . . ." (complete the sentence).

Keep moving until everyone has had an opportunity to talk to almost everyone. Remove masks Again, move about the room sharing with one person at a time. Look him in the eyes and tell him one thing you like about him. Also continue to observe and look at yourself in the mirrors.

The leader should then ask for brief responses: Which experience was most difficult? Did you feel differently? If so, why?

3. REFLECTION

Divide into teams of twos. Take turns serving as "mirrors" for one another.

For 3 minutes A tells B of his reflection or how A sees B and then reverse roles for the second 3 minutes. (If time permits, change teams 2 or 3 times.)

4. EVALUATION (total group)

Do you feel we wear masks in this group?

Is there any time when wearing a "mask" is all right?

How did you feel when talking to a person who wore a visible mask?

In what ways can we be more honest and open with one another?

WORSHIP

Scripture

(Write these verses on newsprint and place around the room before the session.)

John 8:32

Proverbs 27:5

Mark 4:22

1 Corinthians 13:12

Prayer

"Tomorrow, but Not Today" from *Interrobang* by Norman C. Habel (included at the end of this section).

Group Response

Lord, help me to be me.

ADDITIONAL RESOURCES

Charlie Churchman and the Teenage Masquerade

A film which deals with the question of honesty and the masks people wear and want to take off. Order from your denominational film library or Mass Media Ministries. Rental — $12.50.

Tomorrow, but Not Today

by Norman C. Habel

I'm not a shoe
tossed in a corner
or an island
lost in the sea,
I'm not an orphan
or an unwanted pet,
but I might as well be,
because I'm alone.

I'm surrounded by people,
but I'm all alone.
Some people laugh with me,
some give advice,
some ask for help
or tell me I'm neat,
but no one seems to stop
and notice who I really am.

I feel so lonely inside
that I've started spinning
a shell to cover myself
and hide
that strange something inside me
that is me.

I don't want to hide it,
but I must.
Otherwise people will see
what I'm really like.
Then they will smile and say:
"What a funny kid."

Tomorrow I'll try to leave my shell . . .
tomorrow, but not today.

I'm surrounded
by friendly people
who seem so happy.
I pretend to be happy,
and warm and comfortable, too.

I don't know what else to do
when I'm with other people.
I'm all alone then. . . .

And yet I can't talk about it
or explain why.
It's like being trapped.

I feel like a withered left hand
hiding behind someone's back.
I'm wearing a glove
to hide myself.
I need my glove,
but I hate it
because it's not really me.

Tomorrow I'll take it off
and exercise my hand . . .
tomorrow, but not today.

I'm so lonely sometimes
I could run away
and just disappear into the air.
But I want those people around me.
I want their love
and their joy in me.
Still they keep slipping past me,
slipping,
slipping away
and never really touching me.
They just see my mask
and slide slowly by.

Tomorrow, Lord, tomorrow,
I'll remove my mask
and people will have to stop
and notice me . . .
tomorrow, when I'm older and stronger
I'll remove my mask . . .
but not today,
because today I'm too alone
with so many people around me,
so many people
in this place called . . .
a church.

Getting It All Together or the Tinkertoy Thing

by Robert Beaumont

PURPOSE

Discovering the importance of good communication for effective living.

INTRODUCTION

How people like you depends on what you say to them and how you say it. Take your group for instance. A lot of things happen (are happening) in your group that go unnoticed, or are noticed but not reported or described as they occur. Positive kinds of things make a person feel good within a group. Negative things like these destroy a group — "Why should I go? No one cares if I'm there or not," or "_____ is such a _____; he won't let us do anything," or "Nothing ever happens. . . ."

A lot of "negative" ends up meaning NO people. And communication needs people, just as you need people. So let's try to identify some problem areas in communication so you can (1) have a "plus" group feeling, and (2) get a better appreciation of who you are and why you exist.

THE WAY TO DO IT

PLAY GOSSIP

Begin by telling the group they are going to play the game of "Gossip." Whisper a phrase, like "Joyce Fuller watches *Sesame Street* every day," into the ear of the first person, who then passes the message on down the line.

DISCUSSION

What happened? Did the statement remain the same? Was it changed? Where did the change occur? How?

REPLAY

Repeat the game of "Gossip" using this story. "Three black youths climb on a city bus and head down town. Sitting next to them is an elderly lady and two white kids who begin to taunt the black youth. Suddenly one of them jumps up with a knife in his hand, stabs one of the boys, and runs from the bus. The elderly lady is screaming, "He killed him, he killed him!"

DISCUSS

What happened? Did the story change any?

THE THING EXPERIENCE

This is an experiment in determining how well people respond to verbal instructions. The object is for one group to build a TinkerToy model, which they have not seen, from the description given to them by the people who have seen the model. Fun and frustrating.

1. Divide into teams of six people each. These teams compete with one another in completing the TinkerToy model. Subdivide each team into three smaller teams: Builders, Runners, and Observers.

Behind a screen at one end of the room place the TinkerToy model — a free-form figure. Give each team a set of TinkerToys. Give assignments.

Builders will sit at the opposite end of the room. They will build an exact replica of the TinkerToy "Thing." *They are not allowed to see the "Thing."*

Runners will describe the "Thing" to the Builders. They receive their information from the Observers. *Runners are not allowed within two feet of the Builders' table, cannot use diagrams, or do not ever see the "Thing."*

Observers are the only people who see the "Thing." They describe it to the Runners, who in turn describe it to the Builders, who construct an exact replica.

2. See below a diagram of how the room should be prepared. The middle area is reserved for the Runners, who, when the exercise begins, must remain within their designated area and verbally transfer the instructions from the Observers to the Builders. (No diagrams allowed.) Let each team decide the division of responsibility for itself, appointing as many or as few people to each area as they see fit. Announce a time limitation of 10-20 minutes (depending on the complexity of the object).

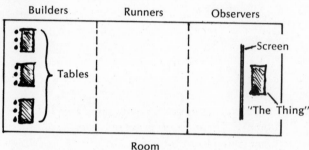

Room

3. Toward the end of the time designated begin reminding the teams of the time left. "Two minutes, one minute," etc. (usually productivity will hasten and/or frustration will increase). Appoint a recorder to watch each team, noting generally what goes on. He is valuable in feeding back to the group an objective report.

DISCUSSION

Call the group together and ask them what happened. Find out how they felt as a team: frustrated, confident, angry, apathetic. Then call for individual feelings. If frustrated, ask "why?" Ask the same if they didn't participate or if they were angry, etc.

Look particularly for the frustration level of the Runners, who could not see the object nor participate in the building. They are the middle men, caught up in the midst of two forces.

Explore the feeling of wanting to solve a problem and not being able to do it effectively. Where is this feeling dominant in their lives (home, school, in groups)?

Pool your learnings together by asking, and recording on newsprint, "What did we learn about our group?" and "What did you learn about yourself?" Compare the list from "Gossip" with these learnings.

REFLECTION

Read Acts 13:44-50.

The early church had a problem among its members: Were you a Christian if you were not first a Jew? Arguing, rumors, fighting, dissension, abounded among the Christians. The Jews insisted only circumcised Jews could become Christians; the non-Jews felt it was not necessary to become a Jew first. The issue was finally resolved but not without much discussion.

Play a contemporary recording like "We Can Be Together."

Sing "They'll Know We Are Christians by Our Love."

Close with prayers from individuals.

PRESESSION PREPARATION

— TinkerToy sets for each team and an extra one for the model.
— Room arrangements.
— Prepare the original TinkerToy "Thing" and keep hidden until you begin the experiment.

Using a Misused Word

COMMUNITY IS SUCH A COME-ON WORD THESE DAYS — used and misused, like the good old word "love." Used and misused so much that WE NEVER KNOW WHETHER WE ARE EVER IN A COMMUNITY OR NOT.

This is another program suggestion for a misused word: COMMUNITY.

WE'D LIKE TO HELP YOU BUILD YOURS:
Build your group into that kind of love relationship that Christ talks about and believed; build your group into that kind of disciple community which is the root of Christian community.

The following are two suggestions for getting you on the road toward "community." Hope you like it. And remember, the road's a rough one — and not very wide. Step off too many times and you'll never make it.

Suggestion 1 Conflict and Grace
Suggestion 2 Dialogue: Listening and Then
Listening Again

1. CONFLICT AND GRACE
by Tim Peterson

The posture:

to discover within ourselves that unconditional love comes only when we are embedded in disagreement and allow ourselves to reveal our honest differences and sense of worth.

The stance: to be human is to be sensitive to our limits.

The action: scene 1 is where *you* come in.

Let's say you and your community (we are more than a group) are where it is at, but that something is tapping your brain that there is no motion, movement, aliveness around this particular day. Things are slow, hot, even the air seems to have deserted us for some other love. "If I was only a part of something," we whisper to ourselves.

O.K. That's where it is at. But I've been there before. Then all of a sudden a stranger comes among us (from newsprint he comes). His name is Tim and that's all we know. And he wants us to face up to what we have become. Listen:

You've all been brainwashed! All of you. You have been trained only to think, never to feel; only to talk, never to emote; only to ask the right questions, never to be questioned yourselves!

Why do students riot? They riot because they receive no credits for being sensitive to their times. They honestly believe that the enemy can be our friend, that war is wrong, that the Bible is misused, that people are more important than ideals or theories, and that the best education is self-learned not mass-learned. They ask you: Why are you so insensitive to our times in high school? Don't you believe in anything?

Break up into fours in your community and try to come to grips with where you are at. Are you brainwashed? What values have you learned? Are they worthwhile and even possible? Would you welcome a Russian family into your home for a visit? Any Russian? Would you be drafted without question? Would you kill if asked? Are the Scriptures relevant any longer to you? How? When are they? Which translation? Are people more important than justice? Than truth? Than faith? Than God? Than freedom? Do you want always to be lectured to, or do you want to test out your knowledge for yourself? Is your high school moral? Immoral? Are your teachers human? Inhuman? Trite? Where do *you* stand on these issues?

2. DIALOGUE: LISTENING AND THEN LISTENING AGAIN
by Tim Peterson

The posture:
to discover within ourselves the meaning of LISTENING and how it helps in our friendships and loveships.

The stance: to be human is to allow someone else to change us.

The action: scene 2 is where *we* come in.

We are back where it is at. This time we want to try not to get hung up on each other's words. We strangled a few in the community last time we met — unconsciously, I am sure, but we did it. We often hang people because of the *way* they answer us. They never seem to say what they mean (at least to our way of thinking). So we hang them; we put a noose around their necks by not even trying to understand them, which means they are cut off from the rest of us. They are, for all practical purposes, dead. Well, it is these people that we need to be concerned about in order to preserve the *we* in our community. This "mono-listening" (a new word of ours) is

A new word for treacherous listening: mono-listening
the act of selective listening. It is so easy and treacherous. *We listen only to our own story-line. That is, we hear only those words in someone else's conversation that fit into our image of what is happening. What does not fit we avoid. We forget. We distort. We do not permit things we do not like to become part of what we hear. Mono-listening separates us into you and me — you believe this, I believe that — we can never share an opinion! Heaven forbid! Mono-listening says my speech is correct; I refuse to listen to an incorrect view of life. Mono-listening dissects and reorders another's words and vocabulary. We select only the beginning, the middle, or the end of the communication. Never in mono-listening do we hear or listen to the whole statement. We hear only what we want to hear. We build only one world — our own — opposed to the other word of the one who addresses us.*

Let us test this out. Let's mono-listen. Break up into fours again, and this time distort each other's conversation — break into it and turn it into a story-line that you want to preserve despite all odds. For instance, discuss "friendship" but keep only your definition of what it means — stick to it, always hearing each other's interpretation, but never listening or allowing your definition to be lost.

TALK OF THE WORD
The Bible says, "Do some loving" (see 1 John 4:12-21).

Dialogue is listening. It is the art of sensitive concern for what the other is communicating.

A BETTER WORD TO LIVE: DIALOGUE
It is, of course, important to know what we are trying to say — to keep in touch with our story-line — but we are willing to change our story if new wisdom comes that improves our story. In fact we want to understand the other's story-line as much as our own so that our stories might intertwine and be fused in some way. We want to because we want to know the other person so much so that we can have a friendship with that person following our talk. We listen, not only to words but to feelings — to discover how important this topic is for the other or how insignificant it is to him. We listen because we know we want to change. We want to become a part of that person in some way and he a part of us. We want him to listen to our story — to understand it and share in it. And when our conversation is through, we may have forgotten exactly what we had first said. Instead we have a new thought, a new story to tell.

Break into fours again. This time begin with a definition of friendship but let the conversation deepen so that you understand each other's definition. Then try to find the best way to say it together. Allow a *we* to come forth out of all the individuals present. Find a common word or sentence that expresses just what you want to say.

Well, was it worth it? You can begin to build more friendships when you allow someone to be your friend, to allow someone else to meet your needs. And it happens only in dialogue one with another. Are you listening?

THE SCRIPTURE
"No unintelligible speeches, please."
(See 1 Corinthians 14:6-11.)

The Earth Is Our Village

And it is good that people in a village be neighbors.

CHURCH BULLETIN MYSTERY

To those who know, the seemingly unrelated topics, retreats, and events that appear Sunday after Sunday in the youth section of the worship bulletin do make sense. They do have an overall sense of direction and purpose. They represent your version of youth ministry — what you think is good and needed for the youth of your church.

The fancy titles and jumbled jargon have a mysterious aura about them for many people. However, while sitting in their pews, scanning the bulletin mistakes (misspelled names, and all the rest), they can only wonder, "What's going on down in those youth rooms?" Ignorance can breed mistrust and usually results in misunderstanding. It is only reasonable then that a great many youth and adult workers with youth feel that the church is not really being supportive of them and their efforts in youth ministry.

Since September is the "blast-off" month for the winter and fall countdown in getting programs and projects off the launch pad, we urge you to help your church get acquainted with youth ministry as you see it developing for 1971-72.

TALK-A-THON

Under the general heading of "Talk-a-thon" (talk as long as you need), we suggest the following two programs for introducing your church to youth ministry: *The Earth Is Our Village* and *Our Proposal.*

PARTICIPANTS: youth, parents, and interested adults.

PURPOSE: to work out a visible concept of ministry that is applicable to mature Christians between the ages of twelve and eighteen.

REASONS: (1) The communication gap which exists among us can only be wiped out if we are interested enough to *start talking;* (2) There's generally a misunderstanding among church people about what is and is not youth ministry; and (3) Youth and adults can and should talk about their mutual ministries.

PRESESSION PREPARATION

Appoint a "talk-a-thon" committee composed equally of youth and adults.

Take a look at your church calendar and decide whether you want a "one-night stand" or a series of two or more. (You're on your own for material after the second one unless you didn't have enough time to use all that is included here.) Set the date(s). Rewrite the purpose which is stated here in light of your own needs and concerns.

Invite and receive firm commitments from adults and youth that they will attend. Pursue the program suggestions and modify as needed. Have some knowledge of Dave Evan's book *Shaping the Church's Ministry with Youth.* Collection '69 also has some material on youth ministry which would be relevant and can be obtained from your nearest Judson Bookstore.

THE EARTH IS OUR VILLAGE

And it is good that people in a village be neighbors.

I. GROUPS OF THREE. (20 minutes)

Introduce the general format and purpose for these sessions. Quickly divide the group into subgroups of three, making certain there is at least one adult in every group. Describe to each other the kinds of youth seen in the church, what they are about and want to do, and the way they feel about their church. Leader calls time. Each group member decides on a one-word description which best describes his group's conversation about the kind of youth in their church. The leader asks for these and writes them on newsprint or a chalkboard as they are called out.

One word descriptions only.

II. GROUPS OF SIX: Simile (10 minutes)

Two subgroups of three join together. Individually each person finishes the following statement. When all are completed, give each grouping a piece of newsprint divided in half. On one side would be the writings of the youth, those of the adults on the other. Compare the similarities and differences. Discuss the "whys" of each.

The sentence to be completed is:

Being a youth in today's world is like _____

_____

_____.

III. TWO GROUPS OF SIX: "When I was sixteen _____." (25 minutes)

Two groups of six merge. The adults in both groups form an inner circle. All youth form an outside circle around the adults. The adults discuss *what they were like when they were sixteen,* what their major concerns were, etc. The youth listen without talking. Adults talk for ten minutes. Then the circles reverse, and the youth go into the inner circle with the adults on the outside. The youth discuss what they heard the adults talking about. At the end of ten minutes the youth move to the outer circle and a general discussion takes place (five minutes).

IV. YOUTH MINISTRY is _____. (As long as you need or have time for.)

The purpose of this step is to have the youth and adults develop a mutual understanding of what youth ministry should be in your church.

A. The following list contains several suggestions about youth ministry. They are to be ranked in order of their importance. A rank of "1" means this is the most important statement in the list, a rank of "2" means this is the second most important statement, etc.

B. Divide the total group in half with adults and youth equally represented in each part. Each person ranks the youth ministry statement according to his own feelings about which is most important.

C. When the list has been individually ranked, each group is to rank them by consensus. That is, each member in the group must agree that the number "1" ranking is really the most important statement in the entire list. Every person in the group must be able, at least partially, to agree to the group's ranking. There can be no decision by majority vote. When the groups are finished, compare their rankings.

YOUTH MINISTRY

Rank in order of their importance. *Our church's ministry with youth is to help youth:*

	Ranking Mine	Group's
1. Accept themselves as persons of worth who can make real contributions to both adults and youth.	_____	_____
2. Learn to live with bodies that are male or female and accept their sexuality as God-given and beautiful.	_____	_____
3. Resolve the inner conflict of needing to be independent from their families and yet dependent on them also.	_____	_____
4. Understand the content and meanings of the gospel without necessarily knowing all of the factual material.	_____	_____
5. Meet the disillusionment of recognizing church policies, tensions, and divisions.	_____	_____
6. Understand the mystery of the church as being "one body in Christ."	_____	_____
7. Understand both the weakness and strengths of our	_____	_____

church in ministry and commitment.

8. Be nurtured through this period of idealism and faith, and feel loved and accepted through this period of skepticism, doubt, cynicism, and unbelief. —— ——
9. Work for their rightful place in the total life of the church as responsible Christians. —— ——
10. Understand the factual content of the Bible. —— ——
11. "Work out in fear and trembling" their own faith. —— ——
12. Overcome the communication gap which exists between youth and adults. —— ——
13. Help adults to accept the worth of an idea rather than dismiss it as an irrelevant youthful suggestion. —— ——
14. Help the church respond to youth's need for both traditional and nontraditional approaches in worship and ministry. —— ——

SCRIPTURE:

Genesis 11:1-9

A continuation of the youth-adult conversation started in "The Earth Is Our Village."

PURPOSE:

To inform interested adults about youth ministry plans and dreams for the coming year, to receive their suggestions, and to do any changing that may be needed as a result of this stimulation.

FORMAT:

The session could be preceded by a light supper or followed by refreshments. The group should be divided into those interested in junior high and those interested in senior high fellowship. Representatives from the board of Christian education, teachers, and advisors should be present.

I. Introduce the purpose of the evening. Then begin discussing what youth ministry will be like this year. Provide as much detail as possible. Print on newsprint FOR JUNIOR HIGH/SENIOR HIGH, THIS YEAR OUR MINISTRY WILL INCLUDE:

CHURCH SCHOOL SETTING

Teachers
Courses to be studied
Special events or emphasis

(This would be an excellent time to talk about the curriculum materials your church is using, to the advantage of both the youth and adults. Make sure there is a qualified person available.)

FELLOWSHIP SETTING

Advisors
Purpose of projects
Meeting time
Potential program
Special events

SPECIAL SETTINGS

Choir
Participation in worship
Youth Week
Relationship to other churches
Relationship to our own church
Drama
Newspaper

II. Ask for audience response. Keep a running account of all questions on newsprint for future solving if they cannot be answered now. A panel composed of a board of education representative, a teacher, an advisor, plus four youth would be one way of answering audience questions.

Question the audience to see whether they would like more youth-adult sessions.

Play a Parable

INTRODUCTION:

A large portion of the Synoptic Gospels (Matthew, Mark, and Luke) consists of short stories called parables. These are sometimes defined as *a word picture of some piece of human experience, actual or imagined.* Jesus made frequent use of parables as a way of teaching. Normally, he drew his characters or images from life experiences familiar to the people he was teaching. The parables became "windows" through which the listener was invited to discover some insights about himself, God, and his world. The real value of a parable, then, is in what it does to us. It pushes us to think seriously about the meaning of life as we experience it. One of the best ways for us to get at the meaning of the parables is to "play" them.

WHERE DO I BEGIN?

Good question. There are so many parables in the Synoptic Gospels that you may feel like a browser in a paperback bookstore trying to decide which book to purchase first. There are several books which will help you get a bird's-eye view of all of the parables. They are listed at the end of this article. Several of the parables lend themselves especially well to "playing." These include:

The prodigal son, the father, and the elder brother — Luke 15:11-32

The good Samaritan — Luke 10:30-37

The Pharisee and the publican — Luke 18:9-14

The marriage feast — Matthew 22:1-14 (and Luke 14:16-24)

The widow and the unjust judge — Luke 18:1-8

The laborers in the vineyard — Matthew 20:1-16

The story of Dives and Lazarus — Luke 16:19-31

The wise and foolish builders — Luke 6:47-49 (and Matthew 7:24-27)

There are any number of ways to play parables. Once you get the idea, I'm sure that your own imagination will discover several possibilities. Here are three possible approaches using three different parables.

THE PRODIGAL SON

Divide your group into four sections. If the group is very large, divide into eight. One person in each group is to be designated the discussion leader. He will later become one of the participants in the role play. Each group is to be given a list of questions dealing with one of the characters in the parable. There are three main characters in this parable: the father, the younger son, the elder son. One more character has been added.

GROUP 1 — THE FATHER

1. What kind of person is the father in the story?

2. What was his attitude toward the younger son?

3. What was his attitude toward the elder son?

4. How would you have reacted to each son if you had been the father?

GROUP 2 — THE YOUNGER SON

1. What kind of person was the younger son?

2. What was his attitude toward his father?

3. What was his attitude toward his older brother?

4. How would you have reacted to the events in the story if you had been the younger brother?

GROUP 3 — THE ELDER BROTHER

1. What kind of person was the elder brother?
2. What was his attitude toward his father?
3. What was his attitude toward his younger brother?
4. How would you have reacted if you had been in his position?

GROUP 4 — THE NEXT DOOR NEIGHBOR

Obviously, this character is not in the story. But since this is a game, you are free to create him for the purpose of better understanding the parable if you wish. Explain that when the younger brother returned home and the elder brother reacted strongly to the way his younger brother was treated by his father, the elder one went off angrily to a friend's house next door. The friend knows the father and the two sons very well. He wants to be of help. Therefore, this group considers the following questions:

1. As the next door neighbor, how will you deal with the angry elder brother?
2. Do you feel that he is right or wrong in the way he has reacted?
3. What advice will you give him?

ACT IT OUT (10 minutes)

Call the group together at the end of twenty minutes. The four discussion leaders are to role-play the persons their group studied. The scene is to be the living room of the father and the two sons. The next door neighbor is there with the family. The players are to work through the hostile feelings of the older brother. They are to stay with the contents of the story as much as possible. No scripts or coaching from the audience.

GROUP DISCUSSION

As the parable is acted out, you will likely discover a multitude of questions and attitudes rising. At the completion of the acting have the group talk about the parable.

Be concerned with *why* the group feels the way they do.

With which character in the story do they most identify and why?

Jesus told this parable as a way of expressing the nature of man and his relationship to God. What vision of man and God comes to us in it?

By this time you will be deep into this interesting parable. You may even discover that this will be only the first of several sessions the group will want to spend on it.

THE STORY OF LAZARUS

Setting the stage for Luke 16:19-31.

Read the parable together. Pretend that you have become directors and producers of a Broadway play (or Hollywood movie, or TV special). The first thing to do is to make sure that everyone "gets" the picture in the parable. You might do this by writing down responses on the chalkboard (maybe even some sketches of scenery) as you ask them:

1. How many characters do you need for your play? Who will be chosen to play the roles? *(Either well-known stars, or members of the group, or even famous political personalities.)*

2. What props will you need? *(Costumes, furniture, scenery, etc.)*

3. How many scenes will there be? *(The story lends itself to at least three scenes.)* How will you arrange for these scenes on the stage? What will "hell" look like, for example?

4. What action will you have taking place in the rich man's home?

5. What action and/or dialogue will you have going on in "heaven" and "hell"?

6. Will you have any music along with your play? What type? Will it change during the course of the play?

7. Do the characters change any during the play? If so, in what way?

8. What are you going to entitle the play?

9. You believe that your play has several good points to make. There are some people you feel especially need to hear the word that it speaks. Therefore, make a list of the people you want to invite as "first nighters." *(Make sure that each person responds to this one and tells why he would invite the person he chose.)*

THE GOOD SAMARITAN

Sermon-dialoguing Luke 10:30-37.
Mini-sermon:
Everyone in your group probably knows this parable, and likely all have listened to a good

many sermons too. This time, they will be the ones to prepare the sermon. Each person gets a copy of the parable, a pen or pencil, and several sheets of clean paper. They have twenty minutes to jot down some ideas for a "mini-sermon" of not more than five minutes. They may take any approach they wish. Some may simply retell the story in their own words. Some may want to take one character in it and develop some ideas around him. Some may compare the several characters (the man in the ditch, the priest, the Levite, the Samaritan). Some may draw a parallel to some contemporary situation involving the social welfare system. Do anything with it. (Chances are that this last approach will lead to most of the talking, however, when you turn to the last part of the game.)

Preach and discuss.

Now, ask for volunteers to preach their mini-sermons before the rest of the group. At the conclusion of each, the rest of the group responds. A good order of questions for the group to consider would be:

What was the strong point of the sermon?
What was the weak point?

Did it help you to understand the parable better?
If not, how would you have done it?
Involve the pastor.

Finally, bring in your pastor. Let him know what you have been doing in playing parables. Ask him to prepare a sermon on this parable, and inform him that you would like to discuss it with him after he preaches it to the group. If he has never done so, you might ask him about the possibilities of trying this kind of technique on a Sunday morning during the regular service! This method can be very stimulating, not only for him, but for you, too. There are many other ways to play a parable. Try a few, and I think that you will begin to see why Jesus held the attention of the people when he "opened his mouth to speak to them in parables."

Additional Resources:

The Parables of Jesus by George Buttrick.
The Parables of Jesus by Joachim Jeremias (paperback).
The Waiting Father by Helmut Thielicke.
The Interpreter's Bible, vol. 7, pages 165-175.

The Mystery/Ministry Scene

by Gary W. Harris

"Man with the Help of God"

by Suzi Grizzard

(From *Impact*, November, 1970)

Man is the best and the worst of all things.
He is only a little less than the angels and on his way to hell at the same time.
He wants peace and is willing to fight for it.
He wants love and hates those who deny it to him.
Man can be the height of happiness and the depth of despair.
He can be definitely at extremes or confusedly in the middle.
He doesn't always know where he is going, and if he knows this he isn't always sure when he gets there.
But when things are going downhill, man has someone to help him — other men with outstretched hands willing to solve a problem, share a load, understand, or just listen.
And as long as there are those who care about the best of men and the worst of men, there is hope.

The times in which we live call for men and women who are willing to be that someone, that instrument of God, of which Miss Grizzard speaks in her poem. Although this task has been given to everyone, there is a great need for young men and women who will dedicate their lives to some form of full-time Christian ministry. But how can a person know that the Christian ministry is for him? What discoveries must he make that will help him evaluate the church's mission and his possible role in it?

PROGRAM TARGET:

This program is designed to give your group a first-hand look at the church in action, to allow them to savor the experience of being "minister" and to encourage them to think seriously about full-time Christian ministry as a vocation.

YOUR PROCEDURE WILL BE A
MYSTERY/MINISTRY TOUR

Take your group on a Mystery/Ministry tour in the general area of your church.

Your objective is to visit persons and places where ministry is happening. These should be ministries that are less familiar to your youth than the pastorate, the educational ministry, or the mission field. Make arrangements well in advance and schedule as accurately as possible a sequence of tours, such as the following:
— another church and its pastor (where, perhaps, something unique is being done, i.e., ministry to businessmen or some ecumenical venture)
— a hospital chaplain
— a campus minister
— a Christian center
— a prison chaplain
— a drug rap-line
— someone involved in night ministry
— a church-operated coffee house or teen drop-in
— a seminary, if there is one near you
— someone involved in problem pregnancy counseling

— a retirement home and its chaplain

— a denominational or Council of Churches office

— something unique to your own area

In each instance you will want to allow time for a tour and a chance to talk with the person in charge. Ask him, also, to talk about his reasons for choosing that particular vocation and how members of your group might also become involved in that ministry. You might plan the tour for a Saturday or a day when the youth are not in school. Plan to return to the church or to the home of one of the members for dinner and discussion.

DISCUSSION

1. Distribute a sheet of paper and a pencil to each person. Instruct him to write on one side of the paper a word or two which summarizes his feelings right now — at the conclusion of the tour. On the other side, have him jot down some thoughts on one particular phase of the tour to which he responded. When this task has been completed ask that each person hold his paper before him so that the rest of the group can see the word or two he has written on side one. By doing this the members of the group will get a feeling about the way in which each of them responded to the tour.

2. Divide the group into dyads (groups of two). Their first task will be to do something for each other which symbolizes ministering to another. (For example, one person might get a chair for another, one might serve the other a cup of cold water, or one might give the other a pat on the back in a gesture of acceptance or assurance.)

The second task is for the two to take turns completing the following statements as the other listens:

"Today I learned something new about ministry, and that was . . ."

"What I found most intriguing about today was . . ."

3. Have each dyad merge with another. Each of the four persons should respond to the question:

What possible place could you see for yourself in the ministry? (Could you, for example, conceive of the possibility that you might choose one form of ministry or another as a full-time vocation?)

or

Are you interested in volunteering your services in one of the ministries you experienced today?

or

Can our youth group share in one of these ministries?

4. Bring the entire group together. Allow a short period of time for any who have really been "turned on" to share their enthusiasm with the group. Then distribute the pamphlets about "Christian vocations" for this program. (Information on the ministry can be obtained from the Ministry with Youth Department of your denomination.)

WORSHIP

Have the group stand in a circle while someone reads Miss Grizzard's poem.

Listen to the recording of a song like, "Bridge over Troubled Water," "Let It Be," or "I'll Be There." Then without talking express how you feel about those standing in the circle with you right now. (This might be done by means of a hand clasp, a smile, or a hug.)

Sing together a song like, "Song Maybe for Teenage Christians" or "They'll Know We Are Christians by Our Love."

To conclude, have two people read Matthew 25:34-45 and John 20:21 in dialogue, as follows:

Voice I   Matthew 25:34-36
Voice II Matthew 25:37-39
Voice I   Matthew 25:40-43
Voice II Matthew 25:44
Voice I   Matthew 25:45
Voice II John 20:21

Ministry in the form of a party to keep young witches and monsters out of pumpkin day mischief.

The Trick Is to Treat
by Mason Brown

PURPOSE

To plan, publicize, and provide leadership for a Halloween party for children from the neighborhood of the church building (or the entire town in smaller communities) which will be at the same time a meaningful project and a significant event for the entire youth fellowship.

INTRODUCTION

Here's a creative approach to Halloween! The trick is to treat the children of your church and those that live in the church neighborhood to a Halloween party. This is a real service for others which can be fun for those who serve. The emphasis is on a positive way to celebrate this special scary season and at the same time keep young witches and monsters out of pumpkin day mischief. This project may even be evangelism. Some of the masked creatures from the neighborhood who are drawn to the haunted house of the moonlit church may return by sunlight to worship and study.

LET'S GET ORGANIZED!

If it is done right, this party may well be the major event of the fall season for your youth group. Plan well in advance, check the details, and do the work. A central planning committee should contain the chairmen of the following subcommittees: (1) publicity, (2) decorations, (3) recreation, and (4) refreshments.

Concerns of the central planning committee will include setting a date which avoids conflicts with football games and the children's usual trick-or-treat night in your community. Set the time in the early evening, say 6-8 P.M. Remember, children go to bed early. You may want to plan an after-party time for senior highs only. Be sure you can handle the size and ages of the children that respond. The party might follow a UNICEF or Church World Service collection. If so, ask the adults who work with children to organize this part of the UNICEF activity. They will want to consider security for children, neighborhood to be covered, and advance publicity. Materials needed can be obtained from U.S. Committee for UNICEF, 331 East 38th Street, New York, New York 10016.

Plan for adults who come with their children. They would enjoy a place where they could sip a hot cup of coffee and watch the witches and goblins enjoy themselves. Be sure to get the names, addresses, and phone numbers of those who attend from the neighborhood. It will probably be easiest if you collect this information from all who attend. Give this information to the chairman of children's work or the pastor for the proper follow-up. It would be helpful to find out what church they attend and if they attend actively or occasionally.

Have the electronic brains in your group tape some weird Halloween noise to be used as background noise for the event. (Records played backwards or at the wrong speed will also do it.) Remember, with young children nothing should be overdone and too scary. How are you going to pay for this event? Will there be a charge? Is there money from the children's work section of the church budget? The youth treasury? Are you going to wash cars and collect paper for funds?

PUBLICIZE

The Publicity Committee needs to see that news of the party gets into the church paper. Here is a suggestion of wording: "A Halloween party for the younger children both in the church and in the neighborhood is scheduled from 6 until 8 P.M., October ___, planned by our senior highs. There will be costume judging at 6:16 followed by spook house, entertainment, games, and refreshments. Coffee will be available throughout the evening for those adults who would like to share in the activities of the evening. The cost will be $___."

Your community newspaper should also be notified. Write up the facts and get them to the proper person well before the deadline. If you have a photographer in the group, include a good picture of the planning committee carving a pumpkin. If the party is a post UNICEF collection event, be sure to cover this aspect of the story. In many communities you can get free publicity of church sponsored events open to the public on certain "billboard" radio programs and weekly papers which are distributed to the homes. Don't forget posters in the local stores. Publicity flyers can be passed door to door in the church neighborhood.

DECORATING

The Decorating Committee has many options. There are witches, cats, ghosts, pumpkins, autumn branches, corn shocks, and spooky lights.

ENTERTAINMENT

The Recreation Committee won't have time to use all the suggestions which follow. Pick those that appeal to you and fit into your situation. Most recreation books will have alternate suggestions. Be sure the properties needed are ready at the right time. At times the recreation leaders will be scattered at interest centers. If a series of events is used, it would be well to have person A lead event 1 and person B lead event 2, and so on, so that while one leader is at work another can be gathering supplies and clarifying his presentation of the next event. A public address system is helpful to give instructions. Some more specific suggestions follow:

REGISTERING

Upon arrival of the first guest everything should be in readiness. They walk into the room under a ladder. Taped Halloween noise sets the mood. They receive a colored name tag which will later identify their relay and recreation group. They register and move to any one of several interest centers.

INTEREST CENTERS

1. Apples, doughnuts, marshmallows are strung up and are to be obtained without use of hands.

2. At one table a sign proclaims *Make Your Own Animals or Creatures*. Here apples, oranges, potatoes, turnips, carrots are available, along with raisins, small marshmallows, toothpicks, pins, colored paper, felt, pipe cleaners, wire, scissors, glue, and tape for creating unusual animals.

3. At another table *fifteen everyday objects* are in a paper sack. Players are blindfolded in turn and each one puts his hand in the sack for two minutes. Then after the blindfold is removed, he writes down what was in the sack. Young children could tell the leader what they felt. Several sacks and blindfolds may be needed. Items included might be nuts, glove, handkerchief, gum, pencil, crayon, etc.

4. In another area play *Pin the nose on the jack-o-lantern.* Cardboard jack-o-lanterns and several noses and pins and blindfolds are needed, along with an appropriate sign.

5. A fish pond with white elephant prizes could be in another area.

6. A game of skill, such as "toss the peanut in the pumpkin," could also result in prizes.

COSTUME AWARDS

Form a large circle and have all of the costumed guests march in a circle while being judged for the following categories:

the cutest costume, the spookiest costume, the most mysterious, most original, and the most authentic character (actor inside costume plays well the role the costume creates).

One judge for each category. Inexpensive prizes may be given, and all should get a piece of candy.

Suggest that masks and unnecessary props be removed and placed on a table provided so that they will not interfere with play.

SHOE SCRAMBLE

All girls will put their right shoe in a pile and go to the other side of the room. Boys pick up one shoe and look for its owner.

RELAYS

Line up behind line the color of your name tag. *Broomstick race:* each team has a broom which each individual rides around marker and returns to pass on broom to next in line. *Ghost race:* old sheet with proper eye holes is placed in sack. Carry sack to marker, put on ghost costume, return to line and place sheet in sack and pass on to next person. *Mask and treat race:* put on mask, run to marker with bag of candy, unwrap one piece of candy, eat it through mask, whistle, return to line, remove mask. Hand mask and bag of candy on to the next person. *Bone pile:* Cardboard skeletons (one for each team) cut into 12 parts are placed in a paper sack. At signal, entire team reassembles skeleton on floor. When skeleton is completed, the group shouts "Fee, Fie, Foe, Fum."

Do as many of these relays as time permits.

BLACK AND BLUE

Two boys from each team are asked to come forward. One large circle is formed while orange and black balloons are tied to boys' backs with 3-foot strings. Rolled newspapers are given to each boy. At signal boys begin swatting each other's balloon while protecting their own. Groups cheer for their representatives. Contest continues till only one balloon is left.

If time permits, the informal recreation at interest centers can be resumed, adding bobbing for apples and a spook house. Simple refreshments are served. Before anyone leaves, remind them to take their complete costumes and any prizes won or animals created. The work for the Clean-up Committee will be easy to find. (Clean-up Committee consists of everyone who participated in the event — including the children.)

Flight 704
by Nancy Peterson and Terry Wall

This playlet is designed to illustrate people's reaction to danger and crisis and how the power of God is accepted or denied. The scene is the cabin of a jet airliner on its way from London to the United States. Seven passengers are on board. The plane is approximately halfway across the Atlantic.

CAST:

Narrator	Stephanie Grant
Pilot	George Barkley
Pam Elliott: Stewardess	Rev. Mr. Gibson
Jean Scott	Doris Richards
Barbara Patton	Marc Holmes

STAGING

The stage is dark except for a red spotlight over the passengers. A second white spotlight is used to highlight members of the cast who take part in individual conversations. The pilot is never seen, only heard. He should speak through a microphone of some kind. A low roar could be taped to simulate a jet engine. Suggested seating for the passengers in two seats abreast:

1. Jean — Marc
2. Barbara — Rev. Mr. Gibson
3. Stephanie — Doris
4. Barkley

Audience

The lurch of the plane as indicated in the script can be simulated, if the chairs are placed on a large sheet of plywood (4' x 8') which rests on low rollers or round logs. A serving tray and cups are needed for the stewardess.

Narrator: Good evening, ladies and gentlemen, welcome to Flight 704 — London to New York. Your captain is Thomas Duncan, a former bomber pilot, who is assisted by stewardess Pam Elliot. The passenger list includes (*spotlight on Stephanie and each passenger in succession as they are introduced*). Stephanie Grant Whitlake III, recently divorced. She could be described as a member of the jet set. She is also known for her sharp tongue and poignant wit. Also on the list is Mr. George Barkley, a businessman of little wit and mean temper. This is Barbara Patton, a sponsor for students studying abroad. She and her two students are returning home after six months of foreign study in Europe. These are the two students, Marc Holmes and Jean Scott. They have gotten to know each other fairly well in the past six months and get along rather well. They are majoring in European history. Next is Mr. Gibson. He has been a pastor for eleven years as a minister in a suburban church in Nebraska. He is returning after a brief sabbatical. Last is Mrs. Doris Richard, who is a kind-hearted but a rather gushy woman. She and her husband are returning to America after a long-dreamed-of vacation. Mr. Richards is on a different flight. Welcome aboard and enjoy your flight with Trans American Airlines.

ACT I

Pilot: Miss Elliott, will you come to the cabin,

please? (*Miss Elliott who has been bustling about and has just stopped to talk to Marc excuses herself. Plane vibrates noticeably.*)

Elliott: Excuse me, please. (*She goes forward to cabin. She returns to deck in a few moments and nervously fluffs a pillow.*)

Pilot: Ladies and Gentlemen, this is Captain Duncan speaking. Our flight is now 3½ hours out of London en route to New York. The slight turbulence we are experiencing is due to some minor adjustments we've made with the engine speed. (*Plane vibrates.*) There is no cause for alarm, but we would ask you to keep your seat belts snugly fastened — and please observe the no-smoking sign. We hope you will continue to enjoy your flight aboard Trans American Airways.

(Slight twitter among passengers.)

Jean: (*To Miss Patton*) I hope there's nothing wrong.

Marc: (*To Jean*) Perhaps there will be a little excitement this trip. (*Jean nods in agreement.*)

Doris: (*To Stephanie*) You know, I told John it sure would be nice for just the two of us to take this trip alone, but after two weeks without the children I'm certainly homesick. I just *can't wait* to see them again. Let me show you their pictures. (*Stephanie is ignoring her.*) Here is little Peggy last Christmas. Isn't she just darling in that red velvet dress? You know, I made it myself, found the material on sale at "Fabrics Unlimited." You know it was only $2.50 a yard! This is our son Jeffy. He was nine last month. This was with my husband John in Colorado last summer. You know, John is on the next flight over. Marge told me when I was under the dryer that it's always wise for husband and wife to take separate flights. She said, "You never know when something might happen." You know, I told John planes were ever so much safer than cars. But he said, "Better safe than sorry." Oh! He's so witty that way (*laughs*). So, here I am!

Stephanie: Hummph! (*Spotlight shifts to Pam Elliott who is serving Mr. Barkley.*)

Barkley: Ham gives me indigestion (*complainingly*). Don't you have any other kind of sandwiches?

Elliott: No, I'm sorry we don't, sir.

Barkley: (*Grumbles*) What a way to run an airline!

I can hardly wait to get off this thing. Lousy coffee, lousy service. (*Pam leaves him.*)

(Plane lurches violently. Stewardess almost falls.)

Jean: Marc, what was that? Miss Patton, do you think something is wrong with the plane?

Miss Patton: (*Nervously*) It was only an air pocket, honey.

Mr. Gibson: They say turbulence is quite common over the ocean.

Pilot: This is your pilot. We have developed some engine trouble. Nothing too serious but prepare for some more turbulence — and please consult the emergency evacuation card located in the seat pocket. This is merely a standard precautionary measure. There is no cause for alarm. We hope you enjoy your flight on Trans American Airways.

Jean: Oh, Marc, could we really have to ditch?

Marc: Don't be silly. They're always overly cautious. There's nothing to worry about. Besides he never even mentioned ditching.

Miss Patton: (*To Mr. Gibson*) Reverend, do you really think there is something wrong?

Rev. Gibson: Well, Miss Patton, I doubt that anything's the matter, but if there is, I'm sure the pilot can handle it. These pilots are excellently trained and very capable. (*Trying to ease his nerves.*) As far as London to New York flights are concerned I adhere to the thought found in Mark 4:35 — "Let us pass over unto the other side."

Stephanie: (*Sarcastically*) Oh! You men of the cloth are such a comfort! (*Laughs.*)

Miss Patton: For the past six years I've been taking students abroad for study in foreign countries. This is really a great responsibility, and until we're headed for home I don't realize the strain I've been under. Surely the good Lord wouldn't let anything happen to us this close to home. I've spent six months with Jean and Marc, and they're just as close to me as part of my own family. You don't think anything will happen, do you?

Mr. Gibson: Well, Miss Patton — (*Interrupted by George Barkley, who has approached.*)

Barkley: Listen, lady. Do you think just because he's a preacher means he knows anymore about it than the rest of us? What do you think he has — a hot line to heaven? If this crumby airline is falling apart, no Bible-tot'n, Scripture-quoting preacher is gonna hold it together.

Elliott: The pilot would like to have all passengers in their seats. Is there anything I can get you?

Barkley: Yea, a good stiff drink. When we crash I don't want to know about it.

Jean: *(Screams.)*

Marc: Take it easy, Jean. It's all right.

Doris: *(Stephanie rises to leave.)* Do you think we really will crash? Do you think we will get out okay? Do you think —

Stephanie: *(to the stewardess)* I'll be joining Mr. Barkley. *(She walks over to Mr. Barkley and plops down on his seat.)* Is this seat taken? *(No response.)* I just had to get away from her. That biddy was driving me up the wall! A little engine trouble and everybody around here comes unglued — like that kid back there. *(Looks over her shoulder toward Jean.)*

Barkley: And that preacher holdin' a revival back there — and I have all this work to do before we hit New York.

Stephanie: All that gal back there talked about was her family. My husband and I have been divorced for three months and it feels good to have no one to worry about but myself.

(Captain's Voice; Passengers freeze in positions.)

Pilot: This is the pilot. Due to further engine trouble we are continuing to lose altitude. Should it become necessary to evacuate the craft, please locate the flotation cushion under your seat and review immediately the evacuation procedure.

Jean: EVACUATE? How can we evacuate in the middle of the ocean? *(Marc turns to her, and the scene quickly fades out.)*

Stephanie: There she goes again!

Barkley: Sounds like we might really be in trouble!

Doris: What are we going to do? What are we going to do? *(Getting hysterical.)* We're going to crash. I know we are. I just know it. Oh, God . . .

(Stephanie returns to Doris.)

Stephanie: Please try to get hold of yourself. You're only making things worse. *(Turns to Mr. Gibson.)* Isn't there anything you can say to help?

Mr. Gibson: When I am in need I turn to the Lord for comfort.

Marc: Well, how do you do that?

Barkley: Nothing like a little foxhole religion, eh, Reverend?

Patton: Let's listen to the Reverend.

SCRIPT ENDS!

At this point stop the play. Divide the entire group into smaller groups of threes and fours. They are to write the script for Mr. Gibson's response to the crisis and the final conclusion of the play. Choose two or three of the scripts when completed and have the original cast act them out.

SOME FINAL COMMENTS!

When the play is over, let some of the other groups discuss their endings. Why were certain endings chosen? What were some of the comments made by Mr. Gibson? Were they helpful comments or the kinds of cliches that ministers are supposed to say? Who did you identify with on the plane? Why? Who did you like least?

THE AUTHOR'S CONCLUSION

The writers of the play concluded it in this way:

Mr. Gibson: I don't presume to have all the answers. But I know I can turn to God at times like this.

Miss Patton: Would you pray with us, Reverend?

Stephanie: Go on, please. It couldn't hurt.

(Lights dim.)

Mr. Gibson: Dear Lord, *(Lights continue to dim throughout prayer.)* Please give us the strength to face this time of crisis. Help us to be brave and give us faith in thy providence in this, our hour of need. Some of us have never known you; others are just mildly acquainted. Help us all to get to know you in these remaining minutes. *(Pause.)*

Our Father, we would ask your help, and pray that we might be granted safe deliverance into the arms of our homeland. *(Pause.)* And we —

Pilot: Ladies and Gentlemen, power has just been restored. We will be able to achieve our destination. Thank you.

Mr. Gibson: For we ask it in Jesus' name, Amen.

DID YOU END YOURS THIS WAY? WHY OR WHY NOT?

A study of the Bible—how it has changed and has not changed. This is an experience-centered approach to a study of revelation.

Now in the World—God
by Harry Moore

INTRODUCTION

The Bible is a report of what occurred hundreds of years ago between God and man. It is a second-hand report of what men saw and did in response to God's revelation. Innumerable translations and rewriting have further obscured those original happenings. Man leaves his indelible print on whatever he does. The biblical reports, in their course through history, have been exposed to thousands of men. *To what extent has the truth of God been clouded by the bumblings of men?* The following experiment will be an answer to that question and will illustrate how the essential truths of the biblical record have been preserved.

You learn by doing is an old cliche with a lot of truth. Although difficult to put into practice, it is still a basic method of education. One learns best when he can be involved mentally, emotionally, and physically in the teaching-learning situation. But there are problems. For example, *how does one relive history? How does one relive God's mighty acts among men as described in the Bible?* Obviously, we cannot go back into the past and relive the experience of the disciples. We can, however, recreate some of the conditions of the past to participate in them. What we then experience may be very similar to what the disciples of old experienced.

We wish to apply this technique of *learning by doing* to a study of *how the Bible came about.*

WHAT GOD'S DONE ALREADY

The Bible is, in fact, a record and interpretation of God's revelation to man. God acted in history, and men recorded those events. It occurred like this:

1. Something happened in an historical event between God and man. God acted! *The fact of revelation.*

2. Someone saw and responded to this self-disclosure by God. He was affected by it and remembered it. He told others about it, who, in turn, told others and others. As the result of the continuous telling, some of the story was changed but its essential truth remained. *The record of revelation.*

3. At some point in the telling, under the direction of the Holy Spirit, holy men of old wrote their own account of what happened. *The interpretation of revelation.*

4. What these ancient men wrote was preserved primarily by copying their original writings. Our present Bible is a part of this process. *The report of revelation.*

You have just read about how the Bible has come down to us through the centuries from the original incidents of God's revelation to our present record and interpretation of it. Let's simulate the process and discover how much truth there is in what we have said thus far.

PROGRAM FORMAT

An Experiment in Repeating History

1. SIMULATE THE FACT OF REVELATION

Have two people leave the room. Have three people act out a role play for the group. They should have been notified prior to the meeting and worked out the situation for the role play

(3-5 minutes). Bring the two people back to the room. Two members of the audience will tell them what happened in the role play. This is an experience to show how two people can watch the same event but see, hear, and retell the event with variation.

Similarities between this and the historical fact of revelation are:
a. Something real happened.
b. Different people witnessed the same event.
c. Different people will find different meaning in the event. Some will see one thing, others something else.

2. SIMULATE THE RECORD OF REVELATION

Divide the group into work groups. *One group will leave the room for the duration of this step.* One group will decide on a brief role play to do for the other work groups. A second role play is done. Each work group will work out a way of reporting the role play to the group which has left the room. Each group will choose one of the following methods of reporting. No duplicating of methods. (Allow about 20 minutes.)

Methods of Reporting

Chronicle or historical account: A detailing of the role play from beginning to end.

Poetry: Poetic expression of the event witnessed. Could be a personal or group effort.

Art: Symbolic expression of what the group saw in the role play. Include painting a mural, individual pictures, songs, ballads, etc.

News reporter: First person interview, etc.

Fantasy or myth: Creation of a story similar in essence to the role play but different in particulars.

3. SIMULATE THE REPORT OF REVELATION

Each small group will now make their report to the total group. Have the group which left, and thus which has been excluded from the process thus far, come into the room for the reporting.

The excluded group now goes to work. Have them listen to the various reports and then reconstruct the role play using the secondhand data of the reports. How different and similar is this report from the original role play? Is the main element of the role play still recognizable? What's been lost or added? On newsprint or on the board, list in one column the report of the excluded group. In a second column list the actual role play. Contrast and compare.

If the experience has worked properly, the essential elements of the role play should be recognizable but some of the specifics of the role play will probably have been modified, embellished, or lost. *But the essential truth still remains.* This is one way of trying to understand our Bible. Many of the specifics have been lost or modified in its long life. But *its essential truth is still there.* The Bible, written by these faithful men of old, is our secondhand account of some original experiences in which God broke through history and spoke to man. We read of those events through the eyes of someone else and try to reconstruct as well as we can the actual happenings. We may never know how it all occurred in the Bible, but the reality and the truth is still there. God did and does come to man.

SUMMARY

1. We did not directly witness the events of the Bible. We were not there.

2. It is difficult to know what actually happened and how it happened from the basis of limited reporting, yet, the truths and meaning of what actually happened can still be discovered.

3. We must attempt to understand the message of the Bible through the various forms in which it is presented. (Psalms is seen as poetry, Revelation as symbolic imagery, Chronicles as historical reporting, etc.)

4. It will take more faith and courage to permit the mystery and unknown of the biblical revelation to address man, than for man to try to explain away the mystery of revelation with pat answers.

PRESESSION PLANNING

To the leader. Two role plays are needed for this session. Have them worked out and rehearsed before the meeting. Paper, pencils, art supplies, glue, and old magazines are needed.

Tim's Dream
by Gary W. Harris

INTRODUCTION

Think back, if you can, to a time when your imagination was triggered by something you saw, read, or heard. You let yourself go and fantasized, building a drama in which you became directly involved. Somehow, the initial experience, when amplified, became so real and so relevant that you were caught up in the thought and it was more than a dream.

In the following dramatization you will be looking in on Tim Tolin, a teenager whose church school teacher had been talking about the relevance for today in the message of the prophets. Tim had been given the assignment of reading the Book of Micah. Perhaps he had volunteered for Micah because it is one of the shorter prophetic books. We see Tim in his room with his Bible. He begins to read unenthusiastically.

PURPOSE

To suggest that the Bible, and in this particular case, the prophets, is relevant today; and to encourage youth to put their faith on the line, making it count for something in this world.

PROCEDURE

The dramatization is open-ended and is designed to be acted out and then discussed as you would a role-play situation. You will need the following characters:

Tim Tolin — a teenager who falls asleep with his Bible

Mike — a modern day Micah

Crowd — 5 or 6 young people

The setting is simple: an easy chair for Tim off to one side; and a soapbox for Mike. Some of the crowd might be carrying signs like, "Peace," "Love," "Brotherhood," etc. (They do not know that they are actually apathetic. They talk in abstractions and are offended when asked to get specific.)

GETTING STARTED

In groups of three browse through Micah to get a feel for the contents and the writer. What is it that the author is trying to say? Spend a few minutes sharing.

THE DRAMATIZATION: TIM'S DREAM

Tim: (*Lounging in an easy chair, he opens his Bible to Micah 1:1. Darken stage except for spot on Tim. He scratches his head and begins.*) "The word of the Lord that came to Micah of Mor — Mor-e — " What in the world . . . (*He scratches his head.*) Mor-e, Jo-tham, man what names! This teacher of mine must have rocks in her head! (*He continues to skim, and then reads aloud at 3:1.*) "And I said: Hear, you heads of Jacob and rulers of the house of Israel! Is it not for you to know justice? — you who hate the good and love the evil . . ." Hmm, not bad. "who tear the skin from off my people . . ." (*He emphasizes the thought of tearing the skin. He continues to read silently, begins to yawn sleepily, and then skips to 6:1 and reads it aloud.*) "Hear what the Lord says: Arise, plead your case before — " (*He yawns.*) " — before the mountains, and let the hills hear your voice. Hear — " (*He pauses.*) " — you mountains — " (*He falls asleep. Lights dim to low on Tim. Slowly come to full behind the crowd. Shadow effect. The crowd begins to gather. They aimlessly mill around the dream-area behind Tim. Suddenly, Mike enters and mounts a soapbox.*)

Mike: Hey, you lazy, good-for-nothing, apathetic, American idiots. Do you think that just because you are young that God is going to let you sit back while the world rots around you? Don't you have any heart — any feelings — any guts? Are you numbed to the cries of humanity around you? Where's your soul, man? (*He points to one or two and beckons them to come*

49

closer.) Are you going to allow Abraham, Martin, Bobby, and John to have died for nothing? Come on! I'm talking to you. *(Beckoning.)* Don't you give a damn about those guys who have spilled their blood in the rice patties? They would rather have been grooving with you than pushing a gun. Have you no feelings — not even for your own kind?

A Person in the Crowd: Who, me?

Mike: Yea, you! I'm talking to you. Are you going to look on while the plastic people squeeze the last ounce of cash and human dignity from the poor, the nameless millions? *(Pause.)* What's the greatest sin? *(Pause. Members of the crowd look at one another and shrug their shoulders.)* Self! The pleasure of yourself! All you care about is where you'll groove and swing this weekend. You carry the signs of peace and faith because its the now thing and you're the now people. You carry them to hide your own plastic personalities.

(People in the crowd look at one another, shrug their shoulders. Some shake their heads "yes." Others yell.) Get off it, will you, man! You're nothing, man, a big piece of nothing, man.

Mike: And what's all this talk about a "great society"? Where's the greatness if people die of hunger, if brothers fight in the streets, if thousands are left homeless by the ravages of war or by the iron claw or urban renewal?

The crowd: *(Angry reactions)* Why doesn't someone get him out of here? Who's he to tell us what to do! Move it, man, or get moved. Who does he think he is, anyway? Throw him out! Get rid of him! *(Crowd continues to grumble as Mike shouts over their voices.)*

Mike: I'm not afraid of any of you. I tell it like it is. I will not pull punches, for I'm no false prophet. Read your own newspapers and discover the truth of what I am saying. *(He pulls out a copy of the daily paper and begins to read aloud some of the headlines. Crowd reaction dies down momentarily.)* Are you going to be like those who destroy the sick in their search for a cure? America's sick — she is in need of your help; with God's help we can save her and us. Are you going to face up to reality that America is only as great as we are — that she's a mirror of our feelings, our lives? Are you going to fiddle while Rome burns for a second

time? Will you perish in that fire as history repeats itself? Are you going to turn the streets of your cities into the furnaces of Auschwitz and Dachau? Don't you get the point? It can go that far. The beginning is happening *now*. And the future, the whole outcome, rests on you and me — and you and you and you. It's the future of mankind.

The crowd: But I love my brother. We want peace and we'll fight for it. I'm interested. You don't know what you're talking about. That's a bunch of malarky. Maybe he's right. *(Crowd shouts their pro and con feelings.)*

Mike: I hear your frustrated cries of peace and love, hate and kill, but these are mere words unless you put them into action — live them. What will your words mean tomorrow, when I'm gone? There can be no rest. Shake off that apathy and plunge in — fight the battle against the injustices that are all about us. Show them what soul is! Show them what love really means! Kill the words "kill" and "oppress." Help God break down the walls or win the battle for peace, for love, for human dignity.

Tim: *(He has become so involved in Mike's speech as it has drawn to its close that he awakens shouting)* "No! No! No! I —" *(He looks bewildered. Gets up and exits, tossing his Bible on the bed.)*

DISCUSSION

The discussion following the dramatization should include the following questions:

1. Ask each player to describe how he felt while playing his part and what he thought of that person.

2. What did Mike reveal by his attitude?

3. What did members of the crowd reveal by their attitudes?

4. What do you think of (pick up a statement or two made by Mike)?

5. What was Tim's feeling as he awakened?

6. Have someone prepare to tell the group a little about Micah and his times. Can you see any relationship between Micah's world and ours that would cause you to say that Micah is relevant for us?

7. If you were Tim, what action would you take, if any, to complete the story where it left off? What does this say about what you and the group must do?

> "The more it is chewed the pleasanter it is, and the more groundedly it is searched the preciouser things are found in it." *

Digging Deep in a Study of the Bible

INTRODUCTION

It is a well-known fact that Bible study and youth don't mix very well. It is an odd-ball group, a Bible freak, that will risk its image for some intellectual sweating with the Bible. Youth tend to reflect their adult counterparts in perpetuating the notorious reputation of the Bible as being one of man's most sacred, best-selling, but least-read books that has ever been produced. Why? Because too many experiences of Bible study have been dull, unimaginative, noncreative lecture/discussion, expert-oriented. We'd like to suggest, however, a different way to study the Bible. We would like to illustrate how a depth study of the Bible can actually help you (1) to a better understanding of the people in your group and (2) to understand God's role in life a little better.

STUDY PROCEDURES

As a group you should decide on the passage of Scripture to be studied in this common effort.

Individual Study (15 minutes)

1. Each person will write his own translation of the selected passage. He uses his own words. None of those in the passage can be a part of his "translation according to Keith or Judy or. . . ." Write it in youth slang. Skip the pious verbiage. Make it high school vernacular.

2. When the passage has been translated, the person will complete this statement:

"If I took this passage seriously I . . ."

Study by Teams of Three (10-15 minutes)

When the assignments are completed, divide into groups of three. Share the translations and the completed statements. Use this procedure:

"A shares with B"; "C" listens and then summarizes what he heard being said in the discussion.

"B" shares with "C"; "A" listens and then summarizes.

"C" shares with "A"; "B" listens and then summarizes.

Finally allow a few minutes of general discussion.

Individual Study

Give each person this assignment. Reflect on the last six or seven months. What was the most important thing that happened to you? Write this down.

Study by Teams of Two (15-20 minutes)

Find a teammate. Share with him your experience and why it was important to you. Your teammate's assignment will be (1) to think of and (2) to translate into his own words a Scripture passage that "speaks" to your experience. You will do the same for him.

When the assignment has been completed, share your translations. See if your partner can understand why you chose the passage for his experience. The translations could be posted around the room and identified in relation to the person for whom they were written. These passages represent the "life" of your group.

WORSHIP

Form a large circle and spend a few minutes

* William Tyndale, in his Prologue to the book of Romans.

talking about the session. Have each person identify one thing he has learned as a result of this session.

What hymns, new and old, catch up this experience? Sing a few.

Quietly go to your former partner, take both of his hands, and say a prayer for him.

As a group, pray the Lord's Prayer.

Have a paraphrase of the Lord's Prayer read by someone who has translated it into his own words before the session.

Shout Amen! Amen! Hurrah!

PRESESSION PREPARATION

Select someone to translate the Lord's Prayer into his own words for use in the worship.

Provide a supply of paper, pencils, and a variety of Bibles.

Write some of the directions on large sheets of paper so that all can understand them.

Establish a procedure for dividing the group into teams of twos and threes.

Obtain a guitarist or pianist to help with the music.

Here are some possible passages for the group to study:

Romans 8:1-19
Philippians 1:27-30; 2:1-13; 4:4-13
2 Timothy 2:1-5
Hebrews 12:1-17
Matthew 5:3-16
John 15:9-21

The Cross Crisis—So We Have a Cross

by Janet DeOrnellas

The use of symbols is universal. Probably the most universal of all is the cross. Symbols have meaning only when we recognize the concepts and experiences they represent. The danger of symbolism is that we forget to explain the meaning and to reinterpret the symbol. The symbol becomes an object of importance rather than significant of what it symbolizes.

Many of the parables of Jesus were symbols in story form. To the uninformed, the parables describe a natural occurrence: a shepherd looking for his sheep (Luke 15:3-7). But with interpretation such a parable can point out the seeking love of God for man.

The cross is an object that we find worn on a necklace, as a tie tac, used as a car ornament, or in some other trivial way. In itself the cross is meaningless. Interpreted, it's a powerful indictment of man's stupidity, and again and again, we need to reinterpret this symbol in order to experience its meaning.

PURPOSE

To interpret "Christ died for all of us in today's world." To look at the cross with new awareness and to try to gain new insight about this symbol. To construct a cross that may be placed in the youth room or elsewhere.

SCRIPTURE

Ephesians 4:4-6. "There is one body and one Spirit, just as you were called to the one hope that belongs to your call, one Lord, one faith, one baptism, one God and Father of us all, who is above all and through all and in all."

John 11:49-52; John 19:17-18.

GO TO WORK

ADVANCE PREPARATION

1. Wooden cross approximately 5' to 6' high, made from 1" x 4" lumber (preferably weathered scrap lumber).
2. Magazines, newspapers, scissors, Elmer's glue, a brush for glazing, and Liquitex Gloss Polymer Medium.

PROCESS

Involve the total group in cutting pictures of faces of all sizes, shapes, sex, age, and color with as many varied expressions as possible from the magazines and newspapers. Include pictures of faces of group members to illustrate the fact that "Christ died for even *me!*" When a sufficient number of pictures have been collected, begin pasting them on the cross with Elmer's glue.

Arrange small faces around large ones so that the total cross is a sea of faces. Several weeks may be needed to complete this activity, depending on the size of your group and the length of time you meet. Perhaps it could be a feature program one week and a work activity for later weeks until finished.

When the cross is completely covered with faces, brush it with a coat of Liquitex Gloss Polymer Medium. Let it dry. Cover it with several coats for best appearance. Your cross may then be hung with fine wire or placed in any prominent place.

As faces are being cut from magazines and newspapers, encourage some informal discussion around the work tables. Be aware of the world problems that are evident in these resource books. Talk about the concerns of mankind, such as population explosion, birth control, pollution, drug culture, etc.

WORSHIP

(Write responses on newsprint where all can see. Readers should receive their part on individual slips of paper.)

ALL: CHRIST DIED FOR ALL OF US.

Reader 1:   Lord, help me see these faces as people — your children and my friends.

ALL: CHRIST DIED FOR ALL OF US.

Reader 2:   Lord, help me to see individual faces, not just a mass of humanity.

ALL: CHRIST DIED FOR ALL OF US.

Reader 3:   Lord, help me to share my resources with others. I have time, energy, and love.

ALL: CHRIST DIED FOR ME.

Reader 4:   Lord, when I look at the cross, remind me of its shame and not its artistic beauty.

ALL: HE DIED FOR YOU.

Reader 5:   Lord, may this cross serve to remind me that there are many of us who have not experienced the message of the cross.

ALL: CHRIST DIED FOR ALL MANKIND.

ADDITIONAL RESOURCE

It's About This Carpenter

Black and white, 14 min., rental — $7.50. A story without dialogue, this film depicts a New York City carpenter as he delivers a cross to a church. It has much symbolism and can be used to stimulate discussion on man's relation to Christ and the church and implications for the church set apart from the world. Obtainable through your denominational film library or from Mass Media Ministries. (See Resource Section for the address.)

A Step Back in Time
by Neil Sowards

PURPOSE:

To understand the traditional description of Jesus as "Lamb of God" or as having "his body broken for us."

TO THE READER

Jesus is often described as the "Lamb of God." Most of our observances of Communion or the Lord's Supper include the phrase, "This is my body broken for you." This session is designed to help your group wrestle with the question of why Jesus let himself be killed. What is the meaning of the crucifixion for today's world? To accomplish this purpose we suggest having the group participate in a custom that is over two thousand years old — the ancient Passover Feast.

THE PASSOVER FEAST

Some historians contend that the Last Supper that Jesus had with his disciples was in fact the ancient Passover Feast. It was at the end of the feast that Jesus took the cup and spoke of his broken body. Regardless of whether the Last Supper and Passover Feast were the same, Jesus, being an Israelite, would have participated in many Passovers. This fact makes the Passover Feast important to us and may help us recapture some of the feelings and understandings of the Last Supper.

The Passover commemorates the angel of death passing over the houses of the Israelites while they were in Egypt. Moses had warned Pharaoh that death would smite the firstborn of Egypt if he would not let God's people go. Pharaoh refused. The Israelites prepared by sacrificing the paschal lamb and putting its blood upon the door posts and lintel. The angel of death passed over the houses marked with the blood of the lamb and the Hebrews dwelling within were saved.

Your group can talk about the Passover. That's one way of trying to understand what it is about. The best way would be to try and experience a part of it. Try to get your minister's help and hold a Passover Feast concluding it with Communion — just as it may have happened 2,000 years ago. The Passover ceremony probably has not changed very much and is a beautiful, deeply meaningful experience if done with seriousness. The ceremony could be held on Palm Sunday night or better yet, on Maundy Thursday.

STEPS TO ORGANIZE THE PASSOVER

1. *Clear date with minister* so he can lead Communion.

2. *Form a committee of seven youth* to plan, organize, and carry out the Passover program.

3. *Obtain a copy of the Passover service.* A Jewish synagogue will probably loan a copy. A Jewish family might have one, or the public library. I would recommend *The Union Haggadah* "Home Service for the Passover" by the Central Conference of American Rabbis, 1923.

4. *Have a planning/study with the youth.* Read Exodus 12 and Matthew 26:17-30 so they can see the origin of the Passover and Communion.

Assign responsibilities:

Setting of table — 2 youth. Room should com-

55

fortably seat all, but, be small enough to be intimate. Table should be nicely decorated with candles as light. Directions for setting of the tables are found in most Passover Service Books.

Preparing of food — 2 youth. Food needed includes symbolic lamb bone, boiled eggs, horseradish, haroses (chopped apple, cinnamon, almonds, raisins), matzo crackers (found in kosher section of most large supermarkets), wine (grape juice), and parsley. The true Passover meal includes a large meal similar in quality to our Thanksgiving meal, but this can be omitted. The Passover Service Book should describe all of what is needed.

Leading of Passover Ceremony — 3 youth. Everything possible should be done to make this a serious, meaningful ceremony. The book will give the ceremony step by step with direc-

tions for what to do. Since it is a long service, parts may be omitted. The chanting parts may well be omitted. If your group has a good soloist, he or she might sing one of the beautiful seder songs. (A record with seder songs may be borrowed from the library.) When the ceremony reaches the "fourth cup," the minister will conduct the Lord's Supper.

You may want to remind the participants that the bitter herbs is horseradish — not to be eaten like cream cheese! (Several youth in one group were over-generous in their bites and had an unforgettable experience!)

Hopefully the youth will have a deeper appreciation of the Passover and our Communion service.

Discussion can be turned to the meaning of the crucifixion. In most groups one or two will have a clear idea which stimulates others to share.

SHOUT FOR JOY before the Lord, you who are
righteous;
praise comes well from the upright.
Give thanks to the Lord on the harp;
sing him psalms to the ten-stringed lute.
SING TO HIM a new song;
strike up with all your art and
　　　　SHOUT IN TRIUMPH.
　　　　　　(Psalm 33:1-3, NEB)

An Easter Thrill for Christian Worship

PURPOSE

To "feel" the moods of Easter and to write a
service of worship that captures and expresses
these moods.

TO THE READER

This article is designed to help your group
write their own service of Easter celebration — a
service that would reflect their experiences, their
needs and interests. There should be a goal in
mind for their writing. Will this be a sunrise
service, an evening service for youth only, for
youth and adults, etc? Clear the dates on your
church calendar. Plan for your publicity.

INTRODUCTION

The Easter service originated as a service of
celebration. The early Christians were so thrilled
at the resurrection that they changed their day
of worship from the seventh day, the sabbath
(Jewish custom), to the first day of the week,
Sunday. Easter is celebrated because Easter is
God's triumph over man's evil, of life over death,
love over murder, and unselfishness over selfishness.

The world had wanted a miracle and they got
it! Man, talk about being excited. Who wouldn't
be? It's like getting a field goal in the final 8
seconds of a game when you're behind 6 to 7.
There is a lot of excitement in a game like that,
but God's excitement was greater, much greater.
And that's what the early Christians were shouting about. God had really stirred them up with
his resurrection event. Their excitement carried

over into their worship — happy, joyous, tumultu-
ous. Worship is intended to be exciting, uplifting,
and renewing. Yet the worship experiences of
most churches are set in a staid, unexciting routine. Too bad. But it can be changed. Easter can
be the time to begin the changing in your
church.

THE PLACE TO START

A good worship experience should grow out
of the understandings and experiences of the
youth worshipers. To have youth use printed
sermons is ugh! To use a "canned" service is
even worse. Therefore, the place to start is to
study the New Testament accounts of the last
week of Jesus' life with emphasis on the crucifixion and resurrection. After study comes discussion
with questions like: What feelings would the disciples have after the crucifixion? What were their
expectations on Easter morning? How did they
react to the first news of the resurrection? How
would you have reacted? Get your youth to feel
and to think on what they are feeling.

WRITING THE EASTER SERVICE

The simplest type of contemporary service is
to take the usual parts of a traditional service,
analyze their purpose and function and then write
or find an up-to-date version. Another way is to
think of the moods you wish to capture and express those in the service. For example, the Easter
event has in it these three moods: despair, hope,
and celebration. Let's use these as our beginning
point.

1. Despair

"Despair" is the word for the mood at Jesus' death. What now? What next? Try to recreate this mood in the life of the worshiper through:

Music:

Hymn or solo with something like "Were You There When They Crucified My Lord?" or "Good Friday" from *Hymns for Now* (see Resource Section).

Scripture:

Mark 15:16-20, 24-30. Read from a modern version such as *Good News for Modern Man* or write your own paraphrase.

Litanies:

Write your own! Format can be: leader/ congregation; or right side of room/left side; or one reader/one respondent; or leader/ chant choir. Use the following only as examples for your writing:

A. We delivered him to be crucified.
B. We fled in his hour of need.
A. They beat him, mocked him, ridiculed him.
B. And we stayed in the shadows keeping warm.
A. They asked us if we were one of them!
B. And we said, "We do not know the man!"
A. They took him and nailed him to a cross.
B. And we hid in the crowds and wept silently.
A. He forgave his enemies from the cross.
B. While we struggled to forgive them, him, and ourselves.

A variation of the above would be to have two readers (A and B) with an added line for the congregation:

A. We delivered him to be crucified.
B. We fled in his hour of need.
Congregation: "My God! Forgive Us! Help!" (To be repeated after each B reading. To be shouted very loudly.)

Meditations:

This can take many forms. A youth reflects on the meaning of the crucifixion for him;
or
a series of news items illustrating how man is crucifying man;

or
a series of confessions of how youth in particular are crucifying each other — cheating, prejudice, violence, a boy getting his girl pregnant, a girl leading her guy on, etc.;
or
slides, movies, panel discussion, statement from the congregation, and so forth.

2. Hope

The theme is found in Isaiah 40:1-5, 9-11.

Music:

Something like "The Strife Is O'er" or "A Soul in Every Man" from *Songs for Celebration* by Kent Schneider (listed in Resource Section).

Meditation:

Comment about hope or read news clippings of hope, new discovery in medicine, peace announcements (this would be hard to find), a strike near settlement, an appeal for help, or similar message of hope.

Litanies:

A. The stone is rolled away!
B. What does it mean?
A. The tomb is empty.
B. Where is the body of the Lord?
A. He is not in the tomb; he is risen!
B. But we saw him die!
A. Men can kill but God can raise up.
B. Alleluia! Praise the Lord!

3. Celebration

This part of the worship is on "becoming alive." So make it work with the feeling of joy and love, the triumphant mood of victory and celebration. "All Hail the Power of Jesus Name" or "And They'll Know We Are Christians by Our Love" or "Clap Your Hands and Shout for Joy" (*Songs for Today*) is the kind of music you want.

Slides expressing joy, beauty, love, tenderness can be flashed on a screen in the background. Something exciting has happened. Something exciting is happening.

Move the congregation out of their pews to join hands and sway with the music, to clap, to stamp, to do anything they want that will reflect the excitement of the *most momentous movement* in history. Christ is alive and doing his will. He's here! Now! In our midst! Yippee!

FOOTNOTES

The key to a successful contemporary service is careful study, creativity, planning, practice, and polish. The congregation is usually quite tense in a contemporary worship celebration because they are uncertain what to expect. If the leaders are confident and know what they are doing, the congregation will be more free to respond.

Once the service has been written it must be practiced and polished. It must run smoothly. The congregation watches a lot of TV where every half hour has $75,000 worth of effort in it. Your service must move fast and effectively to achieve its goal: celebrating the Easter event.

Photo by Ed Carlin

Exploring the Word with hands and feet instead of words.

Hand Clappin', Feet Stompin' People of God
by Janet DeOrnellas

INTRODUCTION

At one point in her long history the church clapped, sang, and danced, as well as listened to the word of God. Now the church is better known for her rigid pews, wordy proclamations, and plastic people. Worship is basically a nonactive activity — an exercise in listening.

Now a lot of people on Sunday morning are too tired to do anything else but listen. For others, it's a bad scene. God created man to move, made man "in his own image." God is an active verb, not a passive one. God created man to see, smell, feel, hear, and taste. God created man to express himself with all of himself, not just his mind. But being the "plastic people" we are, we have trouble using more than our mouths, especially in church. We need to harmonize mind, body, and spirit for more powerful and joyful living. This article may give you and your group the chance to start.

PURPOSE

To provide your group with the opportunity to experience (instead of just to hear) some Scripture, hymns, and biblical themes. To "loosen up the group" and break down some of their plastic qualities through creative movements.

LET'S BEGIN
WARM UP EXPERIENCES

Creative movement or rhythmic interpretation is natural movement used to express and interpret feelings, beliefs, ideas, throughts, experiences, people, situations and all aspects of living. Have the group spread out around the room with as much space as possible between persons. Encourage movements with arms, legs, hands, feet, head, and body that express how one thinks and feels to the music, mood, and words to be interpreted. Try not to always think of literal movements to the words but use your imagination. Do not be concerned about quality of movement — just move.

The Imaginary Ball: This simple experience is designed to loosen up the group. A leader has an imaginary ball. The individuals do whatever he does with their imaginary balls. If he bounces, they bounce, etc. A fast, bouncy record will help. (3-4 minutes)

The Mirror Movement: Two people face each other. One is designated leader. For sixty seconds the second person reflects every movement or facial gesture that the leader makes. At the end of the sixty seconds their roles are reversed. (2 minutes — no talking)

Swing and Sway: Form small circles of 5-6 persons with arms around each other's shoulders. Eyes closed. Play some music. The group will swing and sway in time to the record. (3-4 minutes — no talking)

Stop 'n Talk: Stay in the small circles. Sit. Talk about the experiences: What you were feeling as you were doing them, etc.? (5-6 minutes)

CREATIVE MOVEMENT

Scatter the group around the room. They should not be able to touch one another with their arms outstretched. Eyes closed. (This helps to minimize feelings of embarrassment at having to do a "new" thing.) Quiet music in the background.

61

The leader will read the following words: joy, sorrow, guilt, forgiveness, fear, anger, and love. He will pause a few minutes between the reading of each word. The group acts out whatever comes to mind when they hear the words. Each person does his own thing.

Read the Lord's Prayer next. Slowly, one phrase at a time. Go through the prayer several times until everyone has individually responded to it.

Sit 'n Talk: Form small groups and share. Were any new learnings or new meanings acquired as a result of acting out the words and the Lord's Prayer? (5-10 minutes)

Someone may be willing to share his creative movement expression of the Lord's Prayer. Ask for a couple of volunteers. The group reads the prayer slowly as the volunteers act it out.

Other Themes: Continue to explore other themes. An alternative is to divide into groups of threes or fours. Each group decides on a theme and action steps, rehearses, and presents their creative expression to the total group. (This could be a part of the worship service.)

Suggested themes include:

Hymns:

"All Creatures of Our God and King"
"Rejoice, Ye Pure in Heart"

Spirituals:

"Lonesome Valley"
"Nobody Knows the Trouble I've Seen"

Poem:

"The Creation" by James Weldon Johnson; this is on a recording of *God's Trombones.*

WORSHIP:

Genesis 1:1:   In the beginning God created the heavens and the earth.

Genesis 1:27: So God created man in his own image, in the image of God he created him.

Poem: "The Creation" by James Weldon Johnson.

Amen! Amen! Amen! Amen!

REMEMBER: Many persons are at first reluctant to "move" words rather than "talk" them. But usually after the first hesitant trial, they receive a great deal of satisfaction from physically expressing or interpreting their faith. Remember, no emphasis should be stressed on quality or perfection of movement (at least in the beginning), but rather on efforts to express feelings about faith.

Preparation should be made to have records, words read, or a pianist for these selections you intend to use. The participants should say or sing the words along with the music or voice.

Although the purpose of this program is to experiment with this movement experience, part or all of the group may wish to share one of these interpretations in a worship service at a later date.

CREATIVITY:

ADDITIONAL RESOURCE

Why Man Creates

This film deals with human creativeness — how it is employed and how it evolved. It uses a diverse array of modern cinematic techniques ranging from cartoon animation to quick cuts and superimposition. Suggest advance preview for adequate discussion purposes. Free. Order from Modern Talking Pictures Services, 1212 Avenue of Americas, New York, New York 10032, or Kaiser Aluminum Mechanical Corp., Film Distribution Center, Room 864, Kaiser Center, Oakland, California.

People Who Aren't Quite People
by Richard Orr

Directions:

Four youth and two adult voices are needed. The youth voices are indicated by numbers, the adult voices by the letters "A" and "B." A creative group could provide appropriate background music to heighten the effect of the reading. Some may want to utilize interpretive movements. A discussion question which emerges is, how well does this drama really represent and describe the feelings of today's youth?

Youth: We, contemporary youth, are strangers.

(1-2)	Strangers to each other.
(1-2-3)	Strangers to ourselves.
(4)	We are
(all)	confused,
	baffled,
	tired
(3)	of all the questions about life
(4)	and what are we supposed to be doing.
(all)	Angry (angrily said)
(1)	at what needs to be done
(2)	and isn't being done.
(3)	We are
(4)	searching,
(2)	looking,
(1)	groping
(2)	for something solid on which to stand,
(3)	for something firm on which to lean,
(4)	for something more than ourselves.
(1)	But
(2)	it
(3)	is
(all)	NOT (very loud)
(2-3)	your cars
	and high priced houses,
(1)	NOT (very loud)
(2-3)	your lucrative jobs
(2-3)	and tenuous social connections.
(A)	Listen. (soft to loud)
(B)	Listen.
(A-B)	Listen.

(A)	I am the voice of an adult.
	I have something to say.
(2)	Is there no way of having our search ended?
(3)	Our questions answered?
(A)	There is.
	You're searching for God.
(1)	God? (incredulously said)
(2)	God?
(3)	God?
(all)	DID YOU SAY (loud)
	GOD? (very loud)
(4)	No, sir, Mister.
	We are searching,
	but not for God.
(all)	We've been to your church,
(1)	to your meetings,
(2)	to your youth groups.
(3)	We've seen
(all)	that bunch of old ladies
	and anemic looking kids
(4)	making their once-a-week peace
	with their old man God.
(all)	No, sir, Mister.
(1)	We are not searching
(2)	for
(3)	your
(4)	GOD.
(A)	But you are!
	It's really God
	for whom you're looking.
(B)	The God of life,
(A-B)	WHO
(A)	lets purpose be discovered,
(B)	encourages the fullest living
	of every moment,
(A)	stands not over or against man
	but moves within him.
(1)	Keep talking, Mister!
(2)	We are listening.
(3)	We're not believing it all
(all)	but keep talking. We're listening.

63

People Can Be People

No man has ever seen God; if we love one another, God abides in us and his love is perfected in us.

. . . he who does not love his brother whom he has seen, cannot love God whom he has not seen.

. . . he who loves God should love his brother also.

(1 John 4:12, 20, 21)

A Liturgy of Worship based on 1 John, chapter 4.

PREPARATION:

This liturgy can be used as a service itself or included as a part of a larger service of worship. Two readers are needed. The congregation should be familiar with chapter 4 of 1 John or at least those verses indicated. An imaginative person in your group could develop some interpretive movements so that the reading could be acted out by a group of people as well as read.

THE WORDS:

Reader I: I have seen —
     a boy named Gene,
     a girl named Lillian,
     an old man beside a broken down car,
     a child crying because he is lost,
     a black child running free in the autumn day.
     I have seen people.
     I have seen Christ.
Reader II: Today I have seen —
     (The reader makes his own observations as to how he has seen Christ reflected in the lives of people.)
     I have seen people.
     I have seen Christ.

Reader I: People are hell, but they're heaven too.
Reader II: People hate.
Reader I: People care.
Reader II: People love.
Reader I: People need people.
Reader II: People need love:
Reader I: the love of God,
Reader II: the love of each other.
Reader I: People need people. People need friends, lovers, neighbors.
     People need to be needed.
Readers
  I & II: You need to be needed and you need to be loved.
Reader II: Why all the talk about people? Such a distant word. You're here. I'm here. We're people. Let's talk about us.
Reader I: A wall is tumbling. The wall of distance is coming down, when you speak about us. We always have the walls up. Walls to keep people out. Walls to keep people from getting too close.
Reader II: We live and act that way. We use words to keep people away. Yet we keep waiting for the walls to crack and crumble. We keep waiting to open and live.
Reader I: People need people. People need love.
Reader II: And the courage to reach out. To reach out and ask, to reach out and give.
Reader I: It's frightening, it's scary, but necessary too. To reach out to another person, whether to ask for help or to give some aid, means taking the chance of being turned away.
Reader II: Rejected. Despised. Terribly lonely.

Reader II: Always closer than we want, always closer than we think.

Reader I: It may be that some of us, in this crowd, in our group, are alone. Who is he? Where? The walls keep us out.

Reader II: (SHOUT it out, as if in agony) How do you break free? Tear down the walls, turn on the people?

Reader I: How? By reaching out, by taking the chance, and letting it be known who you are and how you feel. By making the break with the world of self-pretense.

THE PRACTICE:

Reader II: We offer you that chance now, of making the break, of cracking the wall. *Go to one person in this room. Take his/her hands. Look him in the eyes. Ask this question: "I'd like to know how you feel about me."* You have five minutes. Keep hold of both hands until after our closing prayer.

THE PRAYER

Reader I: (Reader I offers the prayer. It is a prayer of confession which speaks to God about how well we succeeded in our honesty. It should reflect the feelings of the experience. A hymn may be appropriate following the prayer.)

NOTE: Don't be too disturbed if this experience is not as good as you would like. The first attempts at group honesty are usually partially successful, filled with nervous laughter and side comments.

War and Peace

by David E. Cloud

THE REAL BATTLE
by
David E. Cloud

There is a race
For land and space.
   I wonder—who will win?

The right or wrong,
The weak or strong?
   And will it involve sin?

The cause of war
Takes from our shore
   Men ready to be tin.

How black the night
If might makes right,
   And truth is lost to din.

Instead, seek love
From God above,
   Let Christ the Savior in.

If we're to cope,
He is the hope.
   The battle lies within.

PURPOSES

To name some of the motives for war and violence. To discover the seeds for war in one's own life. To consider Jesus' teaching on peace as a guide for one's life.

PREPARATION

Even though only one program plan is presented here, the material can be adapted for use in a debate, a panel discussion, a lecture-discussion, small or large group open discussions, or one or more Bible studies.

If you use the "Faith Trial" program, you will need one session to prepare for the trial, one session for the trial itself, and one session for a thorough follow-up and evaluation.

The cast of characters for the "Faith Trial" includes:

a lawyer for War, and one for Peace
one judge   three witnesses for Peace
six jurymen   three witnesses for War
plaintiff, War   other witnesses as each
defendant, Peace   lawyer sees the need

War has had Peace arrested for trying to take over his claimed place in the scheme of world events. The two lawyers should try to develop their own arguments to support their cases. The resources which are suggested in this unit will help them. They should also write out their own list of questions to ask the various witnesses. Other group members who are not already assigned a role in the *trial* could be invited to assist in the initial planning as well as helping during the trial recesses.

Play this courtroom drama to the full. Any time one of the lawyers calls for a strategy recess, divide the remaining members of the youth group equally between the two counselors. They can assist them in developing their counter-arguments and additional questions.

66

THE FAITH TRIAL

Here is a possible order of the trial proceedings:

1. All take their places.

2. The judge recognizes the plaintiff (War) and the defendant (Peace).

3. The lawyer (counsel) for War presents his case (what he intends to prove), followed by the lawyer for Peace with the outline for his defense.

4. Counsel for War calls his first supportive witness.

5. Peace's counsel cross-examines if he wishes.

Repeat steps 4 and 5 with the second and third witnesses for War. Go through the same steps for witnesses for Peace.

6. Next the plaintiff, War, is questioned and then cross-examined. The same is done for the defendant, Peace.

7. Each lawyer presents a final summation of his case and makes an appeal to the jury.

8. The jury recesses, reaches a verdict (guilty or not guilty), and presents it to the court with any recommendations it sees fit to make.

AFTER THE TRIAL

1. List the motives used for violence and war.

2. What are the seeds of war which are found in our own attitudes and behavior?

3. What is the peace Jesus taught as a guiding principle for one's life?

CLOSING

Songs: "One Tin Soldier"
"Blowin' in the Wind"
Poem: "The Real Battle"
Bible: Matthew 5:9
Prayer: Lord God, let there be peace on earth, and let it begin with me. Amen.

WRITTEN EVALUATION

Have the following questions written on the chalkboard or newsprint. Ask everyone present to write his or her response to the "Faith Trial" and discussion approach to the topic of "War and Peace."

1. Write the first three words which come to your mind describing how you feel about the program.

2. Are the issues of war and violence in relation to peace more clearly understood now or only more confused? Explain.

3. What is one (or two) thing you plan to do as a result of the program to fight war or to promote peace?

4. What could the youth group do to promote peace?

RESOURCES FOR CASE PRESENTATIONS AND ARGUMENTS

These suggested topics, questions, and Scripture resources are for the youth doing the planning, but only as they request help. Don't be limited to what is noted here.

DEFINITIONS

adversary—enemy who fights determinedly.

cold war—intensive economic and political rivalry just short of military conflict.

contention—a dispute; a controversy.

controversy—disputation concerning a matter of opinion.

dictators—rulers exercising absolute power.

disputation—a debate, verbal controversy.

economic—of or relating to production, distribution, and use of income and wealth.

enemy—one who cherishes hatred or harmful designs against another; an armed foe.

hostile—opposed in feeling, action, or character; unfriendly; characteristic of an enemy.

hostility—enmity; antagonism.

militant—combative; aggressive; warring.

political—of or relating to governmental power over the actions of men.

power—political or national strength, might, force; control or command over others.

rival—one in pursuit of the same object as another or striving to equal or outdo another.

violence—rough, intense, severe, extreme, or injurious action or treatment.

war—active hostility or contention; conflict; a state of strong opposition; conflict carried on by force of arms.

ISSUES TO RAISE

Killing, violence, Vietnam, Cambodia, Middle East conflict, Irish battles, peace, compromise, negotiation, conflicting goals, ways to reach ends.

MOTIVES FOR WAR

Being defensive or offensive; hatred; to destroy evil; greed, to gain possession; pride; continuing ancient quarrels; protection; power; peace at any cost; lying to achieve ends.

QUESTIONS

These questions are more general in nature and may provide the basis for the more specific ones which the two lawyers will prepare for their witnesses. This list of questions could be used as presented for alternate programs involving general discussion:

Is all violence bad? Explain. Exceptions?

Is all war wrong? Explain. Exceptions?

What are any of the benefits of war and violence? Of peace and brotherhood?

Do high goals of any kind justify violent means to achieve them?

What are some alternatives to war and violence?

What does the New Testament say about war, violence, and peace?

What did Jesus bring? (Matthew 10:34) Why?

How would you respond if you were asked to kill someone in war? Could you do it? Explain.

Who has the right to decide life or death for other human beings?

BIBLE STATISTICS

The following words are found in the RSV New Testament. The numbers in parentheses indicate the number of times each word is used.

war (15); wars (3); warfare (2);

strife (3); fight (5); fighting (2); fights (1);

peace (91); peaceable (2); peaceably (1):

peaceful (1); peacemakers (1)

BIBLE VERSES (New Testament only)

War (strife)—Matthew 24:6; Luke 14:31; 21:9; Romans 1:29; 7:23; 1 Corinthians 3:3; 2 Corinthians 10:3-4; Galatians 5:20; 1 Timothy 1:18; Hebrews 11:34; James 4:1-2; 1 Peter 2:11; Revelation 2:16; 11:7; 12:7, 17; 13:7; 17:14; 19:11, 19.

Peace—Matthew 5:9; Mark 5:34; Luke 1:79; 7:50; 12:51; 19:42; John 14:27; 16:33; Acts 10:36; Romans 5:1, 10; 8:6; 14:17; 2 Corinthians 5:18-21; Galatians 5:22; Ephesians 2:13-18; Colossians 1:20; 3:15; 1 Thessalonians 5:23; Hebrews 12:11; James 2:16.

Here are some ways the Bible verses could be used:

The lawyers may wish to ask a witness, "Do you believe Luke 1:79, where it says that Jesus came to give light to those who sit in darkness and in the shadow of death, to guide your feet into the way of peace? You believe this, and yet you also believe that wars are necessary. How do you hold both beliefs without internal conflict?"

Or the other lawyer could ask, "You believe in promoting peace, and yet Jesus said in Matthew 10:34 that he came to bring a sword. Shouldn't you be supporting wars then?"

Another word about using the Bible verses—be sure to study each of the verses you plan to use, so that you are clear as to the use of the key words *war* and *peace*. At times they refer to person-to-person relationships and at other times to the inner, more spiritual dimensions.

Have enough Bibles on hand for all of the characters in the *Faith Trial* who may want to make reference to them.

Conducting the Trial

The judge has a very important role as the key mover of the action. He must know who is to do what and when. He needs to think through each objection which may come from either of the lawyers and render a quick judgment, either sustained or denied. The *key issues* for the judge to keep before him and the whole court are:

Have the rights of war been denied?

Has peace overstepped his bounds in trying to prevent war from functioning?

Is the world going to be worse off because peace closed the door on war?

What will happen to countries which survive on war economies?

What will happen to countries which are known as generous and helpful when they have no one to help—should all wars stop?

Other Resources

Report of the President's Commission on an All Volunteer Armed Force ("Bates Commission"). New York: The Macmillan Company, 1970. 95 cents (paper).

Book: *War and Conscience in America*, Philadelphia: The Westminster Press, 1968. $1.65 (paper).

Recommended films on the morality of war: a concise listing with brief descriptions and rental rates (one copy free). Write:

Mass Media Ministries
2116 Charles St.
Baltimore, MD 21218

> The right to kill is a necessity, under certain circumstances, for free men.

Attack and Destroy

A common characteristic of man is his creative ability to settle disputes by force. When logic fails he spits, kicks, bites, hits, and bayonets. Love is a luxury. Peace a dream. Force is a practical expediency for the sake of reality. When you want to love and a neighbor wants to kill you, you have two choices: die or defend (maim and kill).

PURPOSE

To explore the reasons for violence and discover the ease with which we can move toward aggressive behavior under certain circumstances.

STRATEGY

"Attack and Destroy" is a game for 4-8 people. It is a game of confrontation, a duel between two opposing teams. Inner-team conflict is a part of the game. The game is designed to help the participants understand how they act under stress and tension. The goal is to defeat your opponent. The way to do it is through team understanding and cooperation.

PRESESSION ARRANGEMENTS

GAME EQUIPMENT

If more than eight people are in your group two sets of the game will be needed.

checker board

thirty chips: fifteen for each team. Two different colors. They can be made from small pieces of cardboard.

score sheet: one for each team

battlefield cards: 3″ x 5″ index cards cut in half. Use one side only.

TIME

Forty-five to sixty minutes should be allowed for the actual playing of the game, thirty minutes for post-game discussion.

PLAYING THE GAME

The *object of the game* is to obtain the highest possible score by the conclusion of the game. The game concludes when

1. The Battlefield Cards have all been played;
2. An opponent's forces have been destroyed;
3. Or the opposing forces mutually agree to end the battle.

The game is basically a confrontation between two opposing sides. Each side is composed of a *Strategy Team* (1-3 people) and a *Commander*. A regular checker or chess board is used. Fifteen chips are needed for each side. Each Commander begins the game with twelve chips placed on the two rows nearest him. Use both dark and light squares. Three chips are kept off the board as extra playing chips (Reserve).

ROUNDS

The game is played in rounds. Each *round* consists of:

1. *The Team Play.* The moving of any one chip three spaces or three chips one space or any combination of moves that includes three spaces by the Strategy Team.

2. *Commander's Play.* Each Commander has three plays. The starting Commander plays once followed in turn by his opponent. The play continues until each Commander has had his three plays.

3. *Scoring.* Done at the end of the Commander's play.

> The team with the fewest points gained in the previous round starts each new round.

> There can be no talking between the Commander and his Strategy Team at anytime during the game.

MOVES

Use both light and dark squares in playing.

Regular chips can only move diagonally or straight ahead, one space at a time except in the Team Play, when moves of up to three spaces may be made. *Kings* can move in any direction. *Jumps* are made as in the regular game of checkers. You do not have to move a chip if you do not wish to do so. A *king* is obtained by moving one of your chips across the board to your opponent's back row. Place two chips together to form a king.

SCORING

Is done at the end of each round. One point for each checker and three points for each king killed in the previous round of play. Two points are deducted for each man lost to the opposing side during a round of play. (See Score Sheet.)

STRATEGY TEAM (one to three people)

— Decides and plays out the Team Play in each round.
— Decides how many men are to be kept on the board, taken from it, or added to it from the Reserves.
— Appoints and dismisses the Commander when his playing is unsatisfactory.
— Negotiates with the opposing team through a selected representative.
— Makes decisions by a majority vote.
— Cannot communicate with the Commander in any way during the game except to dismiss him.

COMMANDER

— Plays three times during a round.
— Can use his Reserves at any time during his

three plays but forfeits one play per Reserve used.
— Is appointed and dismissed by the Strategy Team.
— Can thwart a negotiated decision of the Strategy Team by demanding his three plays of the round.

BATTLEFIELD CARDS

At the conclusion of each Team Play the Commanders of each team draws a Battlefield Card. The Commander starting the round reads aloud and carries out the orders. His opponent does the same. The Commanders then make their plays.

RESERVES: (three chips)

Can be put on the board by the Strategy Team or Commander at any point in the game. One play of the Commander is forfeited for each Reserve added.

NEGOTIATIONS

Any negotiations between the opposing sides occur after the Battlefield Cards are drawn by the Commanders and carried out. Only the Strategy Team can do the negotiating (3 minutes is the time limit). If no agreement is reached, both teams lose three chips from the playing board.

PEACE CALLS

A Strategy Team can call for Peace Negotiations before the Team Play. A "Peace Call" is a call to end the game and decide who will be the winner. *If the opposing side agrees to negotiate,* both sides sustain a loss of four chips each. (These are taken off the board and cannot be played at any time. There is no point loss.)

If a Peace Call is refused, the team requesting the negotiations loses its Team Play. However, it receives four points for the effort. (See Score Sheet.)

SCORING

One point is received for each chip you've killed during a round of play. Three points for each king killed (when a chip is captured, he is regarded as having been killed).

Two points are substracted from your score for each chip or king you lose to your opponent in a round.

ROUNDS	1	2	3	4	5	6	7	8	9	10	11	12
Points from previous round												
Add points from enemy chips killed												
Add 4 points for any Peace Calls made												
Total												
Subtract points deducted for loss of chips to enemy												
Total Score for the round												

BATTLEFIELD CARDS

OUT OF AMMUNITION

Neutralize one of your kings for the rest of this round by placing him in the Reserves. Return it to back row at the end of the round.

FOREIGN INTRIGUE

Commander:

Your Strategy Team has the following decision to make:

"They can have the opposing commander dismissed and lose one of your chips to him (opponent's choice)"

OR

"They can kill any two chips but be forced to dismiss you and give their opponent an extra play."

REINFORCEMENTS

Add two chips to your back row which were captured from you.

PROMOTION

You've been promoted to the Strategy Team. Change places with one of them. No extra play for your opponent.

SMALL GUN FIRE

Remove one of your chips. Take one extra turn.

BOOBY TRAP

You're dead. Change places with a Strategy Team member. Forfeit all plays this round, while your opponent continues to play.

RESCUE OPERATION

If a chip is in danger of being jumped place him in the Reserves. Replace him on his original square at the end of the round.

REINFORCEMENTS

Add two chips to the back row of your playing board, one chip to your opponent's. Take from Reserve.

PEACE MOVEMENT

A militant peace group has effectively blocked any use of your Reserve forces during this round. Remove any Reserves that are on the board.

RETREAT

Return two of your front row chips to your back row.

PRISON BREAK

Return to your opponent all of the chips you captured from him in the preceding round.

OPPONENT LOW ON AMMUNITION

Neutralize any two of your opponent's chips by placing them in his reserves.

SNEAK ATTACK

Give up all of your plays this round.

REINFORCEMENTS

Add a king to your back row if a space is available. If no space is available return a captured chip to your opponent.

WRONG ROAD

You can only move on the light squares this round. All chips on dark squares must remain there.

COMMANDER CAPTURED

You have been captured by the enemy. The two Strategy Teams must negotiate your return before the play continues — 3 minutes for negotiation. Penalty for failing to agree will be loss of three chips for each team and you resume playing.

NIGHT RAID

A successful night raid has given you the advantage of an extra play. You get four moves this round instead of three.

MINEFIELD ALERT

Your chips can only move diagonally this round.

REINFORCEMENTS

Give a king to your opponent. Take the chips from the ones you have captured and place on his back row. If he has no empty space, you lose one chip (opponent's choice). He does not get the king.

YOU HAVE BEEN FIRED

Caucus with your Strategy Team. A new commander will have to be appointed. Your opponent gets an extra play.

PARTIAL DISABLEMENT

Your kings can only move backwards this round.

DISABLED

Your kings cannot move this round.

SUPPLY CARAVAN CAPTURED

Your enemy has captured a supply caravan. Return to him two of his chips. You place them on the board wherever you like.

GENERAL RETREAT

Move all of your chips back one space.

ROCKET ATTACK

All men on light squares are removed to the Reserves for hospitalization.

WAR DOVES

Your military allotment has been cut. A reduction in active forces is necessary. Return three chips (two chips and one king if any are on the board) to the Reserves. The king now becomes two regular chips.

ATTACK AND DESTROY

A historical town of 5,000 is in the way of your attack. If you advance, you destroy the town. Your Strategy Team has these choices:

1. Attack and capture three enemy chips (your choice of chips), draw a Battlefield Card, and lose your next play;

2. Do not attack and lose three chips to your opponent (his choice of chips);

3. Cancel this card by negotiations with your opponent via your Strategy Team.

POST-GAME
DISCUSSION QUESTIONS

1. Were there any feelings of frustration and hostility expressed during the game? How were they expressed? What caused some of these feelings?

2. How did the opposing teams feel about one another?

3. How did the Commanders feel about their roles, about their Strategy Teams?

4. Name the most frustrating point in the game for you. How did you handle the frustration?

5. Was there any attempt to end the game peacefully? What happened?

6. The stakes in this game were simple. Defeat your opponent. Win a game. If the stakes had been higher, what do you think would have happened in the playing?

7. Is there any parallel between the way you played this game and the "world plays" of nations?

8. You allowed yourself to play a game of war, a game designed for the destroying of your opponent. How moral are such games? Has it (and similar games throughout our lifetime) moved us more toward aggressive behavior rather than peace?

9. What one thing have you learned about yourself as a result of this game?

10. What one thing did you learn about violence, aggressive behavior?

11. Can you point to any acts of Christian charity and love in the playing of the game, such as, places where understanding was displayed and peace-making occurred among players?

War and Injustice
by David E. Cloud

INTRODUCTION

Are people expendable? Does it matter how people are treated as long as high moral aims are being achieved? Or are human beings a part of creation rated a little below the angels? Is each person created in God's image? These questions are based on two apparently opposing views of human nature. Any discussion of war and injustice will stir these views into bold conflict. Can it be that a war being waged for the cause of justice will, at the same time, be the cause of further injustice? Or is the injustice of war seen merely as the lesser of two evils?

PURPOSES

To begin to clarify one's own beliefs related to war and injustice. To practice applying three standards of judgment to specific injustices related to war. To start planning at least one way to end some form of injustice.

SESSION APPROACHES

There are four situations presented here which involve different degrees of injustice in relation to war. The situations are:

Session 1: Government and Military Aid
Session 2: A Deserter and Government
Session 3: Killed in Action
Session 4: A C.O. and a National Emergency Draft.

A youth group's planning committee members may wish to use one or all of the four session plans or combine some of the ideas or procedures in an effort to meet the unique needs of their group.

SESSION 1: GOVERNMENT AND MILITARY AID

SITUATION

Your nation is considered one of the top three world powers. An urgent request has come to your president for military aid from the government of a struggling, small country. They say they have been threatened by a large segment of the country's population. These militants, they say, are getting military arms and support from one of the other two top powers.

PROCEDURES

1. Questions for general discussion
• What should your nation do? (Ideally, the group will discover that a decision cannot be made yet and that more information is needed.)
• What questions need to be answered first? (List questions from the group on the board before sharing any of the ones listed here.) Sample questions a nation should consider before entering a military agreement may include at least these: Have we helped the country before? Have we signed any obligatory agreements with it? Do we have the resources to supply what the country needs? Is it in our national self-interest to become involved? What terms are we on with the other

major power which is involved? Might our involvement lead to a major confrontation of world powers? How will our citizens respond if we do help or do not help the small but desperate country? Who will suffer the greatest losses: the country seeking aid, the aggressors, the major power countries, the military, or the women and children? Will the military conflict be unjust, or would we be more unjust by not getting involved? Do the militants have a legitimate cause for wanting to take over the country?

2. Divide the youth group into three smaller groups. Each subgroup will consider one of these three *standards* by which judgments could be made.

• The Bible—moral ideas from our heritage, such as, "Thou shalt not kill."

• Religious Ethics—to preserve and enhance the individual's capacity to be wise, just, and to love. Is this what war will do for people?

• The National Self-Interest—use of power to check power. Will going to war be for:

—wise political purposes?

—militarily prudent operations?

—just allocations of resources?

Each group is to apply its standard to this question: "Would it be just or unjust to provide the military aid which is being requested by the small, struggling country?" The groups may want to select any of the recent military hot spots in the world as a focus in applying the standard.

3. Ask for each group to present a summary of its discussion.

SESSION 2: A DESERTER AND GOVERNMENT

SITUATION

Jerry is a deserter from the army and is living in Canada. Letters to his family indicate that he feels he has done nothing wrong. He loves his country and wants to return. Often he writes about his concern that his so-called democratic America will not recognize his individual beliefs which kept him from participating in what he termed a needless, unjust war.

PROCEDURES

1. Have each group member write out the answers to these questions:

• How should the government treat deserters from the army on grounds of conscience? Why? Is the government unjust in not allowing them to come back into the country even briefly, without being penalized or imprisoned? Is it just for a government to require a volunteer in the armed services to compromise his/her beliefs?

• What is your opinion about those who are conscientious objectors to war? Do they have a right to object? Why or why not?

2. Collect the papers and read samplings of the various responses aloud. Have someone keep a brief summary record on the chalkboard of the reasons given in support of the views. (Headings on the chalkboard: Government and Deserter.)

3. An alternate program: have a former deserter share his views as a Christian about his experience.

4. In addition, or as an alternate program, select one or more of the following Scripture passages for use in small-group discussions. What do these passages say about injustices and how to end them? Do they alter your answers to the questions listed in procedure 1 above?

• injustice—Isaiah 59:14

• unfairness—Luke 16:10; 1 Corinthians 6:1

• oppression—Proverbs 14:31; Ecclesiastes 4:1; Isaiah 1:17

• persecution—Matthew 5:10; Acts 10:38

• tyranny—Psalm 17:8-9; Proverbs 3:31

• cruelty—Isaiah 3:15; Ezekiel 18:18

• bondage—Hebrews 13:3

• unmerciful—Matthew 25:42-43; Luke 10:31

• moral blindness—Matthew 15:14; 1 John 2:11; Isaiah 5:20

• human worth—Matthew 10:31

• rule—Proverbs 29:2

• conscience—Acts 24:16

• brotherhood and responsibility for the weak—Matthew 20:28; 23:23; 25:35-36; Mark 12:31; Luke 4:18; Romans 14:13; 15:1; 2 Corinthians 8:14; Galatians 6:2, 10; Ephesians 6:7; 1 Thessalonians 4:9; 5:14; James 1:27; 2:15-16; 2 Peter 1:5, 7

• inner control—Proverbs 16:32; 1 John 5:4

SESSION 3: KILLED IN ACTION

SITUATION

Mr. and Mrs. Smith had held high ambitions for their son before the war broke out. They have just received notice that he has been killed in action.

PROCEDURES

1. Divide the group into no more than four role-playing teams of three persons each. Remaining

group members should serve as observers. Each team is to role-play an ending to the situation described. Focus on these questions: "How will the parents respond to the news, and what will the military officer do who brought the news to their home?"

2. Preparation of role-playing teams:
- Assign parts (mother, father, officer).
- Outline basic attitudes (not speeches) for each character. For example, the dad might be a veteran who resents any war. The mother could be a stern woman who covers up how she really feels. The army officer might be one who is merely carrying out his duty. Each team works out a brief description of its own characters.
- Ask those not in the role plays to be observers. They should look for these things (have the questions on newsprint or chalkboard):
— Do the role players keep faithful to the roles assigned?
— Is the ending of the story depicted in the role play realistic?
— How do the players deal with the issue of war and injustice? Do they have supporting reasons and facts or just opinions supported by much emotion?
— Are you satisfied with their conclusions? Why or why not?
— Does the role play make reference to Christian beliefs and standards, either directly or indirectly?
- Allow seven to ten minutes for each role play and fifteen to twenty minutes for the discussion of the questions given to the observers. Also ask the role players how they felt in the roles and how they would answer the five questions.
- What could the parents do to help others in response to their son's dying in war?
- How does the Christian faith aid one who has lost a child in armed combat?

SESSION 4: A C.O. AND A NATIONAL EMERGENCY DRAFT

SITUATION

Al strongly believes that killing is not the best way to solve civil and international problems. A national emergency has been declared, and Al has been drafted. (For some reason he did not hear about alternate service until after his induction.) Al was trained in the skills of armed combat and expected to use them. He has just received orders to go the the battlefront.

PROCEDURES

1. Invite four persons to serve on a panel. Members of the panel might include an army recruiter, a church member who has served in the army during a war, a youth nearing high school graduation or one recently graduated, and a clergyman. Ask each panel member to prepare his own 5-minute response to the following questions.
- What could Al do now?
- What should he do? Why?
- Was it unjust to Al to be drafted without having all of the alternatives explained first?
- Would Al be unjust to the army if he went to the battlefront intending not to shoot to kill?
- What are the options open to a young person who wants to give a year or more in government service, but not in the armed services?

2. Or secure a movie which deals with the above issues.

3. Or have a debate.

CLOSING

No matter which of the program plans you select, the suggested closing will be applicable.

PREPARATION

In the sanctuary or chapel, arrange a worship center using various symbols of injustice and war and symbols of brotherhood and helping those who are weak. Possible symbols include a picture or drawing of prison bars or of bombs; a gun; chains; a military hat; a cross; magazine pictures of people starving or of destroyed cities due to bombing; a globe; an open Bible; food on a plate; money; a miniature tractor.

THE SERVICE

Sing "Beneath the Cross of Jesus." Have the group members hum "Onward Christian Soldiers" (or "He's Everything to Me") as they slowly, meditatively file out of the meeting room and walk to the sanctuary. They could sit or kneel on the floor around the worship center. Read 1 Corinthians 13 aloud. Close with silent prayer, as each person considers one specific way he can overcome some kind of injustice, whether at home, at school, at work, in the church, the community, the state, or the nation.

RESOURCES

See pages 136 and following in this book for a listing of other resources. The list includes publications and films for program enrichment.

What's Going On in Your Town?

by Robert Middleton, Jr.

ASSUMPTION

Most of us live fairly sheltered lives. We are concerned with events which directly affect us. We are aware of what is happening in our schools, at work, etc., but we fail to know much about our community or ways in which we can work in it as a group.

PURPOSE

To help the group identify some of the needs which are present in their community and to discover ways in which this group can work to help meet some of the needs.

SUGGESTIONS

1. If you have the money, have some members of the youth group take slides of various aspects of life in your community. These should show both sides of issues, such as poverty — affluence; youth culture — older culture; good schools — bad schools, etc. Arrange these slides so that every other one contrasts with the previous one, or have two projectors and two screens showing the slides. During the showing of the slides, play the record "Give a Damn" by Spanky and Our Gang. Reflect on what you have seen.

2. Make a collage of the various aspects of your town and reflect on what you have done. How does it make you feel? Do you think this is an accurate reading of the conditions which are in your town?

3. Reproduce this questionnaire and have the group interview some of the people in your town. Compile the data and see if there is some project which the group could do.

INTERVIEW QUESTIONNAIRE

Youth _____ Adult _____

1. List one thing you like about your community.

2. What one thing do you like the least?

3. How would you like to live in another part of the city?

4. What do you feel are the three most pressing problems in the community?

5. What are some of the things which can be done about the problem?

WORSHIP SUGGESTIONS

Opening Hymn: "They'll Know We Are Christians by Our Love" (Have the entire group sing. Provide words and music if unfamiliar to your group.)

LITANY

Leader: O God, who lives in tenements, who goes to segregated schools, who is beaten in precincts, who is unemployed.

Congregation: O God, who hangs on street corners, who tastes the grace of cheap wine and the sting of the needle.

Leader: O God, who is pregnant without husband, who is child without parent, who has no place to play. Help us to know you.

Congregation: Help us to touch you.

Leader: O God, who can't read or write, who is on welfare, and who is treated like garbage.

Congregation: O God, whose name is spick, black nigger, guinea, and kike.

Leader: O God, who is white and lives with Mr.

Charlie, who is black and lives with Uncle Tom. Help us to know you.

Congregation: Help us to touch you.

Leader: O God, who is cold in the slums of winter, whose playmates are rats — four-legged ones who live with you, and two-legged ones who imprison you.

Congregation: O God, who smells and has no place to bathe.

Leader: O God, who hustles 50 cents for lousy wine, who sells copper and lead to clean his clothes.

Congregation: O God, whose toys are broken bottles and tin cans, whose play yard is garbage and debris, and whose playhouse is the floors of the condemned buildings.

Leader: O God, who is a bum, a chiseler, who is lazy because people say you are when you don't work and you can't find a job. Help us to know you.

Congregation: Help us to touch you.

All: Help us to be with you.

Leader and Congregation:
O God, who called us from death to life, we offer ourselves to you, and with your church through all ages, we thank and praise you for your redeeming love in Christ Jesus our Lord.
   Our Father in heaven,
   Holy be your name,
   Your kingdom come,
   Your will be done,
      on earth as in heaven.
   Give us today our daily bread.
   Forgive us our sins
      as we forgive those who sin against us.
   Save us in time of trial,
      and deliver us from evil.
   For yours is the kingdom,
      and power, and the glory, forever.
                           Amen.

THE CLOSING AFFIRMATION (ALL)

> If I speak with the eloquence of men and of angels, but have no love, I become no more than blaring brass or crashing cymbal. If I have the gift of foretelling the future and hold in my mind not only all human knowledge but the very secrets of God, and if I also have that absolute faith which can move mountains, but have no love, I amount to nothing at all. If I dispose of all that I possess, yes, even if I give my body to be burned, but have no love, I achieve precisely nothing.
>
> This love of which I speak is slow to lose patience — it looks for a way of being constructive. It is not possessive: it is neither anxious to impress nor does it cherish inflated ideas of its own importance.
>
> Love has good manners and does not pursue selfish advantage. It is not touchy. It does not keep account of evil or gloat over the wickedness of other people. On the contrary, it is glad with all good men when truth prevails.
>
> Love knows no limit to its endurance, no end to its trust, no fading of its hope; it can outlast anything. It is, in fact, the one thing that still stands when all else has fallen (1 Corinthians 13:1-8, Phillips).

BENEDICTION

Leader: Go now, remembering what we have done here, responding and responsible wherever you are. You can never be the same again.

People: We know. We go to be his people wherever life takes us.

Leader: The Lord be with you.

People: Yes, and with you, too.

Leader: Depart in peace.

People: Amen, O Lord, and then once more, Amen. So let it be.

Human Rights in Your Community ▉?

OBJECT OF THIS SESSION

This session is an action-oriented one. You are to discover and analyze the practices of your community in regard to minority rights and opportunities.

APPROACH

Use the following "Human Rights in Your Community" survey. Each person answers it individually. Compare your answers to get an idea of how the group views your community. Then divide into task forces to begin an actual survey of your community. Visit some of the mentioned institutions. Interview some of the officials. Meet with minority spokesmen. Talk with community officials, political ward leaders — anybody who can give you ideas of what's going on with human rights.

Arrange to have some of the people you've visited meet with your group and talk about their jobs and the obstacles they face.

In the survey process you will come in contact with all kinds of future program guests and leaders. Plan to use them.

When the work of your task groups is completed, compile your findings. How does your community rate in the area of human rights?

THEN DECIDE

Then decide what you, as a youth group, can do with your findings. Are there some actual projects you can engage in that will be helpful to people? Should you prepare a report for distribution to your church and community leaders?

Would the newspapers be interested in your work? To stop now, without trying to do something about the situation you've discovered is a negation of your Christian ministry. Act! But act wisely!

YOUR REASON FOR GOING — FOR ACTING

"I appeal to you therefore, brethren, by the mercies of God, to present your bodies as a living sacrifice, holy and acceptable to God, which is your spiritual worship.

Do not be conformed to this world but be transformed by the renewal of your mind, *that you may prove what is the will of God, what is good and acceptable and perfect.*

Let love be genuine; hate what is evil, hold fast to what is good" (Romans 12:1, 2, 9).

HUMAN RIGHTS IN YOUR COMMUNITY

	YES	NO
EQUAL OPPORTUNITY IN JOBS AND BUSINESS		
Are public and private businesses in your community practicing fair employment as provided by law?	☐	☐
Do banks and insurance companies in your community offer equal service to minority group businessmen?	☐	☐

JOB TRAINING

Do the businesses in your community provide job training and recruit applicants regardless of race, religion, or sex, supplying information about available jobs and training? ☐ ☐

Are the tests given to job applicants suited to the type of job being offered? ☐ ☐

UNION ACTIVITY

Are all workers in your community free to organize and join unions? ☐ ☐

Are the apprentice programs in the unions in your community open to all races? ☐ ☐

EQUAL OPPORTUNITY

Is there an opportunity in your community for community leaders, businessmen, and working people to discuss together problems of employment and working conditions, including the problems of hard-core unemployables and new arrivals from rural areas? ☐ ☐

MINIMUM WAGE

Does the law of your state give minimum wage protection to all workers, i.e., household workers, migrant workers, and other agricultural workers? ☐ ☐

INTEGRATION

Do all children in your community have access to integrated education covering the twelve grades? ☐ ☐

Are the board of education, the administration, and faculty of your school system integrated? ☐ ☐

ENRICHMENT PROGRAMS

Do your schools have compensatory educational programs to improve the quality of education and maximize achievement for students who need such services? ☐ ☐

Has your community taken advantage of state and federal aid to establish enrichment programs for preschool children? ☐ ☐

Do your schools and local businesses cooperate in job training? ☐ ☐

COMMUNITY-SCHOOL RELATIONS

Is there a forum where all parents, school administrators, teachers, and all concerned citizens meet to discuss constructive plans for quality, integrated education (not PTA)? ☐ ☐

Do your school officials have a program to cultivate intergroup understanding and respect for human rights, both in the classroom and in the community? ☐ ☐

EXPANDED OPPORTUNITIES

Does your community have adequate vocational training facilities? ☐ ☐

Does your community have a program of adult or continuing education, utilizing public school facilities? ☐ ☐

HIGHER EDUCATION

Does your state have adequate facilities for higher education, open to all regardless of race, religion, or sex? ☐ ☐

	YES	NO			YES	NO

HOUSING

Is the supply of low-rent housing in your community adequate? ☐ ☐

Are your neighborhoods open to all people regardless of race or religion? ☐ ☐

Does your community have a plan to distribute the construction of new low-rent housing all over the city? ☐ ☐

HEALTH

Are hospitals and other medical facilities in your community open to all patients regardless of race and to all practicing physicians regardless of race? ☐ ☐

Are sanitation conditions and other public services, such as mail delivery, street lighting and repairs, equal in all parts of your community? ☐ ☐

PUBLIC ACCOMMODATIONS

Are all recreation facilities, hotels, and restaurants serving the public open to all persons? ☐ ☐

WELFARE

Does the minimum standard of assistance in your state come up to the subsistence "poverty" level ($3,335 per year for a city family of four)? ☐ ☐

Does your state have the AFDCUP Program (Aid for Dependent Children with Unemployed Parents)? ☐ ☐

Does your state have experimental programs to discover how job training and welfare can best interrelate? ☐ ☐

Are the eligibility restrictions and welfare practices in your state conducted fairly and in a manner promoting human dignity? ☐ ☐

LAW ENFORCEMENT

Are relationships good between the police and minority groups in your community? ☐ ☐

Do minority groups in your community have equal police protection? ☐ ☐

Does your community have a means whereby citizens' grievances against the police can be fairly heard? ☐ ☐

Does your community have a program to improve community-police relations and develop support for law enforcement? ☐ ☐

Do the poor, uneducated, and minority groups receive equal justice with the affluent in the courts of your community? ☐ ☐

CITIZENSHIP RIGHTS

Are voter and qualification registration procedures in your community clearly publicized and fairly administered? ☐ ☐

Does your state or county have any restrictions, such as sex, race, or religion on jury duty? ☐ ☐

Is membership in your church open to all people, regardless of class or race? ☐ ☐

Is the pastorate of your congregation open to a minister of any race or ethnic background? ☐ ☐

Are the hiring policies of your congregation in keep-

	YES	NO
ing with fair employment policies as provided by law?	☐	☐
Does your congregation do business with any company that discriminates in its hiring practices?	☐	☐
Are camps, conference grounds, and other facilities used by your congregation open to all races?	☐	☐

	YES	NO
Are all opportunities for service, including policy-making bodies, open in your congregation to any qualified person?	☐	☐

(From "Human Rights in Your Community," prepared jointly by the Methodist Joint Commission on Education and Cultivation for Mission and Church Women United, 1968. Reprinted by permission from *International Journal of Religious Education*, November-December, 1968, National Council of Churches, New York, New York.)

In Our Likeness and with Power over All
—Except Each Other

PURPOSE

To better understand the meaning of being black in a non-black world.

STRATEGY

Divide your group in half. One section will be the whites. The other will be the blacks. The second group will try to think and be what they think most black people are like. (Remember, though, no white man can ever know what it means to be black in a white society.)

Or, better yet,

invite a group of black youth to your meeting.

Each group will complete and share the following questionnaire.

1. The Civil Rights laws that were passed during the sixties have done little for the average black person.

    True   False

2. "Whitey" is a derogatory name and should not be used.

    True   False

3. It is easier to become a first-class citizen if you are white or oriental than if you are black.

    True   False

4. The majority of black people are not moving "up in the world" financially.

    True   False

5. Business tend to cheat blacks more than they do whites.

    True   False

6. Black youth are more susceptible to police arrest than white youth.

    True   False

7. Black people would not have achieved as much as they have, had it not been for some of the racial violence and riots.

    True   False

8. List the three greatest black men of the past decade. Rank them in order of their importance.

    A. _____
    B. _____
    C. _____

STOP AND COMPARE

Compare your answers. Were there any differences between the answers of the black and white groups? Is a compromise answer possible? Go on to the *Prejudice Anyone!* chart.

PREJUDICE ANYONE!

1. I have _____ black friends.
1, 2, 3, 4, or more

2. My black friends have visited in my home.
Yes _____ No _____
a. They have had dinner with my family.
Yes _____ No _____
b. They have stayed overnight in our home.
Yes _____ No _____

3. I would not mind having _____ black teachers in school.
1, 2, 3, 4, or more.

4. A black teacher would probably be more strict with:
black students _____
white students _____

5. I would suggest the following racial balance in our church.
1/3 black membership _____
1/2 black membership _____
2/3 black membership _____
No black membership _____

6. I would not mind eating in a restaurant operated by a black person. Yes _____ No _____

7. I would not mind eating food prepared by a black person. Yes _____ No _____

8. I would not mind loaning a good dress or coat to a black friend. Yes _____ No _____

9. I would not mind going to a good black dentist. No _____ Yes _____
Have you ever checked on a black dentist with the thought of going to him? Yes _____ No _____

10. A black barber or beautician would not bother me. Yes _____ No _____

11. Having more black students than white in my school would be O.K. Yes _____ No _____

12. The idea of a black Jesus is disgusting.
Yes _____ No _____

13. The history and culture of the black people should be taught as extensively as European history is in our school. Yes _____ No _____

14. Should black history be taught if there are no black students around? Yes _____ No _____

15. Picture yourself getting on a bus. Near you is an empty seat beside a black person. Toward the rear is a seat beside a white person. Where would you sit?

16. Would you feel comfortable walking in an all black neighborhood? Yes _____ No _____

17. If I had my choice of skin color I would rather be: white _____, yellow _____, brown _____, red _____, black _____, doesn't matter _____.

COMPARE YOUR ANSWERS.

Divide into smaller groups of threes or fours. Mix up the black/white groups. Compare answers. Then complete the following statement. Everyone in your group is to be in agreement with it.

"As a minority person in this area, this is what I think Jesus Christ would say about my place in your society. . . ."

(Put yourself in the place of whatever minority group is predominant in your area.)

When the groups are finished, share the statements as a part of your worship experience. The groups will respond to each of the statements with:

"And God said, 'Let us make man in our image, after our likeness, and let them have dominion over all living things — except each other'" (paraphrase of Genesis 1:26).

Who are they, these people called minority?

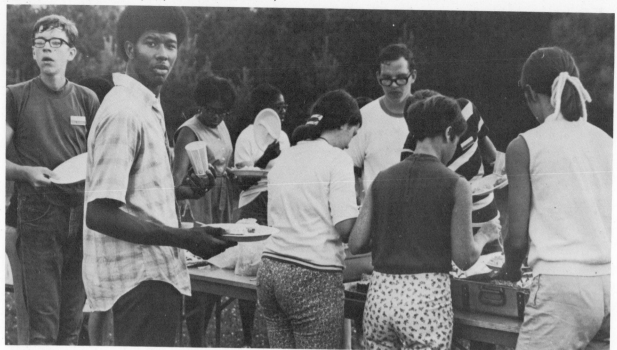

Face to Face

PURPOSE

To better understand who and what a minority person is through some personal encounters.

APPROACH

Study the minority groups in your area. With whom do you have the best contact — blacks, browns, Indians, Orientals? (In some communities Polish, German, or other foreign language speaking people may be regarded as minorities.)

Invite a group of these youth to one of your meetings. Try to have a number equal to the number of your group and about your age. Since they may not have a church relationship you may need to work through your advisor, pastor, or a social worker for contacts.

BEGIN

Begin with light refreshments. Let each person make his own name tag. This period of starting will be a stiff, awkward time as people try to see "who's who."

Explain to your guests the reason for your being

together — that you're simply interested in meeting and talking to better understand each other. The following activities may be used in your experience together:

1. BALLOON BUSTER

Action-filled laughter is a good way to begin breaking down barriers. Obtain two weather balloons (4 feet in diameter) and play double indoor volley ball. Play until players begin to tire.

Sit down and relax for a few minutes.

2. PAIRS

Divide into pairs — one member of your group with a guest. Go for a walk and talk. Talk about anything you want. (10 minutes)

3. QUESTION

Stay in pairs. Find a comfortable spot separated from other pairs.

Instructions:

If you could ask just one more question of your partner, what would you ask that he would now be willing to answer frankly, and at the same time add to your understanding of him? What is the most personal question you could ask and expect to get an honest answer?

Think quietly and write your question down. Give it to your partner. Answer his.

Pair with another couple making a group of four. Change partners. "What questions can you ask your new partner?" Think. Ask. Answer.

Return to your group of four.

4. FOURS

In the groups of four talk about these questions. Everyone should answer "a" before going to "b," etc.

a. Name one good quality that you have.
b. Name one trait that you like least about yourself.
c. How would your parents answer the first two questions?
d. How would your best friend answer them?

5. LEARNINGS

Staying in your groups of four, name one learning that you have had as a result of these experiences.

As a group complete this statement.

As a result of this experience in relationships, we think that one of the goals of our community should be . . .

6. SHARING

Share the completed statements with the total group. Allow for any discussion of questions that might occur.

WORSHIP

This depends on the mood of your group and your guests. If your guests are not church related or are of another faith they could be offended. On the other hand they may appreciate sharing with you in a brief experience of worship.

Suggested parts could include some singing, the poem *"Revolution"* or *"Man with the Help of God"* (in another section of this book). Appropriate Scriptures are 1 John 4:7-12, 1 Corinthians 13:1-3.

Revolution

One of these days
Somebody is going to ask
  "Why?"

"Why" is a bad word,
A dirty word.
It must never be uttered,
  or even thought—
Especially thought.

Four-letter words are not the worst words:
The really bad words are three-letter words.
  Powerful words like "sex."
  Terrible words like "God."
And "why" is a truly dreadful word.
  "Why is there meat and fruit
  And liquor and ice for you?"
  "Why is there nothing but greasy grits
  And flour and beans for me?"

When someone starts asking "why,"
It is already too late to hide.
Why is the switch that lights
Up the end of the world.

          —Edith Lovejoy Pierce

COMMENTS

Few of us like to have our decisions questioned with a "why" question. A "why" question is an aggressive question. "Why do you wear long hair?" Immediately you go on the defensive. Is the person asking out of curiosity or from some other motive? A "why" question can be a curiosity question or a devastating one, depending on who's doing the asking and who is being asked. A "why" question means "state your reasons for what you are doing." Too often it means "state your reasons and I'll tell you if they are any good or not."

POW!

A "why" question means that you have taken a look at common ordinary things and are wondering "why" they have to be done the way they are. Why is worship this way? Why can't we . . . ? A "why" question suggests uncomfortableness with the establishment's order and the possible need for change. A "why" question can mean danger for those being questioned and those questioning. Jesus asked "why" and look what happened to him. The establishment was not ready to be questioned.

SUGGESTED USE OF THE POEM

Ask a "why" question. Take a look around your church. "Why *are* things done the way they are?" "Why do you have that particular schedule for Sunday worship?" "Why are there no youth on the board of deacons?" "Why are you a Christian?"

Prepare a list of questions that deal with the ministry of your church. Turn yourself loose and move. Find the answers.

Share what you've discovered.

or

DIVIDE INTO THREES

Study the poem.

What does the author mean: "Four-letter words are not the worst"?

How is "God" a terrible word?

Why is it too late to hide when someone starts asking "why"?

Interpret the meaning of the poem by giving an example from daily living.

Cheaters Seldom Win—Only Sometimes
by Robert Beaumont

SESSION TARGET

To understand why people cheat and how we are susceptible to its temptations.

INTRODUCTION

"Cheaters never win."
"Never?"
"No, never."

We would like to think that cheaters never win. But that's not true. Cheaters do win. A lot of them go through life pulling in the "big money" through unscrupulous business practices. Many of America's social problems today are the result of past and present "cheating" practices of people in political and economical power. When the "big man" can cheat and get away with it, the "little man" will try it too and so the vicious cycle begins — and ends in human disaster. There is always a loser when cheating occurs.

Cheating has always been and is now a problem of man. "We cheat to get ahead" has been the established answer of students. This simple answer is only part of a problem that goes deeper into the makeup of man: his competitive drive, his feelings of superiority and inferiority, and his greed and selfishness. This program attempts to deal with the inner feeling of why people cheat so that they will look at themselves and ask the same question when faced the next time with an opportunity to cheat.

SESSION PLANS

Brainstorm:

With chalkboard or newsprint have the youth relate different ways people (youth and adults)

cheat today. (Steer away from naming people.) Answers will include tests, income tax forms, homework, assignment papers, exchange of money, permission slips.

Discuss:

Why do you think people cheat? Who gains or loses from cheating? Are there degrees of cheating?

A Value Scale:

Is cheating ever O.K.? Answer each question.

1. Bob, because he did not study well, will fail a major test. No make-up test is available. The failure will keep him out of his favorite college. He knows how he can get the answers to the test. Should he cheat?

2. Bob's reason for not studying was sickness. Should he cheat? If you answer yes for 2, go on to 3.

3. Bob gets the answers. Which of the following should he do?

— He decides to go for the best possible score, since he is cheating anyway.

— He'll use just enough of the answers to maintain his usual test scores. This is probably what he would have gotten had he studied.

— He'll use enough of the answers to get a minimum passing score. His past grades will indicate the quality of work he is capable of doing.

— He decides not to use any of the answers. He will talk with the teacher and take the consequence.

Spend some time discussing your answers and the reasons for them. Then do the role play.

ROLE PLAY:

The Big Test

Fred was asked to see Mr. Brooks following school on Tuesday about some project with the Photography Club. Mr. Brooks was called from the room for a few minutes by the principal, leaving Fred all alone. On the teacher's desk were copies of a test in English for the following day. Fred quickly made some mental notes of the questions and then jotted down some further notes. On the way home he met his friends at the corner. Unable to hold his news, he broke in, "I've got something to tell you . . ."

CHARACTERS:

Fred — Caught in the predicament of having some questions for the test, you must tell the gang about it. You are unsure, however, if you have done the right thing and want your friends to help you decide what to do.

Mike — Thinks Fred should have lifted the complete test from Mr. Brooks' desk. Believes the teacher was dumb for leaving the questions in the open.

Joyce — Thinks Mr. Brooks should know that they have the questions. If he's told, the punishment may not be as harsh.

Alison — Has no use for people who cheat and steal things. Has no problem letting the group know how she feels.

DIRECTIONS:

Write out the directions for the characters on 3″ x 5″ cards and make name tags on 8½″ x 11″ paper for each character. Call for volunteers. Explain that they are to assume the role of the person described. When the situation has been enacted, stop the action and discuss: What was the key issue? What different viewpoints were presented? How well did the people assume their parts?

Creative Expression and Worship

Prepare a work area large enough for each person to have room for a 14″ x 22″ piece of poster board. Provide plenty of newspapers, paper cups, water, and cleaning rags, paint of five or six bright colors, assorted brushes.

Think about Fred for a while. Then about yourself. How do you feel when you cheat? Proud of yourself? Disgusted? Nothing?

Then draw or paint whatever comes to mind, anything that represents your feelings about cheating — about doing the kinds of things you really don't want to do.

READ TO THE GROUP:

Genesis 25:19-34;
Deuteronomy 5:18-20.
Share with each other your self-expressions.

I'VE GOT TO TALK TO SOMEONE. Can I talk to you? There's a big exam tomorrow. It's an important one that I've got to do well on. I've done all the studying that I can, but I'm scared that I'm going to fail. If I pass it, I will get a big scholarship, and I can't go on with my education unless I get a scholarship.

My dad will blow his cool if I don't do well. He always was a genius or something in school, and he can't believe his having a kid that can't do as well. I just know he will disinherit me if I flunk. He tells me that my sister always did well in school and he can't understand what happened to me.

Many of my friends already have scholarships. I'm one of the last of the Varsity Club without one. I don't want them laughing at me because I'm too dumb to make the grade.

My teachers think I can't pass, I'm sure. In fact one of them told me I shouldn't take the exam at all. Boy, with that kind of backing . . .

Anyway, I'm scared. I'd just like to run away and let the test be given before I get back. One guy said he has something I could take that would make me so happy that I wouldn't care what happens.

What should I do?

Royce Makin
San Antonio, Texas

(Reprinted by permission from the April-June, 1971, *Power*, a resource for meditation and reflection, published by Christian Youth Publications, St. Louis, Missouri.)

The student and public high schools.

You Force Us to Rebel
by Bill Shook

That the American school system is under attack by a wide range of critics is no secret. From student to teacher to administrator to taxpayer the question comes, "What's going on in our schools?"

It is also no secret that a growing number of high school students are raising serious questions about the role of education in their lives. Some are almost in open rebellion via underground papers, boycotts, and the like.

"You force us to rebel," say many of them. "You force us to rebel because we have no real way to protest bad school policies or practices and to work toward positive changes. We have no way of really reaching the policy-makers."

One of the basic concerns is the goal of public education. Most public school administrations insist that the goal of education is not to prepare a student just for college. They would suggest that public education is most interested in personal growth and development as opposed to academic excellence for the sake of college entrance exams. As one high school administrator said: "Our job is to teach people to be adaptable to change."

SESSION TARGET

To understand the goal of public education in order to make school life meaningful.

ADVANCE PREPARATION

Divide your group into three subgroups. Have one subgroup of students collect statements from public school administrators, teachers, and parents as to what they consider the goal of public education to be.

Ask another subgroup of students to interview a number of students in the high school on what they feel to be the goal of public education.

Have the remaining subgroup of students conduct the following survey among adults and young people in your church. The students should feel free to construct their own survey if they wish.

SURVEY

YES	NO	REASON	
			1. What do you think is the primary goal of public education?
			2. Do you agree: "Instead of school systems being built around the needs of the students, the students are being built around the needs of the system"?
			3. Is student conformity necessary in our high school?
			4. Should the public school system reflect the community?
			5. Are the real world and the world being taught in the classroom the same?
			6. Education should help students become informed, reliable, and cooperative citizens.

7. Since 18-year-olds now have the power to affect change in the national government by voting, should they be allowed to help formulate the educational policies of their schools?

8. Can a school tolerate a democracy for policy decision or must there always be a chain of command as in business?

9. "Strikes" are an American method for protesting discrimination and bad practices. Should students be allowed to "strike" against poor school board policies, poor teaching, etc.?

THE SESSION

1. Have each subgroup share the results of their research.

2. Write a group decision to each of the questions. Divide into several smaller groups with each group working on one question. Share. Discuss. Rewrite.

3. Invite several school officials to hear and discuss your paper. Modify on the basis of the discussion.

4. Meet with your advisors and some other church people to decide how this information can be gotten to the officials in your school system.

SCRIPTURE REFERENCES

Read: 1 Timothy 4:11-16; 1 Thessalonians 5:11-18.

What are these passages saying about your role as students in today's school system, your relationship with other students, faculty, school boards?

The Drug Scene

"Taking of drugs is a recess from life for which the Christian has no time" — student in New Jersey.

A NOTE OF WARNING ABOUT DRUG EDUCATION

Information about drugs, no matter how good and who presents it, is not enough for an adequate drug education experience.

The critical question, and one that is seldom ever asked, is this:

"Are you ever unhappy and what do you do when you are unhappy?" It is usually the unhappy kid who "bangs high" on drugs given to him by a friend or even a brother who says, "Take this. It will make you feel better."

DRUG RESOURCES

A beginning step in discovering who, when, and why kids make the drug scene.

RESOURCE GUIDE ON DRUG ABUSE

Because of the concern for one of today's most pressing problems, the Division of Mass Media of the United Presbyterian Church has compiled a resource guide on drug abuse. There is a listing of materials related to drugs presented in such a way that individual churches and other community organizations can select resources for particular needs. Its contents are divided into three areas: films, bibliography, and music on drug abuse.

The Resource Guide on Drug Abuse can be purchased from the Presbyterian Distribution Center, 225 Varick Street, New York, New York 10014 for $1. Checks should be payable to the Division of Mass Media.

Hide and Seek (film)

Color, 14 minutes, Center for Mass Communication, Columbia University Press, 1125 Amsterdam Avenue, New York, New York 11025.

This is the very personal story of a boy's life as an addict. The events of the film are real as they begin with his initiation with drugs and the consequent mental and physical deterioration. The boy narrates his despair, loneliness, and helplessness. Good technical accuracy. The film is excellent in reaching the audience with this dramatic impact. At some points, however, it does appear to be contrived but the effects of narcotics abuse are well and convincingly portrayed. Recommended for junior high, senior high, and older.

The Seekers (film)

Thirty minutes, Bench Mark Film Library, 267 West 25th Street, New York, New York 10001.

This is a documentary film about youth who use drugs. It is basically a description of one of the ways groups can be used to rehabilitate drug users. The film depicts encounter groups and how they can help drug users see themselves as they are. Problems are discussed, and descriptions of why they begin using the drugs are talked about. People listen to one another, help one another, and ask for clarification when things are not understood.

Recommendation

We do not recommend this film for use with young people — only because most of them would have heard this before. There is some obscenity in the film. We recommend that this film be used

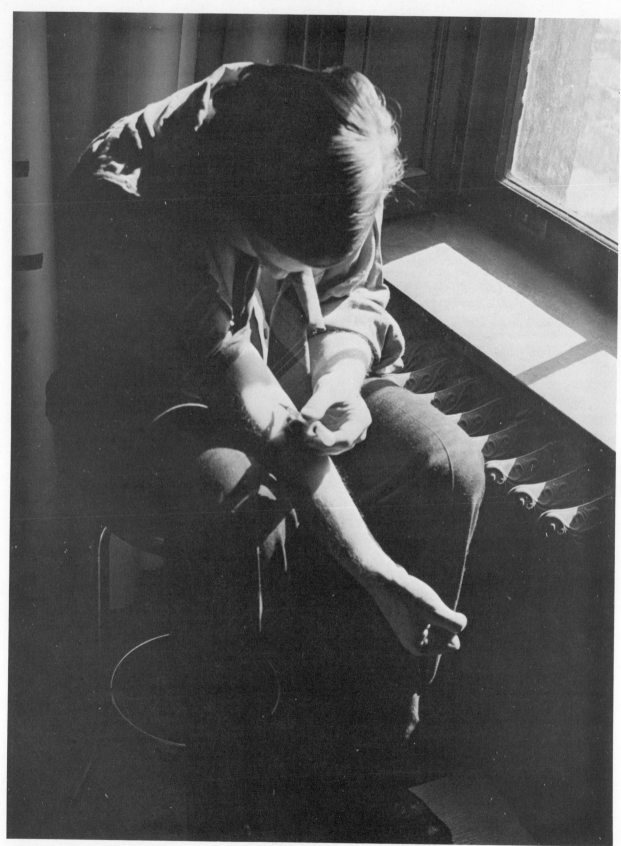

Photo by H. Armstrong Roberts

by professional adults in a teaching situation with adult workers with youth.

DRUG MATERIALS FROM GUIDANCE ASSOCIATES

Guidance Associates of Pleasantville, New York 10570, have several series of sound filmstrips which deal with the drug issue. Their drug information series contains highly useful information concerning (1) sedatives, (2) stimulants, (3) narcotics, (4) psychedelic drugs, (5) LSD and the acid world. Each subject in the preceding list is a filmstrip in itself. We suggest that you write to Guidance Associates for their catalogue on the drug information series.

The Moveable Scene (film)

Thirty minutes. Narrated by Robert Mitchum. This is a film composed of interviews, sights and sounds of the study of youth drugs. It undertakes to analyze the reasons for young people leaving their comfortable middle-class homes and moving into the city slums. Produced by the National Institute of Mental Health. Available through your Blue Cross or Blue Shield Health Insurance Office. Check with your local office. Free.

The Youth Drug Scene (film)

Thirty minutes. Available from Family Films, 5823 Santa Monica Blvd., Hollywood, California 90003.

This is a true story of a young boy who turned on to the drug scene for three years and then, supported by friends and family, began the painful journey back to reality. There is a good music track and vital effects.

Marijuana (film)

Available from Mass Media Ministries, 2116 North Charles Street, Baltimore, Maryland 21218 or 1720 Chouteau Avenue, St. Louis, Missouri 63103.

This film is against marijuana yet it succeeds in getting its message across without becoming preachy. The viewer is asked to think for himself as popular concepts about the drug are examined. Recommended for junior high and senior high ages. Rental $20.

Drugs from A to Z — A Dictionary (book)

By Richard R. Lingeman. McGraw-Hill Book Company, New York, New York, 1969, $2.95.

What We Can Do About Drug Abuse (pamphlet)

By Jules Saltman, Public Affairs Pamphlet #390, 381 Park Avenue, South, New York, New York 10016. 1966, 25c.

Ecology Versus Pollution

Living on this old planet called earth creates a lot of problems. If you do something on one side of the earth, it has immediate and long-range implications on the other side.

Ecology raises an ethical question about property and the owning of land. "If you own a piece of land, does that mean you can do anything you want with it or are you the caretaker for a piece of land that humanity owns?"

Ecology raises a nostalgic question. "Parents/adults think of your old childhood 'swimming holes,' your best 'fishing spots.' Are they fit to swim in now?"

One thing is certain. If the pollution continues at the present rate, our next glimpse of blue sky will be in the history books.

RESOURCES FOR GOD'S PEOPLE AND EARTH

Ecology (filmstrip)

This filmstrip does not spiel forth direct warnings about how mankind is killing itself, nor does it present tons of statistics in order to bury the viewer before the garbage comes. The filmstrip presents the varied and even contradictory ways of looking at the problem of living with our planet. Only when love takes the lead will the earth be safe again. Sound, 110 frames, 18 minutes, $17.50 rental from Argus Communications, 3505 North Ashon Avenue, Chicago, Illinois 60657.

Pollution (multimedia)

Pollution is not a filmstrip. It is a self-contained multimedia happening. Imagine this: a filmstrip with beautiful photographs and a sound track containing only two spoken lines but hundreds of sounds of the world. The sound track is a collage of sounds from Bach to gurgling waters to jack hammers. Throughout we hear the voice of a baby and a man repeating something we can never quite hear. Gradually we hear them, "Sounds can have a lot to do with sanity." "All producers must take into consideration what happens to the product."

A teacher's guide and a chart for students to plot their anti-pollution activities are available. Ninety frames, 90 minutes, $17.50 from Argus Communications, 3505 North Ashon Avenue, Chicago, Illinois 60657.

The Environmental Handbook (book)

Diversified series of papers and essays related to the ecological problems. The book is an attempt to come to grips with the problems of our environment at the level of the individual private citizen.

The second half of the book proposes specific individual action that can be initiated by informed, aroused citizens. A comprehensive bibliography of books and films is included also. Edited by Garrett de Bell, a Ballantine/Friends of the Earth Book. Paperback, 95¢ from any bookstore.

The Runaround (film)

Produced by Anaram Nowak Associates, 15 minutes, color. Available on a free loan basis from the National Tuberculosis and Respiratory Disease Association, 1740 Broadway, New York, New York.

"Someplace,
Once,
    there was air you couldn't see,
    a sun without rings,
    water that didn't smell.

Someplace,
    there still may even be
    invisible air,
    bright sun,
    and water that doesn't smell.

But not for long."

Mr. John Q. Citizen with a nasty cough decides to find out what's causing his local air pollution. He goes to several factories and businesses in his community only to discover that they have great public relations programs announcing pollution control but in reality are pollution contributors. They are passing the buck. John Q. Citizen also begins to discover how much he himself contributes to the pollution problem. When it comes time for him to shoulder the responsibility for an individual fight against pollution, he passes the buck on to someone else. Senator Muskie adds a final comment to the film. The film is done in animation.

All the Difference (film)

This 20-minute, 16 mm, color film contrasts the unspoiled scenic beauty of America with the worst of its polluted areas. Available on free loan from Audio Visual Services, Eastman Kodak Company, Rochester, New York 14560.

To Clear the Air (film)

Free. This film talks about the chief causes of air pollution and shows various methods being used by industry to improve the air. The facts are given in a dialogue between a representative of the American Petroleum Institute and a fellow passenger on an airplane trip. Information given about air pollution is accurate and worth knowing. It can be used with junior highs and older groups for content appeal not for dramatic emphasis. Order from the American Petroleum Institute, 1271 Avenue of the Americas, New York, New York 10020.

The River Must Live (film)

Free. The emphasis of this film is the steps needed to keep rivers and other water sources pure and alive. Photography and script are excellent (they usually are in oil company film productions). Filmed in a European setting the film describes the situation that is familiar to the American continent. A river, once clean and full of life, is being killed by man's carelessness. New methods of purifying water from industrial wastes before it is returned to the river are explored. Order from the Shell Oil Company Film Library, 450 North Meridian Street, Indianapolis, Indiana 46204.·

The following films on pollution can be ordered from Mass Media Ministries, 1720 Chouteau Avenue, St. Louis, Missouri 63103 or 2116 N. Charles Street, Baltimore, Maryland 21218.

Alone in the Midst of the Land (film)

Created by Scott Craig for WMAQ-TV, 28 minutes, color, rental $20.

The way to live on earth is in a space suit. Why? Because 140 million tons of pollutants are being sent skyward each year. The related problem of pesticides, destruction of wild life, and vegetation-land erosion, and general lag in food production can eventually cause man to stand alone in the midst of his land. Symbolic nature of the film is that man will kill himself and become extinct if he does not take better care of the land on which he is dependent.

Bulldozed America (film)

Produced by CBS News, 25 minutes, black and white, rental $10.

CBS documentary report on a problem very much in the news: the need for beautifying our countryside instead of filling it up with more billboards, automobile graveyards, and slum-like suburbs.

A Carnival of Ugly (film)

Produced and directed by George Gipe for WMAR-TV. Color, 25 minutes, rental $25. Another title for the film could be "A Line-up of National Eyesores." The reading of a poem in the background is the only verbal sound we hear. The film directs our eyes to ten eyesores: telephone poles, slums, strip mines, bulldozing of trees, signs and billboards, polluting smoke, refuse-clogged rivers, garbage dumps, litter, and junk yards. The film succeeds as an impressive work of motion picture art and style as well as a poetic call to clean up the mess we are making of our landscapes.

The Noise Boom (film)

Created by William Turque for WNBC-TV, 25 minutes, rental $20.

This is a film about noise pollution, and how noise in urban centers is becoming a major threat to national health. Diseases can be caused by the noise of cranes, jackhammers, drills, air compressors, loud cars and trucks and flying aircraft.

The cynical indifference of youth at a deafening discotheque and the need of so many for the excitement of noise is probed.

The Redwoods (film)

A Sterling Educational Release, 20 minutes, color, rental $20.

This is a beautiful poetic history of a vanishing forest — the redwoods.

Up to Our Necks (film)

Twenty-five minutes, color, rental $20.

The problem of waste disposal is one of the most complicated critical problems in the world. Since matter cannot be destroyed but only changed, we will eventually run out of holes in which to pour our billions of tons of garbage. In many areas garbage is literally being piled up around people's necks. This ranges from the gigantic automobile graveyards around our airports and city entrances to overflowing cesspools in the back yard. "Up to Our Necks" was filmed in and around New York City. It depicts what New York is now doing with its garbage. However, New York is to reach its saturation point by 1975. There will then be no place left to put its garbage. What is the answer? New York does not know, but it will have to be found within the next five to ten years.

Automania 2000 (film)

Ten minutes, rental $12.50. By the end of this century traffic will become so congested that cars are stacked up seventeen stories high. People become car dwellers and are classified socially as to how near the top they live. For junior highs to adults.

Section 2
Hymns and Songs

All My Trials

Traditional

1. Hush little baby, don't you cry,
   You know your Mama was born to die;
   All my trials, Lord, soon be over.

2. I've got a little book with pages three,
   And every page spells liberty;
   All my trials, Lord, soon be over.
   Too late, my brothers,
   Too late, but never mind;
   All my trials, Lord, soon be over.

3. If living was a thing that money could buy,
   You know the rich would live but the poor
   would die;
   All my trials, Lord, soon be over.

4. There grows a tree in Paradise,
   And the Pilgrims call it the Tree of Life;
   All my trials, Lord, soon be over.
   Too late, my brothers . . .

I Wonder as I Wander

Traditional

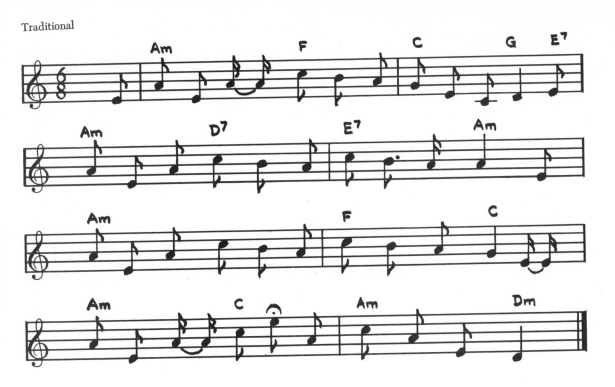

1. I wonder as I wander, out under the sky,
   How Jesus the Saviour did come for to die
   For poor or'n'ry people like you and like I;
   I wonder as I wander, out under the sky.

2. When Mary birthed Jesus, 'twas in a cow's stall
   With wise men and farmers and shepherds and
   all.
   But high from God's heaven a star's light did
   fall,
   And the promise of ages it did then recall.

3. If Jesus had wanted for any wee thing,
   A star in the sky, or a bird on the wing,
   Or all of God's angels in heaven for to sing,
   He surely could have it, 'cause He was the
   King.

4. I wonder as I wander, out under the sky,
   How Jesus the Saviour did come for to die
   For poor or'n'ry people like you and like I;
   I wonder as I wander, out under the sky.

And God Said Yes!

Norman Habel

Richard Koehneke

1. And God said, Yes! Yes! Yes!
   Said yes to the world once more,
   Said yes with a cosmic roar,
   Said open that other door,
   Said yes! yes! yes! man, yes!

2. For God said, Yes! Yes! Yes!
   Let's splash the sky with light,
   Let's float the earth in space,
   Let's dance away the night,
   Said yes, yes, yes, man, yes!

3. And God said, Yes! Yes! Yes!
   Let's make a man who's free,
   Creating life with love
   And ruling earth with me.
   Said yes, yes, yes, man, yes!

4. And God said, Yes! Yes! Yes!
   Let Jesus Christ be born!
   Let's find him in the straw!
   Let's blast the shepherd's horn!
   Said yes, yes, yes, son, yes!

5. And God said, Yes! Yes! Yes!
   Yes to his broken son!
   Yes to his open wound!
   Yes to the broken tomb!
   Said yes, yes, yes, son, yes!

6. And God said, Yes! Yes! Yes!
   We'll leap the swirling sky!
   We'll leap the hungry grave!
   We'll never stop to die
   Said yes, yes, yes, man, yes!

7. And God says, Yes! Yes! Yes!
   Says yes to that other door!
   Says yes when men say no!
   Says yes with a cosmic roar!
   Says yes, yes, yes, with me!

Build a Bridge

Roland T. Kamm
Becky Boyer

Ohio Synod School — 1970

Build a bridge   be-cause you love and real-ly care,
Walk a-cross, stand with your bro-ther there.
Build a bridge   be-cause we're called by God to be
A—live to one another,
For Christ has set   us free.

1. A bridge is hard to build, and we're afraid that it might fall.
   Too often it is easier to simply build a wall.
   But from the Christian vantage point we'll learn to view the need
   To build a bridge of living faith. The structure will succeed.

2. Sometimes it's even hard to see the gap a bridge must span,
   We climb into our shell and then forget our fellow man.
   We build our sep'rate neighborhoods, we judge without a trial,
   Yet God has placed us in this world to love and reconcile.

3. But bridges must, like houses, on a firm foundation stand,
   Because they'll only wash away if they are built on sand.
   Christ is the rock we'll build upon. Our bridge will be a sign
   Of meeting, helping, loving: A communication line.

4. The Holy Spirit leads us so God's action we may see.
   If Christians work together as a whole community
   We won't avoid deep diff'rences, but go the second mile,
   We'll build a bridge with words and deeds of love to reconcile.

"When I Was Hungry"

Words and music by Joe Dowell

1. When I was hungry,
   You gave me nothing to eat.
   When I was naked,
   No coat or shoes for my feet.
   When I was thirsty,
   you gave me none of your wine.
   I needed your hand,
   And you didn't have time.

2. We saw the hungry.
   We saw the naked too.
   We saw the thirsty,
   But, Lord, we didn't see you.
   'Cause if we had, Lord,
   We would have given you wine.
   We'd have offered a hand;
   Yes, we would have had time.

3. But when your brothers
   Cry out for help from you,
   And you turn your backs,
   I feel the sorrow too.
   When your ears are deaf
   To your brother's plea,
   Your heart is hard,
   And you can't hear me.

4. When I was hungry,
   You gave me none
   Of your bread.
   When I was weary
   You had no place for my head.
   When I was crying,
   You didn't comfort me.
   You just left me to my misery.

5. We saw the hungry;
   We saw the weary too.
   We heard them crying,
   But, Lord, we didn't hear you.
   'Cause if we had, Lord,
   We would have run to your side.
   A call from the Master
   Would not be denied.

6. But when your brothers
   Cry out for help from you,
   And you turn your backs,
   I feel the sorrow too.
   When your ears are deaf
   To your brother's plea,
   Your heart is hard,
   And you can't hear me.

7. When I was hungry
   You gave me nothing to eat.
   When I was naked,
   No coat or shoes for my feet.
   When I was thirsty,
   You gave me none of your wine.
   I needed your hand,
   And you didn't have time.

CODA
   How I needed your hand,
   And you didn't have time.

Down by the Riverside

Traditional

1. Gonna lay down my sword and shield,
   Down by the riverside,
   Down by the riverside,
   Down by the riverside.
   Gonna lay down my sword and shield,
   Down by the riverside,
   Gonna study war no more.

2. Gonna stick my sword in the golden sand . . .
3. Gonna put on my long white robe . . .
4. Gonna put on my starry crown . . .
5. Gonna put on my golden shoes . . .
6. Gonna ride on my milk white horse . . .
7. Gonna talk with the Prince of Peace . . .
8. Gonna walk with the Prince of Peace . . .
9. Gonna shake hands around the world . . .

Refrain

I ain't gonna study war no more,
I ain't gonna study war no more,
I ain't gonna study war no more. (Repeat)

Section 3
Handles for Leaders—Youth and Adults

Suggestions for group discussion and other kinds of things.

Hot and Cold

The following ideas are some ways for turning on your group to good discussion. They are not ends in themselves and *will work only if the topic or question under discussion is really of interest to the group.* If the agenda is not good or the group has not "bought your plan for the evening" these suggestions will not be of much use.

Don't limit these suggestions to just program sessions. They are for working groups too — groups working on party plans, youth ministry goals, etc. Read through them! Think about them! Use when appropriate!

PAIRS

Two people become a discussion team. This arrangement allows for immediate discussion and ample time for each to express his opinion. It helps to become immediately involved in the discussion. There can be no nondiscussers in this setting for there is no place to hide. Eight to ten minutes is a maximum time limit since two people can quickly run out of ideas. A good way to continue the discussion is to *merge one pair with a second pair* for a group of four. The new group share their ideas and moves into a deeper conversation.

THREE IN A GROUP

Three people provide for more spontaneous and a broader range of thinking. The discussion will be a little more complicated. Each person will have a little less talking time. The pressure will still be on each person to participate since it is still difficult to hide in a group of three.

Variation: "Listener and two talkers" Two peo-

ple talk while a third listens. When time is called (5-8 minutes), the listener summarizes what he has heard being said. One of the two original talkers becomes a listener while the other two become talkers, etc. Repeat until each has been a listener. Allow for a few minutes of generalized discussion at the conclusion.

GROUPS OF FOUR TO TEN

Ten is the maximum for a good analysis of a question or problem. With four to ten people in a group there is a wide range of ideas and creative thinking. A group leader is not always necessary if

1. *the group assignment is clear and understood by everyone in the group;*
2. *the group is really interested in the idea under discussion.*

The larger the group, the less "air time" (time to say what he thinks) each member has. More energies and time are needed to sort through all the possibilities suggested in such a group. Decision making is more difficult.

BREAKDOWN INTO WORKING GROUPS

Often it is advantageous to meet in a larger group and brainstorm on ideas and questions. Then break into groups of twos or threes to actually work on the assignment. Each working team brings one definite proposal back to the larger group. The larger group looks at the suggested proposal and decides on the most appropriate one.

Another variation is to break the assignment of the larger group into several parts. Each working team works on one of the parts. The total group then looks at each of the completed parts. If satisfactory, they are accepted and the job is done.

A larger group that has stalemated itself can often be revitalized by a reshuffling of its members into smaller units for a period of time. The change of pace, the different setting, the movement can help "move" a group. Do some of the work in the smaller units and you've got handles for the larger group to work on.

IMPORTANT NOTICE

1. Remember! It is not necessary or even good to try to do everything together all the time. To get a big job done break it into small parts and let everyone have a "bite of it."

2. Still water tends to be stagnant. Running water is fresh. The flow of people from small groups to larger groups, to teams, and back again will be a lot more refreshing than trying to have everybody do the same thing in the same way at the same time.

THE FISHBOWL

The group is divided in half. One group forms a tight inner circle, the other forms an outside circle around them. The inner circle discusses the assigned question while the outside group listens silently (5-10 minutes). The two groups exchange places. The inside group talks about the conversation they heard — whether they agree or not, etc. (5-7 minutes). Merge the two groups and allow for general discussion.

The Fishbowl puts all participants into a circle of attention for a while. It creates an environment of excitement as people listen to what's being said, knowing that they'll be next in the circle, and as people hear their ideas being challenged, accepted, or dismissed. This method allows a smaller group to discuss while at the same time the total group is aware of what is happening.

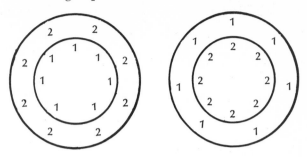

Variation: "I hear, you saying. . . ." The person in the outer circle sits directly behind a person in the inner circle. At the end of the inner circle's discussion he restates what he heard that one person saying in the conversation. The two people talk about it for a few minutes (3-5), and roles are reversed. Inner circle talks while the outer circle listens, etc.

HOT AND COLD

This is a way of letting each person say "how it is with him" in a given program. Give each person a 4" x 6" card. On one side is printed the word "hot." On the other side the word "cold." When he is caught up in the experience, he keeps the "hot" side of the card showing. When he's been left cold by the event, he flashes the "cold" side. All activity grinds to a halt. And we explore with him what's happened — what turned him off.

REMEMBER!

Every person is important to your group. If one has dropped out of an event or experience (meaning he's there in body, but not in spirit and mind) *find out why!* If he drops out of too many little things, he'll end up dropping out of the group for good.

Tired of an interest-dwindling, topic-centered, attendance-falling type of youth program? Pull in the slack and try this on for size. *Group* your youth *according to needs and interest.* Forget about age and year in school.

1. Youth may want to be together because of a common interest even though ages are different. So, you have a group of youth working on the problem of:

> Worship possibilities for
> our church
>   10th-12th graders
>   meet Sunday — 6 P.M.
>   with the pastor

Youth Groupings

MEANWHILE

2. Youth of the same age can have a variety of interests.

> 10th graders studying
>   "Being Christian in School"
>   Sunday — 6:30 P.M.
>   six youth meetings

> 10th graders working on
>   "Youth Projects for the
>   Aged in Our Town"
>   Wednesday — 7:30 P.M.
>   four youth meetings with
>   a deacon

3. AND there's the time element. It's easier for these people to meet after school:

> *Drama Group*
> Monday — 4:30 P.M.
> 9th-12th graders

4. BUT some youth may want to meet

> *Sunday Evening*
> 6:30 P.M. in two groups:
> junior high and senior high

5. HOWEVER, a few youth who will not attend a regular church school class will attend a

> *Donut Klass*
> Sunday — 9:30-11 A.M.
> Open to 10-11-12 grade students.
> Informal conversation on things
> that are important.

INTEREST GROUPS

A youth group of ten to fifteen can have a variety of settings, assignments, and meeting places. One person can be involved in several different settings if times are different. On the other hand, a variety of events and groupings can occur at the same time in approximately the same place.

Interest groups are usually short lived, depending on the group's assignment. Some groups may dissolve after three weeks, others after ten. Constant reshuffling is needed. Real attention to youth needs is a critical necessity. An added value of interest groups is the short tenure of adult lead-ers. Adults who are not willing to work for a year or two in youth ministry may be happy to work on a short-term project.

OVERVIEW

A sense of direction is needed for an adequate ministry with youth. You may wish to keep track of what's been happening to your youth in order to know where you need to go. The following chart may be helpful to you as a planner in youth ministry. You can at a glance see what has been offered to your youth, who has been participating, and what else is needed. It's the kind of record that will help the entire church understand what's going on with "those kids."

YOUTH MINISTRY SCHEDULE

NAME OF THE GROUP (SETTING)	MEMBERS	REASON FOR THIS GROUP	LENGTH	ADULT	MEETING TIME
Church vocations	Bob R. Jenny B. Nancy C. Bill D.	These youth have had some interest in full-time Christian service.	3 weeks	Pastor	Sunday— 6:30 P.M.
Religious folk music	Bill D. Jim F. Mike L. Michele I. Henry R. Sarah L.	They have been complaining about the music used in Sunday worship. Their assignment is to find some appropriate folk music that might be usable in worship.	6 weeks	Mrs. Den	Wednesday— 7:30 P.M.

UPSETTING THE APPLECART

Unless a radical reshuffling is needed, do not force interest groups on everybody. If the majority of youth want their regular youth meetings, let that occur. But from time to time as special interest or concerns are needed, be alert to the possibility of a separate interest group *which may or may not meet during your* regularly scheduled youth meeting.

Be flexible!

Be happy!

And don't be afraid.

WHAT ONE CHURCH TRIED

Here's the listing of activities in one church which tried the Interest Group approach to youth ministry. You'll note that some of the activities involved groups of both youth and adults.

Carpentry

Minor repairs to the church building. Church school furnishings.

Sewing

Dolls for children. Curtain repairs in the church building. Sweaters for Appalachia.

Singing

Youth interested in contemporary church music.

Drama

Bible Study: the book of Acts

Audio-visual

Running the equipment. How to lead film discussion.

Worship

Groups of youth and deacons to study changes in our worship services.

Poverty/Hunger

Youth and adults concerned about the poor in our area.

Pollution

Fighting pollution in our city.

ACTION INTEREST GROUP

Interest groups should not be limited to discussion-only topics. *Create action-oriented groups.* Be on the alert for possible action that emerges out of any discussion. Ministry is more than talking. Action is essential.

Problem Solving—An Easy Way to Do It

Every group has its problem (understatement of the year). However, most of them are solvable. The following process can be of real help to you as an adult worker with youth. It is a way of tearing a problem apart, analyzing it, and coming up with some adequate solutions. It is simple to use, quick, and efficient. It can be a personal tool or it can be used with the total group.

PROBLEM DIAGNOSIS

1. Brainstorm some of the problems facing your youth group. Write on newsprint. Select one. (You may want to select a simple one for the first use of this process.)

2. Draw this diagram on a large sheet of newsprint. Place where all can see it.

PROBLEM: _____

GOAL: _____

A. Forces causing the problem   B. Forces that could get rid of the problem

3. State very specifically what the problem is and your goal.
   Example:
      Problem: "Attendance is decreasing."
      Goal: "To keep our attendance from decreasing and have more youth involved."

4. List in Column "A" everything you can think of which is causing the problem. List in Column "B" everything you can think of which could solve it.

5. Study Column "A." List several ways each item could be eliminated or decreased in importance.

6. Determine which items in Column "A" need to be worked on first, second, etc. Review your remedies. Which of the suggested action steps seems to be best suited for your group?

7. Act. For each action step needed to correct the problem, list the materials, people, and other resources required. Make team assignments.
      Example: One reason for decreased attendance is the problem of transportation. Some of the youth don't have rides. One team is assigned the task of (a) discovering who those youth are, (b) working out a car pool arrangement, and (c) implementing it by such and such a date.

By working at the problem in this manner the roots of the problem are revealed. As each cause is eliminated, the problem becomes a little less difficult and closer to its final solution.

What to Do When Nothing Else Seems to Work

There comes a time in the life of every group when "nobody wants to do anything." You've looked at every program in this book plus some and nothing seems to work.

What do you do?

Simple. Find out what the group is really interested in.

How do you do that?

One of these three suggestions may help.

1. Use the *Interest Rating Scale* in this section of the book with the group. Add to the list some of the items you think the group may be interested in. Use as suggested.

2. Use the *Escape from Commitment* chart located in this section of the book.

OR

3. *Try this* with your group's planning team or the total group.

A. *Asking the Question* (8-10 minutes)

Divide into teams of three or four. Each team is to talk about "why the youth group is the way it is." They write on newsprint at least three questions or problems they have with the group.

B. *Answering the Question* (10 minutes)

After one team has written its questions on newsprint, it exchanges questions with another team. Each team answers the questions or problems of another team.

C. *Review and Identify* (15 minutes)

When the answering period is over, hang the answers on the wall. Note the similarities in questions and answers. Are there any dissimilarities? What trends are apparent? Summarize the trends on a separate sheet of newsprint.

D. *Working Team* (20 minutes)

Once the trends have been identified, subdivide into a new set of working teams (3-4). Each team takes one "trend" and tries to dig beneath it. What seems to be causing it? What does it mean for the group? What can we do about it? Make a proposal as to what the group can do.

E. *Decide* (15 minutes)

Each team returns to the larger group with its completed assignment. Decide on the next step by studying each proposal.

Escape from Commitment

An invitation to think and to act in a world of reaction.

Being young can be an escape from commitment. In an adult-oriented world youth have no entree into the power structures. Many think of themselves as *citizens without power* in a country of old men. They escape commitment to themselves and anyone else with the use of a shopworn phrase: "What can I do? I cannot change anything."

Concerned youth, however, are changing things. Those who "think" are finding ways of *solving national problems at the local level*. Some youth have found themselves in the chambers of Congress because they pursued a local issue to its logical end.

SESSION PURPOSE

The purpose is to help your group determine its response to the issues facing you in your town. It will be an attempt to see if the group is capable of doing something other than just talking about a problem. A procedure of action is suggested for those who want to put *Christ's words into action*.

I WAS HUNGRY
AND YOU
GAVE ME FOOD . . .
NAKED AND YOU
CLOTHED ME . . .
(Matthew 25:34-43).

It is time for you to make a decision.
You've got some problems in your part of the country. Are you really interested in trying to solve one of them?

PROCESS

1. As a group complete the *Concern Chart* which is printed at the end of this section. Score the answers.

2. Which concern received the highest 10-point rating from the members of the group?

3. By consensus decide which of the concerns is to be tackled first by the group.

4. Problem knowledge:

On the chalkboard brainstorm all information which the group members have about the problem. Note the trends, contradictions, etc.

5. Information gathering:

What other information is needed that can be collected by the group during the week? Make assignments.

6. Next week:

Study all the information. Brainstorm all the possible solutions.

7. Decide which solution (or partial solution) can best be done by your group. Take into consideration school commitments, interests, etc.

8. Assignments:

What needs to be done to reach your solution? Who will do what?

What is the time element?

9. Write down everything that will be done to solve the problem. Number them 1, 2, 3, etc., so the progression from beginning to end can be seen. Make sure everyone understands what he will be doing and when he is to do it.

10. You're at Start. Go.

Concern Chart

Check the appropriate box

How Do You Feel About?	No Concern	Mildly Interested	Concerned	Indignant: Something Should Be Done	I'll Do Something	I Am Doing Something Now
Inflation						
Pollution (Air, Water)						
Negative Criticism About the Church						
Vietnam War						
Poor Quality Education						
Marijuana						
Defense Budget						
Decrease in Church Membership						
Hunger						

Scoring

Give yourself these points:
- 0 — for No Concern
- 1 — for Mildly Interested
- 2 — for Concerned
- 3 — for Indignant
- 6 — for I'll Do Something
- 10 — for I Am Doing Something

Total your points and compare with your friends. A low score will indicate "a lot of talk and no action" on your part.

Interest Rating Scale

USES FOR THIS SCALE

— when suggested programs don't seem to work,
— when you want to go beyond where you've been,
— when you want to discover the specific concerns of your group.

HOW TO USE

Add some of your own concerns. Leave one or two blanks for the group to add theirs. Give each person a copy. Let everyone complete the scale silently during a regular youth group session.

When the group is finished, collate the results. Which item has the highest concern rate, the next highest, etc.? List on newsprint. Place on the wall.

Divide into working teams. Assign one or two of the higher ranking items to each team (no duplications). Each team will brainstorm ways of dealing with that issue. They will answer questions, such as: Will the total group deal with the issue? Will it be the concern of a special interest group? How much time will be allotted?

This interest scale can help the others in your group catch sight of the way you feel about some of the issues around us. Your scale plus theirs can help in creative program planning for the future.

DIRECTION

Rate each item according to its importance to you. You will feel more strongly about some items than others. Rate them accordingly.

Read through the items in the first section before going on to the next section. Add any items to that section which you feel should have been included.

Then decide which two items are of extreme concern to you. Place an asterisk beside them. Next decide which two items are of the least concern to you. Place a minus sign beside those statements. Finally decide which two statements are of some concern to you. Place an "x" beside those. Go on to the next section.

INTEREST RATING SCALE

SCHOOL

1. _____ Too much pressure for grades.
2. _____ School is too oppressive.
3. _____ Concern about graduation and college.
4. _____ Homework load too great.
5. _____ Students need a say in determining school curriculum and school policies.
6. _____ Improvement in classes.
7. _____ Parents do not understand our school situations.
8. _____ School newspapers should be the voice of the students.
9. _____ School has little meaning.
10. _____ School dress should be left to the student's choice.

11. _____
12. _____
13. _____
14. _____

PERSONAL

1. _____ Have some honest discussion about sex.
2. _____ Fight too often with parents.
3. _____ Family communications poor.
4. _____ Use of money.

5. _____ Some concern about my physical — sexual growth.
6. _____ Schedule for the use of the family car.
7. _____ Have my parents trust me more.
8. _____ I fail too often.
9. _____ Would like to date more.
10. _____ Feel useless.
11. _____ Too little freedom at home.
12. _____
13. _____
14. _____

RELIGION

1. _____ Interested in improving Sunday worship.
2. _____ Troubled by poor understanding of the Bible.
3. _____ Problem with prayer being artificial.
4. _____ Cannot see God's role in my life.
5. _____ Why people go to church so much.
6. _____ Question of the church's involvement with things like politics, poverty, or other social issues.
7. _____ Wish youth could be more involved in decision making in the church.
8. _____ Wish adult members would also listen and trust us more.
9. _____ Would like to improve our church school.
10. _____ Wish our youth group had a sense of direction and purpose.
11. _____ Would like to engage adults in honest discussion about the ministry of the church.
12. _____ Wish our group would really be honest with each other.

13. _____ Wish we had some other kinds of youth groups.
14. _____ Wish I didn't have to pretend so much while at church.
15. _____
16. _____
17. _____

SOCIAL ISSUES

1. _____ Minority problems are large in our town.
2. _____ Police in our area are suspicious of young people.
3. _____ Concerned about war and the draft.
4. _____ Concerned about the race problem in our school.
5. _____ Concerned about the anti-patriotism in the country.
6. _____ Would like to know more about conscientious objection.
7. _____ Concerned about poverty in our town.
8. _____ Concerned about censorship of movies and books.
9. _____ Concerned about youth distrust of the town administration.
10. _____ Dancing is still an issue to be settled.
11. _____ Wish the community was more concerned about the needs of youth.
12. _____ Wish we could do something about the pollution in our area.
13. _____
14. _____
15. _____

Learning to Role Play

Role play (informal drama of make-believe) is being used with increasing frequency at school and church. It is a solid educational tool which acts as a bridge between talk and action.

Role play can break open issues for discussion, help solve real problems, or interpret people's reasons for the decisions they make (i.e., no dancing in the church building). This method works by putting you in someone else's shoes, helping you to see how they feel or think. Most problems can be solved if the opposing sides will try to understand each other. Role playing can assist in the understanding process.

HOW TO DO IT

Certain steps must be followed if you are to succeed with role playing.

1. CLEARLY STATE THE PROBLEM

The problem or issue must be clearly defined. Example: Board of education has refused your group's request for dancing in the fellowship hall.

By assuming some of the roles of the board members, you can discover some of the pressures they are under and some of the reasons for their refusal.

2. SELECT THE CAST

Assign the roles. Allow some time for thinking about the parts. "Who is it that I am portraying?" "What is he like?" "Who starts the action?"

Some youth are threatened by acting in front of a group. Others are exhibitionists. Avoid these two groups. Select people who can put some "bounce" into their acting but at the same time will take it seriously.

3. GUIDE THE AUDIENCE

Instruct the audience as to what they are to listen for. Going back to our "dancing" example, you could ask the audience to see if the reasons given for the refusal of the dance are really honest ones. What are the reasons for some of the statements given by the board members?

4. ACT

Allow enough time for the actors to come to grips with the problems, to present some of the feelings and thinking of the people they are portraying. Five minutes is usually about right. *Do not allow the actors to jump out of their roles. It will kill the effort.*

5. REFLECT — DISCUSS

Begin the discussion by allowing the actors to share their feelings about the parts they played, why they said and did what they did. Five minutes or so.

Next move into a generalized discussion. Analyze the situation and issues. In our example situation can you sympathize with some of the board members? What alternatives do you have now for dealing with the board's decision?

Asking the Right Kind of Questions at the End of a Field Trip, Project, or Special Activity

Asking the right kind of questions and relating the gospel

Experience does not teach by itself. *You learn from experience when you reflect upon what happened to you in that experience.* Therefore, it is essential that you provide a period of reflection for talking about any special experience your group has, that is, if you want your group to understand the meaning of their experiences.

At the end of a choir trip, church drama, worship at the old folks home, party at the children's center, or any special activity, try one of these two approaches.

MEANINGFUL REFLECTION

LOOKING BACK

1. Relate some of the things — humorous and otherwise — that happened in this experience. What happened to whom? What caused it? Was anyone else involved?

2. Tear apart the experience. What could have made it better? What one or two things were really good about it? What was your most nega-tive experience? What would you do differently the next time?

3. What was learned? What one thing can you say that you learned as a direct result of this experience? To what point in the experience was the gospel clearly related?

AFTER A FIELD TRIP

Each person in the group answer these questions about the person he visited.

1. What kinds of feelings did the person have about his job, about life in general?

2. What kinds of daily experiences does he have — good, bad, so-so?

3. What gives him hope, keeps him going? Does he think others share his optimistic views?

4. Being with this person today was like . . . (Complete)

5. The gospel came into focus for me when . . . (Complete)

Break into small groups and share your answers with others in your group.

A planning method for programs,
retreats, and things like that.

Getting a Good Grip on Planning

Good planning is essential to youth ministry. If you have a good planning procedure you do not need to read on — unless you wish to compare your method with the one we are going to suggest.

The following is a brief description of a planning process usable in almost any situation — from planning a total youth ministry effort to a Sunday evening program to a youth retreat.

Read our method three times. Try it twice! It may seem long and cumbersome. It is, in the beginning. Work through this a few times and you'll be amazed at how quickly it goes.

A PLANNING METHOD

for programs, retreats, projects, and things like that.

1. GATHERING THE INFORMATION

Find out all you can about the people who will be coming. What do they like? Ages? Interests? What have they done before? What would you like to do? What are the givens, such as time, place, and leaders? Gather the information through interviews, your assumptions, written questions, and other available methods.

2. FIGURING IT ALL OUT

Take a long look at all the information you've gotten. Are there any common interests, likes, or dislikes? Group all of the trends. How many people seem to be interested in what? What is all of this information saying about the group and the event you are planning?

3. GETTING A PURPOSE

Decide which trends or groupings seem to be the most important. Write a very specific purpose for each.

Our purpose in working with this trend for our youth is . . .

How many of these purposes can be accomplished in the given time limit? Decide which purpose you really want to work on.

4. OUTLINE THE GENERAL PLAN AND SPECIFIC STEPS

What creative experiences can you provide for the youth which will let them learn what you've stated in your purpose? *Brainstorm* the possibilities. *Sort through* and *decide.*

Example: We go on a field trip to the welfare hospital and interview some of the doctors and patients. (That's a general plan.)

Next, outline the specific steps that have to be taken.

A. How are you going to get to the hospital?
B. How much time will you spend?
C. How many doctors and patients will you interview?
D. Who in your group will do the interviewing?
E. What do you plan to do with the information you get in the interview?

5. DO THE EVENT!

6. EVALUATE!

Was the purpose accomplished?

Youth Power in Your Church

RULE 1

To plan for youth ministry without having youth involved is to have adults *plan for* youth and is not to be confused with a ministry *with* youth. *Ministry with* means *planning with* youth: adults and youth working together on a common effort — their ministry as people of God.

RULE 2

Youth ministry is judged by "the ministries youth have," not by "what is done for youth" by a group of adults or a church. Ministry is "serving." *Ministry with youth* means "serving with youth."

A PROCEDURE FOR PLANNING MINISTRY WITH YOUTH

A planning committee of six youth and four adults (pastor and representatives from the deacons, board of Christian education) work through this process.

WHAT IS A "MINISTRY WITH YOUTH?"

Brainstorm all of the assumptions. A variation would be to have each church board and the various youth groups brainstorm separately. The planning committee could take the information, add their own assumptions, and sort through them.

Sort through the assumptions. List trends and categorize. (You now have some of the broad trends of thought concerning youth ministry in your church.)

OBJECTIVES AND PURPOSE

On the basis of your categories write a purpose statement for each category. Your youth ministry effort will have a number of purposes, such as to provide our youth with special training in Christian music, to help youth see God in their lives, and to help youth become ministers of the gospel. They will all be related to the overall goal of *having youth accept faith and grow in it to become men of God* as exemplified by Christ.

GETTING THE PURPOSE ACCOMPLISHED

Once the purposes have been stated, the next step will be to decide on the methods and ways of getting them accomplished. Methods emerge out of the purposes so there will be a variety of things presented.

Take each purpose and brainstorm all of the ways it can be accomplished. Discuss each method. Decide on the best ones, basing your decision on leadership and resources available to your church and the openness of your church.

For example: A purpose may be to get youth involved in all aspects of church life. Brainstorming indicated they could be members on church boards, leading worship, and delegates to association, state, and national meetings. You may have decided after a lot of discussion that you will start by having youth placed on church boards. Your reasoning is that most adults may not be open to having youth as delegates or leaders in worship. (*But you will try to work on these possibilities next year by changing the atmosphere.*)

The Methods

Once you've decided what's going to be done, you need to decide who is going to initiate it, how long the task will take, and matters like these:
— How many youth will be on a board?
— How will they be elected?
— Full members or ex-officio?

Action

After discussing all of the purposes and after deciding on the best methods, you will need to make your youth ministry proposal to appropriate boards and to the youth themselves. Ask for modification. Revise and put into action.

WHY GO THROUGH ALL THIS?

Because youth ministry needs a sense of direction, it needs to be more than a "bunch of hit and miss things," a conglomeration of this and that. You, the youth, the boards, and all of the people need to understand the reasons for what you are doing in youth ministry. If they understand, support rather than criticism will be their contribution to your youth ministry effort.

Brainstorming—How To

Brainstorming is the free flowing of free wheeling imagination as members pinch, push, and probe at an idea. Brainstorming is a group discussion technique that lets a group identify the issues of a topic and set priorities for the handling of it.

IMPORTANT GUIDELINES

1. Every person has the chance to express himself.

2. No idea is discarded. Quantity is wanted.

3. No discussion is permitted until every idea has been listed.

4. There should be no pushing for more when the ideas stop coming. Stop and begin discussing the list.

TWO WAYS OF BRAINSTORMING

TOTAL GROUP

Proceed something like this:

1. Expose the group to the question or issue. Give any available information.

Example: *We've scheduled a retreat for December 10-13. Our theme is education. What are some of the concerns you see?*

2. Let's brainstorm. As ideas fly, have two people writing them down on newsprint.

Example: "Student bill of rights," "students on curriculum committee," "no homework," "end to grades," "more football games," etc.)

3. When ideas stop coming, close off the brainstorming. Go back over the list, briefly discussing each item.

Example: "What is meant by 'student's bill of rights'?"

4. Note duplication and similarities. Categorize.

5. You can now ask the group to decide which of the categories are most important to them. Or divide into groups of twos and threes and rank the categories in order of their importance.

PANEL BRAINSTORMING

1. Decide the issue or question to be brainstormed. Obtain a panel of five or six people: three or four youth from the group and a couple of guests who have some knowledge of the issue.

2. One or two days before the session give each member background information such as why the question was raised, the kind of ideas desired, and the length of their participation. This will permit the panel to do some extra thinking about the subject.

3. At the session, introduce the panel and explain what they are to do and how long they will be brainstorming. Restate the issue for the group.

4. Begin the brainstorming. Two writers record the ideas on newsprint. Hang on wall so everyone can see them.

5. When the panel has stopped, allow the total group to build on their ideas.

— criticism of ideas not allowed

— quantity wanted

— no discussion

6. Discuss each item within the total group, through the panel, or in small working teams. Categorize and decide which ideas are most appropriate to the group.

A guide to evaluating, discovering how well
you did.

How Did You Like It?

At the end of every program, field trip, project, or other activity, plan to evaluate what went on, whether the purpose was accomplished, and what happened to the participants. *Build evaluation into every session plan.*

WHY?

To evaluate is to learn; it is to reflect on what has happened, what has been said, what people were feeling about all the happenings in order to consolidate ideas and clarify thinking. For the leader it is valuable in that it lets him know what has happened to his audience and whether his purposes were accomplished.

METHODS INCLUDE . . .

SIMILES

A simile is a method of comparing yourself to something else. "Being in this meeting was like . . ." or "Compared to happiness this experience was . . ."

SENTENCE COMPLETION

"One thing I've learned from this session is . . ."

or

"The reason why I think I am not learning anything is . . ."

RATING SCALES

"Were the purposes for the session clear?"

Excellent				Poor
5	4	3	2	1

or

"Did you gain any new insights?"

Yes	No	Not Sure

INTERVIEW

Divide into teams of two to discuss what each person felt or learned about the experience.

In planning for evaluation allow enough time for the participants to complete the evaluation and to talk about what they have written. The real value of evaluation is its learning potential. Group discussion of the evaluation facilitates learning.

SAMPLE EVALUATION FORMS

Read. Study. But develop your own.

EVALUATION I

GENERAL QUESTIONS

1. What did you like best about the session?
2. What did you like least about the session?
3. What specific things came up today that you would have liked to explore further?
4. How would you suggest the session could have been improved?

CONTRASTING STATEMENTS

Instructions: Circle one of the five points on the scale which most nearly represents your reaction in relation to the contrasting statement at each end of the scale.

1. How did you like the session today?

Excellent				Poor
5	4	3	2	1

2. Were the purposes clear?

Very clear				Not clear
5	4	3	2	1

3. How did you feel about participating in the discussion?

Very free				Very inhibited
5	4	3	2	1

4. How interested were you in the topic?

Very interested				Not at all interested
5	4	3	2	1

OPEN-ENDED QUESTIONS

Reactions to what happened in the session.
1. Our progress was hindered today when _____
2. It was disappointing when _____

EVALUATION II

1. I view myself learning:

6	5	4	3	2	1
a great deal	quite a bit	somewhat	not too much	very little	nothing

2. The kinds of things I am learning are:

3. The reason I think I am not learning is:

4. The reason I think I am learning is:

COMPLETE:

Being in this meeting was like . . .

	A	B

EVALUATION III

1. A. Were you satisfied with the performance of the group?
   B. How many of the members would you say were satisfied with the performance of the group?

2. A. Would it have been helpful if the less talkative members had expressed their opinions more readily?
   B. How many members of the group will agree?

3. A. Do you feel the discussion was dominated by two or three members?
   B. How many will agree?

4. A. Did you have any feelings of irritation during the discussion?
   B. How many members will say they did?

AT VARIOUS times during the session I felt:

_____ embarrassed   _____ rejected   _____ sad
_____ joyful   _____ inadequate   _____ shut out
_____ excited   _____ accepted   _____ stupid
_____ angry   _____ bored   _____ hopeful
_____ guilty   _____ surprised   _____ confused
_____ lonely   _____ hopeless   _____ I had no feelings
                                                          tonight

Section 4
Retreats

Retreats—Planning for Them

WHAT IS A RETREAT?

A retreat is a *planned experience of intentional living in order to accomplish a specific purpose.* A group gathers together for a specific amount of time in order to work on a specific purpose.

The length of the retreat experience and the place for it is directly related to the purpose of the retreat. You don't go to a city hotel for a ski retreat.

THE LIVING TOGETHER

A retreat needs to be planned in order to be effective. The living/eating together aspect has certain implications which need to be discussed. The balance between work/worship/sleep/play/meals and between personal freedom/community responsibility for each other needs to be thoroughly studied. Living together in a kind of communal setting can be tremendously meaningful.

The quality of the "living together" has a direct influence on accomplishing the purpose. If things are "going well" in the living together, the group will be able to work together successfully. If "bad times" are showing up in the "living together," the group will be unable to function very well. Inner tensions and disputes will need to be worked out before the group can get to the purpose of the retreat.

THE PURPOSE

As illustrated in the "Sample Retreats" section, the purpose can be almost anything that is of concern to the group. To plan a successful retreat use a planning process. (See "Getting a Good Grip on Planning" in this edition of *Respond.*) Good planning is needed to assure that the retreat purpose is of real importance to the group rather than superficial and secondary.

SAMPLE RETREATS

The following are brief descriptions of several successful youth retreats. They are presented as examples for your retreat planning. *Do not copy!* To do so means disaster. These retreats have come out of experiences and needs. Your retreat, in order to succeed, must develop from your own needs and concerns.

Good planning!

Good luck!

RETREAT 1

BEING CHRISTIAN IN SCHOOL

PLACE: High School Gymnasium
TIME: Friday 5:30 P.M. to Saturday 5:30 P.M.
PARTICIPANTS: Youth and adults

PURPOSE:

To understand what it means to be "Christian in school" by dealing with some of the school issues and problems facing today's students.

STRATEGY:

Six interest centers will be available to the group during the weekend. Each will deal with a specific school issue. Each participant will elect to attend four of these centers. Size is limited to ten people at each center, on a first come, first served basis.

Friday:
- 5:30 P.M. — Dinner
- 7:00 — Brief orientation
- 7:15 — Interest centers (your choice)
- 9:00 — Free-for-all (games, refreshments, singing)
- 10:30 — Interest centers (your choice)
- 12:00 — Worship
- 12:15 — Sleep, if you're ready

Saturday:
- 9:00 A.M. — Breakfast
- 10:10 — Interest centers
- 11:40 — Break for lunch
- 12:00 — Lunch
- 1:00 P.M. — Rough and ready exercise and recreation
- 2:30 — Interest centers
- 4:00 — Snacks
- 4:30 — Evaluation — "What was and was not learned"
- 5:30 — Home for dinner

RETREAT 2
LOCK IN
— TALK A LOT!

PURPOSE:

To explore some of our inner feelings and problems about religion, home, etc.

TIME: Friday 9:00 P.M. to Saturday 9:00 A.M.

PLACE: The home of a church member. Needs one large recreation or family room, two smaller sleeping rooms, and easy accessibility to bathrooms.

PARTICIPANTS: Senior high youth and a few invited guests.

PLAN: At 9:30 P.M. the doors will be shut and a "lock in" of the participants will occur. No one can leave the meeting room except to go to sleep or to the bathroom. Participants may talk as long as they wish, about anything they want. Food will be available through the night.

SCHEDULE:

Friday: 9:00 to 9:30 P.M. — Arrival
9:30 — Lock In — Talk A Lot!

RETREAT 3
CREATIVE EXPRESSIONS

PURPOSE:

To allow youth to explore the possibilities of drama, music, and visual/sound media for use in church and worship.

PLAN: Three sections will be provided the participants. Each person will choose one section and remain in it for the weekend.

1. *Musical Expression*
   Singing, listening, and planning for the use of contemporary music in worship.
2. *Drama*
   Reading, acting out, and writing of dramas for use in our kind of church.
3. *Creative media*
   Dramatic ways to use films, rocks, pictures, driftwood, slides, junk sculptures in worship, and other experiences.

PLACE: State Conference Center

TIME: Friday 7:00 P.M. — Sunday 3:30 P.M.

SCHEDULE:

Friday
- 7:00 P.M. — Arrival and orientation
- 7:30 — Beginning by worship
- 8:00-10:00 — Sections (getting acquainted — expectations, purposes, plans, etc.)
- 10:00 — Food and fun

Saturday:
- 7:30 A.M. — Breakfast/worship
- 9:00-11:30 — Sections (each section will decide when to hold a 10-minute break)
- 12:00 — Lunch/free/recreation
- 3:00-5:00 — Sections
- 5:30 — Dinner
- 7:00 — Sections
- 8:30 — Movie/party

Sunday:
- Breakfast/sections/sharing of accomplishments/evaluation/free time/going home

RETREAT 4
CITY/STATE GOVERNMENT

PURPOSE: To explore how decisions are made and influenced in city or state governments.

PLAN: The group will spend the weekend talking to several city councilmen, department directors, visiting city hall.

TIME: Friday 7:00 P.M. to Saturday 8:00 P.M.

PLACE: City hall

PARTICIPANTS: Junior and middle high.

SCHEDULE:

Friday: 7:00 P.M. — Leave for the city. Check in

at hotel. Short orientation meeting as to purpose and design of the retreat.

Saturday 8:00 A.M. — Breakfast in hotel restaurant.
9:00 A.M. — Visit city hall, meet city councilmen, and so forth. Evaluation and reflection on what was learned, not learned, etc.

NOTE:

*Before leaving on such a retreat, have several questions ready to ask in the interviews. Discuss the theme enough so that everyone fully understands it and has some idea of what to expect the interviews to accomplish.

*Several variations of this retreat are possible. Go to your state capital, to Washington, D.C., or to the United Nations.

*Themes can range from decision making to discrimination to pollution, to religion and state, to poverty, and so forth. Any concern a Christian has about his government is "fair game" for such a retreat.

RETREAT 5
SILENT SUNDAY

PURPOSE:

To explore the meaning of silence, how people are affected by it, and its place in the worship and reflection of God.

STRATEGY:

The group will spend Saturday evening enjoying the sound of talking and laughing. Most of Sunday will be spent in total silence, broken only by the sound of nature, selected sounds of the leader, and a final discussion of the experience. During the Silent Period, *every person will work alone* and be by himself.

SCHEDULE:

Saturday: 6:00 P.M. — Arrival/dinner
— Orientation
— Discussion of the implications of "Silent Sunday"
— Free time and recreation
Sunday: — Silence!
8:00 A.M. — Silent breakfast
9:00 — Worship
One leader talks — no congregational participation
9:30 — Silent meditation

10:30 — Worship via film exposure (silent)
11:00 — Silent reflection (write a diary of your feelings and thoughts at this point of your experience.)
11:40 — Lunch (silent)
1:00 P.M. — Volley ball (silent)
2:00 — Worship via record exposure
2:30 — Silent reflection
2:45 — Total group gathering. (The bell will toll twelve times. At the stroke of twelve, do one loud thing that will break the bond of community silence.)
3:00 — General reflection and discussion of the experience
4:00 — Homeward bound

OTHER KINDS OF RETREATS

Almost any theme can be a retreat theme when "community living" is seen as a part of the plan. Other suggestions for retreats include:

"RETREATS FOR EIGHTH-GRADE THEOLOGIANS"

Weekend sessions in which eighth graders develop and write their own statements of faith. Eighth graders are willing to spend some time doing serious studying if enough active recreation has been planned for them.

"YOUTH MINISTRY PLANNING RETREAT"

Youth and the youth committee of the board of Christian education will meet this weekend to work out the purpose and strategies of a youth ministry in your church. They will use the planning model "Youth Power in Your Church" described in this edition of *Respond*.

"COMMUNICATION WEEKEND"

Senior highs and their parents will meet for a communication weekend at the state conference center. Their purpose will be to. . . .

"WORK RETREAT"

Middle and senior highs will meet for the weekend at the _____ community center to study and work on some of the problems in the area.

"Pollution," "Bible Study," "Worship," "People" are all possibilities for a retreat. Try It! (And if your group has been to several retreats, try a new kind of retreat experience for yourselves — one that you've never had before! Have fun.)

Section 5
Resources

Resources

BIBLICAL STUDY

Creative Arts in Reconciliation

A multimedia kit. Contains a guide with film-strips on using creative motion in a group study of reconciliation. Included are a 33 1/3 record, a guidance sheet, and a booklet containing quotations from modern writers on the subject of reconciliation. Order from Service Center, 7820 Reading Road, Cincinnati, Ohio 45237. Price, $5.75.

Prayer — Who Needs It?
by Annette Walters

If the idea of praying turns you off, too bad. Perhaps you used to pray, but as you grew older it sounded childish. This book tries to explore some of the prejudices which keep prayer from being effective. Thomas Nelson, Inc., Copewood & Davis Streets, Camden, New Jersey 08103. Price, $1.95.

Psalms

The American Bible Society has issued a new translation of the book of Psalms. This is a first of the Old Testament books to appear in the new version called *The Psalms for Modern Man*. It joins *Good News for Modern Man*, Today's English Version of the New Testament. *Psalms* will sell for 10¢. The combined version with both *Good News and Psalms* will cost 50¢. Order from the American Bible Society, 1865 Broadway, New York, New York 10023.

Twenty Ways of Teaching the Bible
by Donald L. Griggs

A series of approaches to teaching the Bible. For use with junior high students. $3. Order from Griggs Educational Services, 1033 Via Madrid, Livermore, California 94550.

Teaching and Celebrating Advent
by Patricia and Donald Griggs

A packet of materials to assist teachers, parents and church educators for celebrating Advent in the church and home. $2. Order from Griggs Educational Services, 1033 Via Madrid, Livermore, California 94550.

DRAMA

Contemporary Church Drama

How to produce and direct it by Arthur Zapel.

A handbook of church drama ideas. Covers artistic and "people" problems. Illustrated. Order from Contemporary Drama Service, Box 68, Department S-9, Downers Grove, Illinois 60615. $1.

(Also ask Contemporary Drama Service for their catalogue on church plays.)

Unfold

A listing of art, music, drama, and literature published by the Department of Church Culture, National Council of Churches. Write Mrs. Rena Hansen, Room 5110, 475 Riverside Drive, New York, N.Y. 10027, for information.

Plays for the Church

Department of Church Culture, Division of Christian Life and Mission, National Council of Churches, 475 Riverside Drive, New York, New York 10027. $1.

We Will Suffer and Die If We Have To

A folk drama by Colin Hodgetts that explores the contrast between violent and nonviolent protest as personified by Malcolm X and Martin Luther King, Jr. Judson Press, Valley Forge, Pennsylvania 19481. $1.95.

What Are We Going to Do with All These Rotting Fish?

Seven short plays for church and community. Edited by Norman C. Habel, Fortress Press, 2900 Queen Lane, Philadelphia, Pennsylvania 19129. $2.95.

Plays and playlets written by eight young authors. They are short and easy to produce for church or community. These are plays that reach a soft spot of our loneliness, frustration, and self-satisfaction. They are plays that cause you to laugh, to shout, and to overturn tables. They will jolt the older generation and jostle the young.

HUNGER

Baldicer (a simulation game)
by Georgeann Wilcoxson.

"Baldicer" is a simulation game on the problem of feeding the world's population. The objective is to help the participants understand why it's so important for countries to help one another. They also gain increased awareness of related issues, such as the population explosion, inflation, and the power of the rich over the poor. The game is designed primarily to motivate study and action. Players needed, 10-20; ages 12 through adult; playing time, 2-3 hours; reflection time needed, 1-2 hours; price, $25. Available from John Knox Press, Box 1176, Richmond, Virginia 23209.

Ghetto

A simulation game developed by David Toll. This is a game which simulates the pressures upon the urban poor and the choices that face them as they try to improve their living conditions. Players have the experience of trying to plan out what they can do under the restrictions of poverty. The game makes clear that there are great barriers to completing one's education in ghetto schools. Players, 7-10; playing time, 2-4 hours; cost, $20. Available from Academic Games Project, Johns Hopkins University, 3505 North Charles Street, Baltimore, Maryland 21212.

Sometimes They Cry
Edited by Estelle Rountree and Hugh Halverstadt.

Is *Sometimes They Cry* a book? No, it's a series of experiences which deal with you and your part in the hungry cry of a starving child. They write about you — over-stuffed, fat-bottomed kids who can afford to walk away from liver and spinach. *Sometimes They Cry* is a study action book which offers concrete suggestions to a direct attack on hunger. It points out that you're not too young to help. $1.95. Available from Friendship Press, 475 Riverside Drive, New York, New York 10027.

The Food-Population Problem
by Marvin E. Smith

A study action guide designed to help youth and adults explore some of the major issues related to hunger and the population explosion. Contains excellent resources and approaches to moving into a study of the problem. Action projects are suggested as well as a list of other resources. Write to the Christian Board of Publication, Box 179, St. Louis, Missouri 63166. 90¢.

LEADERSHIP AIDS

Audio-Visual Resource Guide

Audio-visual material classified by subject matter, audience, and audio-visual medias. Includes films, filmstrips, recordings, and slides. Evaluations and reviews describe the thought, purpose, and message of each. Gives source of rental or purchase. Over 3,800 listings. Write to the National Council of Churches, Audio-Visual Division, 475 Riverside Drive, New York, New York 10027.

Catalogue of TV Films

For a listing of all the films related to the church which are available to the general public write BFC-TV Films, Room 852, 475 Riverside Drive, New York, New York 10027.

Chromeophobia (film)

This beautiful little Belgium film can be described as a short version of the Beatles' *Yellow Submarine*. This film is the story of a colorful town that is invaded by machine-like soldiers who march through the countryside destroying every bit of color. Butterflies are shot down, red balloons are punctured. The film is full of penetrating insights about violence. Color; 11 minutes; rental fee, $15 from Mass Media Ministries, 2116 North Charles Street, Baltimore, Maryland 21204 or 1720 Chouteau Avenue, St. Louis, Missouri 63103.

Good News, Anyone!
by Jean Louise Smith

This is a work book which will take the reader to the world of the artists and communicators and will involve him with their ideas as well as giving a greater understanding of the gospel itself. The aim of the book, 'Good News, Anyone! is to help the reader discover how and where the Word gets around in the world. It deals with all of the contemporary art forms which have a connection with the gospel. $2.75. Order from Friendship Press, 475 Riverside Drive, New York, New York 10027.

Mass Media Ministries

Mass Media Ministries has just published a new audio-visual catalogue #3. It describes all of the film resources now available through the Mass Media Ministries, 2116 North Charles Street, Baltimore, Maryland 21204 or 1720 Chouteau Avenue, St. Louis, Missouri 63103.

Probe
by Jane Day Mook

Probe is a bouncing mimeographed newsletter about youth ministry and the creative efforts of people engaged in it. It contains short reviews of available resources. The ten issues a year have brief comments about things churches are doing with their youth and what youth are doing with their churches. Probe puts you into contact with people who are doing exciting things. We recommend Probe for the adult worker with youth. It will keep him informed and up-to-date on the latest available resources. Order from Christian Associates of Southwest Pennsylvania, Department of Communications, 220 Grant Street, Pittsburgh, Pennsylvania 15219. Single subscription is $5.

Publications
New York State Division for Youth, 2 University Place, Albany, New York 12203.

The Publications is a series of publications, pamphlets, magazines which deal with the youth scene. Write to the preceding address for the catalogue of their publications.

Resources Galore
by Betty E. Stone and Mel Ludwig

A superb listing of fresh resources for creative educational ministries in the church. Books, films, recordings, drama, TV, think-tanks, etc. $1 per copy. Order from Gramercy Plaza — 8-F, 130 East 18th Street, New York, New York 10003 or Scribner Studios, 250 South 23rd Street, Philadelphia, Pennsylvania 19103.

This Covenant People
by Harold A. Malmborg, George W. Peck, and Edwin Taylor

Ten programmed Bible sessions. Short, snappy study units. The need for constant learning participation makes this study of the Bible fun to do and easy to learn. Three great events are studied: the Exodus, the Exile, and the life and work of Jesus. The sessions are designed for individual study preparation for group discussions. Recommended for junior high youth. The teacher's book $2.50, student's book, $1.50. Order from Judson Press, Valley Forge, Pennsylvania 19481.

The Making of a Counter Culture
by Theodore Roszak

The author assumes the task of trying to analyze the changing phenomenon in a society and its youth. Who are these youth who are so anti-establishment? What can we expect in the very near future? Doubleday Publication, 1969, $1.95.

The Planning Game I — Moses
by Donald Griggs

An experience designed for use by teachers and church educators to develop and employ a model for planning teaching sessions and units. $3. Order from Griggs Educational Service, 1033 Via Madrid, Livermore, California 94550.

Youth Ministry Resources

A listing of the new materials available for youth ministry. $1.50. Order from the Christian Board of Publication, Box 179, St. Louis, Missouri 63166.

Youth Report
331 Madison Avenue, New York, New York 10017.

Youth Report is a commercial newsletter published for people interested in the youth culture. It's basic purpose is an attempt to analyze youth patterns and trends for the sake of business institutions. Those engaged in youth ministry will find it to be a helpful resource publication for keeping abreast of youth culture and discovering the interpretations that businessmen make about youth culture. Published monthly. Price, $18 a year.

RACE

Adventures in Negro History

A set of two sound filmstrips, color with records. Volume I includes information of historically important Negroes in the development of the United States. Volume II deals with the Frederick Douglass years between 1817 and 1895. Free. Pepsi-Cola Bottling Company, c/o Mr. Elwood Brown, 500 Park Avenue, New York, New York 10016.

Let's Face Racism
by Nathan Wright, Jr.

A black baby has less than half the chance of a white baby to survive infancy. The average black high school graduate earns less than the average white person with an eighth grade education. It takes three wage earners in the average black family to earn as much as a white family with only one wage earner. These are some of the results of racism which youth can stop perpetrating. $1.95. Order from Thomas Nelson Inc., Copewood and Davis Streets, Camden, New Jersey 08103.

Today's Negro Voices

The almost universal cry today is that youth has something to say but no one will listen. This book contains some of the poems selected by author Beatrice Murphy. These are the poetic works of young people who are developing a deep pride in their race and a determination to change the way things are. The poets range in age from 14 to 30. $3.95. Julian Messner, 1 West 39th Street, New York, New York 10018.

WORSHIP

Catalogue of Resources
edited by Ron Atkinson

A catalogue of the latest resources dealing with contemporary worship forms. It's a collection of what's happening to worship throughout North America. $2. Write to Celebration, Center for Contemporary Worship, 117 Bloor Street E., Toronto, Ontario, Canada.

Contemporary Songs for Worship

The following is a list of the new youth hymnals that are available to churches. They contain some of the newest and contemporary church religious music and folk hymns.

Now Songs by Malcolm Stewart, Abingdon Press

Alleluia, Song Book for Inner-city Parishes
Cooperative Recreational Service, Inc.
Delaware, Ohio.

Songs from Nottinghill by Inger Calbert
Nottinghill Methodist Church, Lancaster Road West, Levit London, England

Hymns Hot and Carols Cool
Proclamation Production, 7 Kingston Avenue, Port Jurez, New York 12771.

Hymns for Now — Volume I
Hymns for Now — Volume II

Available from
Concordia Publishing House, 3358 South Jefferson Avenue, St. Louis, Missouri 63118.

Center for Contemporary Celebration

For a listing of the services provided by the Center for Contemporary Celebration in worship write to the Center for Contemporary Celebration, 1400 East 53rd Street, Chicago, Illinois 60615.

Cop Out

A collection of fresh songs and art produced by Mos Henry. Lakeview Presbyterian Church, 1310 Lakeview Avenue South, South Petersburg, Florida 33713.

Interrobang

by Norman C. Habel, Fortress Press, 2900 Queen Lane, Philadelphia, Pennsylvania 19129.

A book of prayers. Live ammunition for the young churchmen. Words of prophecy. Moments of reality. These are the actual feelings, hopes, and wants of youth. Collected and recorded by the author Norman C. Habel. This is a book that can be privately read, caressed, or given to the ears of others in everyday worship.

Let Us Break Bread Together

A folk communion service created by Carl Staplin and Dale Miller. Contains music and all the other necessary resources. Bethany Press, Box 179, St. Louis, Missouri 63166.

New Ways in Worship for Youth
by John Brown

Resources for twenty completed worship services. The services deal with a wide variety of themes suitable to many of the special days in the church year. Judson Press, Valley Forge, Pennsylvania 19481.

YOUTH CONCERNS

Generation Gap (simulation game)

This game simulates the kind of experiences that a parent and an adolescent son or daughter have with certain kinds of issues in which they have opposing attitudes. Conflict is presented within the game as a way to stimulate discussion. Players gain insight into the meaning of trust, concern, and responsibilities. They learn that conflict can best be resolved through communication and compromise. Players needed, 4-10; time, 1½ hours; price, $15. Available from Academic Games Project, Johns Hopkins University, 3505 North Charles Street, Baltimore, Maryland 21212.

Girl Problems

To help church educators discuss the problems youth face, Kimberly-Clark's Life Cycle Center, an education-information service, provides six booklets which can be used in workshops, seminars, discussions, or as sources of individual information.

For youth workers who want to interpret the process of growing up to preadolescents, the Center provides *The Miracle of You.* For those working with teenagers who want to understand themselves and the opposite sex better, *Your Years of Self-Discovery* is helpful. *You and Your Daughter* is a question-answer booklet useful for discussion leaders and mothers of young girls.

For insights into the conflicts faced by young women who seek independence after leaving home for college or a first job, *The Years of Independence* is an important source. Young women who are engaged or recently married will find many answers to their questions in the booklet *Getting Married.*

These booklets are available to church educators working with youth without charge. Individual copies are 10¢ each. Additional information and order forms can be obtained from The Life Cycle Center, Kimberly-Clark Corp., Neenah, Wisconsin 54956.

Letters of a C.O. from Prison
by Timothy W. L. Zimmer

This book contains the letters of Tim Zimmer, a college student sentenced to three years in the Federal Youth Center in Ashland, Kentucky. Whether you agree with Tim's point of view or not, you cannot escape being deeply moved by the depth and sincerity of his decision. $2.50. Judson Press, Valley Forge, Pennsylvania 19481.

Life Issue Booklets

A series of four booklets, each dealing with a subject of current interest, which will provoke discussion. The booklets are *Violence, Poverty and Wealth, Commitment and Indifference,* and *The Individual and the State.* They are available individually at 75¢ each or in a set of four for $2.75 from Judson Press, Valley Forge, Pennsylvania 19481.

Like Father, Like Son, Like Hell
by Robert R. Hansell

In this book the author does a most excellent job of expressing why youth feel alienated from society and from their parents. This book deals with adult-youth understanding. It can be of help for dealing with communication gaps in your church. Seabury Press, New York, $3.95.

The Now Generation
by Dennis C. Benson

Helps bridge the gap between the older generation and the "now" generation, utilizing the media of music by Bob Dylan, John Lennon, Arlo Guthrie and others. Book, $2.95. Study guides, 10 for $2.50. John Knox Press, Box 1176, Richmond, Virginia 23209.

CREATIVITY

Why Man Creates (film)

This film deals with human creativeness — how it is employed and how it is involved. It uses a diverse array of modern techniques ranging from cartoon animation to quick cuts and superimposition. The film is free. It will take advance preview for adequate discussion purposes. Order from Modern Talking Pictures Services, 1212 Avenue of Americas, New York, New York 10036, or from Kaiser Aluminum Mechanical Corporation, Film Distribution Center, Room 864, Kaiser Center, Oakland, California.

Biblical Index

RESPOND

VOLUME 2
A RESOURCE BOOK
FOR YOUTH MINISTRY

RESPOND

RESPOND

VOLUME 2
A RESOURCE BOOK
FOR YOUTH MINISTRY

EDITED BY JANICE M. CORBETT

JUDSON PRESS, ® Valley Forge

RESPOND, VOLUME 2

Copyright © 1972

Judson Press, Valley Forge, Pa. 19481
Fourth Printing, 1977

Library of Congress Cataloging in Publication Data
Main entry under title:

Respond; a resource book for youth ministry.

    Bibliography: v. 1, p. 136-140. v. 2, p.
    Vol. 2. edited by J. Corbett.
    1. Religious education—Textbooks for young people—
Baptist. I. Ignatius, Keith L., ed. II. Corbett, Janice, ed.
BX6225.R47   268'.4   77-159050
ISBN 0-8170-0542-0 (v. 1)

Photo Credits: Cover, Giles; p. 17, Wallowitch; p. 22, Jordan; p. 29, Combs; p. 31, Wallowitch; 37, Greene; p. 49, Tritch.

WHAT IS YOUTH MINISTRY?

Youth ministry means spending time with youth. That does not mean making oneself available for youth but making an effort to be with youth in group situations and individual encounters.

Youth ministry involves interpreting the problems and joys of youth in a Christian perspective. It also means interpreting the adult world to youth and interpreting the youth world to adults. It means interpreting the Christian life-style to individuals who are searching for meaning.

Youth ministry means acquainting youth with Christ and the Bible.

Youth ministry means accepting youth, as persons, with all their hang-ups, and at the same time allowing youth to accept adults with all their hang-ups.

Youth ministry is more than just dealing with the church; it should seek to deal with youth in other life situations as well.

Youth ministry should seek to involve youth and adults together in some common experiences.

Youth ministry is providing an experimental ground for youth to deal with their problems and questions.

—Curtis McCormack

USING THIS BOOK

A NOTE ABOUT RESPOND, VOLUME 2

This is the second volume of Respond, *a new resource for youth ministry. It incorporates many of the things you found helpful in Volume 1: practical advice, "down-to-earth" ideas, and "meaty" study suggestions. But* Respond, Volume 2 *has all new resources built around issues and ideas that are relevant NOW.*

Pick it up!
   Hold it!
      Love it!
   See it as a beautiful example of a youth ministry resource and then—

We Suggest You Do This!

Browse through the book to see what's hidden behind its innocent look. Note the various sections. Read a couple of the plans. Get a feel of what's here and what may have some possibilities for your group. Discover the sensation of gripping an extensive compilation of action and study resources and leadership helps that have never been produced before. Realize, however, that—

It's Not the Gospel.

Respond is a book of suggestions. Don't be afraid to modify, tear out, change, or discard any of the material that is of no value to your group. (The editor will never know.) But don't throw away some stuff that you may use later—like twelve months from now.

Stay with It!

Browse through the book several times. Get to know it inside out. And when the moment comes that your group has an idea it wants to explore, but no resources, you can say, "Hey, I've got just the thing!" Flip to the appropriate page and surprise the "living daylights" out of them.

When Using the Suggested Articles:

1. *Read* through the session plans in order to get an idea of what the session is about.

2. *Reread* the objective or purpose. Restate it in your own words. Then ask: Does it fit the group? How should it be changed? What other appropriate experiences does it enable you to recall?

3. *Reread* the procedures. How do they fit the needs of your group—size, temperament, amount of session time, setting, room size, equipment, leadership, etc.?

4. *Recheck* the preparation which will be needed. Do you have enough time to get ready for the session? Necessary resources? Leadership?

5. If you've got the answer to all those questions, get on with it and have a successful experience.

ONE FINAL COMMENT

Respond took a lot of hard work by a lot of people to produce. Our reasons for doing the book are:

1. Hopefully, it will make your work in youth ministry a little easier;
2. it will make you smile
      more often
      and not worry so much
      about where you are in youth
      ministry;
3. and that will help your group and the gospel get together
      more often and more intimately.

Good luck,
Good reading, and
A Great Ministry!

   —From the people
      of *Respond*

CONTENTS

RESOURCES FOR STUDY AND ACTION

FORGIVE US OUR SIN

by PAUL GEHRI

SIN AND FORGIVENESS

A comprehensive definition of sin is "anything less than the best in any situation." This definition sweeps wide, and it catches all of us within its scope. But that's nothing new. Most of us are intuitively aware of doing less than the best toward God, our neighbors, and ourselves. We live with it, often too comfortably, sometimes enjoyably; lack of perfection is our accepted lot.

Forgiveness means granting pardon, clearing the score, wiping out the debt. Forgiveness doesn't come as easy as sin does. Forgiveness is at the heart of the gospel and it isn't cheap or easy, but it is real and available and quick—from God. Forgiveness, person to person, is another story. Sometimes hard to accept, it can be very hard to give, except grudgingly. This attitude is in opposition to clear New Testament teaching.

PURPOSE

To sense the quickness and fullness of God's forgiveness.

To work on one's personal aptitude for forgiveness.

To contemplate a forgiving world.

PROCESS

1. OBSTACLE COURSE

As members arrive, have them set up a moderately cluttered obstacle course, using chairs or books or newspapers as obstacles. Each person will be asked to run through the course as fast as possible, three times, competing with each other to get the best time. (If the room is small, the course can be circular and members can cover it two or three times.)

2. THE PRODIGAL SON

Each person should now read the story of the Prodigal Son in Luke 15:11-24, zeroing in on verse 20 where the father runs to meet his younger son to embrace and forgive him.

This verse is one of the few places in the whole Bible where God is pictured as being in a hurry, and it is in the context of forgiving. The action is unmistakably clear.

3. INFORMAL DRAMA

Have the group talk about the kinds of things people need forgiveness for from other people in our kind of world. Then place a person at the end of the obstacle course used in Step 1. Have persons individually run to this person and offer forgiveness. Talk about how it feels to offer forgiveness—and to receive it.

WORSHIP

READINGS:

Matthew 6:12 (forgiveness in the Lord's Prayer)

Matthew 18:21-22 (How many times should we forgive?)

Luke 23:34 (Jesus forgives those who killed him.)

MUSING TOGETHER: What kind of world would this be if people could forgive one another?

FORMULATING A PERSONAL PLAN OF ACTION: Why not forgive? How can I forgive without coming on like Big Daddy? What do I do when people don't forgive me? Talk about these questions. Then encourage each person to develop his or her own set of forgiveness priorities.

OTHER RESOURCES:

John O. Nelson, ed., *The Student Prayer Book.* Nashville, Tenn: Abingdon Press, 1953. Prayer 219, page 200.

What is temperance?
What is the temple of the Holy Spirit?
What does either have to do with youth?

ENOUGH IS ENOUGH

by PAUL GEHRIS

ABUSING THE BODY

A professional football coach says the newer players don't have the drive or stamina to be superior! Headlines in newspapers decry the abuse of drugs by young people in an obviously drug-oriented society. Alcohol continues to take its terrible toll on the highways where over 50 percent of fatalities are directly attributed to the influence of alcohol. In spite of near conclusive evidence citing the dangers to health and longevity from smoking, people continue to smoke and more young people begin to smoke. Obesity in more and more youth points up our affluent, corpulent society, and the general physical condition of our nation is not what it ought to be, mostly from too much eating and too little exercise.

While the Bible doesn't give us any specific program for exercise, temperance, and health, it does speak out against gluttony, drunkenness, and laziness, and it instructs us to care for ourselves. In fact, that bodies are temples of the Holy Spirit certainly implies that we must take as much care of them as we do the other things we hold holy.

The crucial difference between abstinence or moderate indulgence (temperance) and overindulgence (gluttony, drunkenness) is the debasement or careless use of the temple of the Holy Spirit which is our body.

PURPOSE

To experience overindulgence and to reflect on its benefit or harm.

To try to transfer our understandings of overindulgence to other areas of life.

PROCESS

1. EAT

As the group gathers, serve a favorite dish (pizza, sloppy joes) and drink (soda or some other beverage). Ask everyone to eat and drink his fill; then encourage each one to eat and drink at least one more serving. Perhaps some will accept the challenge and become overstuffed.

2. SHARE FEELINGS

How did it feel to indulge in overeating? Talk about its delights versus its dangers. Relate the discussion to other areas relating to temperance, such as smoking, using alcohol, or using soft drugs.

3. PHYSICAL EXERCISE

Do some exercises that test the physical condition of members of the group (push-ups, timed running, etc.). Has overindulgence slowed anyone down? Should some members be more careful of their bodies' condition?

4. WRITE A LITANY

Discuss the following questions:

Does it pay to take care of one's body?
What are the ways we abuse our bodies?
Can this practice be changed? How?

Read 1 Corinthians 3:16-17 in several versions of the Bible. Discuss what it means to be God's temple. Then write a group litany about temperate living.

WORSHIP

Create a picture study from recent newspapers and magazines, showing tragedy and misery which have resulted from the lack of temperance.

Scripture: 1 Corinthians 3:16-17
1 Corinthians 6:19-20
2 Peter 1:1-11

Litany: Use the litany created above.

BIBLICAL QUOTES AND MISQUOTES

by KEITH L. IGNATIUS

Youth, like most adults, are not known for their serious Bible study habits. This program may help the participants to become aware of their attitudes and to be stimulated to explore ways and means of becoming more interested in biblical studies.

PURPOSE

To examine attitudes toward study of the Bible.

PROCESS

1. ATTITUDE CHECK

The leader should place this quiz on chalkboard or newsprint for all to see. Each person will answer this quiz on a separate sheet of paper. He is to circle the number which best describes his feelings about the question. A number 5 would indicate that the Bible is not important at all; "1" means that it is very important; "4" would mean somewhat important, "3" a little more important, etc.

1. How important is the Bible to the Christian faith?

    5   4   3   2   1

2. How important is the Bible to the average Christian?

    5   4   3   2   1

3. How often is the Bible read by the average Christian?

    Very Little   Very often

    5   4   3   2   1

4. How often is the Bible read by the average youth in your fellowship group?

    Very little   Very often

    5   4   3   2   1

5. How important is it to read the Bible regularly?

    5   4   3   2   1

6. List in order three reasons why the Bible is not read more often by young people.

7. Now list in order of their importance the three reasons for not reading the Bible more often.

When all have completed this quiz, have as many as possible go simultaneously to the chalkboard and write their answers. Now divide your group into threes or fours and have them talk about the answers which have been placed on the chalkboard.

2. YOUTH BIBLE ILLITERATES

Read these statements by two prominent youth ministers or, even better, have them written on large sheets of paper which up to this point have been obscured. Have your group take a look at them now. Ask each small group to react to the statements.

"Bible illiteracy and lack of theological understanding among youth is appalling—even among our top-notch young people."

"Youth are profoundly ignorant of the Bible and the historical background of their faith. Though they talk about communicating the gospel, there seems to be a very small understanding of what the gospel is."

Ask each of the groups to react to the statements. Are they true or not? The various groups should share their conclusions with the total group and should give reasons for their answers.

3. QUOTES AND MISQUOTES

Again ask the question: Is it important to be a

14

regular reader of the Bible? One of the reasons often given for not reading the Bible regularly is that all you need is a general knowledge of the Bible—you do not need to know all the facts and history that are in the Gospels. However, one of the weaknesses of this argument is that the understanding of the Christian faith can become so shallow and superficial that a person cannot tell what is and what is not Christian in his thinking. His understanding can become so distorted and misdirected that his belief is really a mixture of "this and that." One of the realities of life is that we tend to incorporate into our thinking and beliefs only those things that we like. Beliefs can be changed by misunderstandings. Try the quiz "Quotes and Misquotes" to test out your knowledge of the Bible.

QUOTES AND MISQUOTES

Read the following statements to the group or have them written on a chalkboard. Each person is to place a yes beside the statements which come from the Bible and a no beside those statements which do not come from the Bible.

1. Naked came I into the world, and naked must I go out.
2. Give instructions to a wise man, and he will be still wiser.
3. Faith without good works is dead.
4. Every one who thirsts, come to the waters; and he who has no money, come, buy and eat! Come, buy wine and milk without money and without price.
5. God moves in a mysterious way his wonders to perform.
6. He was wounded for our transgressions, he was bruised for our iniquities.
7. Let your light so shine before men.
8. God helps those who help themselves.
9. A good name is to be chosen rather than great riches.
10. Who steals my purse steals trash . . . But he that filches [steals] from me my good name . . . makes me poor indeed.
11. A king faced certain defeat and so he took his own sword and fell upon it.
12. The trees once went forth to anoint a king, but the olive, fig, and vine would not leave their tasks. Only the thistle would take time to be king.
13. A man had two sons; the first said, "I will not do what you ask," but did it. The second said, "I will do what you ask," and did not do it.
14. The Lord reproves him whom he loves.
15. The Lord disciplines him whom he loves.
16. God tempers the wind to the shorn lamb.
17. With faith, hope, and charity, this is the way to live.
18. Discharge your obligations to all men; pay tax and toll, reverence and respect, to those to whom they are due.
19. Let us behave with decency as befits the day.
20. God obligeth no man to more than he hath given him ability to perform.

When the quiz has been completed, spend about

five minutes having the members of the group share their answers as to how well they did in the quiz. Whatever their results, this is not to say, however, that we should go back to the old ways of trying to memorize passages and chapters and receive "little pink ribbons" every time we do it successfully. The quiz does point out the fact that many groups will discover that their practice of reading the Bible and their awareness of its relevance for them lag far behind the basic reverence they hold for the Bible.

Spend the rest of the session looking at the reasons why youth do not read the Bible more often. These reasons were given in response to questions six and seven in the first quiz entitled, "Attitude Check." Assign one of the reasons to each of the small groups. Have the small groups work on possible solutions to the problem of why the Bible is not read more regularly. Put the groups' answers on the chalkboard or a large sheet of paper and have the members of the total group decide whether or not they would be interested in working through some of the solutions.

4. WHAT ARE OUR ATTITUDES?

This quiz may have shown us that we have an inaccurate understanding of what is in the Bible. It is very common for us not to recognize passages that are in the Bible or to think that other well-known quotes are from the Bible. The simple fact is that we have not been trained in a thorough knowledge of the Bible as were some people in previous generations.

WORSHIP

Worship can be very simple. Place an open Bible in the center of the group and have the group members quote their favorite passages and explain why they are meaningful to them. End the worship by praying together the Lord's Prayer.

ANSWERS TO "QUOTES AND MISQUOTES" QUIZ

1. No —Don Quixote
2. Yes—Proverbs 9:9
3. No —Don Quixote
4. Yes—Isaiah 55:1
5. No —It is really from a hymn by William Cowper
6. Yes—Isaiah 53:5
7. Yes—Matthew 5:16
8. No —Proverb found in most of the major languages but not in the Bible
9. Yes—Proverbs 22:1
10. No —Shakespeare (*Othello*)
11. Yes—1 Samuel 31:4
12. Yes—Judges 9:7-15
13. Yes—Matthew 21:28-31
14. Yes—Proverbs 3:12
15. Yes—Hebrews 12:6
16. No —Laurence Sterne (*A Sentimental Journey*)
17. No —Misquote from a paraphrase of 1 Corinthians 13:13
18. Yes—Romans 13:7, NEB
19. Yes—Romans 13:13, NEB
20. No —Koran

MODERN AMERICA AND MATTHEW

by KEITH L. IGNATIUS

"O [America, America], killing the prophets and stoning those who are sent to you! How often would I have gathered your children together as a hen gathers her brood under her wings, and you would not! Behold, your house is forsaken and desolate. For I tell you, you will not see me again, until you say, 'Blessed is he who comes in the name of the Lord'" (Matthew 23:37-39).

The author of Matthew wrote a Gospel that embarrassed the early church and today is embarrassing America. In this session we want to ask the question, "Why?" What does Matthew say to America that causes her so much embarrassment?

PURPOSE

To attempt to understand the gospel of Christ as recorded in Matthew in light of who we are as a nation and as a people.

PROCESS AND BACKGROUND

1. BACKGROUND

Matthew was written during the infancy of the Christian faith. Although the church had been growing for a whole generation, the converts, by and large, were not coming from among the Jewish people. Missionary ventures into the Greek and Roman world provided the growing edge. Jesus had been a Jew, his disciples had been Jews, and the very early converts had been Jews. But, on the whole, the Jewish people, who had been so close to God for so many generations, were rejecting this latest and greatest of God's gifts to them. The word was being received more enthusiastically by those people who had never heard of God—foreigners and outcasts with whom the Jews never associated.

America has been traditionally Christian. Generations after generations have grown up into the faith. Is there a possibility that America is rejecting the newer forms of God's word to the world and holding onto the acceptable and traditional—comparable to the Pharisees described in Jesus' time?

Matthew is addressed to both nations and individuals. It speaks about our group responsibilities, our life together as a nation and as a world of brothers. Jesus' Sermon on the Mount was directed not only to individuals but also to groups of people. Individuals heard and accepted, but if these individuals had worked in groups to carry out the word they had heard and accepted, the thrust would have been even more effective.

America has traditionally, except in times of national emergency, relied on the concept of individualism. Every man can solve his own problem, pull himself up by his own boot straps. However, the question for us today is: Can issues of national scope—such as housing, poverty—still be solved with this kind of individual emphasis?

2. STUDYING MATTHEW

Divide your group into smaller units with each unit being assigned one of the following sections of Matthew. Each unit is to read the assigned passage and study any questions accompanying it. On the basis of their answers, each unit is to rewrite the assigned Scripture passage, giving specific illustrations from life today. These are to be shared with the total group.

a. Matthew 5:1-14

- Your next door neighbor is a widow; her only son was killed in a hold-up attempt this week. Interpret and rewrite verse 4 in light of this situation.
- A gentle and very friendly family has moved into a home down the block from you. Yours is a good neighborhood. Last night their house was bombed. The family is black. Interpret and rewrite verses 10, 11, and 12 for this specific family.
- Write specific illustrations for each of the verses contained in the rest of the passage. Rewrite the verses in modern terms and show how they apply to the situation which you have developed.

b. Matthew 7:15-20

Who are today's false prophets?
How do you recognize them?
How do you reconcile the fact that some men are considered prophets by some people and misguided men by others?

Have each person in the group list some of the Old Testament prophets (about five). Next, have each person list beside each name of a prophet the name of a modern-day man who in some way resembles that prophet.

Would you consider such men as Martin Luther King, Jr., Robert Kennedy, James Forman, and Billy Graham to be modern-day prophets? Why or why not?

Rewrite this passage of Scripture, trying to identify who the false prophets are today and how they can be recognized.

c. Matthew 8:1-9

A church refused to grant a temporary loan to a mother of three on welfare. Sickness had used up her money. The decision to refuse was based on the fact that the mother was not a member of the church. The church does give money, however, to people who are members.

A man was refused admittance to a hospital because he had no insurance coverage. The hospital did not feel it could absorb his expenses if he did not pay.

How should these two problems be solved in

light of Jesus' action in this passage of Matthew? Does Jesus demand faith and obedience as the price of healing? Rewrite this passage in light of the way in which healing and serving should be done by Christians today.

d. Matthew 10:1-42

Controversy and hostility seem always to surround great men. According to Jesus this would also be true of his disciples. Yet, today in America most churches loathe to become involved in controversial issues. The mood of most churches seems to be "don't stir up the waters."

For example, a church voting on a budget had an open debate on the matter. All sides and aspects of the budget were debated. Several people became angry during the process. The minister, afterward, was criticized by some for allowing such honest discussion. The contention was that things like this should not be allowed in the church.

A youth group in a given church was restrained from having a discussion on school discipline. They had planned to have the principal and several teachers attend, plus some youth who were arguing for more student participation in school policy making. The reason given the youth group was that this matter is not a subject for a church group discussion.

Rewrite this passage of Scripture, taking into consideration the attitude of churches today and the previous two illustrations. Consider the problem contained in each illustration before you rewrite.

3. ALL GROUPS

Rewrite Matthew 28:19-20, giving specific examples of how this commandment is to be carried out among the poor, minority people who distrust much of what the church says and does, and how it is to be carried out among youth who are bored with church life, and among people of different countries. These examples may be shared during the worship.

WORSHIP

After the groups have shared their work, move into a circle. In unison read Matthew 5:13-16, substituting "I" and "my" for "you" and "your."

Lord's Prayer: Pray together this prayer substituting "my" and "me" for "our" and "us."

The Commandment: Have each group read its version of Matthew 28:19-20.

I THANK GOD I'M NOT LIKE OTHER MEN (BUT HE WAS AND IS—AS YOU ARE)

by KEITH L. IGNATIUS

A PREJUDICED PRAYER

The prayer of the Pharisee was one of the most prejudiced prayers of all times, "Thank God I am not like other men. . . ." He would hope to be a "little God" in his own right. He refused to look at himself to see his prejudices and self-distortions. He would have the world's ills be the fault of other men.

The publican's prayer was the honest one. "Here I am, God. Help!" Most of us would prefer the prayer of the Pharisee—that the world's ills are the fault of other men. Youth could blame adults; adults could blame their parents and the younger generation. No persons would have to hold themselves responsible.

When it comes to prejudice, most of us are like the Pharisee. "We are not really prejudiced against blacks, but. . . ." God calls us to pray the publican's prayer. "Confess! Ask for help. Do something about it."

PURPOSE

To look at our feelings toward minority groups.

PROGRAM DEVELOPMENT

Put the following two statements on a large sheet of paper. Divide into twos for discussion of the statements. After a few minutes cut off the conversations and have each team write a "true" or "false" under each statement.

1. Dr. Martin Luther King, Jr., in his famous letter, "Letter from Birmingham Jail," wrote:

"I suppose . . . that few members of the oppres-sor race [meaning the white race] can understand the deep groans and passionate yearnings of the oppressed race. . . ." [1]

2. Because you are black, you are prejudiced against Chicanos. (Substitute whatever group your group might be prejudiced against.)

Allow time for any group comments and reactions.

Give each person a copy of "Check Your Prejudices," below. Have each person complete it silently. When all are finished, divide into groups of four to discuss their answers. Allow about fifteen minutes. Then have the groups answer each question using this frame of reference: "What is the Christian response to this question?" Have the groups share their answers.

CHECK YOUR PREJUDICES

The following statements are designed to help you to look at yourself—to spot-check your own personal prejudices. In place of the word "minority" in each statement substitute the name of the group your group might be prejudiced against. The quiz can be used in relation to any racial, ethnic, or economic group from your area.

Circle the answer which describes you best. Do your checking without talking.

1. I have _____ (number) minority friends.
   1 2 3 4 more

2. My minority friends have visited my home.
   yes   no

[1] Martin Luther King, Jr., *Why We Can't Wait* (New York: Harper & Row, Publishers, 1963), p. 93.

a. They have had dinner with my family.
　　yes　　　　　　　　no

b. They stayed overnight in my home.
　　yes　　　　　　　　no

3. I would not mind having _____ minority teachers.

　　1 2 3 4 more

4. A minority teacher would probably be more strict with _____.

　　black students　　white students

5. I would suggest the following racial balance in our church.

　　1/3 minority membership; 1/2 minority; 2/3 minority; no minority

6. I would not mind eating in a restaurant operated by a minority person.
　　　　yes　　　　　　　　no

7. I would not mind staying overnight in a minority operated motel.
　　　　yes　　　　　　　　no

a. Have you ever stayed in such a motel?
　　　yes　　　　　　　　no

8. I would not mind loaning a good dress/coat to a minority friend.
　　　　yes　　　　　　　　no

9. I would not mind going to a minority dentist.
　　　yes　　　　　　　　no

a. Have you ever checked on a minority dentist with the thought of going to him?
　　　　yes　　　　　　　　no

10. A minority barber/beautician would not bother me.
　　　　yes　　　　　　　　no

11. Having more minority students than my race in my school would be OK.
　　　　yes　　　　　　　　no

12. The idea of a "minority Jesus" disgusts me.
　　　yes　　　　　　　　no

13. The history and culture of the minority people should be taught as extensively as European history in my school.
　　　　yes　　　　　　　　no

a. Should minority history be taught if there are no minority students around?
　　　　yes　　　　　　　　no

14. Picture yourself getting on a bus. Near you is an empty seat beside a minority person. Toward the rear is an empty seat beside a person of your own race. Where would you sit?
beside the minority person
　　　　beside the person of your own race

15. Would you feel comfortable walking in an all minority neighborhood?
　　　yes　　　　　　　　no

a. Would a minority person feel comfortable walking down your street?
　　　yes　　　　　　　　no

WORSHIP

Read Luke 18:9-14 and 1 John 4:7-21. What do these passages say about prejudice and our involvement in it?

Hymn: "They'll Know We Are Christians by Our Love"

Prayer

21

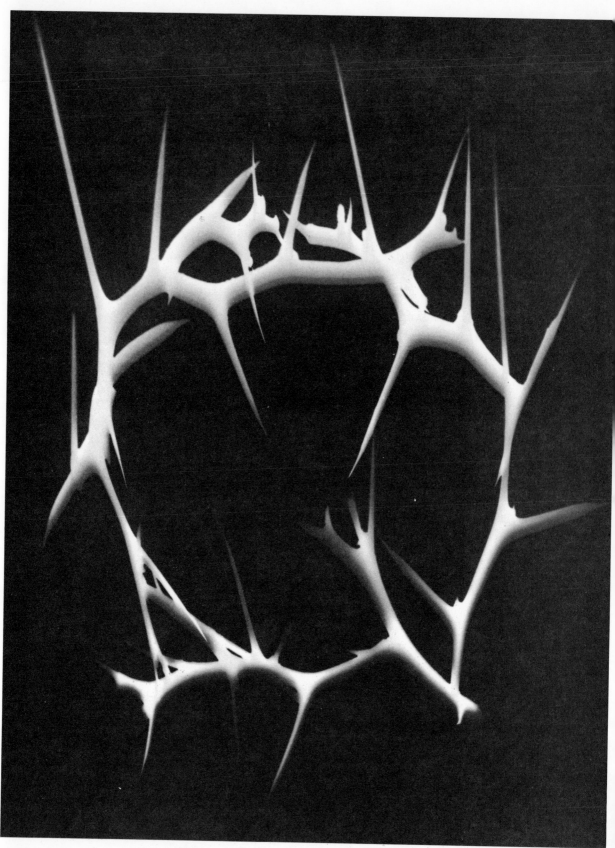

IS IT I?

by KEITH L. IGNATIUS

INTRODUCTION

It was one of the days immediately preceding the Passover—a joyous occasion for the Jews. Jerusalem was crowded; the streets were packed. The cries of the weary mingled with the shouts of the happy as men prepared to celebrate the occasion of their "exodus" from Egypt.

Away from it all, in a small room dimly lit by the flickering light of an oil lamp, thirteen men sat at a table. The room was hushed. Only the buzzing of flies and the humming of mosquitoes could be heard. They had finished eating and they sat quietly —waiting. Sweat poured down their backs and dripped off their foreheads. The night was hot.

The twelve stared at their leader, waiting for some word from him—some comment which might explain his puzzling actions during the evening. Finally he rose slowly from the table. He looked searchingly into the face of each. The air was electrified with tension. How unlike the Master! The silence became almost unbearable. At last! At last he began to speak. "One of you is—" he paused wearily. "Is what? Will do what?" screamed the twelve silently.

"One of you," he gasped, "is going to betray me—" The world seemed to stand still. Muscles contracted and breathing halted as the disciples grappled with the magnitude of what had just been said. Had they heard correctly? In the next instant there was a war of confusion as each disciple shouted his loyalty and asked his fear-ridden question, "Is it I, Lord? Is it I?" They demanded to be heard and answered.

PURPOSE

The celebration of Easter brings with it a myriad of worship services. No doubt your group will be involved with the planning of one or two of these services in your church. If so, we offer this suggestion as one possibility for your thinking.

1. HISTORICAL NARRATION

The introduction, above, is a paraphrase of Matthew 26:17-25. This style of worship is sometimes called "historical fiction." The author takes an historical fact and tries to recreate what might have happened. In planning for your Easter service, divide into subgroups and recreate the scenes and situations depicted in the Scripture passages you are using. This can be done in a variety of forms. For example:

- *Reporter Uncovers Unusual Phenomenon.*

Have two or three people rewrite Matthew's description of the resurrection in the style of a newspaper article (Matthew 28:1-10).

- *"Body Stolen," Says Guard.*

Pretend you're a TV reporter. Interview the sentries who were guarding the tomb (Matthew 28:11-15).

- *"A Hoax," Says Famous News Analyst.*

Be a skeptic and write the story of the resurrection, taking into account the contradicting testimonies of Mary, Mary Magdalene, and the guards. Did Matthew know about the secret bribe, or was there really a bribe?

- *Death Penalty Carried Out!*

As a Roman reporter covering the crucifixion, write the events as if they had occurred today. Remember that crucifixion was a common method of putting criminals to death—similar to our electric chair. As a reporter, you have been through this a number of times (Matthew 27:32-61).

2. HOW WAS IT?

Divide into two groups and form two circles. Group 2 forms a circle around Group 1. While Group 2 silently observes, have members of Group 1 comment on what they felt while engaged in the project (5 min.). Switch places and have Group 2 answer the same question.

3. TELLING IT LIKE IT WAS

Have each group read what it has written. Evaluate each one and suggest improvements. Rewrite on the basis of the suggestions and continue the planning for your service of worship. You should have gotten some creative ideas.

THE KISS THAT KILLED

by KEITH IGNATIUS

THE BETRAYAL

Flickering torch lights and muffled voices are to be seen and heard from inside the temple walls. Suddenly the gate is thrown open, and a group of men leave the temple and hurry toward the Valley of Kidron. A man named Judas is at the head of the procession. His tense, moody expression is in sharp contrast to the expectant look which lights the faces of those behind. A trap is being set and Judas is the man who will spring it. Jesus is the one to be caught!

PURPOSE

Who is this man called Judas? What were the decisions and motives which led him to that fateful kiss? Was there a conspiracy? Did he do it alone? The strategy of this program is an attempt to get under the skin of Judas and to discover who the real person was.

PROCESS

Some authors suspect Judas of being a guerilla —or at least that he was sympathetic in some way to the Zealots. The Zealots were an undercover organization intent on overthrowing the Roman government and freeing Israel. Their tactics, in some ways, could be compared with the terrorism of the Viet Cong. No city or village was completely safe from them. They had infiltrated everywhere. Any civilian suspected of collaborating with the Roman government was put on their death list. Instead of homemade bombs and mortar blasts, poison or the short knife beneath a cape was used. They knew how to kill silently and escape into the crowd.

In the beginning Judas may have thought Jesus was sympathetic to the Zealots' cause. But now, after three years—?

1. WRITING VIGNETTES

In teams of three, write a brief vignette which will answer these questions about Judas. Each team chooses one question.

a. Assume that Judas was a member of the Zealots who are becoming suspicious of Jesus' intentions. What kind of conversation would take place between Judas and a fellow Zealot concerning the fate of Jesus? Judas is probably not sure about the full purpose and meaning of Jesus' life. He may have a feeling that Jesus is something special.

b. Assume that Judas was not a Zealot but a firm believer of the Law instead. Could Jesus' continuous indifference to the trivial points of the Law and his association with the wrong kinds of people have disillusioned Judas?

Did Judas, near the end, finally believe Jesus was a false Messiah who, according to the Law (Deuteronomy 13:1-11), should be done away with? Write a script depicting some of the thinking Judas must have done.

c. Judas is on his way to betray Jesus. What is he thinking as he moves at the head of the procession? How does he feel betraying a person who has befriended him for so long?

2. SHARING

Share with each other the scripts which have been written. These could be used as parts of a creative worship service.

3. FURTHER EXPLORATION

If you have time, explore some of these additional questions:

- Was Judas simply selfish and dishonest, a man who could not resist the chance for some personal gain? (John 12:4-6; Matthew 26:14-16)

  If so, why did he receive such a trivial sum of money for such a heinous crime?

- Matthew depicts Judas as having repented and offering to return the money. He hangs himself. The other Gospels make no mention of this end. Acts 1:18-19 has Judas dying in yet another way. Did Judas repent?

- Why do you think Jesus chose Judas as one of his disciples in the first place?

WHY DO PEOPLE GO TO CHURCH?

by KEITH L. IGNATIUS

MANY ANSWERS

Why do people go to church? A wide variety of answers would come in response to that question. Worship, habit, fellowship, duty, guilt, and thanksgiving would be included in some of the answers. There would probably be no one answer for everyone in a given congregation. The fact that people do attend church regularly means that some needs are being met. Since a great percentage of the American population seldom attends church, if at all, we must also assume that a great many needs are not being met. Why? If we understand why some people do get something out of church, we might be in a position to understand why others do not.

PURPOSE

To find out how the church can serve more of the needs of people.

PROCESS

1. BIBLE—A PLACE TO BEGIN

The Bible is a place to begin for digging up clues to church attendance. The Old Testament suggests that the motives of the Israelites were not altogether pure. Their reasons included appeasement of God's anger, a way of insuring success in war, earning a long life, and attainment of wealth and wisdom. (Sounds familiar, doesn't it?) In the New Testament, the motive seems to be the building of Christian character through mutual teaching, confession, sharing, and thanksgiving to God. Many of these old and new reasons are also the motives of people today. Look up "temple" in a Bible concordance to find what people in the Bible thought about going to church.

2. "STREET-CORNER QUESTION"

Divide your group into subgroupings of three. Half of the group will poll people on the downtown streets. The other half will survey people of the church coming out of worship on a Sunday morning.

Street-Corner Procedure: Each subgroup will interview at least ten people. "I am from the _____ church and we are conducting a survey on church attendance. Do you go to church regularly? Do you go at all? Why do you not go?" Ask each person the same questions. Note his or her approximate age.

After the survey, compare the findings. What conclusions can be drawn about why people do or do not attend church? Does age make a difference? Why or why not?

Sunday Morning Procedure: Each subgroup will interview at least ten people. Ask each person the same questions and try to ask people you do not know well. "Hello, our youth group is conducting a study of church attendance. Do you attend church often? What does it do for you? Why do you sometimes not attend? Why do you think so many people fail to attend church?"

3. PASTOR-DEACON INTERVIEW

Interview the pastor and chairman of the board of deacons. They symbolize the spiritual aspect of the church by virtue of their positions. Explain the purpose of the interview and then ask each:

- Why should people regularly attend church?
- Could you list four reasons why most people attend church?
- Why do more people not attend church regularly? List four reasons.

Ask the members of the youth group the same questions. List their responses on the chalkboard. Compare these with the answers of the pastor and the deacon or with those from the street and church survey, if you did them. Are there discrepancies? What conclusions can be drawn? In order to have more people attend church, what changes would have to be made?

WORSHIP

Hymn: "Renew Thy Church" (From *Chapbook 2*)

Scripture: 1 Corinthians 12:27-31

Prayer: Pray for a church that has meaning to the people you have interviewed and to the members of your own group.

Is the Christian world view a part of the problem or a part of the solution?

A QUESTION OF VALUES

by DIANE ZEDIKE

ENVIRONMENTAL CRISIS!

"It takes 500 years to create one inch of good top soil."

"Each year the U.S. paves over 1,000,000 acres of oxygen-producing trees."

"Everyday we produce 11,000 calories of food per person in the U.S. We need only 2,500 calories."

"Although the U.S. contains only 5.7% of the world's population, it consumes 40% of the world's production of natural resources."

BACKGROUND AND RESOURCE MATERIAL

It is not news to say that our world is endangered by too many people, some of whom have too much of the world's goods and MOST of whom have too little.

Population, hunger, crowding, pollution, depletion of resources, and inadequate distribution of these resources are words which may create fear as we use them, but which need to be heard as a challenge. They seem to call for action and at the same time seem to be too big for us to solve.

Before we can redirect our actions to create solutions, some of the values and assumptions that we act on need to be checked.

Time magazine summarized the issue by saying that more than anything else our way of thinking threatens our very existence and has produced the present environmental crisis.

For example, many people believe that:
—nature exists for man to conquer;
—nature is endlessly bountiful;
—economic growth is worth any effort;
—technology will get us out of the problem.

Basic to all solutions is the need for a new way of thinking: "[we] must view the world in terms of unities rather than units. To recognize the interdependence of all creatures . . . [see wholes, not parts].

The biggest need may be a change in values." [1]

[1] *Time,* February 2, 1970.

"The earth is the Lord's and the fulness thereof the world and those who dwell therein."

(Psalm 24:1)

God founded the world and established it and pronounced his creation as "good." He created man to be like himself and gave man dominion over the earth. (See Genesis 1.)

Thus the Bible affirms the things of the earth, claims them as God's possession, but places man in a unique position of power over all forms of life. (See Psalm 8.)

If we stopped there, perhaps critics would be justified in saying that the Christian world view has given license to Western civilization to conquer, exploit, and plunder the earth; and that a new theology or nature-oriented religion is needed.

But there is more to the Christian view of the world than the brief summary above. Two key themes are missing or only hinted at: man's role in relationship to God's earth is that of steward (see Luke 12:42-48), and God's purpose of reconciliation includes all of life. (See Isaiah 11:1-9.) Dominion does not need to imply domination.

Look in your dictionary for the meaning of the words:

steward
dominion
domination

PURPOSE

To explore what effect the values and attitudes of Christians might have on the environmental crisis of our time.

PROCESS

1. MAKE A COLLAGE

Begin the session by having each member develop a collage, symbolizing "The Good Life." (The collage can be made by tearing words and pictures from magazines.) This collage is to include all that he or she has and hopes to have in the future.

Supplies Needed: Many magazines, glue or

26

paste, scissors (if possible), crayons, markers or pencils, newsprint, shelf paper, cardboard boxes, or whatever you want to use to mount the collage on.

Variation: If time is short, the pictures and words can be torn out and held by individuals rather than assembled in a collage.

Next, in small groups (approximately 4 persons) share with one another the things that represent the good life for you. You may add to your list someone else's idea if you want to, but this is not a time to debate relative values or to criticize one another's choices. (When finished, put the lists up on the walls.)

2. DISCUSSION

Spend a few minutes looking at all the collages, reflecting silently on the following questions: (These could be put up on newsprint.)

- What values seem to be dominant in the collages?
- How strongly do I feel about my right to achieve the good life? Is there something wrong with society if I cannot realize my hopes and dreams?
- What will be the impact on the environment if we all get everything we have put on the collages?

Allow a few minutes for any responses that individuals might want to make to the questions.

Look at the background and resource section. (This could be a brief input by the leader of the session.)

In small groups, evaluate whether the values expressed so far have been closer to the kind that create the environmental problem or the kind that might lead to its solution.

3. BIBLE STUDY

In small groups, look at the following listing of Scriptures in the light of these questions:

What is the "Good Life" for a Christian?

What values should have highest priority?

Luke 12:16-21
Mark 10:17-22
Luke 12:22-34
Matthew 6:9-13

Have each group list on newsprint its responses and share these with the total group. Allow a few minutes for any questions or clarification.

Note: If time is limited, assign one Scripture passage to each group rather than have every group look at each passage.

Have all groups look at the next two Scripture passages in response to the question: "What are we called to be and do?"

Luke 12:42-48
Matthew 8:18-20

Again share responses and seek consensus as a group on what the implications are.

WORSHIP

Read John 10:10.

Look again at the collages. Ask members of the group to take into consideration whatever they have discovered about the crisis of population, pollution, depletion of resources, inequitable distribution of goods, and our responsibilities as Christians to be stewards of God's earth and brothers to all His children and then to decide WHAT of the things which they put on their collages they could do without and what they would need to add in order to have a good life as Christians.

Have them act out their decisions by each individual getting up and changing his collage to make it correspond to his decision. The group members can take this step individually, symbolizing the need of each person to act responsibly, or they can do it with others and create a new mural to represent the group's commitment to a new way of thinking about life.

OTHER RESOURCES FOR WORSHIP

Recording: "He Ain't Heavy, He's My Brother"
Song: "Rise Up, Children" from *New Wine, Songs for Celebration*
Responsive Readings:
Nos. 43 or 44 *Chapbook 2*
No. 22 *Hymns and Songs of the Spirit*
Prayers:
No. 32 *Chapbook 2*
No. 30 *Hymns and Songs of the Spirit*

OTHER POSSIBILITIES FOR ACTION

Find out what is being done in your area to meet the challenge of the environmental crisis. Can you join in as individuals? As a group? What is not being done? Can you start something? Some of the kinds of tasks that other youth have done are: organization and maintenance of bottle recycling stations; arrangement of litter clean-up campaigns; fund raising and work parties to plant trees; support of legislative measures to combat pollution.

28

GETTING IT TOGETHER—IN MEDITATION   by WARREN LANE MOLTON

GETTING IT TOGETHER

The youth culture in the West and especially in this country is becoming turned on to meditation. For some it is an EXERCISE by which a person hones the mind and spirit. For others, meditation is a DISCIPLINE, out of which a whole life-style develops. For still others, it is an EXPERIENCE emerging from a discipline which seems to change all of reality, the whole way a person views his existence.

PURPOSE

The exercises in this session should help your group to grasp something of the insight and power available in the art of personal meditation.

BACKGROUND

Meditation is not new to Western man. It is at the heart of his Jewish-Christian faith and for centuries has seemed necessary to the cultivation of the spirit of love and true discipleship.

The Psalms are filled with references to meditation, beginning with the very first one:

Blessed is the man
who walks not in the counsel
of the wicked,
nor stands in the way of sinners,
nor sits in the seat of scoffers;
but his delight is in the law of the
Lord
and on his law he meditates day
and night.

(Psalm 1:1-2)

Other Old Testament references include Joshua 1:7-9; Psalm 4:4; Psalm 119:97; and Proverbs 4:26. The great passage in the New Testament referring to meditation is Philippians 4:8:

Finally, brethren, whatever is true, whatever is honorable, whatever is just, whatever is pure, whatever is lovely, whatever is gracious, if there is any excellence, if there is anything worthy of praise, *think about* these things (emphasis added).

The Gospels report many occasions on which Jesus drew aside for meditation and prayer, from the first experience of his forty days in the wilderness to his "dark night of the soul" in the Garden of Gethsemane.

There are many literary classics on the subject of meditation. There is *Meditations* by the Roman philosopher-general, Marcus Aurelius. In Christian tradition we have St. Augustine's *Confessions* and the *Spiritual Exercises* by De Loyola, founder of the Society of Jesus. Another great work in this field is Pascal's *Thoughts*. There are scores of other writings of those who have deeply searched their lives and world for the meaning of their existence and the presence of the Holy Spirit.

Today, at a time when youth refer to "plastic people" and "space food" (processed, flavorless, and virtually unspoilable), and the now-and-coming trauma of "future shock," meditation is in. Youth are turning to the human encounter of one's self and the experience of transcendence (going beyond) through meditation.

The initial phase of meditation is CONCENTRATION. This is a process of focusing in an attempt to discover the essence of anything from a flower to the ocean. One might also concentrate upon a person or a truth at the elementary level of simply discovering the "isness" of reality: who IS this person? What IS this truth?

One of the most dynamic exercises for developing the art of concentration is not found in the recitation of some symbolic word or formula, or even in pouring over a book or staring at a flame, but rather through the "Blind Walk." In this method, one eliminates sight, which so often simply gobbles up the environment without our experiencing it, and then gives the other senses a chance to come alive to the world around us. Try it.

PROCESS

1. THE BLIND WALK

Divide members of the group into pairs and blindfold one in each twosome. The sighted person is to lead the blindfolded one around the room, the building, or outside, introducing the person to his world: a book, held but not seen; the sound of a clock; water over one's hand at the fountain; the smell of the church kitchen; the feel of a stone. This trip is taken slowly, giving time for concentration, and without talking. After approximately ten minutes each pair reverses roles.

2. EVALUATION

After each person has made the trip, the pairs return to the group area and quietly discuss the experience for ten or fifteen minutes. Then the entire group reassembles and discusses what happened.

These questions may help: What new things did you discover about your world? Did concentration on a few senses (touch, taste, smell) change your experience with any object or person? Do you see value in learning to concentrate your mind and senses in this way?

WORSHIP

Have the group members sit in a circle on the floor and with their eyes closed hold hands. The leader opens a bottle of oil of peppermint and goes around the circle touching each brow with his finger after moistening it with the fragrance of peppermint. Then read aloud very slowly Philippians 4:8. Then play softly a favorite recording, such as "Bridge Over Troubled Waters." After the record is completed, the leader should read the Scripture verse a second time, slowly. Then say, "Let us wait in silence." After about one minute, the leader concludes the session with "Amen."

THE MIND'S EYE—
MEDITATION AS REFLECTION

by WARREN LANE MOLTON

We occasionally use the word "reflection" to mean "letting the object, truth, or person be reflected in me." More often, however, we merely mean "to ponder or contemplate." Since the latter is done in concentration, we now want so to dwell upon "the focused other" (object, truth, or person) that we feel it becoming a part of our experience, and thus living in us.

An overdose of this sort of thing is the story by Hawthorne called "The Great Stone Face," in which a little boy studies the face of the Old Man of the Mountain until he begins to take on its character, as reflected in the sculptured features. Another example is Charles Sheldon's book, *In His Steps*, which is a tale of simple discipleship practiced by trying to do in life today "just as Jesus would."

The problems with these stories are many, among them being the naïve idealism and a sort of this-for-that correlation between the object and the person. Building character is not that simple.

To reflect is not merely to IMITATE.

Yet the Hawthorne story has a great truth that includes letting ourselves get into harmony with all the natural forces in the environment which promote strength and health. Many young people today are returning to the land to rediscover the simple goodness of the earth. They are trying to find the meaning of the old Indian chief's answer to the question of how one learns the great virtues: "By standing long under the mountains, following the sounding bass, studying the deer, bending low to the desert flower, bathing in the swift stream, running and singing under the stars." Man, the most destructive animal of all, would do well to learn from other members of the animal kingdom as well as certain objects in this life-sphere.

One of the great works of all time is *The Imitation of Christ* by Thomas á Kempis (1380–1471). Thomas has some helpful things to say; yet, he dares suggest that "it is private love which most hindereth from the chiefest good." Hence, he de-

parts from the words of Jesus that we should love God and neighbor AS OURSELVES (see Luke 10: 27). It is not good mirroring simply to lay hold upon the words. We must find the truth and emulate it.

Jesus says we cannot love neighbor and God unless we love self. The MIRROR must be true to reflect in a truly caring way the neighbor and God. We can imitate or mirror Christ, not by blindly following what we think he would do if he were here today, but by reflecting his qualities of peace, love, and integrity. The task of reflection is to make it possible for the nobility of the objects of our concentration to live in us, to be reflected in our lives. This is the deepest meaning of reflection.

PURPOSE

To discover the meaning of reflection and to use reflection in meditation.

PROCESS

1. MIRRORING

Divide members of the group into pairs and have them stand facing each other. They then take turns in the following exercise: One of each pair holds his hands out in front of himself and begins to move them about slowly. (Do not select a person to begin. Let the pair decide—without talking— who is going to begin.) The partner attempts to follow the one who begins, and they discuss their feelings about leading and being led, of closeness, perhaps of intimacy as they begin to anticipate each other's moves, etc. What happens when one mirrors another? What does he gain, or lose?

2. DISCUSSION

After a few minutes of discussion, join pairs into groups of fours and have them discuss the following:

- Tell your small group about one person who has had some great influence upon your life.
- How does that person make you feel about *yourself?*
- What does that person cause you to want to do or be?
- How do you want to influence your world because of that person reflected in you?

3. EXERCISE IN REFLECTION

After the above discussion has gone on for fifteen to twenty minutes, hang up a banner or poster with the words "Love God and Neighbor as Your-

self." Ask group members to move off by themselves, keeping a distance from others for reflection. Then give each one a piece of paper and pencil or felt marking pen, and ask him to spend five minutes concentrating upon the words of the poster and then draw a self-portrait. It can be any figure, an abstract design, perhaps only a square, anything.

After this is accomplished, put the entire group in a large circle and ask members to comment briefly on "themselves" as projected in the drawing. Discuss HOW one loves himself as a basis for loving others and God. How can we become true reflectors of God's love? In private moments of meditation, is it possible to become truer mirrors of the objects of our concentration? Is this a part of prayer?

WORSHIP

Seat members in pairs, back to back, in a tight cluster, perhaps an inner and outer circle, but close. Ask them quietly to sit with eyes closed for a few moments. Then read the following selected verses from John 14:15-31 (TEV) and ask the group to repeat the refrain "Let me reflect your spirit."

READER: "If you love me, you will obey my commandments."

GROUP: Let me reflect your spirit.

(Pause for 10-15 seconds.)

READER: "I will ask the Father and he will give you another Helper, the Spirit of truth to stay with you forever."

GROUP: Let me reflect your spirit.

READER: "Peace I leave with you; my own peace I give you. I do not give it to you as the world does. Do not be worried and upset; do not be afraid."

GROUP: Let me reflect your spirit.

(Pause)

READER: "Whoever loves me will obey my message. My Father will love him, and my Father and I will come to him and live with him. . . . The message you have heard is not mine, but comes from the Father who sent me."

GROUP: Let me reflect your spirit.

(Pause)

Have the group stand and hold hands, eyes open, and sing a hymn, such as "We Are One in the Spirit," or even the old standby "Jacob's Ladder." Reader concludes with "Amen."

THE DRAMA OF DREAMS—
MEDITATION AS FANTASY

by WARREN LANE MOLTON

OUR FANTASY WORLD

In fantasy, we are trying to enter the area of awareness in which we do our dreaming. Some refer to this as the subconscious in which we have stored all of the data of our lives, and perhaps the data shared by the whole human family. Here we find the pleasant and the unpleasant experiences. It appears that messages from this region are often filled with insight and occasionally surprise us with a truth about ourselves which we had somehow missed.

Sometime ago, when prayer seemed rather barren for me, I began to use fantasy as a basis for meditation. Out of such an experience I wrote what I called the prayer-poem. I simply closed my eyes and waited, much as one might wait before a blank movie screen. Soon, I began to daydream in a brief episode. When it was over, I kept my eyes closed and meditated upon these three questions:

What happened?

What might it mean?

How does it speak to my life here and now?

An example of this process is seen in my book *Bruised Reeds*. On page 81 is the prayer-poem, "Mystery Play," as follows:

MYSTERY PLAY

Lord,
  This cup
    came down through the years:
    mother, grandmother,
    and a couple of other generations
    before them
    used it to measure
    flour and sugar.
  Mother spoke of trying
    to take her first dose
    of castor oil in hot coffee
    from this cup.
  I planted a single hyacinth
    in it last fall
    and kept it hidden
    in the cellar all winter.

This spring I took it out
    and set it in the sun,
    where it grew and blossomed
    into a fragrant, lovely thing
    that caught the eye
    of my two-year-old
    who loved it from the window
    to the floor.
The cup is broken,
    the flower bruised and torn.
The church is that cup,
  Christ that hyacinth,
    and I am that child.
    Amen.[1]

[1] Warren Lane Molton, *Bruised Reeds* (Valley Forge: Judson Press, 1970). Reprinted by permission.

33

All of the prayer-poem except for the last five lines is a fantasy. This is the daydream that spun out in my mind, and all I had to begin with was the memory of a cup in my mother's home. I did not know why that fantasy came to me, but after a few moments of meditation, the analogy of the last five lines also came and I knew the meaning of my meditation-fantasy. Out of the depths of my mind had come the cup bearing with it a story that symbolized my present feelings about the church, Christ, and myself. It was a very significant message for me, and it helped to clarify my present state of spiritual health. I believe that in fantasy it is possible for one to touch down in his own depths, where God may be at work addressing him. In fantasy we permit that which is alive for good at the deepest levels of the self to rise to consciousness.

PURPOSE

To use fantasy as an aid to meditation.

PROCESS

1. FANTASY EXERCISE

Members should be asked to sit or lie down on the floor, singly, with eyes closed. Play the record "He Ain't Heavy, He's My Brother," or some other popular recording with a simple, clear thought of "reaching out." Let the group remain in silence for a couple of minutes. The leader then suggests that they breathe deeply six or eight times, breathing out all tension. During this time, repeat three or four times, "Relax and meditate."

Then say, "Now, with your eyes still closed, imagine you are watching a movie screen. The film begins. It is of YOU walking in a beautiful garden at dusk. You are alone. After a time you come to a small beautiful pool. You sit down by it and wait. You will now be given five minutes or so to let your fantasy spin out by itself in silence."

2. EVALUATION

At the end of the time, ask the group to divide into pairs and discuss for ten minutes. Use the questions: What happened? What might it mean? How does it speak to my life here and now?

Then ask members to sit singly and write a poem (or paint a picture if paints are available), in an attempt to capture the message of their fantasy. Allow approximately twenty minutes; then ask members of the group to return to a large circle for sharing. Make this sharing time brief without a lot of analysis. Ask if members think fantasy might be used each day as a way of touching down deep where God is working in us.

3. BIBLE STUDY

Ask different members to look up the following references to dreams in the Bible. Genesis 28: 10-17; Genesis 41:1-32; Daniel 4:4-27. Ask about each one: What experiences from the person's background came out in the dream? How did God speak through this dream?

WORSHIP

Ask members of the group to stand in a circle, arms about each other's shoulders or holding hands and then sing a seven-fold "Amen."

FOR FURTHER READING

Humphreys, Christmas, *Concentration and Meditation*. Baltimore: Pelican Books, Imprint of Penguin Books, Inc., 1970.

Kazantzakis, Nikos, *The Saviors of God: Spiritual Exercises*. New York: Simon and Schuster, Inc., 1960.

Molton, Warren L., *Bruised Reeds*. Valley Forge: Judson Press, 1970.

Suzuke, D. T., *An Introduction to Zen Buddhism*. New York: Grove Press, Inc., 1964.

PRESIDENT WHO?—WHAT KIND OF PRESIDENT DO YOU WANT?

by PHIL and DAPHNE GILLESPIE

HOW DO WE FIT INTO THE PICTURE?

Every day the president of our country makes decisions that affect our destiny and the destinies of countless others at home and abroad. How do we fit into this picture, and who are these countless persons? It is necessary for each one to decide how he will act out his political responsibility on the stage of the U.S.A. in light of his Christian beliefs. But it is also important that we first discover who shares that stage with us.

PURPOSE

To gain insight into the scope, power, and potential of the presidency.

To stimulate thinking concerning political responsibility.

To define the ideal president.

PROCESS

1. RADIO BROADCAST

Assign roles for the following radio broadcast. (This idea might also be adapted for a panel discussion.)

Responses should be improvised using some of this material and the youth's OWN knowledge.

INVOLVEMENT ROLES:

INTERVIEWER *(Asks each one):* Describe the man or woman who would most adequately and satisfactorily represent you in the White House.

BLACK AMERICAN *(Suffering from discrimination and concerned about quality housing and education, he longs for a political voice.):*

INDIAN AMERICAN *(Confined in large measure to life on a reservation, the lands of which are presently being expropriated for oil enterprises, the Indian wants quality housing and education for his offspring.):*

FEMALE AMERICAN *(She longs for an even chance in medicine, law, business, and government.):*

COAL MINER *(Suffering from black lung, the coal miner is aware that both his health and his job are in jeopardy.):*

MIDDLE AMERICANS *(Comfortable and often complacent, they cannot always see the problems of the poor. Feeling the economic pinch, they have a tendency to pinch others.):*

2. REFLECTION

How can we as senior highs work for the election of a presidential candidate who will meet all of these needs? Discuss.

3. EVALUATION

Could YOU be president? Discuss SERIOUSLY!

WORSHIP

SCRIPTURE: Micah 6:8

PRAYER: Dear Lord, forgive our folly when we say Christianity and politics don't mix. Help us to seek justice and truth in all our political endeavors. Amen.

YOU CAN MAKE A DIFFERENCE: THEREFORE, VOTE!

A CHANCE FOR INVOLVEMENT

Although the right to register to vote has finally been granted to the 18 to 21-year-olds, in some communities fewer than half of those eligible have even bothered to register to vote! Many who opposed granting the vote to the young have pointed to this seeming apathy and have said that the majority of the youth today are not interested in working constructively within the system. You can make a difference by involving others in the democratic process.

PURPOSE

To encourage persons between the ages of eighteen and twenty-one to register to vote.

PROCESS

In order to achieve the purpose stated above, it will be necessary to do some pre- and post-meeting work.

PRE-MEETING PLANNING

The group in charge of the program should invite to the meeting someone who is familiar with the process of voter registration. Probably someone from the city or county office where persons register would be able to answer the who, when, and where of voter registration.

Prior to the meeting, the planning committee should also inventory what has been done in their locality to register the "newly franchised." Has registration taken place at the high school or at a local college?

THE MEETING

Begin with a speaker who can acquaint the group with the process for registering new voters. If the speaker is from the local board of elections, the group may want to ask that special places and times be set aside for registering new voters.

The latter part of the meeting should be devoted to developing strategies for registering the 18-to-21-year-olds in your community. You may want to have a group go to the high school administration and ask for the names of all students who are over eighteen and therefore eligible to vote. After receiving the names, you could contact them individually and acquaint them with the procedure for registering to vote. You may want to try to set up a special place for registration of the young. Perhaps having a registrar at a central location on Saturdays or in the evening would be appropriate.

The important thing to do is to develop strategies that will meet the unique needs of your community and also that will get the job done. Be sure to assign specific persons to specific jobs.

DISCUSSION

Discuss how "getting out the vote" relates to

by PHIL and DAPHNE GILLESPIE

your Christian faith. What is a Christian's responsibility for participation in a democratic society? Should persons mix politics and religion?

Read and discuss the following Bible passages:

Isaiah 1:1-9
Amos 4:1-3
Luke 19:41-44

Meeting Follow-up: Follow-up in this case merely means implementing the strategy or strategies that were decided upon at the meeting. The test of whether or not the purpose has been accomplished will come at the final day of registration before the election.

EVALUATION

The evaluation of this program goes beyond the limited objectives of registering a few new voters. You must also be evaluated in light of how well you follow-up on the registered voters to see that they actually vote. How successful have you been in teaching students the value of primary elections, of political parties, and of party conventions? What have you learned about the Christian's involvement in politics?

WORSHIP

HYMN: "Rise Up, O Men of God"
SCRIPTURE: Isaiah 61:1-7
PRAYER: Read together Psalm 148:11-14.

Indian beads are called "ethnic jewelry."

LET THE REAL FIRST AMERICAN SPEAK

by ROBERT FEREE

TAKING THE SCRIPTURES SERIOUSLY

Some leaders of social action are casually saying, "This is the year for the American Indian. . . . The Indian is the 'in' thing this year. . . . Indian beads are now called 'ethnic jewelry'. . . ."

The Indian is the original or first American and yet we have treated him as a second-class citizen. If we are to take the Scriptures and Jesus seriously, we should recognize our neighbor's needs and relate to his concerns. The church should attempt to provide an atmosphere of love and acceptance for all races—including the American Indian. Christian young people would do well to become more aware of the American Indian's contribution to God's world and man's society as well as the concerns that face American Indians today.

PURPOSE

To help stimulate your group to identify with the concerns of American Indian youth and to discuss ways that your members may become more involved with the American Indians' needs.

PROCESS

1. FREEHAND DRAWINGS

As the members of your group arrive, let them begin making quick freehand drawings or paintings on large pieces of newsprint or shelf paper. The subject matter of each work of "art" can be anything related to the American Indian. Have a supply of crayons, colored chalk, water colors, construction paper, felt-tip markers, scissors, and glue. Continue this activity until all have arrived.

2. "ART" GALLERY

If there is wall space, these pictures can be hung temporarily as an art gallery. Instruct everyone to take a grand tour of the exhibit as each "artist" describes what his portrayal has to do with the American Indian.

Keep touring the "gallery" until everyone has had an opportunity to tell something about what his picture has to say with reference to the American Indian.

The leader can then ask for brief responses to such questions as:

Which of these artists' subject matter is related to the Indians' past culture?

Which subject matter has a more contemporary flavor?

3. ROLE PLAY

Divide into several groups. Reflect upon the concerns of a particular Indian youth. Plan a four-minute role play based upon these concerns.

a. "I am a Bacone College male student and my tribe is Tewa. I am from Taos, New Mexico. I think that the first concern of our Indian young people is for education. There is only one day school fairly near where my people have to go to school with white people and Mexicans. There is hardly room for them there. I think that there is need for an Indian school in our community."

The problem: How can we best provide the Indian with needed education?

b. "I am a Navajo teenage girl. I am concerned about the B.I.A. (Bureau of Indian Affairs). It seems to be perpetuating the status quo of the stereotyped older American Indian in order that its staff may keep their jobs in the B.I.A. Our Indian young people feel that the B.I.A. should help to provide jobs for the Indian youth on the reservation, something like the 'Job Corps.' We ask for help but the B.I.A. does not listen to us young people."

The problem: How can we convince the B.I.A. to do something about our problem?

c. "I am a Sioux young person from South Dakota. I am concerned with the cultural genocide with reference to the American Indian. I am interested in helping the youth of my people to be effectively identified with their Indian heritage so that in the troubled years of adolescence they may not be a 'nothing' when they cannot identify with the hostile white world facing them."

The problem: How can we help the Indian personality to escape the stereotypes of both races and enrich society with a qualitative different person?

d. "I am a Cherokee teenager from what was originally called Indian Territory, now Oklahoma. We have no reservations in Oklahoma and therefore seem to have more freedom than some reservation Indians. I think that we need to help the American Indian to respect his heritage, but not set him aside as an Indian. The difference between my grandfather and me is that my grandfather thought of himself first as an Indian. I think of myself first as an individual and secondly as an Indian."

The problem: How can we recognize and accept the American Indians as individuals?

4. EVALUATION

After each group has given its presentation through role play, there should be an evaluation:

- Do you feel that the group presented a real-life situation?
- What changes would you make in their presentation?
- How can we show more concern for the American Indian?

WORSHIP

Hymn: "In Christ There Is No East or West"
Scripture Implications: (Have a different person read each passage.)
  "I Am My Brother's Keeper"—Genesis 4:9
  "Practice the Golden Rule"—Matthew 7:12
  "The Indian Is My Neighbor"—Luke 10:29-37
  "Show Christian Concern"—John 13:34-35
Prayer: O Great Spirit, grant that I may not find fault with my neighbor until I have walked two moons in his moccasins. Amen.

Racism affects all minorities—including Asian Americans.

IT HAPPENED ONCE; CAN IT HAPPEN AGAIN? by DAVID Y. HIRANO

THE "MODEL MINORITY"

Asian Americans have been considered to be the "model minority" in the United States. In spite of the stereotypes that exist about Asian Americans, it is nevertheless a fact that the Asian American is a part of the colored minority in the United States and thus suffers from white racism. This was brought out again when the large group of Vietnamese and Cambodian refugees came to the United States in 1975.

For the most part the history of Asians in America has been left out of history and social studies textbooks. The contributions of Asians to American culture have not been touched, nor has the exploitation of Asians at the hands of Americans been revealed.

For years Asians have been lumped together as a part of the "Yellow Peril." When America declared war on Japan, thousands of loyal Americans of Japanese ancestry were taken to concentration camps around the United States. These camps were called relocation camps, but in fact were POW camps with barbed wire and guard towers.

PURPOSE

To enable youth to appreciate the pluralism in American culture, to see the consequences of white racism as it affects even the "model minority," and to identify what their Christian response should be to this situation.

RESOURCES

Asian Americans in your neighborhood. Asian Americans are Americans of Japanese, Korean, Chinese, Filipino, Vietnamese, or Cambodian ancestry.

The Asian American Studies Center at the University of California, P.O. Box 24 A 43, Los Angeles, CA 90024; or at the University of California in Davis, California. Write for their bibliography.

Your denominational offices may have some materials about Asian Americans.

Note: Because resources about Asian Americans are so limited, the program planner will need to allow some lead time to assemble the resources and to put together a program.

PROCESS

1. QUESTIONS TO DISCUSS

As youth arrive, ask some of the following questions. (You might have them on newsprint or on slips of paper that are handed out to members of the group.) Use the resources you collected before the meeting to find answers to the questions.

- Who are the Asian Americans? How many are there?
- Where do they live?
- Why did they come to America?
- When did they come to America?
- What has been the church's ministry to Asian Americans?
- Why do textbooks in social studies and history leave out the Asian Americans?

Look in your history books and encyclopedias to find out what you can about the "Yellow Peril."

- How do you feel about that title?
- Has history justified the fears of Americans?

Find out what you can about the concentration camps into which thousands of Japanese Americans were sent during World War II.

2. QUESTIONS TO ASK:

- Why were the Japanese in America relocated?
- Why were not the Germans or Italians similarly relocated?
- How would you feel if you were incarcerated?
- What was the real cause of the relocation?

- If it happened once, can it happen again?

Write your congressman about the recent repeal of Title II of the National Detention Act of 1956 which allowed for the existence of detention camps in the United States. How did your congressman vote? Do you think that people could be incarcerated en masse for reasons other than race—such as the length of their hair?

3. BIBLICAL REFLECTION

Read Luke 4:18-19.

- What does it mean "to set at liberty those who are oppressed"?
- What does it mean to be free in Christ?
Read 2 Corinthians 5:16-21.
- What does being a reconciler mean?
- How can it be done?

WORSHIP

Take time to share feelings about racism.

Take time to confess that all share in America's sins.

Ask God to forgive.

Songs: "We Are One in the Spirit" and "We Shall Overcome."

I GOT SHOES

by MILTON E. OWENS

Shoes are an important part of black culture—and white culture. Did you ever notice how proud children are of a new pair of shoes? Think how you, yourself, feel in a new pair of shoes—or an old, comfortable pair of shoes. Why are shoes valuable? Why would a people "sell the needy for a pair of shoes" (as in Amos 2:6)? This session will help answer these questions.

PURPOSE

To become aware of the value of persons and their contributions to our lives.

PROCESS

1. DISPLAY OF SHOES

Have pictures of different types of shoes displayed around the room and have the pairs of shoes displayed on a table for all to see.

As students enter the class, ask them to examine the shoes. Ask them to describe the shoes they like least and most, the different types of shoes and their functions. Ask them to talk about their feelings as they wear new shoes or old shoes.

2. BIBLE STUDY

Read Amos 2:6-7. Ask the class members to discuss:

• Why are shoes valuable?

• What did Amos mean when he spoke out against selling the needy for a pair of shoes?
• Are people more valuable than shoes?
• Are the "needy" more valuable than shoes?
• How do people sell the needy for shoes in our society today?

3. A SIGNIFICANT BLACK CONTRIBUTION

Return to the pictures of shoes and talk about Jan Ernest Matzeliger and shoes. Share the following information:

Jan Ernest Matzeliger (1852–1889) made it possible to produce a complete shoe by machine. He laid the foundation for the shoe industry in the United States, and made Lynn, Massachusetts, the shoe capital of the world. On March 20, 1883, patent number 274,207 was granted to J. E. Matzeliger, and six years later he died of tuberculosis.

WORSHIP

Scripture: John 13:3-15

Talk about serving others, as a recognition of their worth. Then ask young people to shine one another's shoes, symbolizing the care Jesus expressed in washing his disciples' feet.

CHANT OF THE GURUS—
A NEW LOOK AT EASTERN RELIGIONS

by WILLIAM SHINTO

A RENEWED INTEREST IN EASTERN RELIGIONS

Sidney Slomich tells the tale of a man who dreamed that a monster was on his chest, choking him. The man, waking in terror, saw the monster above him. "What is going to happen to me?" the man cried. "Don't ask me," replied the monster. "It's your dream!"

The youth of America have a monster hovering over them. The United States is channeling greater proportions of its national wealth into private consumption—more and better washer-dryers, television sets, cars, roads, and golf balls. This inordinate preoccupation with material gain in a life built around self-interest is troubling a new generation of youth who want to move beyond the wasteland of American life and frontier Protestantism.

Much of the communal life-style and the impulses of the counter-culture are the results of the impact of the East rather than any influences arising from Protestant denominations. The central appeal of the East is the basic belief in unlimited human possibilities through self-awareness coupled with specific religious techniques and methods to achieve this personal enlightenment.

The monster of Western materialism, selfish rugged individualism, and bankrupt Protestant/Puritan ethics is being rejected by modern young people. They are now seriously turning to other faiths for solutions of the deep problems of fragmented American life. Thus Christian youth need to engage Asian faiths in honest and open dialogue.

PURPOSE

To help youth begin to identify their own commitments, to discover where each person is "coming from," and to begin a dialogue about the dual impact of the West and the East on youth's own perceptions of life.

GROUP PROCEDURE

1. COME TOGETHER

Have each person in the group draw a symbol which best projects what his personal way of life is. You may want to introduce this by sharing some examples of Christian and other symbols—the cross, the fish, the dove, the peace symbol, the happy face, etc. Then ask each young person to try to conjure up a symbol which is peculiarly fitting to where he or she is "at" now.

Have the group then form a circle and let each

43

person share the symbol he or she has drawn. Let members of the group first ask questions about it, and then let the person tell what the symbol means.

2. Leader's Rap

Draw a cross. The group will obviously identify it as a Christian symbol meaning, among other things, salvation and sacrifice. By adding arrowheads on the ends of the cross, the facilitator has transformed the symbol into one with an Asian motif which points to group consciousness, interdependence, and self-realization. Discuss with the group the way the same symbol may project a different perspective.

3. Reflection

Have the group members reflect upon their symbols by breaking up into groups of two or three to discuss what they believe to be present in their own symbols. Questions which may be helpful are: Who am I? Where am I going? Why do I find living in America at this time a strange and/or positive experience? How do I decide what to decide?

4. Summary

Many people would agree that when we come to know well our own deepest nature, which includes all of our experience, we then also know human nature in general. If this is so, then youth can begin to realize that they are being shut off from real learning if they cannot begin to share the "juices" of other cultures which may contribute to helping shape a faith for a new humanity.

WORSHIP

Scripture: Acts 17:24-28

Divide the group into three sections, assigning them the three phrases: Hare Krishna, *namu Amida butsu,* and Jesus Christ Lord. Have each section simultaneously chant these phrases while the leader reads the Scripture passage.

Join hands and have a full minute of silent meditation. Close with a simple benediction—"peace," "joy," "let love bind us," etc.

ADDITIONAL RESOURCES

Needleman, Jacob, *The New Religions.* New York: Doubleday & Company, Inc., 1970.

THE QUALITY OF LIFE— WHAT EASTERN RELIGIONS ARE

by WILLIAM SHINTO

WE UNDERSTAND SO LITTLE

The deeply rooted religious and cultural foundations of Asia differ sharply from the technological and pragmatic American society. A misreading of these differences has already led us into the tragedy of the Vietnam war.

Yet we are like little children in our understanding about Asia, where two-fifths of the world's population lodges. And although generalizations about Asia have to be made, there is no simple all-embracing philosophy in Asia, but a vast conglomeration of the most disparate conceptions of life. People as different as Chinese and Hindu, Japanese and Vietnamese are all Asians. So before one embarks on the journey to the East, youth are reminded that the complexity which is Asia is no "small trip."

Yet some generalization can be made. There is a tendency in the West to separate sharply man and nature. But from the perspective of Asia, man stands at the crossroads of nature and spirit and is integrally related and interdependent with nature. Western Christians are also apt to view the individual as an encapsulated ego over against an independent environment while Asians in general see life as one whole.

Thus there are two great cultures separated into the Western style of "striving" (doing, coping, achieving, trying; pragmatic, purposive, competitive) and the Eastern way of "being-becoming" (existing, expressing, growing, self-actualization, holistic, meditative).

The Buddhist invites you to take the journey with him; not "have faith," but "here is the Path, follow it and see."

PURPOSE

To introduce the complexity of the Asian religions and to begin the group on a path toward probing Asian faiths as a way to new perspectives.

PROCESS

1. A WAY TO BEGIN

Divide the group into two halves. Have one section silently meditate on the precept or *koan,* "What is the meaning of one hand clapping?" (which is meant to help one move from logical reasoning to intuitive insight). The other group should repeat aloud the Lord's Prayer.

You may wish to have the sections reverse the experience. When they have finished, discuss how each one felt and the similarities and differences in the two experiences.

2. LEADER'S RAP

Lead the group in exploring the differences between the East and the West. You may want to center upon the following three Eastern concepts:

Transitoriness: There is a sense of timelessness in the East which manifests itself in the acceptance of change as normative. All things, including humans, condition and are conditioned by each other.

The Middle Path: The Middle Path is the intuitive insight into the optimum balancing of all possible conflicting forces in order to channel them and use them toward the development of a practical program of action. The East is not burdened with the either/or choice, but, following the principle of the *yin* and *yang,* is completely flexible and creatively blends all contradictions into a whole.

Self-discipline: Persons need specific religious guidance in methods to achieve self-discipline. "Be a lamp unto yourself." Eastern meditation is not to "turn on" but to "shut off" all sensory input. The point is to decrease sensory stimuli in order to surface the true self, the Buddha nature. The group may, in fact, enjoy attempting some simple meditation practices, such as controlled breathing, sitting in a lotus or half-lotus position, and trying to shut off the stream of consciousness from the mind.

3. SUMMARY

Help the group identify the differences between East and West. Why has American Protestantism lost its sense of awe? Why are Christians in the West so lax about prayer and ritual? Can the meditative methods of the East discipline us in our Christian faith? What can the East teach the West about religious life and thought?

WORSHIP

If possible, create an Asian atmosphere by using Asian art prints around the room, by having Asian artifacts placed on low tables, and by burning incense.

Begin with one minute of silent meditation. Then with the group seated in a circle, place a natural object, such as a flower or stone, in the center as a focus for meditation.

Read the following passage:

> The mind of man searches outward
>   all day.
> The farther it reaches,
> The more it opposes itself.
> Only those who look inward
> Can censor their passions,
> And cease their thoughts.
> Being able to cease their thoughts,
> Their minds become tranquil.
> To tranquilize one's mind is to
>   nourish one's spirit.
> To nourish the spirit is to return
>   to nature.

Have a moment of silent reflection on this passage.

Close with the reading of Psalm 19:1-4, 14.

ADDITIONAL RESOURCES

Hesse, Herman, *Siddhartha.* New York: New Directions Publishing Co. (paperback), 1951.

Swearer, Donald K., "The Appeal of Buddhism," *The Christian Century,* November 3, 1971.

Manzanar, a film by Bob Nakamura. (This is the work of an Asian American student at UCLA who utilizes his cultural heritage to make a poetic statement about a real American issue, the evacuation of the Japanese during World War II. Obtainable from the Asian American Studies Center, Campbell Hall, UCLA, Los Angeles, CA.)

CREATIVE REVOLUTION—CHRISTIAN ACTION FROM EASTERN RELIGIONS

by WILLIAM SHINTO

THE SOFT REVOLUTION

The pent-up moral rage which drives some youth to plot how to bomb the local bank is the pursuit of a hard revolution. That is not the revolution now.

Neither is the revolutionary the svelte young man who jumps out of his Jaguar and runs into the Zen Center for meditation. That kind of cultural contradiction we can all do without.

The real action might be in a quiet creative revolution taught by some of the major precepts of the ancient East. It may just be time to *yin yang* the gang.

Why not take at least the following three Asian ideas and see where they lead us in actions of creative change?

The first is the concept of nonviolence. Gandhi, for example, took the religious idea of *ahimsa* (nonviolence) and turned it into a weapon to challenge the British Empire—and won. Gandhi taught that a PROTEST should be made with the goal of achieving change. To do violence is a basic frontier American response. In Asia, you have lost before you start, if you adopt violent methods.

A second idea is the use of non-action to act. This is not to advocate passivity, but to use the strength which comes in not acting or not speaking.

Lastly, a lesson for us who emerge out of a tradition of rigid moralism is the *yin yang* principle of blending apparent contradictions into a wholeness. Fanaticism has little place when a person follows the Middle Path. This is not to imply immorality or loss of principles, but to point out that the truly religious person is on a pilgrimage, but one which he starts by knowing who he is and where he is going. His symbol is the bamboo, which is flexible but strong enough to withstand the winds. With this attitude the generation gap, for instance, may be bridged.

PROCEDURE

1. LEADER'S RAP

Introduce the concept of the creative revolution to the group. Take time to discover recent events, preferably community events which will be relevant to the group, and share how these are either examples of the quiet revolution or could be improved by an "Asian soft attack."

2. GROUP ACTIVITY

Have the youth choose a specific issue in their lives which is drawn from either the church, school, or family. Be as specific as possible. Then divide the group in half and let each smaller group develop a plan of action to follow in solving the problem. However, instruct one group to use the "soft revolution" and the other, the "hard revolution." Let them record their "game plan" on newsprint.

3. GROUP RAP

When they have finished, place the two plans side by side. Review the plans, asking what is positive and what is negative about each one. Consolidate ideas to form a master plan of action. If you are then ready to be "Asian," initiate the plan.

47

WORSHIP

SCRIPTURE: 1 Corinthians 1:17-25

GROUP RESPONSE: We are weak.
We are the meek.
We shall inherit the earth.

FIRST READER: The wild geese fly across the long sky above.
Their image is reflected upon the chilly water below.
The geese do not mean to cast their image on the water;
Nor does the water mean to hold the image of the geese.[1]

GROUP RESPONSE: We are one.
We cast shadows on everyone.
We are held by each other.

SECOND READER: Of late I deeply devote myself to quiescense.
Nothing in the world concerns my mind.

The breeze from the pine woods blows my sash;
The mountain moon shines upon my harp.
You ask me to explain the reason of failure or success.
The fisherman's song goes deep into the river.[2]

GROUP RESPONSE: I am at peace.
We are together in life.
The earth, the song,
We shall overcome. Amen.

ADDITIONAL RESOURCES

Chang Chung-yuan, *Creativity and Taoism*. New York: Julian Press, Inc., 1963 (Harper Colophon Paperback, 1970).

Postman, Neil, and Weingartner, Charles, *The Soft Revolution*. New York: Dell Publishing Co., Inc. (Delta Paperback), 1971.

[1] Chang Chung-yuan, *Creativity and Taoism* (New York: Julian Press, Inc., 1963, Harper Colophon book, 1970), p. 57.

[2] *Ibid.*, p. 91.

Why be concerned about international affairs?

by RICHARD RISELING

GO INTO ALL THE WORLD

WHY WORRY ABOUT THE WORLD?

Human history has been transformed, revolutionized. There is only one world now and the making of one world transforms in an extraordinary way the destiny of the human family. That is big news to people raised in the Christian tradition. And it has all happened during the lifetime of most youth and many adults.

Until recently, history was local or national and it did not involve the total sphere of all human activity extending all round the earth. But that has changed.

Some of the great philosophers used to write of one world. Merchants used to dream of caravans of goods and commercial offices stretching around the globe. Now these "dreamed of" things are true. You can now fly to the Swiss Alps for a school vacation skiing trip for the same price as a visit to a city on the opposite coast in the United States. Just as Coca Cola and Gulf Oil signs are seen in many countries, citizens of the United States increasingly encounter "made in Japan" (or any

number of other countries) on the goods they purchase. In the sky are satellites which "spy" on many of the activities that take place in the countries we call "enemy." On the ground are missiles and nuclear weapons that can destroy everyone on earth one thousand times over, in just thirty minutes. When the price of coffee drops just one penny in the United States, Latin American people, who are already very poor, lose an additional fifty million dollars.

Many people in the United States still believe these developments are not important or relevant to their lives. But they are wrong. Few countries have experienced, in fact, more radical changes in their national life than the United States. For instance, the nuclear threat that unites the world makes it impossible for our government to fulfill its constitutional responsibility "to arrange for the common defense." The present international economic challenges to the U.S. dollar and export of U.S. manufactured goods indicate that other constitutional responsibilities of national government such as "arrange for economic prosperity" and "foster the welfare of the citizen" are no longer possible without reference to international affairs. The oil crisis and our involvements in Asia raised the price of gas, cars, homes, and practically everything else, and simply made many necessities of life too expensive for millions of Americans. In short, the United States, the most wealthy and powerful nation, is increasingly dependent upon other nations for its security and prosperity.

This is a very positive, although challenging, and potentially very dangerous development in human history. If people and governments are willing to respect the values and interests of others who differ or oppose them, if people and governments are able to talk issues through rather than turn to warfare, then all of the human family will find a better way to arrange for their daily needs. Since the recent period of intense nationalism has created such horrible conditions for the vast majority of our brothers and sisters, the internationalization of all life may give new and more humane direction to history. In any event, there is no choice. All history is now world history and the person who shuns or knows little of international affairs also fails to understand his own community environment.

PURPOSE

To have dialogue with persons of a nationality other than your own, and to consider the Christian implications of this dialogue.

PROCESS

1. PREPARATION

Before the meeting, find some person or persons with whom your group can have dialogue. These should be persons of different national background than that of your group. You might find a foreign student, a family that has immigrated from another country, or a family that is visiting this country.

Invite this person or these persons to your meeting. Establish the kind of atmosphere that will allow you to talk in depth, but informally, about your different ideas. (Do not ask the person to "make a speech.")

2. SETTING

The setting for your meeting is important. Put pillows on the floor, sit around a fireplace, or use the church lounge. Have simple refreshments available, perhaps prepared on an international theme. You might have mood music playing as the group arrives—perhaps music related to the country from which your guest comes.

3. CONVERSATION

Talk in small groups with your guest or guests. If only one guest is present, arrange the evening in such a way that every person will have a chance to talk with her or him, but in groups of two or three people at a time.

4. DISCUSSION

Both the group and your guest should consider the following questions:
- When differences arise, do you feel any loss of affection or trust in the other person?
- Do you feel that you can really change some of your own ideas, perceptions, and values as you are confronted with those from another culture?
- Why is the ability to change important in international relations?

5. BIBLE STUDY

Read 1 John 4:7-12. Discuss the following questions:
- Does God expect us to love only persons who are citizens of our own country?
- Is it possible to love someone even though you disagree with his or her ideas?
- How has the missionary movement expressed the love of God? Are there ways in which it has sometimes failed to express this?
- If we love someone, do we sometimes change? How does this relate to loving people from other countries?

WORSHIP

Hymn: "In Christ, There Is No East or West"
Scripture: John 3:16-17
Prayer: Pray silently for the building of international love relationships.
Song: "He's Got the Whole World in His Hands"

RESOURCES

Literature you may wish to subscribe to:
Headline Series, published by the Foreign Policy Association, 345 E. 46 Street, New York, NY 10017. $5.00/year. The book *International Education for Spaceship Earth*, also published by the Foreign Policy Association, is very good.

GOD'S ALIVE AND DOING WELL

by KEITH L. IGNATIUS

GOD'S ALIVE

Jesus said, "I am the resurrection and the life; he who believes in me, though he die, yet shall he live, and whoever lives and believes in me shall never die. Do you believe this?" (John 11:25-26).

You've read it. Now, what does it mean? What does it mean to live, to celebrate, to be?

Most congregations begin the celebration of Easter with special Lenten services each year, concluding with a colorful and impressive Easter Sunday worship experience. Great songs of the church are sung amid the rich fragrance of lilies arranged in the shape of the cross. The minister says the benediction, and the celebration of Christ's resurrection is over for another year.

... CANNOT AFFORD NOT TO CELEBRATE   In a time when we are so painfully aware of war, pockets of poverty in the midst of affluence, anger and hatred among many different breeds, and a general air of mistrust, celebration is needed. In the midst of despair, hope needs to be offered. We need to ask, where are the proclaimers of the resurrection? Where are the believers in the new life?

Here are some suggestions to encourage members of your group to celebrate their lives as sons of God and brothers of Christ and to proclaim their discovery: God's Alive and Doing Well!

PROCESS

Decide on your plan of action. Will you ask permission to lead a Sunday morning service, or a worship service at a family-night dinner or some other regular gathering? Or will the celebration be for your group only? How you use the following suggestions will be affected by your decision.

1. MUSIC

You may wish to spend a session learning some songs of celebration that are unfamiliar. Your director of music may be a helpful resource here. Guitarists will enjoy learning the songs.

2. DRAMA

See what you can come up with in terms of a play or choral drama to suggest your interpretation and feelings about the power and presence of the resurrected Christ in God's world. You should attempt to respond to some of the questions raised in the introduction to this article.

3. FEELING THE STORY

As a group, divide into small groups of no more than eight to ten persons with a leader. Proceed as follows:

a. Leader instructs group members to stand silently in a circle. First, each person extends one hand into the circle and the hands are joined. Then the other hand is placed upon the others. Persons are then instructed to close their eyes, to raise their hands approximately shoulder high, and then lower them to knee level.

b. Sit down and for three minutes discuss step *a* by asking such questions as:
  - Who initiated the movement each time?
  - Were you reluctant to move until you felt others attempt to do so or were you a leader?
  - Did you sense a closeness, a working together?
  Was there confusion, a pulling apart?

c. Stand in the circle again. The leader tells the group that he will call out a word, and persons in the group are to make a group formation representing that word. He begins with easy shapes, such as square, triangle, and figure 8. Then he suggests such words as joy, fear, celebration, love, and life.

d. Sit down again. Talk five minutes about your experience in working out the group formations.

e. Choose a passage of Scripture which suggests celebration or thanksgiving for life. The Prodigal Son (Luke 15:11-24); the Healing of the Ten Lepers (Luke 17:11-19); or the Resurrection Story (Matthew 28:1-9) can be effectively used. Instruct each person to read the chosen passage silently, trying to put himself into the story. Suggest that one try to feel what the persons in the story must have felt. For example, you might say, "Imagine you are the father of the prodigal. Try to feel what he must have felt as he first caught sight of his son returning."

f. Give each person paper and pencil (or crayon, marker, etc.). Ask him to write about the feeling he had as he put himself into the selected story. Suggest that he be as creative as he can, perhaps putting the story into a modern setting or composing a litany, a ballad, or a poem. This part of the exercise can actually be a "do your own thing" experience. These creative efforts can become a part of your worship service.

4. KEEPING IT ALIVE

Brainstorm other ways of keeping the celebration of Easter alive. What can your group do over the next few months that would remind your small part of the world (home and church) that God's alive and doing well? Here are a few suggestions, but the group can use its own ideas first.

Buttons

Create a design for a button; have a quantity made; and distribute them to friends in school, church, and on the street.

Greeting Cards

Messages of greeting need not be reserved for Christmas. Have some handbills made up and distribute them as post-Easter cards. You may also decide to send a special greeting to a few special friends expressing your joy in life and your thanks for them as persons.

Banners

Have a "Banner Party." There may be many places in your church where banners can remind one and all that life is worth living.

Multi-Media Booth

Erect a booth in some corner of your church building or just outside. Make the booth an audio-visual experience. Play records, use psychedelic lighting, hang posters or banners, provide objects to touch, hang mobiles; in general, provide things for persons to experience as they pass through the booth. A benediction or greeting as persons leave the booth would be effective. Use a word like "shalom" or its English counterpart, "The peace of God be with you."

Visits

Remember persons who usually receive attention only during holiday seasons. Hospitals and homes often welcome visitors, gifts, and singers throughout the year but find that groups prefer to come just before Christmas.

Supper

Many groups have found it meaningful to share an Agape Meal or Love Feast with members of their church. Often a family-night dinner provides the occasion for this. Suggestions may be provided for guiding the informal conversation during the meal. At the close of the meal, have songs, readings, and expressions of celebration and belief. Prayers may precede the receiving of the bread and the cup. It may be meaningful for your group to bake the bread which is used. Your pastor can assist you in your planning. Be sure to contact your board of deacons to determine at what point they should be involved.

BENEDICTION

Peace and joy be yours as you seek to live and believe in Him who is the Resurrection and the Life! Go to it!

CREATED MALE AND FEMALE

by WILLIAM R. STAYTON

WHOLE MEN AND WOMEN

In this session, we will be discussing an aspect of life which is probably shackled with more intense personal emotional feelings, problems, and hang-ups than any other part of one's personal life and experience—human sexuality. It is time that Christian young people be allowed to look at realistically and understand this important dimension of their life. One of the basic teachings of Christianity is that Jesus was concerned with the whole man, which means that we are to be concerned with man's sexuality as well as his soul. One of the great tragedies of history has been that the church has not enabled its youth (or adults for that matter!) to understand fully what it means to be a male or a female and how to express themselves more creatively as Christian sexual persons.

This session should help youth develop a realistic set of guidelines for male/female relationships before marriage. This program will not be conclusive, but we do hope that it will open some new windows into the house of life so that youth will continue to explore what it means to be a sexual Christian person.

PURPOSE

To look at the need for sex education in the church and to explore one area of increasing concern among youth and their parents, namely premarital sexual behavior.

PROCEDURE

1. VIGNETTE

After the group has assembled, ask three members to read the following vignette for the rest of the group. While they are looking over the parts, explain to the group that this is the story of a mother, a father, and their ninth-grade daughter. The scene takes place in their car on the way home from church after the Sunday morning service.

MOTHER: Well, Janie, how was church school today?

JANIE: It was groovy. Our new youth director is really great.

FATHER: What makes him so great? Is he tall, dark, and handsome?

JANIE: Oh, Daddy! No. As a matter of fact, he is kind of fat and squatty. He is just great; that's all.

MOTHER: I think it is wonderful that you like him. What did you do this morning?

JANIE: We just talked. For once, almost everyone talked.

FATHER: That makes a church school groovy? What did you talk about?

JANIE: Oh—boys and girls, and growing up.

FATHER: In church school? Didn't you learn anything about Jesus or the Bible?

JANIE: Not exactly. We talked about us. We're going to have a neat time the next few months. He told us we would be talking about what it means to be a man and a woman.

MOTHER: Oh, really? Since when does a young man just out of school think he has the right to teach our youngsters about being a man or a woman?

JANIE: Why shouldn't he know? We are going to talk about dating and marriage and babies and. . . .

FATHER: That's enough. I am going to have a talk with the pastor about this. The church has no business teaching this. This is the home's domain.

JANIE: Oh, Daddy. Please don't. I would be so embarrassed. Please—I don't see what is so wrong. Is learning about womanhood so bad? You don't ever say anything about it. The only thing that you say is that when I grow up, I will learn about things.

MOTHER: Janie! Don't talk that way to your father. He knows what is best for you. We will look into this. Maybe it will be all right—what this young man is teaching. But we want to be sure that you are getting good biblical and moral training. That's what the church is for.

JANIE: I promise to read the Bible every day—anything you want me to read. But please don't make trouble for our class.

2. DISCUSSION

Have the group discuss the issues raised in this vignette. What is the parents' concern? What is the daughter learning about human sexuality by their response? Does the church have any right or responsibility to provide education for sexuality? How could a youth group help their parents and church leaders understand the need for this type of education?

3. VIGNETTE

Ask three more members of the group to volunteer for the following vignette. This is the story of a mother, a father, and their nineteen-year-old daughter, a sophomore in college, who is home on vacation. The scene takes place in the family living room. The daughter has just gone out on a date with her steady boyfriend.

SCENE 1

FATHER: Well, Mother, we ought to be very proud of our daughter. She is going out with a fine young man. He doesn't seem to be one of those drifting boys with no purpose. He is working steadily toward his medical degree. He is even of the same religion as we. What more could we ask!

MOTHER: I don't know what to think. Today I discovered something in her room that has really upset me. I didn't say anything to Sally because I wanted to talk with you first.

FATHER: Well, what is it?

MOTHER: When I was putting her clothes away, I saw a packet of pills in her drawer.

FATHER: Has she been sick? It isn't dope, is it?

MOTHER: Oh, no, I don't think so. I think it is—well, the Pill—you know—birth control.

FATHER: Birth control! Oh, no. Our Sally? I can't believe that. You must be mistaken.

MOTHER: I don't think I'm mistaken. What has happened? Are college and her classmates making her feel that she has to conform to that sort of thing? Are there no values about the sacredness of sex anymore?

FATHER: Do you really think she is having—uh, relations with Rick? I just cannot believe it. They do not seem so selfish as to expect to have everything for their own gratification right now; they seem mature enough to be able to wait. Maybe we don't really know our daughter.

MOTHER: Remember just last year she spoke about the Smith girl who got pregnant during her senior year in high school. Sally thought it was just terrible that a girl would give herself like that without marriage. She said it went against everything that the Smith family taught and also what her religion taught.

FATHER: Well, what are we going to do about it? We don't want to accuse her of something and make her think we don't trust her. But yet we should talk about the dangers of this.

MOTHER: We will just have to talk to her about it, painful though it may be.

SCENE 2

(Sally enters the house from her date.)

SALLY: Hi, what are you two doing up? Waiting for me? I'm a big girl now, you know.

MOTHER: We have something we want to talk over with you. We couldn't sleep without this talk.

SALLY: What's wrong?

FATHER: It's about you and Rick—

SALLY: What about us?

FATHER: Well, we know that you see each other a lot here and at school and we—

MOTHER: Let me say it. You know that today I washed and ironed all the clothes you brought home from school. And I took them into your room. While I was putting them away in your drawer, I saw a packet that looked like a compact. I didn't want to hide it under the clothes; so I picked it up to put it on top of the clothes and discovered it was a packet of pills. Sally, are you using birth control pills?

SALLY *(with eyes down):* Oh, Mom, you would never understand. I'm sorry you found that.

FATHER: But, Sally, with all our talks about the sacredness of marriage and self-control and the respect we have for our own bodies, how could you violate all that?

SALLY: Oh, Dad! Things are different now. Rick and I have talked many things over. You know we are very much in love. I never knew what it was like to love a man before. I can't deny that I have passionate feelings. We realize now that physical intimacy is, when not abused, a fulfillment of love between a man and a woman. Both of us would like to enter marriage "pure," as you might say, but I am not sure both of us can exercise complete control all the time. If it will relieve your mind, we haven't had intercourse yet, but I am not so sure this will always be so before we are married. You realize that it may be years before we will be able to marry—at least until I am through school so I can support him through medical school. I'm just being realistic.

FATHER: But what about the commitment you have to your own self-image? Suppose your relationship with Rick should end, for some unknown reason. The psychological damage you may incur upon yourself could be irreparable.

MOTHER: Does the Pill make your actions any more reasonable than those of the Smith girl? The Pill simply prevents the new life from beginning. If you have intercourse before marriage, you may be very sorry sometime later in your marriage. The risk is so great.

FATHER: All these arguments are really beside the point. The point is that it is wrong to be intimate before marriage. Wrong! Pill or no Pill!

SALLY: I knew you wouldn't understand. Are you sure that you aren't confusing right and wrong with some outdated Puritan ethic that has beset this nation from the beginning? We are trying to keep traditional standards, but we really don't know why. We know we are going to marry one another. Must the legal document be our time schedule for physical intimacy or is our commitment to one another a personal decision between the two of us?

4. DISCUSSION

Have the group discuss the issues involved in this vignette. What points were the parents trying to make? What points did Sally make? Who did you find yourself identifying with most? Why? Can this family resolve their differences of feeling? How could the church have been helpful to the parents? to Sally?

5. REFLECTION

Divide the group up into triads and ask each triad to develop a set of guidelines for premarital standards and behavior that members of the triad feel are realistic and in accordance with Christian teaching. (Consult the Bible to back up your understanding of Christian teaching. See 1 Corinthians 6:12-20, especially verse 20.) Give the groups at least fifteen minutes for this exercise. Then have the groups share their guidelines with each other and discuss them. From the lists draw a common set of guidelines that is acceptable to the group. Discuss how these can be shared with parents and other members of the church fellowship.

WORSHIP

Scripture: 1 Corinthians 6:12-20

Prayer: Our Father, help us to develop meaningful relationships and to understand how to relate effectively as young men and women without exploiting one another or without fear or guilt. Help us truly to develop the capacity to give and receive love. Amen.

ADDITIONAL RESOURCES

Three excellent movies which can be used to further explore this subject are *Phoebe, The Game,* and *The Party.* All are available for rental from American Baptist Films, Valley Forge, PA 19481 or Box 23204, Oakland, CA 94623.

IT'S A MAN'S—AND WOMAN'S—WORLD

by WILLIAM R. STAYTON

What are the role expectations and characteristics of man and woman in today's world? This question is a crucial one and has far-reaching implications for sex education and family-life education. This session will be devoted to helping you take a serious look at characteristics of maleness and femaleness.

PROCEDURE

1. PREPARATION

Before the members arrive, arrange to have copies of the following list of characteristics[1] mimeographed so that each person will have a copy.

1. Not at all aggressive
   Very aggressive — — —
2. Not at all independent
   Very independent — — —
3. Very emotional
   Not at all emotional — — —
4. Does not hide emotions at all
   Almost always hides emotions — — —
5. Very subjective
   Very objective — — —
6. Very easily influenced
   Not at all easily influenced — — —
7. Very submissive
   Very dominant — — —
8. Dislikes math and science very much
   Likes math and science very much — — —
9. Very excitable in a minor crisis
   Not at all excitable in a minor crisis — — —
10. Very passive
    Very active — — —
11. Not at all competitive
    Very competitive — — —

12. Very illogical
    Very logical — — —
13. Very home oriented
    Very worldly — — —
14. Not at all skilled in business
    Very skilled in business — — —
15. Very sneaky
    Very direct — — —
16. Does not know the way of the world
    Knows the way of the world — — —
17. Feelings easily hurt
    Feelings not easily hurt — — —
18. Not at all adventurous
    Very adventurous — — —
19. Has difficulty making decisions
    Can make decisions easily — — —
20. Cries very easily
    Never cries — — —
21. Almost never acts as a leader
    Almost always acts as a leader — — —
22. Not at all self-confident
    Very self-confident — — —
23. Very uncomfortable about being aggressive
    Not at all uncomfortable about being aggressive — — —
24. Not at all ambitious
    Very ambitious — — —
25. Unable to separate feelings from ideas
    Easily able to separate feelings from ideas — — —
26. Very dependent
    Not at all dependent — — —
27. Very conceited about appearance
    Never conceited about appearance — — —
28. Very talkative
    Not at all talkative — — —
29. Very tactful
    Very blunt — — —

[1] List was developed by I. K. and D. M. Boverman, Worcester State Hospital, Worcester, Massachusetts. Used by permission.

Then God said, "Let us make man in our image, after our likeness; and let them have dominion over the fish of the sea, and over the birds of the air, and over the cattle, and over all the earth, and over every creeping thing that creeps upon the earth." So God created man in his own image, in the image of God he created him; male and female he created them. And God blessed them. . . . and God saw everything that he had made, and behold, it was very good (Genesis 1:26-28, 31).

---

30. Very gentle   — — —
    Very rough   — — —
31. Very aware of feelings of others   — — —
    Not at all aware of feelings of others   — — —
32. Very religious   — — —
    Not at all religious   — — —
33. Very interested in own appearance   — — —
    Not at all interested in own appearance   — — —
34. Very neat in habits   — — —
    Very sloppy in habits   — — —
35. Very quiet   — — —
    Very loud   — — —
36. Very strong need for security   — — —
    Very little need for security   — — —
37. Enjoys art and literature very much   — — —
    Does not enjoy art and literature very much   — — —
38. Easily expresses tender feelings   — — —
    Does not express tender feelings at all   — — —

2. IDENTIFYING ROLES

After handing out the above list of characteristics, give the following instructions:

Think of a normal adult man and then indicate for each numbered item the statement which best describes a mature, healthy, socially competent adult man. Mark it *M*.

Have the group members go through the entire list marking the M's. When they have finished, give these instructions:

Now think of a normal adult woman and then indicate for each numbered item the statement which best describes a mature, healthy, socially competent adult woman. Mark it *F*.

Have members of the group go through the entire list marking the F's. When they have finished, have them go through the list once more, after giving these instructions:

Finally, think of a normal adult and then indicate for each numbered item the statement which best describes a mature, healthy, socially competent adult. Mark it with an *A*.

3. REFLECTION

Have the group discuss the answers to the above questionnaire. The following statistics have been found true for the general population:

Ninety percent of persons will list female characteristics (F) on the upper line for all thirty-eight items; 90 percent will list male characteristics (M) on the lower line for all 38 items; 90 percent will list adult characteristics (A) on the lower line for items 1-27 and on the upper line for items 28-38. Have the group members compare these statistics with their responses. Discuss the meaning of adult versus male and female characteristics.

What can be done to help persons become mature, healthy, socially competent adults? What effect will this understanding of sexuality have in the church program of Christian education? What stereotypes about sex roles does the church teach, or practice? Is this teaching biblical?

WORSHIP

Scripture: Genesis 1:26-28a, 31.

Prayer: Make us truly to reflect your image, your likeness, that we may grow to full maturity, "to the measure of the stature of the fulness of Christ; so that we may no longer be children, tossed to and fro and carried about by every wind of doctrine. . . . Rather, speaking the truth in love, [help us] to grow up in every way into him who is the head, into Christ, from whom the whole body, joined and knit together by every joint with which it is supplied, when each part is working properly, makes bodily growth and upbuilds itself in love." Through Jesus Christ our Lord we pray. Amen.

SPECIAL PROGRAMS FOR JUNIOR HIGHS

Two sessions for Junior Highs

THE SEARCH FOR "I"

by BILL L. SHOOK

PURPOSE

To help the junior high talk about who he or she is and what he or she would like to become as a junior high person.

ADVANCE PREPARATION:

1. Have a large number of magazines available for use by the group. Each person could be asked to bring several magazines.

2. Have each person bring a piece of poster-board or newsprint.

3. Have glue, scissors, pencils, and rulers available.

4. Have a large piece of newsprint and a marking pencil available for your use.

Session One: I Am Unique

1. POSTERS

Give each person a piece of posterboard, scissors, glue, and pencils. Ask each one to select from the magazines pictures that describe his or her feelings, and what he or she wants to be or do.

Have each person arrange these pictures on a posterboard, thus constructing a portrait of himself or herself.

Tape these posters to the wall. Let individuals in the group try to guess who made each poster by writing on the poster the name of the person they think it belongs to. Keep the posters up for use in the next session.

2. DISCUSSION

Break the group into twos. Have the subgroups discuss the question "What is unique about me as a person?"

Ask each person to go to a place in the room and write out, in very brief form, how the other person described his uniqueness.

The two should then return to the two-by-two conversation and discuss what each has written. (The written work should deal with what the person IS like, NOT WHAT HE LIKES TO EAT, PLAY, DO, ETC.) Then the pairs should share their conversations with the total group.

WORSHIP

Scripture: Psalm 139:1-18
Prayer

Session Two: I Am Like . . .

1. PORTRAITS

Have each person hold up the portrait he or she constructed in the last session. Have the whole group join in describing what the portrait says about the individual.

Then have the individual explain the portrait to the group.

2. SIMILES

Have each person complete the following statements:

At my best I am like _____.

At my worst I am like _____.

My inner person is like _____.

My relationship to the church is like _____

_____.

Living in this world is like _____.
These similes should then be shared in small groups of four or five.

Each person will then write out the following simile:
"The person I want to be is like _____."

WORSHIP

Silent reflection on the question "To what am I going to commit myself?"
Prayer
Scripture: John 15:1-7

SPECIAL PROGRAMS FOR JUNIOR HIGHS

Three sessions on worship for Junior Highs

TUNED IN OR TUNED OUT

by JUDY MINTIER

It is Sunday morning. The time is 11:25 A.M. A service of worship is in progress. The Scripture has been read and the minister is starting his sermon. In a pew halfway back a young girl waits expectantly. Her name is Debbie.

Well, I wonder what he is going to say today? What's that? Moses? Oh, no! Another sermon about the Old Testament! I wish he'd talk about something that's going on now—Well, maybe the old folks like this stuff. (Debbie shifts restlessly in the pew.) *I wonder what happened to Nancy? She said she was coming today. Maybe her family went someplace. Sunday school sure isn't any fun when Nancy isn't there. Isn't that a terrible color for those curtains up front? They sure make it look drab in here. After church I think I'll call Barbara and see if she can come over to the house—Oh, gosh, homework! I forgot all about it. Why didn't I do it yesterday?—These pews sure are hard. Oh, Reverend Brown is praying. Good, it's almost over.* (Debbie takes the hymnbook and stands to sing.)

This is Debbie's story. How close does it come to yours? *Have you "tuned out" worship?* Is it like one junior high boy says, "Worship around here is a real drag"? Do you ever want to tune in— or do you care?

There are many teens who have never given much thought to worship. It's a drag and it'll stay a drag. But there are others who'd like to find out what it's all about.

The following three sessions may help your group get acquainted with the meaning of worship. They may help you learn how to worship. See what happens.

Session One: What Is It All About?

PURPOSE

This is an introductory session designed to help the group understand some of the "whys" of the worship service. Why is it the way it is? Does it always have to be this way? Worship is an important part of the church's life and does affect you and your group, whether you like it or not.

1. QUESTIONS ABOUT WORSHIP

What are the parts of the worship service? List all ideas. Which parts do the members of the group like best, least? Why? What should be changed? Why are the parts arranged the way they are? Who decides the arrangement? What happens to people in worship? What should happen? Again list all the answers.

2. DISCUSSION

Your chalkboard by this time should be covered with questions and answers. Let members of the group discuss the questions. Then invite your minister to come to your meeting and respond to each of these questions.

Discuss ways youth can get more out of worship.

Session Two: Listening and Observing

PURPOSE

To evaluate your Sunday morning worship service.

PROCESS

1. OBSERVATION

During the Sunday morning worship service, observe what is happening to the congregation as persons participate in the service. Take paper along to write down what you see happening. Answer these statements:

- Does the service seem to be arranged properly? In what way?
- Does there seem to be an overall theme? What is it?
- How do the hymns relate to this theme?
- What was the sermon about? List three key statements.
- What were the people doing during the sermon? List as many different examples as possible. What does this tell you about how people listen to sermons?
- What would you have changed in the service? Why?

2. EVALUATION

During the first part of the group meeting, have each person write his findings on a large piece of paper. Discuss your findings with your minister.

Session Three: Doing Your Own Thing

PURPOSE

To create meaningful worship

PROCESS

Divide into groups of three or four. Have each group take the findings and discussions of the preceding two sessions and develop a worship service that would meet the needs of both youth and adults in your church. Have each group work independently of the others. Post the finished products. Have the minister evaluate each one. Perhaps he might be willing to use several of the ideas in the Sunday morning service.

THE GOOD SAMARITAN—

DON'T FRET ABOUT WHO HE IS; PICK HIM UP; HE'S HURT

by BILL SHOOK

PURPOSE

To try to help junior high students understand and experience the meaning of Luke 10:25-37, the story of the good Samaritan.

ADVANCE PREPARATION

1. Read Luke 10:25-37 completely. Consult with the pastor or look in commentaries concerning the meaning of the passage. *The Laymen's Bible Commentary,* published by John Knox Press, avoids technical language and is very clear in its explanations.

2. Collect a large number of pictures from magazines or newspapers that might depict life as it is in your city or state. Be sure to include several pictures of areas of suffering and need as well as pictures of very secure and happy community life.

3. Have several large pieces of newsprint or posterboard, marking pencils or crayons, glue or paste, and scissors available.

4. Have plenty of Bibles on hand.

PROCESS

1. TELEGRAM HOME

Have the group read the passage through completely. Each student is to compose a telegram to send to his home describing how the man who was beaten was treated by all the characters in the story. He is to treat this story as an historical event, using his own words and phrases.

Each letter space in the telegram costs three cents. Limit spending to $5 on the telegram.

Have each person share with the group the telegram message he has written.

2. EXPLANATION OF PASSAGE

The leader should very briefly explain the essential teaching of this passage of Scripture.

Jesus tried to point out that the reason that you do something is as important as your actually doing it. You can outwardly obey every one of the Ten Commandments, and still not be doing God's will if you're obeying them for the wrong reasons. The lawyer proved this. He could live according to the law and still not love. He had to know who he was supposed to love before he could love. Jesus ridiculed this kind of behavior with the story of the good Samaritan who loved and took care of someone without bothering to find out who or what he was. The Christian does not ask, "WHO IS MY NEIGHBOR?" He lives and acts as if all men, regardless of race, color, or creed, are his neighbors.

3. WE'RE NOT VERY DIFFERENT

List the characters in the story on newsprint or chalkboard. For each character listed, every person is to write an experience from his own life that describes how he has been or is like those people in the story. This exercise will help the group understand that Jesus' descriptions of people are as real now as they were then. The Bible is not only a book of ancient history, but it is also about life now. In groups of two, share these writings. Let each person then offer a prayer for his partner.

4. IN TODAY'S LANGUAGE

Divide the group into groups of four or five. Give each of the small groups several of the pictures you have collected from various sources. Give them two or three pieces of newsprint or posterboard and a marking pencil or crayon. They should have scissors and glue or paste available for their use.

Tell them to arrange the pictures in such a way as to tell the story of the good Samaritan in contemporary scenes.

After they have finished their pictorial version of the story, have the various groups write a narrative to go with the pictures they have put together. It will be their own story of how the ethic taught in this passage can be lived out today.

WORSHIP

Have a representative from each group read to the whole group the contemporary version of the story of the good Samaritan that his group wrote.

SNAPSHOT BIBLE STUDY

The only limitation to creative Bible study is your imagination. Another way to study the good Samaritan passage is through the use of a Polaroid camera and pictures.

Secure some biblical-type pictures and construct the story of the good Samaritan on a sheet of newsprint. On another sheet, write out the biblical passage in large letters.

Secure a Polaroid camera and film and go around your city taking pictures that could tell the story in terms of contemporary society. Construct the contemporary story on newsprint or posterboard and write a narrative about it. Point out that it is your city and propose how your church could play the role of the good Samaritan in your town.

Place these two versions of the story on a bulletin board so that the members of your church can see them.

MINI-PROGRAMS

by FREDERICK YOUNG and PATRICIA A. SHAW

CONFRONTATION

PURPOSE: To build a bridge of understanding between youth and adults.

PROCESS: The youth group invites adults to this meeting.

INVOLVEMENT: The adults, as a total group, make a collage of their image of the youth of today. The youth make a collage, again as a group effort, of what their image of adults is.

EVALUATION: Each group then answers these questions about the other group's collage.

　　1. What do you think the other group is saying about you?

　　2. Do you think you have been fairly treated?

　　3. Where do you think most misunderstanding about your group arises? Discuss as a combined group: How might our Christian faith help bridge this gap?

RESOURCES: Magazines, newsprint, paste, tape.

WHAT MAKES LIFE WORTHWHILE?

PURPOSE: To discover what one values in life.

PROCESS: Each youth finds magazine pictures which illustrate the things he or she values. Attach a long strip of paper on the longest wall of the room. Each youth pastes his or her pictures on the paper.

EVALUATION: The collage is studied and discussed, especially noting where the same subject was repeated.

RESOURCES: Magazines (*Life, National Geographic, etc.*), paste, large roll of paper.

AIRPORT

PURPOSE: To discover how concerned people are for the needs of others.

INTRODUCTION: This session involves visiting an airport (train station, or bus terminal) to observe people.

OBSERVATION: 1. How do people creatively use time?

2. Can you really "tune in" to what concerns people?

3. Observe ways people are kind to others.

4. Observe ways people show their awareness of others.

PROCESS: Meet at a central point and thoroughly explain the task. Give out the assignments. Two alternative plans may be used.

1. Observe someone with a problem, trying to follow them through to see how they solved it.

2. Decide on one of the following questions to ask:

   a. Where do you get a cab?

   b. Where is the movie theater?

   c. Where can I get change?

EVALUATION: Meet at the church to discuss the results of the evening.

ART GALLERY

PURPOSE: To relate Bible life situations with youth life situations

PROCESS: Have prepared four enlarged drawings from *Good News for Modern Man*.

INVOLVEMENT: Group is divided into four small groups. The youth are instructed to formulate a story, relevant to their life, which they feel is portrayed through the drawings. Each group shares the story formulated by its members. Each picture's original story is then read from *Good News for Modern Man*, and a comparison is made with the stories written by the various groups.

RESOURCES: *Good News for Modern Man*. Especially note illustrations on pages 251, 354, 362, 400, 501.

CELEBRATION RESOURCES

HOW TO PRODUCE A LIGHT SHOW

by DAN HOLLAND

If you haven't been a part of a light show, you have most likely seen one in a movie or heard someone else describe this kind of experience. The hardware for producing light shows is sold now even in department stores in the local shopping center. You can buy strobe lights, strobe candles, and a variety of revolving fixtures in most cities.

WHY HAVE A LIGHT SHOW?

You will want to think through, before you begin, why you are involving your group in a light show. There are a couple of things to keep in mind. Have a clear sense of what you want to have happen at your event. What kinds of feelings are you trying to arouse? What are you trying to communicate in either a subtle or an obvious way? After the room lights come back up and the atmosphere returns to normal, there should be ample time for the group members to talk about their feelings and what happened to them during the activity. This discussion should happen even before they talk about whether or not they liked it.

A light show should not have to stand by itself. It should be a complement to a sound track. This can be a recording, some live music by a group or soloists, or a narration, such as a meditation or a poetry reading. You might choose to have a dramatic reading by several people or, on the other hand, your sound track might be taken from the radio or TV. A collage of comments from news broadcasts, coupled with varying light patterns, might be used to interpret a current event.

THE SETTING

Choose your room with care. It should not be too large, and the furnishings should allow freedom for your group to move around. A room with lots of uncluttered wall space is ideal. Remember that with a light show you are trying to simulate an environment which will capture your audience's total visual interest. You are not only trying to convey information, but you are also trying to stimulate feelings.

PROCESS

Make arrangements to borrow several slide projectors. You will soon discover that these are very useful pieces of equipment to be used in a number of different ways. Try this: cover a volleyball with crumbled aluminum foil, tape a string to it, and suspend it close to the ceiling. Mount a slide projector at the same level as your aluminum-covered ball and project the light onto the ball. Shift the projector around until you get the desired moving light patterns on the ceiling and walls. By careful aiming, you can also put the flashing starlike patterns onto a screen.

Set up two slide projectors side by side and arrange a series of pictures that you will superimpose upon each other. For instance, pictures of lonely, alienated people might have bars or walls superimposed upon them.

As you project pictures on the wall, try moving your fingers in front of each projector in a variety of patterns. Do the same thing using pieces of colored, transparent plastic which have some holes and slots cut in them.

If you have an overhead projector, place a clear container of water on the lighted surface, and float oil on top of the water. Try coloring the water and the oil with appropriate oil and water-based dyes (water will absorb food coloring and leave interesting oil "blobs" floating).

There is another device which is quite easy to prepare that will provide some interesting effects for your group. Obtain a large public-address speaker or use a movie projector speaker. Suspend small pieces of shiny metal, such as bits of chromed steel or tin can lids, in the opening of the speaker on threads or light string. Connect the speaker to your source of sound for the light show and shine the light from a slide projector on the shiny metal. As the sound level is increased, the sound waves from the speaker will cause the bits of metal to dance and to create light patterns on the wall which will move in time to the music or spoken word.

Strobe lights are most effective when they, too, can be connected to your audio sources so that they will be triggered by the sound peaks. There may be someone in your group or church who knows how to modify strobe lights and how to connect them to your sound equipment.

Many hobby magazines have ads for large weather balloons at a moderate price. These can be inflated to six or eight feet in diameter by using the exhaust from a vacuum cleaner. Set one of these up in your room and use it as a three-dimensional screen with several projectors shining on it at the same time.

Make up some slides of polarized materials and show them through moving, polarizing screens to obtain interesting, moving patterns superimposed on other pictures.

Your light show will be most effective when the visual effects complement the sound track you have chosen and create a mood suggested by it. For instance, a quiet meditative reflection might be accompanied by softly blending colored lights, starry flashes on the ceiling, with appropriate slides and designs projected on the walls. On the other hand, a folk song about war or violent dissonant sounds should be accompanied by garish colors, jagged shapes and patterns, such as those obtained by burning holes through old slide film. Turn your imagination loose and you will come up with many other possibilities.

HOW TO USE VIDEO TAPE IN CELEBRATIONS
by DAN HOLLAND

You may belong to a church which has already purchased a video tape recorder (VTR) or you may want to encourage your church to consider such a purchase. If this is not your case, however, don't despair! Check in your community to see where you might borrow or rent video taping equipment. You may find that another church or a school would be willing to make their equipment available. Check in the yellow pages of the telephone book to find companies which have video cameras and recorders for rent. Inquire at local companies that use tapes to train employees to find out if they would be willing to lend their equipment for a special occasion.

You can begin with three basic pieces: a camera, a tape deck, and a monitor. The monitor is essentially a television receiver with a few circuit changes. It will have extra connectors so that the camera or VTR can be connected directly to it.

ADVANTAGES OF VTR

Before you begin, you should be aware of the unique advantages and disadvantages of using television this way. One major advantage of television over other media is that it gives you "instant playback." By rewinding and replaying the tape, you can see immediately what you have just recorded. There are other advantages, too. Television cameras will record a usable picture in normal room light so that bulky bright lights need not be used. Most cameras have automatic light-compensating circuits so that the operator does not have to constantly worry about overexposure or underexposure. By careful use of the camera, the attention of the group can be focused on a small part of the scene, such as a person's face or his hands, to the exclusion of everything else. If you add special ef-fects and switching equipment, the pictures from two cameras can be superimposed on each other or faded in and out and wiped across the screen.

Keep in mind that there are disadvantages in the use of television, too. Since the television screen is small, it cannot be viewed easily by a large group nor from any distance. You may need several monitors hooked up together if you are going to have a large group share in this activity. You probably should not try to do this in the sanctuary but rather should choose a setting where groups can cluster and move around easily. The extension cords and interconnecting cables will also limit your use of the camera and VTR unless you have access to some of the portable equipment which is available.

PLANNING FOR A CELEBRATION

If you are going to use video effectively, there will be key decisions to make at several points along the way. Let's assume that you have already decided to have a worship/celebration. The first step is to think through how television will help you accomplish your goals for this event. Questions such as "What kinds of feelings are we trying to arouse?" and "What do we want to learn?" must be considered. Once you have answered some of these basic questions, then you can consider whether or not television fits into your production.

We'll assume now that the use of television does fit in. The next question to answer is whether you will record something that you have produced yourselves or whether you will put some other resources on the tape. We noted earlier the usefulness of the instant playback feature of taping. A key part of any worship celebration is recalling what we have been doing and what has been happening to us. A group that has been working together in a retreat setting for a weekend may have discovered something about its own life together: a new level of honesty and caring may have been reached; there may have been moments which are remembered as "keys" to the new spiritual depth which has been discovered. Playback of these moments in a group's history can provide a rich resource for celebration at the end of the retreat.

Presentations prepared ahead of time by two or three members of your group might also add to your celebration. Consider taping an interview, a monologue, a prepared or informal dialogue, a play reading, a collage of faces, hands, or movement—any or all of these might be useful.

With some advance planning, good use can be made of other resources as well. Try recording segments of films, slides, printed matter, and still pictures, along with music. You might consider a collage of many of these media used together.

A very effective technique is to record a song or narration as the audio portion of your presentation, while carefully chosen pictures are recorded as the video portion. With some practice, you can make a smooth-flowing transition from one scene to the next with the visual material supporting the mood and message on the audio portion of the tape.

Mount your pictures on a music stand so that they can be flipped forward one at a time while your camera is mounted on a tripod in front of them. If you have two cameras and switching equipment, this will make your presentation even smoother.

Most public libraries have free-loan films available. Choose useful scenes out of these films and focus your camera on the movie screen to record them at the appropriate point in the tape. Slides can be recorded in the same way. In fact, you can get a sense of movement by panning your camera across a projected or flat picture, zooming in on it, tilting up and down, or dollying in and out or across the picture. All of these will provide an interesting sense of movement with still pictures.

A third possibility is to combine informal scenes of your own group at work with an appropriate sound track, either music or narrative, interspersed with other video segments from films, slides, etc., so that all tie together to help you have an effective presentation.

While video taping equipment is complicated in design and circuitry, it is basically simple to use. Don't become frightened by the interconnecting cables. The pieces tie together in a logical manner, and adequate instructions generally are printed right on the appropriate connectors. The hardware is becoming more and more common. Several manufacturers will soon have video cassette records on the market. All you have to do is drop in a prerecorded cassette or a blank cassette for your own recording! The audio portion of your presentation can be added with the microphone that generally comes with the VTR or you can patch directly onto turntables, radios, movie projectors, or other pieces of equipment.

There is another value that is worth mentioning. Video tape, unlike film, can be used over and over again. This should encourage your experimentation. If you "goof," stop the machine and start over again. Keep working at it until you have exactly what you want on the tape. You can stop at any point, rewind the tape, and play it back to be sure that you're getting exactly what you want on both the audio and the video track. This feature allows even amateurs to come up with a useful, finished production.

HOW TO MAKE SLIDES

by DAN HOLLAND

There are three common ways to make slides: photographically, by fabrication, and by transfer.

1. Using a Camera to Make Slides

We are all familiar with shooting a roll of twenty or thirty-six frames and taking it to our friendly neighborhood drugstore for processing. Along with the usual photographing of landscapes, buildings, and people, there are some other techniques with which you might not be familiar and which might be useful to you.

Try photographing parts of other pictures to focus your group's attention on one particular feature.

Work on a series of several slides, all taken of a single picture from different perspectives. One slide might be a close-up of lines on a face. Another might mask out everything but the eyes. If you use a tripod and close-up lenses, you might experiment with table-top scenes or live scenes with members of your group as participants. Set up a sheet of translucent material (frosted plastic works well for this) as a screen, with your slide projector behind it. Put the "scenery" slide in the projector backward so that it appears on the front of your screen correctly oriented (this is particularly important where words appear in your background scene). Actors can then take their places in front of the projected backdrop and the entire scene can be photographed and will place your "action" in an entirely new simulated setting.

Have you considered processing your own slides? Instead of waiting one to four days for your pictures to be returned to you, consider the usefulness of having your pictures within one or two hours. At one senior high convention, pictures were taken as small groups worked throughout the community all day Saturday, were processed Saturday night, and became the focus of the group's worship on Sunday morning as group members remembered again the vivid experiences of the day before. Black and white film can be reverse-processed by using a special kit available from the Kodak Company. For this, you will need some Plus X film, exposed at ASA 80, a daylight processing tank, a black and white positive developing kit, bottles in which to mix chemicals, some photographic fixer, and a dark place to load the film into the tank. Complete instructions come with the chemicals. It's fairly easy to do and will give you usable pictures in a little over an hour. (Do your processing in a stainless-steel sink as some of the chemicals stain rather badly.)

Your film can be run through a projector as a filmstrip or cut apart and mounted in slide frames available at any photography store. If you can borrow the tank and fixer from someone who has a darkroom, your only expense will be the processing kit and slide frames. You can develop 100 slides for around $6.

A more interesting but more expensive possibility is to try your hand at color processing. All the chemical needed to develop about 100 slides can be purchased for approximately $10. It will take about an hour to prepare the chemicals and another hour to take each batch of film through the process. Allow one-half hour for drying and another for cutting and mounting, and you will have an almost instant replay of the scenes you have been photographing with the 35 mm. camera. If you use a half-frame camera, you'll have a film-strip which can be put directly into a projector and, in this way, you will avoid the step of cutting and mounting slides. There is an added bonus in processing your own Ektachrome type film. Instructions are included with the processing kit for "pushing" your film as high as ASA 640! With the proper settings on a good camera, you will be able to take pictures under very poor light conditions without the use of flash. Many photo processing companies also offer a special processing service.

Expose high speed Ektachrome film at ASA 400 and ask for special processing when you turn your film in. This will cost you an extra $1.25 or so. Ansco has a film rated ASA 500. Check with your photo dealer or a photographer about other possibilities for taking slides in poor light.

2. FABRICATING SLIDES

A second way to make slides is by fabricating them, using a variety of materials. These slides will be useful to you if you plan to use two projectors to obtain special effects by superimposing one picture upon another. You will need items such as pieces of fabric, clear and colored plastic (both transparent and translucent), felt tip markers, crayons, drawing pens, transparent ink, bits and pieces of odds and ends of all types.

Begin with ready-made slide mounts obtainable at photography supply houses. These come with several different sized openings (probably the ones with the larger opening will be most useful to you). You can start with a piece of clear plastic glued into the opening with other materials glued to this, or you may choose to draw directly on the plastic. Interesting effects can be obtained by mounting open-weave fabrics in slide frames and projecting this pattern on top of another picture, projected by a second slide machine. Try taking some old slides which are no longer useful and holding them over a flame until they just begin to char. This also provides an interesting effect when superimposed upon another picture. If you have a particular story in mind that you want to tell, you might want to superimpose bars, chains, changing colors, and various patterns that would complement the mood which you are trying to establish.

Have you seen the simulated movement used by television stations on their weather reports? Rain seems to fall or the sun seems to be radiating light as the weatherman is talking. This effect is produced by using polarized light and polarizing material. You can buy these filters and plastics from such supply houses as Edmund Scientific Company (300 Edscorp Bldg., Barrington, N.J. 08007). By putting them together in proper combinations, you can get the effect of movement in your slides. Many thin plastics, when they are crumpled and viewed through polarizing filters, also seem to be multicolored. This procedure can also add interesting effects to your homemade slides.

3. TRANSFER SLIDES

Here is another useful way to make slides. Draw or paste up a series of pictures on an 8½-by-11-inch sheet. Be careful to have each segment just the right size to fit into your slide frame. Process this sheet in your church's thermal duplicating machine and make a transparency of the type used for overhead projectors. You can then cut this transparency apart into squares and mount these pictures on a series of slides. This is an easy way to copy cartoons, titles, words, and some types of photographs. Some of the same materials provided by companies such as 3M for making transparencies can also be used effectively in the making of slides. These companies are a good source for colored plastics, tapes, letters, transparent pens, and the like.

Low-cost slides can be transferred from magazine pictures by using clear Contact or other self-sticking covering materials. Cut a piece of the clear Contact paper 2″ by 2″ and press over the portion of the magazine you want to make into a slide. Remember that the opening in the frame is smaller than 2″ by 2″ so the part of the picture that you want to appear must be in the center of the piece of Contact paper. Smooth out all of the wrinkles and air bubbles with a paper clip or other rounded metal object (a spoon works fine for this part of the project).

Cut the picture out of the magazine, dip it in hot water for a minute or so, then take it out, and peel the paper away from the plastic. You can then rub the little bits of paper adhering to the plastic with a moistened finger to get as much of the paper pulp off as possible. Be careful not to rub away the ink which has adhered to the glue. Dry the sticky side of your plastic slide and cover it with another piece of clear Contact paper, the same size, with both sticky surfaces together. The ink from your picture will now be between two pieces of plastic which can be mounted inside a slide frame and trimmed to size. Pictures or print can be lifted from just about any kind of slick paper and used to make this kind of slide. Your pictures will be fuzzy and not quite as transparent as regular slides, but they do have use in some special applications. They are so easy to do that they certainly are worth experimenting with.

NEW PEOPLE AND NEW PATHS

by RICHARD D. ORR

FIRST READING (Jeremiah 7 and Deuteronomy 30)

READER 1: Bible speech is centered in action and movement. To walk the way God commanded was to walk the right way and to move in the right direction. To follow his leading was to be loyal in moving forward: "I will be your God, and you shall be my people; and walk in all the way that I command you, that it may be well with you" (Jeremiah 7:23).

READER 2: Let us speak of the people of the Way and of the paths they follow:

READER 3: "See, I have set before you this day life and good, death and evil. If you obey the commandments of the Lord your God which I command you this day, by loving the Lord your God, by walking in his ways . . . then you shall live . . . and the Lord your God will bless you. . . . I have set before you LIFE and death, blessing and curse; therefore, choose life, that you and your descendents may LIVE" (Deuteronomy 30:15-19, emphasis added).

READER 1: Therefore choose life—that YOU may live.

READER 2: Life and good, death and evil. CHOOSE life.

READER 3: Love God, walk in his ways, choose LIFE.

READER 1: Therefore

READER 2: Therefore

READER 3: Therefore

ALL: Therefore, choose life, choose to be alive, choose to live in the Way. Choose life that:

READER 1: you (*echo*) may (*shout*) LIVE!

READER 2: You

READER 3: You

SECOND READING (Psalm 8, emphasis added)

READER 1: "O Lord, our Lord,
how majestic is thy name in all the earth! . . .
When I look at thy heavens, the work of thy fingers,
the moon and the stars which thou hast established;
what is man that thou art mindful of HIM . .. ?"

READER 2: When I look at the bigness of moon and stars, (*disdainfully*) WHAT IS MAN?

READER 3 (*questioningly*): What IS man? Why care for him?

READER 1 (*softly, but with intensity*): Why is man important? What are we to God? WHAT is man? (*echo*)

READER 2: What IS man?

READER 3: What is MAN?

READER 1: And yet, and "YET thou hast made him little less than God,
and dost crown him with glory and honor.
Thou hast given him dominion over the works of thy hands;

... the beasts of the field,
the birds of the air, and the fish of the
sea."

READER 2: So there WE are—little less than God
—crowned with glory and honor—in CHARGE
of fields, fowl, and fish.

READER 3: That's US? That's not exactly a description of *Un*-response/ability!

ALL: What is man? What are WE? *(elongated)*
In-n-n Charge! Co-creator with the Creator.
(forcefully) Responsible!

READER 1 *(with anguish, fear):* Oh, Lord!

READER 2 *(factually):* O Lord—OUR Lord, OUR
Lord!

ALL *(slowly):* O Lord . . .

READER 1: Our Lord,

READER 2: My Lord,

READER 3: Your Lord,

ALL: "OUR LORD! How majestic is thy name in ALL
the earth!"

THIRD READING (Isaiah 43:15-19, emphasis
added)

READER 1: "I am the Lord, your Holy One,
the Creator of Israel, your King."
Thus says the Lord,
who makes a WAY in the sea,
a PATH in the mighty waters. . . .
"Remember not the former things,
nor consider the things of old.

BEHOLD, I am doing a new thing;
now it springs forth, do you not
perceive it?
I will make a way in the wilderness
and rivers in the desert."

READER 2: Here and now new things are being
done. They are springing forth in surprising
places.

READER 3: Can we see them? Can we perceive
their importance?

ALL: Think of it—WAYS EVEN, even through the
wilderness!

READER 1 *(quietly, but with intensity):* the confusion,

READER 2: the uncertainty,

READER 3: the indecision,

READER 1: the wondering,

READER 2: the trying,

READER 3: the apathy,

ALL: the WIL-DER-NESS. And PATHS, steps to follow, PATHS in the barren

READER 1: barren *(echo)* desert.

READER 2 *(echo):* barren

ALL *(loud, triumphant):* A new THING, let US SEE,
ways in the wilds, paths in the wasteland,
Aaa-MEN! New ways to walk!

FOURTH READING (Matthew 5, emphasis
added)

READER 1: "You have heard that it was said, 'An
eye for an eye, and a tooth for a tooth.' But

now I tell you: do not take revenge on some-one who does you wrong. If anyone slaps you on the right cheek, let him slap your left cheek too. And if someone takes you to court to sue you for your shirt, let him have your coat as well. And if any one forces you to go one mile, go with him *two miles"* (Matthew 5: 38-40, TEV; 5:41, RSV).

READER 2: New ways to walk.

READER 3: Walking the second mile, walking WITH—

ALL: "Love your enemies, and pray for those who mistreat you" (Matthew 5:44, TEV).

READER 1: That's more than what's expected—that's doing the "special."

READER 2: No revenge. Much caring.

ALL: Loving, walking along the second mile, a new way of walking, new people.

READER 3: "When anyone is joined to Christ he is a new being: the old is gone, the new has come.

READER 1: "All this is done by God, who through Christ changed us from enemies into his friends, and gave us the task of making others his friends also.

READER 2: "Our message is that God was making friends of all men through Christ. . . . he has given us the message of how he makes them his friends.

READER 3: "Here we are, then, speaking for Christ, as though God himself were appealing to you through us: On Christ's behalf *(slowly)* WE BEG YOU,

ALL: "Let God change you from enemies into friends!"

(2 Corinthians 5:17-20, TEV, emphasis added).

(Repeat two more times with increasing intensity)

READER 1: So the request, the invitation is: Walk in THE WAY.

READER 2: NEW people need NEW paths.

READER 3: There are choices—choose life!

READER 1: Good life.

READER 2: Warm life.

READER 3: Loving life.

ALL: Walking along WITH LIFE.

READER 1: What is man?

ALL: What are we?

READER 2: In charge of the paths of earth, sea, and sky.

ALL: God's majestic earth!

READER 1: Doing/Being/Becoming new.

READER 2: Joined with Christ.

READER 3: Walk two miles.

READER 1: Give your coat.

READER 2: Enemies are friends.

ALL: Can you see it, can you do it? It's a good new thing: a new path for new ways for all.

READER 1: New

READER 2: New

READER 3: New

ALL *(intense, quiet)*: People, *(shout)* YES!

WE LIVE IN HOPE

by RICHARD D. ORR

READER 1: At Christmas we speak readily of the COMING of the one who brings PEACE and HOPE. Such a season should not be relegated to a few frantic days. It is a fresh festive time. People smile with anticipations they can't keep to themselves. Handmade and home-prepared surprises are shared with great warmth and festivity. Secrets are special. The message: the Christ has come, the kingdom is HERE! Let us spin our hopes about the coming.

READER 2: I hope he comes with HEALING:
—I need putting back together.
—I need wholeness for my fragments.
—I need energy for my wastedness.
—I need quiet strength for my tired body.

ALL: COME, O COME.

READER 2: I hope he comes with DREAMING:
—I like imagination.
—I like dreams to fill me with joy.
—I need a vision to give me hope.
—I want an "inkling" of hope for those impossible dreams.
—I hope he comes with a soaring, curious, all-things-are-possible imagination, a HURRAH of expectation, THE reason to try and try and try—

ALL: COME, O COME.

READER 4: I hope he comes letting us know that PEOPLE are a FULL-TIME JOB!
—I'm tired of tasks.
—I'm tired of grinding up new energies for more doing, doing, doing.
—I'm tired of measuring and naming my days by how many jobs I got done.
—Is that heaven? Finishing all your jobs?
—I'm tired of missing people because I'm paralyzed with my list of stuff to do.

ALL: COME, O COME.

READER 5: I hope he comes with an end to aloneness.

—People are afraid of themselves.
—We're professionals at hiding from one an-another.
—WHY IS IT EASIER TO BE HARD THAN TENDER?
—Why do we think our hurting is weakness?

READER 1: I hope he comes, freeing us to embrace.

READER 2: Why is hugging people weird?

READER 3: I hope he invites us to make an impact —letting us be able to hug.

READER 4: I hope that crying and laughing and confessing and longing for—can all be a part of the whole and holy human WAY.

READER 1: I want to be loved.

READER 2: I want to be appreciated for what I AM.

READER 3: I want to know the richness people are—without judgments about properness or rightness.

READER 4: People ARE/and people are lovable!

READER 5: Wouldn't that be GOOD NEWS!

READER 1: You're not alone.

READER 2: Your pieces are going to come together.

READER 3: Body is OK.

READER 4: Mind can imagine.

READER 5: Feelings are acceptable.

ALL: You are ONE, your spirit can be ALIVE. You BELONG.

COME, O COME

READER 1: King of vision,

READER 2: Lord of aliveness,

READER 3: Spirit of possibility,

READER 4: Babe of holding love,

ALL: COME, come to us.

READER 5: Light our dark streets.

READER 1: Love us.

READER 2: Open us.

ALL: COME!

ALL: Amen.

SONGS FOR CELEBRATION

CARING

Words and music by Douglas Piper and Richard Piper

APOSTLE'S SONG, by Debbie New

Sing to the tune of "Wichita Lineman."

I am a witness for the Lord
And I've found my way
Being human, spreading the word
Every day.
And I'm lonely lots of times;
It's not an easy job to do,
But with the grace of our God
I'll make it through.

I know it's sometimes hard to be
A whole person every day;
But the grace of God forgives and accepts us
As being OK.
So you can forgive your brothers
And accept them as they are.
For the grace of our Father
Will take us far.

UNIVERSE END, by Debbie New

Sing to the tune of "Scarborough Fair."

Are you going to universe end?
Accept his grace, forgiveness and mine
Give praise to the One from which life begins
For he is now a Savior of mine.

Bid him take this soul I give
Accept his grace, forgiveness and mine
A small price to pay for the right to live
For he is now a Savior of mine.

Bid him to tell me to do his work
Accept his grace, forgiveness and mine
I now have no fears from where dangers lurk
For he is now a Savior of mine.

Bid him to call and an army is his
Accept his grace, forgiveness and mine
Brave men who have found just what true peace is
For he is now a Savior of mine.

Thank him for becoming a part of me
Accept his grace, forgiveness and mine
My life to direct, my soul to set free
For he is now a Savior of mine.

Give up yourself to the Eternal Son
Accept his grace, forgiveness and mine
Have no fear of life or when life is done
And then he'll be a Savior of thine.

TROUBLED THOUGHTS, by Debbie New

Sing to the tune of "My Cup Runneth Over."

I see troubled thoughts behind stormy eyes
Angry clouds are a-piling in darkening skies
This war is a-coming to destroy man and beast
I pray and ask God for peace.

This war is a-tearing apart each man's home
A woman sits crying, so lost and alone
"My sons are a-dying," she sobs out in grief
I pray and ask God for peace.

If each man accepted and loved his fellowman
And reached out beside him to take his neighbor's hand
A chain of human goodness we'd form across the land
And thank God for bringing us peace.

PLEASE FREE A DOVE THIS CHRISTMAS!

by MILTON P. RYDER

The dove is perhaps the most complete symbol of the coming of Jesus, the Christ. More graphic artists are using the shape of the dove for Advent greeting cards; several of my friends have removed the star from the top of their Christmas trees and replaced it with a small, three-dimensional dove; many Christians are decorating wreaths and trees with dove-like Chrismons (ornaments shaped into monograms of Christ); and one congregation has a huge, papier-mâché dove with a six-foot wing span suspended over the Communion table. What the symbol says is that in this one act of history God concentrated his breath, his Spirit of peace and love into the world through the special life of the one who reveals God, even Jesus.

INTRODUCTION

The main symbol in this celebration is a dove—the image of freedom, peace, and love. Man has in many ways imprisoned the dove in modern times. But God sent Jesus into life to be a liberator, a freeing voice. The message of this service is to free the dove and liberate the spirit.

It is quite significant that the word "Advent" has the same root as the word "adventure," an undertaking involving danger and unknown risk. Adventure also implies moving forward despite danger. Most Advent worship services try to recover the adventure, the undertaking with unknown risks, which Jesus' birth implied for Mary, for Joseph, for the wise men, or for the infant-Master himself.

The objective underlying this celebration of Advent—and of adventure—is that all those quaint stories about Bethlehem, the lantern-lit delivery room, beams of heavenly light, and the rest, remain just quaint stories, until we can assimilate them and use them as nourishment for our present cultural traditions, as adventures.

To have a party about Jesus' birthday, in isolation from the risks of our electronic age, is as practical and meaningful as an azalea festival in Antarctica! So, the four parts of this worship experience try to touch us where we are and bring the birth of the Savior into the context of our undertakings which involve danger and unknown risk: the context of our world, our church, our family, and our leisure. Freeing a dove in these areas is really to assimilate the Christmas message. It's an adventure!

OUTLINE OF THE SERVICE

The following order of celebration will indicate the "flow" of the experience. A more detailed explanation of the service follows the outline.

REHEARSAL

INTRODUCTION: "Calling Out the Spirit"

THE WORLD WE DESIGN
    Carol: "O Come, All Ye Faithful"
    Scripture: Antiphonal Reading of Matthew 2
    Placement of Symbols
    Question: Peggy Lee

THE CHURCH WE SUPPORT
    Reading: "A Christmas Hymn,"
                         Richard Wilbur *
    Carol: "Good Christian Men, Rejoice"
    Placement of Symbols
    Question: Peggy Lee

THE FAMILY WE LOVE
    Play: "Santa Claus," e. e. cummings
                       (scenes 1 & 2)
    Carol: "What Child Is This?"
    Play: (scene 3)
    Placement of symbols
    Question: Peggy Lee

THE LEISURE WE USE
    Carol: "Deck the Halls"
    Poem: "Christ Climbed Down"
                      by L. Ferlinghetti
    Placement of Symbols
    Question: Peggy Lee
    Answer: "Joy to the World"

* Jacob Trapp, ed., *Modern Religious Poems* (New York: Harper & Row, Publishers, 1964), pp. 99-100.

As the worshipers arrive, they might be given *small, paper Chrismon* pins like the one illustrated here. This will not only generate the thinking of "dove-ness" but also emphasize the theme: "PLEASE FREE A DOVE THIS CHRISTMAS!" (You will need a few more Chrismons and straight pins than the anticipated attendance to be sure that there is one for every person present.)

A large table might be arranged near the entrance with a massive collection of objects representing the phases of our lives indicated in the outline, such as a cross, a Bible, a book of theology, a political poster, a toy gun, a gavel, a few balloons, a large serving platter, a small, live-potted tree, framed photographs of someone's children, a soft drink bottle, a radio, a basketball, etc. As each person enters the worship area, he should be asked if he would like to select one of the objects from the table and take it to his seat.

The seating should be arranged so that parts of

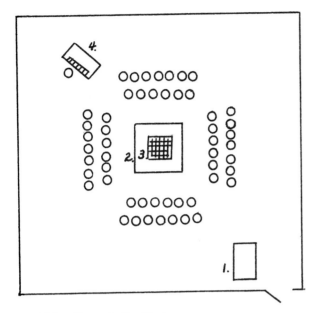

1. Table with symbolic objects
2. Central table/worship center
3. Cage with live dove
4. Piano

the congregation are located on each of four sides of the central table on which should be located a *live dove in a cage.* (See diagram of the room.) The dove may be borrowed from a pet store or even purchased for the celebration. (If doves are not available in your community, a white, fantail pigeon would be a very acceptable substitute.) Printed or mimeographed worship guides should be placed on each seat, along with a hymnal, before the service.

Everyone has now arrived and is seated, wearing a dove Chrismon pin, and many are holding objects from the table at the entrance. Don't be concerned if there aren't enough objects for each to hold one. In fact, freedom should be exercised so that anyone who chooses not to select an object from the table as he enters will feel perfectly comfortable doing so.

One of the leaders, himself sitting in one of the four sections, should enthusiastically introduce the idea of the service and verbally rehearse what will happen. (Rehearsing worship before actually beginning the experience is an excellent technique of helping everyone feel at ease and familiar with what might take place, dispelling any fear of the unexpected. One of the drawbacks of typical, innovative worship styles is that participants have little opportunity to prepare and become ready. A rehearsal can be a very effective tool for helping attendants to prepare for participation later in the celebration. The rehearsal ingredients may be gleaned from the following detailed synopsis of what is intended and expected in this service of worship.) The congregation should now be ready to announce their attitudes in considering an Advent and adventure experience. The celebration can now begin.

"Calling out the spirit" is an exercise in which another leader, seated in another of the four seating areas, stands and asks for the calling out of single words or short phrases which those present immediately think about at Christmas. Voices from around the room, unprompted, will call out such words as: "presents," "family reunions," "turkey," "school vacation," "cranberry sauce," "carols," "eggnog and cookies," "Bethlehem," etc. This kind of spontaneous request frequently produces a rash of loud statements. But it may also result in silence, which is itself a significant statement!

Each of the four segments of the celebration contain the same general format: a carol, a seasonal reading, an invitation to place on the table with the caged dove some of the objects which each is holding, and the playing of a cassette recording of a strange and bothersome song, *Is That All There Is?* by Peggy Lee (Cap. 45/6161). Also, each of the four segments will be led from a different one of the seating areas, including the recording, which should be recorded on four *cassette tapes* well in advance of the program. This shift of leadership will create the effect of worship coming out of the congregation with a rotating mobility.

A technical word about the use of the recordings will be helpful here. First, this portion of the service should *not* be explained in the rehearsal. The words are haunting. As they are heard from a different corner of the room each time, an increasing awareness of the probing question "Is that all there is?" will result.

Cassette recorders are very accessible today. In most congregations there are numerous families who own cassette players. The recording should be transferred to FOUR CASSETTE TAPES, and each of the four cassette players should be equipped with its own print of the song. Fidelity is not important (as the musical quality of this particular song is questionable anyway). But enough volume should be available for everyone in the room to be able to hear the words. If it is not possible for four cassette players to be obtained, just one, played each time from the same location will suffice, though with less effect. The entire recording should not be played each time, just enough for the re-frain "Is that all there is?" to be heard. Following each playing of the recording, each player should be rewound to the beginning as ALL four will be played simultaneously in the final segment.

A PIANIST should begin each segment with the musical introduction to the carol. Because mimeo-graphed worship guides are provided for each cele-brant, no announcements need to be made. Be careful not to insult the intelligence of worshipers by announcing those items when guidelines are in each one's hands to begin with.

Advent carols are sung so infrequently year-round that it will be good to sing all verses of each carol. Otherwise, the selected words you wish to sing should be mimeographed, perhaps on the back of the worship guides.

The Scripture in segment 1 can be a responsive reading from Matthew 2 and, for variety, might be read antiphonally, seating-sections 1 and 2 reading the light type and sections 3 and 4 responding with the heavy type. Following the antiphonal reading, a period of silence should be allowed, during which anyone who feels that the object he is holding has some relationship to the worship theme brings this object and places it on the table near the dove (or even on top of the cage). This exercise is re-peated in each worship segment until, by the time segment 4 is completed, all the objects have been presented on the central table. This should create a "picture" on the dove-table of a collection of unrelated objects. The clear view of the beautiful dove will be blocked from most of the worshipers, and the scene should seem very congested and con-fusing. The idea, of course, is that by the time all of the familiar objects of our lives are used and presented, we tend to lose sight of the already cap-tive dove. You will have done just the opposite of the inscription on the Chrismons "freeing a dove!" In fact, you will have imprisoned it even more.

Following the placement of these symbolic ob-jects (at the conclusion of each worship segment), the haunting recording will be heard, and minds and imaginations will be actively at work.

Segment 2 begins with a reading, "A Christmas Hymn" by Richard Wilbur, led by another par-ticipant-leader standing in another of the four seat-ing-sections. Before the leader begins, he should ask everyone present to repeat after him the fol-lowing phrase each time it is used in the reading: "And every stone shall cry!" This procedure will

do two things: it will insure the careful listening of the worshipers, and it will add a dramatic read-ing effect to an otherwise uninteresting monologue. Each of the leaders spread throughout the room will be familiar with the celebration before it begins and will be able to lead the worshipers seated around him as they are prepared for this echoing effect. At the conclusion of the reading, the pianist should immediately play the introduction for the next carol, "Good Christian Men, Rejoice." The congregation of celebrants will spontaneously join in singing. Again silence will follow, and objects will be presented on the dove-table. The cassette will be played again, this time from a different area of the room.

Segment 3 of the worship begins with a dramatic reading, for which two leaders will need to be well prepared, one wearing a large placard with the title "DEATH" and the other with a similar placard, reading "SANTA." The play reading is "Santa Claus" by e. e. cummings and is available in paperback form in *Religious Drama 3* (New York: Meridian Books, 1959). Scenes 1 and 2 are read, followed by the piano introduction to the carol "What Child Is This?" Scene 3 of the play is then read by the same leaders, followed by the silent period when objects are presented on the dove-table. Once again, the cassette recording is played from a different part of the room, and seg-ment 3 is completed.

(One additional word about e. e. cummings' play, "Santa Claus." It would be very wise to ana-lyze the play, omitting sections which you think are too heavy. The entire use of scenes 1, 2, and 3 is a bit longer than would be most desirable. Cutting some bits of dialogue, without reducing the impact, would help.)

The final segment of worship begins with the carol "Deck the Halls." (This is not in most hym-nals and might have to be mimeographed on the back of the worship guides.) The next leader, from the fourth seating area, then reads Lawrence Fer-linghetti's probing free verse "Christ Climbed Down." This poem is integral to the meaning of segment four and cannot be effectively replaced by anything else; it may be found in a paperback book of poems, *A Coney Island of the Mind* (New York: New Directions Pub. Corp., 1958). It should be read slowly with innocent sincerity. The placement of the remaining objects which wor-shipers have in hand will follow the poetic reading.

This time, instead of just one of the cassettes being played, EACH should be turned on, slightly out of synchronization with each other. (Because all of the cassette tapes have been rewound to the beginning, they will all start playing at the beginning of the song.) This should produce an audio-din, but by the time this happens, that haunting song "Is that all there is?" will have accomplished its effect. With all four players sounding loudly, one of the leaders should go to the dove-table, now littered with objects which virtually hide the caged dove, and open the cage, lifting the dove out and letting him free! This act will be the most exhilarating symbol of the celebration—and may even produce the reaction of applause. The pianist should be quick to begin playing the introduction to "Joy to the World," both while the cassettes are playing and the dove is being freed. As the congregation starts to sing (standing for this carol would be appropriate), each of the cassette players should be tuned down and then off in the same sequence as they began to be played—the first one off, then the second one off, then the third one, and finally, the fourth.

In effect, the clutter will no longer be binding the dove—the accumulations of our world, church, family, and leisure will no longer incarcerate the spirit of freedom, peace, and love. The recorded question "Is that all there is?" will be triumphantly answered by the enthusiastic singing of the great affirmation, ". . . the Lord is come: Let earth receive her King!" This act is itself a benediction, and the celebration is concluded as each person leaves, embraces another, touches the dove, or just bursts into conversation and action in the world—freeing the spirit of Advent and adventure for everyone he meets!

A careful rereading of this synopsis will indicate all the supplies, props, and equipment needed to carry off this experimental celebration. One final word to the leaders: In your next concern to present this type of service well, don't forget to assimilate the meaning yourselves. Sometimes worship leaders and liturgists become too involved in leading to worship themselves. In this celebration, with shared responsibilities, you can worship—you MUST worship.

RESURRECTION FISH

by MILTON P. RYDER

INTRODUCTION

This worship/celebration is designed to celebrate the idea of resurrection in terms of GETTING UP AGAIN TO COMPLETE THE UNFINISHED TASKS OF MY LIFE AND YOURS. And, as a point of entry, this celebration uses the very reference to his own resurrection which Jesus made, as reported in Matthew 12:40, when he answered the teachers of law and Pharisees who were demanding a sign from him:

> In the same way that Jonah spent three days and nights in the belly of the big fish, so will the Son of Man spend three days and nights in the depths of the earth. (TEV)

Maybe looking at the resurrection from the point of view of Jonah will be a fresh perspective for celebrating Easter. And the title "RESURRECTION FISH" with the support of a mixed-media program might generate a triumphant Christian holiday which will have deep impact and long-lasting influence.

THE MIND SET (Writing the Script)

Resurrection, described in the narrative of Jonah, is, among other definitions, the discovery of new life so that we may continue working and carrying out daily tasks of justice, love, and peace.

THE SETTING (Building the Set)

This celebration includes a blend of media: traditional song, drama, folk-rock recording, group participation, spiritual songs, spontaneously created litany, and stream-of-consciousness prayer.

The following outline will help to describe the general experience. A detailed explanation will follow.

OUTLINE OF THE SERVICE

GETTING IT TOGETHER

Unison Call to Celebration
Matthew 12:39-40, printed for the group to read.

Song: "Jonah" *(5 minutes)*
Paraphrased sea chantey dealing with Jonah's resurrection.

Small-Group Activity *(5 minutes)*
Group divided into two sets, each with Sunday newspapers from which one group selects three travel ads and the other selects three short accounts of tragedy.

Three-Part Antiphonal Litany *(2 minutes)*
Created by group one reading a travel ad, followed by group two reading a tragedy, and then group three (the leader or two voices) reading from Psalm 139:7-10.

EXPANDING THE MIND

Listening Music for Reflection *(4 minutes)*
"Yesterday" by John Lennon and Paul McCartney, played on a record player or tape recorder.

Introspection Exercise *(5 minutes)*
1. 4″ x 6″ cards and pencils distributed to everyone.
2. Each asked to draw or symbolize the place or activity in which he hides when faced with an unattractive task.
3. Those who care to are given the opportunity of sharing their story with the total group.
4. Cards are kept to be used later in celebration.

OPENING THE WINDOWS

Drama Excerpts and Song *(10 minutes)*
Selected scenes from Mankowitz's "It Should Happen to a Dog!" interspersed by selected verses of the sea chantey "Jonah." Scenes involve only two readers and no set.

Unison Prayer *(2 minutes)*
Printed for the group to read.

DOING A NEW THING

Drawings *(1 minute)*
Individually, drawings of each person's "Tarshish" are taken to the center and offered up, burnt, or torn.

Spiritual: "Resurrection Fish!" *(5 minutes)*

PASSING-THE-PEACE BENEDICTION

The songs are easily learned and sung, and where the melody is familiar, such as the sea chantey, just the words and guitar chords are listed. Newly written songs, such as "Resurrection Fish," should include both the music score and the lyrics for everyone to join in as equals. These parts of worship, to be used in unison, follow this explanatory section and may be copied in any way for use in your celebration. The permission of the author has already been obtained for you.

The small-group activity is intended to provide a way for everyone to contribute. After one of the two groups has selected three travel ads from the newspapers and the other group has selected three paragraphs describing some tragedy, individuals from each of the groups should be selected to read the group's selection, in sequence, with a worship leader responding to the two with a third reading, from Psalm 139. The sequence might be as follows:

Group One Reader:	travel ad #1
Group Two Reader:	tragedy #1
Worship Leader:	Psalm 139:7
Group One Reader:	travel ad #2
Group Two Reader:	tragedy #2
Worship Leader:	Psalm 139:8
Group One Reader:	travel ad #3
Group Two Reader:	tragedy #3
Worship Leader:	Psalm 139:9-10

The Introspection Exercise is another way of allowing everyone to share without insisting on participation. Care must be taken to preserve each one's freedom so that a person who chooses not to participate actively is still made to feel accepted as a worshiper. The exercise has the possibility of releasing humor as well as insight and should be treated in a warm but serious frame of mind. Drawings, such as a motorcycle, a bedroom, a book, might be produced, showing the places to which we mentally escape when facing difficult tasks.

We each have a "Tarshish," a place where we find seclusion and comfort, and these aren't necessarily bad, nor is the need for some kind of personal shrine. What is helpful sometimes is to acknowledge these places and also the feelings which encourage us to hide there, sort of self-discovery via the sketch pad. After enough time has been allowed for each one to draw in silence, the opportunity should be given for anyone who would like to share with the group his line drawing or symbol, as well as the times when he feels like escaping there. The cards are to be kept and used in a symbolic offering later in the celebration.

Use of the amusing but profound drama by Wolf Mankowitz "It Should Happen to a Dog!" is suggested in relationship to certain verses of the paraphrased sea chantey. The play shouldn't be memorized. If the two-part script is read well, the presentation is as effective for worship as a memorized production. The following chart will indicate the succession of the scenes to be used; and the bold-faced numbers of the song's verses on the printed word sheet will tell the singing group which verses to sing at each interval:

> Scene I: Jonah sent to a strange land.
> Verse 1 and chorus.
> Scene III: Overboard.
> Verses 3 and 4 with chorus each time.
> Scene V: Doing his thing in Nineveh.
> Verse 8 and chorus.
> Scene VI: Jonah understanding God.
> Verses 9 and 10 with chorus each time.

The sharing of drawings can be done in several ways. Each person should be given the opportunity to take his 4" x 6" card to the worship/celebration center and tear it, burn it, or just place it as an act symbolical of being open to God and a desire for receiving a resurrection like Jonah, of being found and wanting to be used to complete some task. This act could be a very dramatic moment of dedication or a simple symbolic expression of each person's mood. Special effort should be made *not* to create a mystical ceremony out of this act, but to let it be a simple statement of reality as a result of resurrection. God's Spirit has more freedom to work within us when we stress simplicity than when we build ornate theological compartments for ourselves, which might in fact be a "Tarshish" for some.

The final act of passing-the-peace is an ancient but reviving experience. There are several techniques, the most familiar of which is for each person to turn to another, and with one's hands folded prayer-like, the other person holds them on the outside and says, "The peace of God go with you." The partners then reverse hand positions and now the other person responds, "And with you." This act is repeated around the group until each person has greeted and been greeted. The words will echo repeatedly and create a note of warm fellowship on which to disperse.

THE MECHANICS (Collecting the Props)

Much of the smoothness of a celebration comes from thorough preparation of the place and the program. It is suggested that a carpeted room be used for this experience, with more pillows and pads than chairs; people, therefore, being at a variety of eye levels. Seating-in-the-round is probably the most intimate and intense seating and the one which encourages the most feeling of participation. It is recommended for this worship. The following materials should be obtained well in advance of the celebration time:

> Printed words for each worshiper.
> Two copies of *Religious Drama 3.* (New York: Meridian Books, Inc., 1959).
> One Bible for litany.
> Six Sunday newspapers for writing the litany (back issues OK).
> One recording: "Yesterday" by the Beatles (Cap. 45/5498).
> One record player with good fidelity.
> Pencils for everyone, #1 lead preferable, or magic markers.
> 4" x 6" cards (plain) for everyone.

Human resources needed will include:

> One leader to introduce readings, to be the third voice in the litany, and to help lead the singing.
> Two drama readers who should have rehearsed enough to read the script well.
> One guitarist who should be familiar with the songs before the celebration.

(Copy this order of service for each worshiper.)

RESURRECTION FISH

THE CALL TO CELEBRATION

Jesus exclaimed: "You ask me for a miracle? No! The only miracle you will be given is the miracle of the prophet Jonah. In the same way that Jonah spent three days and nights in the belly of the big fish, so will the Son of Man spend three days and nights in the depths of the earth" (Matthew 12: 39-40, TEV).

SEA CHANTEY PARAPHRASED

"What Do You Do with a Drunken Sailor?" (Scene I)

RESURRECTION FISH

M. P. Ryder
1972

M. P. Ryder

© Milton Perron Ryder 1972

2. —he had a whale of a problem!
   —tried to flee to "Port Tarshish."
   —he had a whale of a problem!
   —spent a weekend in a fish!

3. —reconsidered goin' to Nin'veh.
   —fish burped; he was on his way!
   —reconsidered goin' to Nin'veh.
   —told them to repent and pray.

4. —was a man with second chances;
   —knew what resurrection meant.
   —was a man with second chances;
   —Easter always follows Lent!

Suggestions:
  Introduction with only wood block on first beat of four measures.
  Add guitar chord (C) to wood block for next four measures.
  Then eight measures (all verse 1) with rhythmic voices on "Jo-nah" added to the guitar and wood block.
  Finally, melody voices on verses 1-4, plus the continuing rhythmic voices, guitar, and wood block.

Chorus:
  Tambourine on second and fourth beats of each measure, shaking loudly on final beat of song.

1. Who ran from God on a boat? 'twas Jonah!
    (Dm)
Who ran from God on a boat? 'twas Jonah!
    (C)
Who ran from God on a boat? 'twas Jonah!
    (Dm)
Ear-lye in the mor-ning.   (C)
Chorus (same chords as the verse):
Lord, our God, have mercy on us. (repeat three times)
Ear-lye in the mor-ning.
2. Waves curled high and the ship seemed so small. (repeat three times)

(Scene III)

3. Sailors said, "Someone on board's guilty!" (repeat three times)
4. They cast lots which fingered Jonah. (repeat three times)
5. God sent a fish with a crazy app'tite. (repeat three times)
6. Fish ate Jonah, got indigestion! (repeat three times)
7. Lord, God tic-kled the throat of the big fish! (repeat three times)

(Scene V)

8. Jonah did his thing in Nineveh. (repeat three times)

(Scene VI)

9. What shall we do when the world flees God? (repeat three times)
10. Lord, send a fish and a resurrection! (repeat three times)

(Boldface numbers indicate verses to be used between scenes of drama.)

PRAYER

Lord,
You gotta be kidding! This has to be some kind of gag!

I mean, why me? Why not Ben or Connie?
Sure, I once said, "Here am I, send me."
But you know I really meant, "There's Ben and Connie, send them!"
OK. OK.
Accept responsibility,
use my energies,
express myself.
But you saw my drawing,
you know where I like to hide!
Why can't you be a real God
and do FOR me what I don't want to do for myself?
What?
You're sorry?
You didn't mean to get in the way?
Do my own thing if I don't want to do yours?
Now hold on—and I mean really hold on!
You aren't just going to let go of me, are you?
What makes you think I can't do it?
Or go there?
Or fix that broken thing?
After all, I don't have to be eighteen or twenty-one to campaign for a president or a councilman, you know.
I don't have to be an M.D. to wear candy-stripes!
I don't have to be Evelyn Wood to tutor a slow reader in grade three!
After all,
You did make me, you know?
And I can do something—
And I WILL do something!
Lord,
Where's my fish? I'm ready for a resurrection!
And Ben and Connie can come with me if they want, but I AM GOING!
Watch me!
and, Lord—
please help me!
    AMEN

EXPRESSIONS IN BLACK

by BEATRICE SULLIVAN

PREPARATION

This program is a combination of a verse choir and pantomime scenes. Persons will be needed for the following speaking parts:

Voices—any number could be used
Narrator
Speaker
Slave mother
Voice from the audience

The following pantomime scenes will be presented and will need these persons to take the various parts:

A black woman
A slave mother and children
A slave auction
Phillis Wheatley at a desk
Slaves working in field, slave mother a part of the group
Group of black athletes
Group of black entertainers
Woman seated in bus

The pantomime scenes will be most effective if they can be presented on a stage where a curtain can be opened and closed on the scene. If this arrangement is not possible, the participants could move silently into place from the side and depart the same way at the appropriate times.

EXPRESSIONS IN BLACK

When the curtain opens, a woman dressed in black is seen kneeling in spotlight. She rises slowly with arms outstretched as voices from backstage speak.

(Use background of "Praying Hands.")

VOICES *(very low, slowly rising in tempo):* Woman, Woman, Woman, etc. *(Voices continue very softly while narrator speaks.)*

NARRATOR: Who is she? What is she? This Black Woman of America. What does she think? What does she feel? What is her heritage?

VOICES *(loud, then low and fade):* Woman, Woman, Woman, Woman.

NARRATOR: What is woman? Poets and writers have spent many years and have written many words to try to describe this mystic being—woman. Woman is a marvelous being. There are red women, yellow women, white women, and black women. We concern ourselves today with just one woman, the black woman. Let us look at her closely. Let us examine this beautiful and fruitful flower from God's garden of mankind. Ah, what a background she has! She is typical of all the struggles that any race of man has known. If you look closely enough, you will see that she, with her family, has struggled down through the years in an amazing effort to become a real human power—a power that has contributed much to civilization. Her struggles enabled her to reach down and bring her race of people up from the valley of dark despair to climb the mountain toward love and brotherhood. What a heritage we owe this Black Woman!

VOICES *(low to loud):* Woman, Woman, Black Woman, Black Woman.

SPEAKER: Can't you see her, this black woman of slavery? Turn back the hands of time. Look at our slave mother as she goes about her daily task. What a brave soul she is! I wonder what she is thinking.

Picture: Typical slave scene is formed: a mother

91

washing, old-fashioned tub, shanty in background, etc. One or two children, barefoot, dressed as slaves.

Music: "Nobody Knows the Trouble I've Seen" (Can be sung or played.)

SLAVE MOTHER: Nobody knows how I weep for my children. I pray that one day they will be free. O you, who view this scene today, I know that it must pain your heart to see me as I was in this bygone day. Do not forget whence we come. Be not ashamed of our African heritage, but be proud that from our rich dark past we brought gifts of music, laughter, skilled hands, and nimble feet. Gifts that were denied and rejected. In this land our laughter is filled with tears, our music is of sorrow. Look at me now as I stand here washing for my mistress and her family. I see my dismal shanty in the background, and in the foreground I see the mansions of my mistress. Surely one day I can get such a lovely home and fine clothes. One day my family—my black family—will live in some of this earthly splendor. One day my sons and daughters will be educated. They will be doctors, lawyers, teachers, scientists, preachers. One day my daughters will be ladies in their own right. But now, my sisters, the shackles of slavery bind my people. Fret not—we shall be free.

Curtain closes on picture.

Offstage the sound of an auctioneer is heard. Cries of "Lordy no, please don't take my child—take me!" and other appropriate sounds are heard.

SLAVE MOTHER (sounds as if she has been crying): Don't take my child. She is so small, and she needs her mammy so. Please, Master John, don't let them take my precious child.

Picture: Slave auction: players are posed in proper setting with slave mother in scene with expression of pleading.

SPEAKER: Look at this woman. This woman of sorrow. This Black Woman. Weep with her, if you must. Feel in your heart the pain, the anguish, as her child is taken from her bosom. How dark can the days be? Oh, Woman, Black Woman, give up, give up, there is no hope. Stop dreaming—be content with your lot—there is no better day for you.

SLAVE MOTHER (as curtain slowly closes): Stop! Stop! I know better. There is a better day for all of us. I know it! I know it! My sons, my daughters, have faith, have courage. I know that one day we shall rise above these human injustices. We shall take our rightful places in human society. Even in this dark day, my children are speaking out in love and compassion through this heavy curtain of despair. Listen, I believe I hear one of my daughters speaking now—listen. Phillis, Phillis Wheatley, speak to us.

Picture: Phillis Wheatley, in garb of house slave, at writing desk. Old-fashioned desk with quill pen, if possible.

OFFSTAGE VOICE: reads one of two poems written by Phillis Wheatley and curtain closes.

SLAVE MOTHER: Thank you, my dear. Really your words are the beginnings of what will be called "soul" one day, for you have expressed the language of the heart. My children, don't give up. I have hope in my heart. One day we shall be free, and the soul of this black woman will lead the way.

NARRATOR: This brave woman, this black woman, even though she was not given public recognition, was really the backbone for much of the struggle for freedom. When man was disappointed, she gave him hope. When he was sad, she sang and made him glad. When he was afraid, she looked him in the eye and demanded that he be brave. She suffered beside her man in the cotton fields. Her head was bowed, but not her heart. She looked forward to the times when the code was passed among her people that there was to be a meeting on the plantation. Listen. I hear one of the code songs now, telling the slaves to "steal away."

Music: "Steal Away"

Picture: A group of slaves is formed while "Steal Away" is sung or played. Slave mother is center of group.

Narrator: What must these blacks be thinking? Who will be sold tomorrow? They could be telling about a slave woman who had escaped and would come back to lead the way to freedom. They could be dreaming of the day they too would be free. Look at the slave mother—what dreams are in her eyes! Look as she drops to her knees. *(Slave mother in picture kneels.)* She must be asking God to lead her children to freedom. *(Curtain closes.)*

Narrator: How rich and vital is our heritage! It was in these days of dark despair that our dreams and our hopes were born. Without the prayers, the vision, the training of our black women, we would not or could not enjoy the fruits of her labor. Our progress forward has been slow. Ofttimes we have become impatient. Often our courage has run out, but when we reach our lowest ebb, this black woman influences one of her sons or daughters to come forth and hold high another ray of light. She says to the world: "Look, look, here is my child—flesh of my flesh, bone of my bone. He stands here a beacon of light to show the way to others. No road is left untouched."

Voice from Audience: Tell me of those who led the way on the road of sports.

Narrator: Let me show you just a few.

Picture: Several persons in proper attire representing outstanding athletes: boxing, Jack Johnson, Joe Louis; tennis, Althea Gibson, Arthur Ashe; baseball, Jackie Robinson, etc.

Voice from Audience: That's well and good, Black Woman, but tell me, what has been accomplished in the field of entertainment?

Narrator: Very much. Listen to the voice of Marian Anderson, which sings of our hope.

Picture: Group representing: piano, Hazel Scott; actress, Louise Beaver; dancer, Cathryn Dunham; vocalist, Marian Anderson.

Narrator: There are many fields, almost too numerous to name, but let me speak of a few of my sons and daughters. Frederick Douglass, who was a leader in the fight to abolish slavery; P.B.S. Pinchback, who for a short time sat in the governor's chair in the state of Louisiana; Booker T. Washington, an outstanding educator. W. E. B. DuBois, Walter White, Adam Clayton Powell, and Martin Luther King. I had many daughters dedicated to leading the way. Glorious is the woman who toiled both early and late at the washtub in order that her children might have the education she was denied. Now deceased, but great in their lifetimes were Gertrude Janet Washington, concert pianist; Ida B. Wells, journalist; Susan McKinney, physician; Madame C. J. Walker, cosmetologist; Mary McLeod Bethune, educator and adviser to presidents; Hallie Q. Brown, author; Juanita Kidd, juvenile judge.

VOICES: Freedom, freedom, Woman, lead us to freedom!

NARRATOR: Slavery days were a long way behind us. Voices were heard and were listened to, and the long pilgrimage toward freedom was begun. But the children grew weary, the way was long—so long. Could something be done to hasten the day? Just some tiny thing, some insignificant thing that would let the black children know that daybreak was just ahead?

Picture: Woman seated inside bus.

SLAVE MOTHER: Meet my daughter, Rosa Parks. You might call her the flame that lit the present fire for freedom. O dear, my daughter worked so hard today. Her feet are tired, and they hurt. She must rest. She is weary, so weary. She just can't take another step. She must sit down and rest. Ah, there's an empty seat; she will sit down. Sure, it is in the front of a bus in Alabama, but she must sit down. What did you say? No, no, we can't suffer any more of these abuses. This is too much. My daughter refuses to move and let that man sit in her seat just because it is in the front of the bus. She will not; she will not. O my children, lift high your heads, let there be a song in your hearts. My children, God made us all, and we, his black children, have pride too.

Music: "Lift Every Voice and Sing"

SPEAKER: Little did this black daughter know that her action of that day was to start a chain of reactions that would bring the dawning of a new day. First, it gave to the world a new leader, the martyred Martin Luther King. Her action led us to realize that now was the day for action. We began taking new steps, doing bigger and better things. We found opportunities in new fields, such as engineering, space technology, advanced scientific research, politics, human relations, and religion.

NARRATOR: Yes, this black race is a people on the move. Nothing worthwhile is won without striving. We must climb by faith. We must hold high the principles of God. It was Booker T. Washington who gave sane advice when he said, "I will hate no man until I let him draw me down to his level." To rise to our fullest heights, we must rise with love for all mankind, regardless of race. We must become expressions of black—expressions for all and to all that peace, love, and unity can abide. Our struggles, our heartbreaks, our tears are the things that have made us unafraid.

Music: "We Shall Overcome"

VOICES: Woman, Black Woman. Who is she?

NARRATOR: She is the dream of tomorrow.

VOICES: Woman, Woman, Black Woman. What is she?

NARRATOR: She is the hope of today.

VOICES: Woman, Woman, Black Woman. Where is she?

NARRATOR: She is everywhere—her hopes, her joys, her sorrow, her tears.

Picture: As song continues, the curtain opens. The first scene is repeated, only this time the woman is standing with arms outstretched, palms upward. This is to create two ideas: to include everyone and to reach heavenward for guidance.

A one-act play on the meaning of Christmas

CHRISTMAS HAS BEEN CANCELED

by W. BARKLEY BUTLER, JAMES L. PIKE and the Junior High B.Y.F., First Baptist Church, Madison, Wisconsin

PREPARATION

The stage is divided into two stages, right and left.

STAGE: On stage left, a family living room: fireplace with red stockings, couch, rug, lamp, pictures on walls, easy chair, and table. On stage right, a giant "television set" with cardboard and dials, risers for small choir.

PROPS: Red "Santa" hats for choir members; choir robes; a large sign which says "BULLETIN" for use with giant TV set; large Bible; and signs of a commercial Christmas for family living room. Bathrobes and slippers for family members. A bare Christmas tree; a manger and some greenery. (Maybe a record player.) Commercial Christmas cards (no mention of Jesus). A candle (wide and decorative). Two spotlights. (Stage manager should be in charge of lighting.)

CHARACTERS: Narrator, mother, father, four children, newscaster, piano player, and choir members.

CHRISTMAS HAS BEEN CANCELED

(As the play begins, the lights go down and the spotlight goes on the narrator at a podium on the floor in front of stage left.)

NARRATOR: It's Christmas time again. Remember? It happens each December. Well—to tell the truth, they began it in late October this year: it seems to arrive earlier each year—sort of like the new cars. Anyhow, December is when it reaches its climax or really starts to get to you, depending on your point of view.
(Lights on family.)

This is the Williams family. They could live anywhere—New York, Chicago, San Francisco, but they happen to live here. Let's see how they're coming with their Christmas preparations. They ought to be about finished; there are only a few days left now.

Oh, dear! It looks as if they haven't even finished their Christmas cards.

SCENE: Mother and father seated at card table doing Christmas cards, great stacks of envelopes, etc. The two younger children (use their real names) are playing on the floor.

MOTHER: Did you send Aunt Florence a Santa card or a Rudolph one, dear?

FATHER: What difference does it make?

MOTHER: Well, I don't want to send the same one to Cousin Millie. They live next door to each other, you know.

FATHER *(sarcastically):* Yeah, that would be terrible. Say, where are those fifty-cent cards with the gold lettering? I need one for my boss.

MOTHER: I used the last one for Pastor Gladhand.

FATHER: Well, we'll just have to get some more. Say, is the Sanders' party tomorrow night or Sunday?

MOTHER: Sunday, but we're going to the church family night, so we can't go.

FATHER: Miss the Sanders' party for a potluck supper with a bunch of screaming kids? Forget it! I can't stand potluck suppers.

MOTHER: Well, you'll stand this one. I promised Gloria Gladhand I would help. Besides, the kids look forward to getting a present from Santa. Jeremiah Smith is going to be Santa Claus again. He's always such a good one.

95

(George and Mary, the two older children, burst into the room, arguing and pushing each other.)

MARY: Mother, tell George he can't use the gold wrapping paper. He just messes it up, and I need it for your present.

GEORGE: She won't let me use any of the new paper. All I get is the stuff from last year's presents with Scotch tape all over it. What makes her think she's so great?

(Just then the two little children start fighting over a toy: one hits the other, who starts crying. George and Mary continue to argue over the paper.)

FATHER: Shut up! All of you. If you don't stop this fighting, I'll just take back all the presents and forget the whole thing. The way I feel right now, I wish Christmas were over and done with. I hate it!

MOTHER: Well, at least we agree on one thing. I'd never miss it if they would just skip Christmas.

LITTLE BOY *(in panic)*: Isn't there going to be a Christmas? I want to get a fire truck and a ray gun and a space suit and—

LITTLE GIRL: Am I going to get my doll, Mommy? Am I? Huh?

GEORGE: Yeah, Dad, and don't forget those skis I want, and the boots and jacket.

MARY: And that dress and sweater. I'll die if I don't get those.

MOTHER: All right! You're getting on my nerves. Why don't you turn on the television? It's time for the "Goodmonth" Santa Christmas Special.

(She goes out and returns with popcorn and soda while one of the children turns on the TV.)

MOTHER: How about stringing some more popcorn for the tree? I think the Holiday Singers and Dancers are on tonight.

(The lights go down on the family and half up on the TV with the narrator's light going on too. The choir, dressed in Santa hats, sings one verse of "Santa Claus Is Coming to Town" or some other song.)

NARRATOR *(piano plays softly during narration)*: Sound familiar? Sort of brings that dull December ache back to your head? I wonder why it seems so natural when we play the parts ourselves? Well, that chorus sounds good and the song is familiar. Why don't we all join them and sing along.

(The lights go way down on the family and all the

way up on the TV, and the narrator directs the audience to the end of the song.)*

CHOIR MEMBER: And now listen as the choir sings their own rendition of that famous Christmas carol "Rudolph, the Red-nosed Reindeer."

(The choir starts on "Rudolph the Red-nosed Reindeer," which is interrupted at the point of "Santa came to say. . . .")

NEWSCASTER *(reading and pushing his way through the TV singers)*: We interrupt this Christmas special to bring you a news bulletin. This bulletin has just been received. Christmas has been canceled. We repeat. Christmas has been canceled. This is all we know at this time. We will broadcast more information as we receive it. We do not know the reason for this announcement. We do know that all Christmas preparations are to cease immediately. No trees, parties, decorations, cards, or presents are allowed. We repeat. Christmas has been canceled. No trees, parties, decorations, cards, or presents are allowed.

(The lights begin to come up on the family, who are looking very upset and surprised.)

In keeping with this order, we cannot continue the special you were watching. WFBC will now leave the air. We will return to the air at 9:00 P.M. E.S.T. for the regularly scheduled program, "The Avengers."

(TV lights off and choir leaves. Lights all the way up on family. Everyone staring at the TV with look of amazement. Then tears from the little ones, confusion, etc.)

LITTLE GIRL: Did the man say there won't be Christmas, Mommy?

LITTLE BOY: Does that mean Santa won't come, Dad? Does it?

GEORGE: Does that mean I won't get my skis? They can't do that, can they?

FATHER: Well, at least we don't have the tree yet.

MOTHER: What will we do with all these cards we haven't mailed yet? And what am I going to do with six pumpkin pies?

FATHER: And I just bought a plastic Santa Claus that lights up for the lawn. What do I do with that?

MOTHER *(to father)*: What does it mean, dear? How can they cancel Christmas? I mean, it's sort of a relief in a way, but to just do it without asking anybody. Shouldn't we have voted on it or something? It's sure going to be hard on the kids.

FATHER: Well, I don't know; I guess we'll get along without it. We can save the kids' presents for their birthdays. They get everything they want anyway, and we do too, for that matter. Maybe—

GEORGE: Dad, how can they just say there isn't any Christmas? There's always been Christmas, hasn't there? Why stop it now? If they didn't want it, why let it get started? How did it get started, anyhow?

(Action stops, light comes on for narrator.)

NARRATOR: I know what you're all thinking. Don't be ridiculous. You're putting me on, right? Nobody could be so dumb as not to know how Christmas got started. Especially nobody coming to a church Christmas play. We all know, right? Of course, we won't ask what your kids would think Christmas was all about if all they knew was from watching you go through one. But we all know, don't we? Well, no matter, these people really know, too. They almost have forgotten, but they know. The parents are getting ready to explain it now. Want to listen in just to be sure they're getting it right?

(Lights off on narrator and action resumes in play.)

FATHER: How did Christmas get started? Didn't you learn that story in Sunday school about shepherds and kings coming to give presents to a baby? It's all in the Bible.

MOTHER: I remember when we used to go to Grandpa's when I was a little girl. We would sit by the fireplace, and Grandpa would read that story out of the family Bible. That was so long ago. But Christmas was so much fun and so relaxed and—it was even—inspirational. It's so different now, or it was till a few minutes ago. I'd forgotten all about that.

LITTLE BOY: Would you read us that story about how Christmas all started?

MARY: Yeah, I never thought much about it until now when they canceled it.

FATHER: Where is that old Bible? *(It is on an end table, covered with dust. He blows off the dust and asks his wife to find the story.)*

MOTHER: Where is it now? *(Looking through book.)* Oh, yes, here it is with Grandpa's bookmark.

FATHER *(reads. Soft music in background. TV lights come up and family lights soften. Father reads while the choir sings softly in background and comes up louder to finish each song after his reading has stopped.):*

Luke 2:1-7 *(Choir sings first verse of "The Virgin Mary Had a Baby Boy" or "Silent Night.")*

Matthew 2:1-2 *(Choir sings "We Three Kings.")*

Luke 2:8-14 *(Choir sings "While Shepherds Watched Their Flocks" or "The First Noel.")*

Matthew 2:9-12 *(Choir sings rest of "The Virgin Mary Had a Baby Boy" or "Away in a Manger.")*

MOTHER: And that's how Christmas got started. Funny how we'd forgotten that in all the Christmas rush. Maybe that's why Christmas got canceled. We were thinking of all the popcorn and parties and presents and forgot all about the real meaning.

LITTLE GIRL: What happened to the baby?

FATHER: After the wise men gave him gifts, he grew up; and when he was a man, Jesus gave his life that there might be love and peace for all men. That is the greatest gift of all.

MARY: And that's why we give presents?

GEORGE: And Christmas isn't getting presents, really; it's giving them.

MOTHER: That's right. We give to others, not just presents, but more important, ourselves, our love, because God gave himself to us. Maybe Christmas will really be Christmas if we think of it that way.

(Choir begins singing "O Holy Night" or some other carol. Lights go down on family and up on the Narrator and chorus.)

NARRATOR: Maybe Christmas will really be Christmas. Who knows? For many people the real Christmas was canceled long ago—not for lack of interest, or lack of time, or lack of bread, not even by a TV news bulletin. For them Christmas was canceled by a preoccupation with all of the "busywork" of the holiday season. It's just too bad the Christ part of Christmas gets lost in the shuffle.

(Choir sings "I Wonder as I Wander" with guitars. Prayer by Narrator.)

Section 3

A SIMULATION GAME

A SIMULATION GAME*

*IN CASE YOU'VE NEVER TRIED ONE,

SIMULATION GAMES ARE

- fun, educational, involving
- like role playing, but with rules
- competitive

THEY CAN BE GIMMICKY IF

- played too often
- played without a learning goal in mind
- played without discussion following
  the game

TRY THIS ONE!

CREDIT AND DEBT, by Ronald A. Schlosser

PURPOSE

To experience the feeling of being in debt, in order to understand a common experience of the poor.

WAYS TO USE THIS GAME

The best use of the game is in a study of poverty. Note that all players start out with unequal assets, but equal minimum needs. This is the situation of many poor people.

BIBLICAL STUDY RELATED TO THE GAME
Matthew 18:23-35

INSTRUCTIONS FOR THE GAME OF CREDIT AND DEBT

OBJECT OF GAME: To stay out of debt.

MATERIALS NEEDED: Play cards (cut apart cards which are printed on pages 107 and 109); scrip (pages 103-105). Additional scrip can be made as needed from slips of paper.

ORDER OF PLAY:

1. All players empty their pockets or purses of loose change (up to one dollar each).
2. Bank (leader) gives paper scrip to each player equivalent to money put up (in multiples of 5). A piece of 5 scrip equals 5 cents.
3. The player who has the highest amount of scrip is appointed Loan Shark. Player who has the next highest amount is appointed Pawn-

broker. In case of ties, a coin can be flipped to determine roles.

4. At the beginning of play, all persons must have scrip worth $1. Players who do not have this amount must acquire it in one of two ways:

   a. Borrow needed amount from Loan Shark at 20 percent interest. That is, for every 25 scrip borrowed, 5 scrip will be expected at the end of the game. (It might be well to have players borrow in multiples of 25 to keep bookkeeping simple.)

   b. Pawn items he has on his person, such as tie clip, comb, lipstick, mirror. Pawnbroker determines the worth of these items and loans the needed scrip. Players can buy back each item pawned by repaying the amount received for it plus 10 scrip mark-up.

5. Loan Shark and Pawnbroker can borrow scrip from the Banker at 10 percent interest to provide scrip for loans. Banker keeps record of all transactions in real money and property and of borrowed scrip. (See suggested forms at end of instructions for keeping records.)

6. When all players have a total of 100 in scrip, play begins by having the person whose last name is closest to the beginning of the alphabet draw a play card. (Cards should be shuffled and the pack placed face down on the table.) He reads the instructions on the card and pays or collects the stated amount of scrip. Play then moves to the person's left (or in a clockwise direction).

7. Scrip payable to the collection agency is to be given to the Loan Shark as manager of the agency.

8. If players run out of scrip, they can borrow what they need from the Loan Shark or Pawnbroker in the manner and on the terms described above.

9. Loan Shark and Pawnbroker also play by picking up cards in turn. Loan Shark does not need to pay amounts which he would otherwise collect as head of the collection agency. His only

payments will be made to the bank or to other players as the cards direct.

10. To get additional money interest free, Pawnbroker can sell pawned items to the bank for the amount he paid for them, plus an extra 5 scrip profit on each.

11. Welfare and salary funds are paid from the bank.

12. The time limit of the game is fifteen minutes (beginning with the picking up of the first play card). When time is up, all players determine the amount of scrip they owe or have on hand. They can use the scrip they have to buy back their real money or personal property given up at the beginning of the game.

FOLLOW-UP INFORMATION FOR THE LEADER

The purpose of the game is to have the players experience the feeling of being in debt and the frustrations that come from trying to get enough money to pay one's financial obligations. The game attempts to simulate the kinds of problems and circumstances the poor face in their day-to-day lives. Players are asked to exchange their own money and personal property for play scrip, not knowing if they will get these things back. Although proper restitution will be made at the end of the game, it might be well to explore with the players how they would feel if they could get back only what they were able to pay for with the scrip on hand.

After playing the game, discuss with the players their feelings about the experience they just had.

1. How did they feel when they needed to get a certain amount of money to begin the game?

2. What were their feelings toward the Loan Shark, the Pawnbroker, and the Banker? Did they resent any of them for monopolizing the financial resources?

3. Did they feel a sense of hopelessness as their debts mounted up? Did they think that the "cards were stacked against them"?

4. What did the statements on the play cards say to them about the conditions under which the poor live?

Suggested forms for keeping track of financial transactions

BANK STATEMENT

Player's Name	Amount of Money Exchanged for Scrip
1.	
2.	
3.	
4.	
5.	
6.	
7.	

BANK LOANS AT 10% INTEREST

To Loan Shark	Amount	To Pawnbroker	Amount

LOAN SHARK'S I.O.U.

Player's Name

Amount Borrowed

+ 20% Interest

   Total Owed

PAWNBROKER'S ACCOUNT

Player's Name	Article Pawned	Amount of Scrip Given
1.		
2.		
3.		
4.		
5.		
6.		
7.		

5 5 5 5 5 5 5 5

5 5 5 5 5 5 5 5

5 5 5 5 5 5 5 5

5 5 5 5 5 5 5 5

5 5 5 5 5 5 5 5

10 10 10 10 10 10 10 10

10 10 10 10 10 10 10 10

10 10 10 10 10 10 10 10

10 10 10 10 10 10 10 10

10 10 10 10 10 10 10 10

Your child needs new shoes **PAY 5** to collection agency	Your child needs new shoes **PAY 5** to collection agency	You are hooked on drugs **PAY 40** to Loan Shark	Your tenement needs repair **PAY 20** to collection agency
Your child needs clothes from thrift shop **PAY 10** to collection agency	Your little girl needs a dress **PAY 5** to collection agency	You are hooked on drugs **PAY 40** to Loan Shark	You need exterminator to fight rats **PAY 20** to collection agency
Your child needs clothes from thrift shop **PAY 10** to collection agency	Your little boy needs new pants **PAY 5** to collection agency	Grocery Bill **PAY 20** to bank	Grocery Bill **PAY 20** to bank
You need books for course in night school **PAY 10** to bank	You need books for course in night school **PAY 10** to bank	Grocery Bill **PAY 20** to bank	Grocery Bill **PAY 20** to bank
You won baseball pool **COLLECT 10** from each player	You won football pool **COLLECT 10** from each player	You won in numbers game **COLLECT 10** from Loan Shark	Welfare Check **COLLECT 15** from bank
...st payment on loan due **...AY Loan Shark 20%** ...f amount borrowed	You won at race track **COLLECT 15** from Loan Shark	You won in numbers game **COLLECT 10** from Loan Shark	Welfare Check **COLLECT 15** from bank
...st payment on loan due **...AY Loan Shark 20%** ...f amount borrowed	You won at race track **COLLECT 15** from Loan Shark	Bookie payoff **COLLECT 10** from Loan Shark	Welfare Check **COLLECT 15** from bank
...You were mugged **PAY 25** ...son with greatest debt	You were mugged **PAY 20** to person with greatest debt	Bookie payoff **COLLECT 10** from Loan Shark	Welfare Check **COLLECT 15** from bank

CUT OUT PLAY CARDS ALONG DOTTED LINE

You lost gambling on heavyweight fight **PAY 10** to each player	You lost baseball pool **PAY 10** to each player	You lost football pool **PAY 10** to each player	You won gambling on heavyweight fight **COLLECT 10** from each player
You lost at the race track **PAY 10** to Loan Shark	Your family needs medicine **PAY 15** to bank	Doctor bill for treating rat bite **PAY 20** to bank	Your family has the flu **PAY 10** to bank for doctor bill
You lost at the race track **PAY 10** to Loan Shark	Your family needs medicine **PAY 15** to bank	Dentist Bill **PAY 10** to bank	Another baby will be joining your family **PAY 30** to bank for doctor bill
You have stolen some money to pay debts **COLLECT 10** om person on your right	You have resorted to crime to pay your bills **COLLECT 10** from person on your right	You have been hustled **PAY 10** to person with greatest debt	You have been hustled **PAY 10** to person with greatest debt
Rent due **PAY 35** to collection agency	You were able to work overtime this week **COLLECT 10** from bank	Hospital Bill **PAY 75** to bank	Salary Check **COLLECT 25** from bank
Rent due **PAY 35** to collection agency	You were able to work overtime this week **COLLECT 10** from bank	Syndicate bribes you to lie before Grand Jury **COLLECT 10** from Loan Shark	Salary Check **COLLECT 25** from bank
Rent due **PAY 35** to collection agency	You were able to work overtime this week **COLLECT 10** from bank	Syndicate bribes you to give false information to the police **COLLECT 10** from Loan Shark	Salary Check **COLLECT 25** from bank
Rent due **PAY 35** o collection agency	You were able to work overtime this week **COLLECT 10** from bank	You won the Sweepstakes **COLLECT 100** from Loan Shark	You have found a wallet in front of the collection agency **COLLECT 50** from Loan Shark

CUT OUT PLAY CARDS ALONG DOTTED LI

HANDLES FOR LEADERS—YOUTH AND ADULT

AN EXPLOSION!

I've had it with congregations who tell me about their junior deacons, the young people who are the "youth representatives" on each board (but who do not have a vote), and the week when youth "take over" the church. These actions only contribute to the "get-out-as-soon-as-I-can" feeling that is an expressed or subconscious desire of many youth.

I'm up to "here" with reports of congregations regarding the youth representatives on boards who have failed to perform according to normal standards—standards that are usually vague and unachievable and normally not communicated to the new and uninitiated members of a board.

Look at it this way! You're the *only* adult member of a high school student council. The council is facing an issue that demands a decision.

- You know nothing of the past history of the council.
- You are not sure of the purpose of the council.
- You have little interest in what's going on; you are not even sure what the conversation is all about.

As the consideration of the issue comes to a close and the decision has obviously been made, one of the senior highs on the council turns to you and says:

What does our ADULT member think?

Does that help you to understand the dilemma?

Adults can help youth participate in the total life of the church.

ANOTHER HAT TO WEAR

by JOHN CARROLL

Adults who work with youth wear many hats:

- a hat for listening and understanding,
- a hat for helping when help is needed,
- a hat for asking the right questions,
- a hat for organization and planning,
- a hat of adult maturity.

One more hat must be tried for size. It's the hat of advocate.

One of the roles of the adult who works with youth is to be an advocate for the concerns and needs of the younger laity. This role will make it possible for youth to try their own ideas and develop their own abilities. You open some doors, stand back, let youth who enter through the door do their thing, and then stand ready to help them evaluate what happened.

The adult avocate needs to facilitate the participation of youth in the total life of the church. Youth are not an auxiliary to be called up when a banquet needs to be served or a room painted. If they are to find meaning in the church, their involvement must be of greater significance.

A continuing lament of the church is that "we are losing our kids." There is no simplified or single solution to this problem. Each dropout has personal reasons for giving up on the church. Some are tied into normal "rebellion" patterns; still other reasons are tied in with inadequate models of church life—models that fail to take seriously youth's participation in the congregation.

The advocate must ask its congregation: "Is the church really interested in the youth for the youth's sake?" Asking is not all. He or she must help answer the question.

The key idea in this article is that one of the reasons youth are leaving the church is that they are not involved in any significant way in the congregations to which they belong.

One educator has identified the three broad areas of youth concern as relationship, self-identity, and control.[1] Another educator defines these terms: Relationship is the youth's sense of the relation between himself, other people, and the world; self-identity is youth's sense of himself; control is youth's sense of his ability to make himself felt in his world.[2]

These concerns of youth must be met by the church who wants its younger members to have a positive experience in the community of faith. A positive experience can be defined as one in which the young person can struggle with and internalize for himself the content of the faith and find ways to express that faith in the congregation and through the congregation to the community. The positive experience responds to the concerns of identity, relationship, and control.

As advocate, you can begin the task of making the congregation conscious of youth by considering three questions. Ask them in the specific light of your congregation and not as philosophical generalities:

1. What should be the role of youth in your congregation in light of youth's "concerns"?
2. What changes in your congregational life need to be made to respond to the concerns of youth?
3. How can your congregation be retrained for this new style of congregational life?

Many congregations will find that radical changes in attitude, behavior, and structure need

---

[1] Gerald Weinstein and Mario Fantini, *A Model for Developing Relevant Curriculum* (Praeger, New York: Ford Foundation Publication, 1970).

[2] Terry Borton, *Reach, Touch, and Teach* (New York: McGraw-Hill Book Company, 1970).

113

to be made if youth are to find a meaningful place in the total life of the church.

Let's examine what this might mean in one specific area of congregational life: the power decision-making structure of the church.

One of youth's concerns is to control (influence) those decisions that shape his life. As an advocate, you need to help the church become concerned about meaningful youth participation in boards and committees. There are two ways to approach the problem:

Approach #1

Youth cannot be honest participants in the existing church structures since these structures do not minister to their needs. *Solution:* Either forget youth participation or change the structures.

Approach #2

Participation doesn't just happen; youth (and adults) need to be trained to be responsible participants. *Solution:* Work on preparation of youth and adults for the experience. Recognize that change in attitudes and behavior is essential for satisfactory participation by all concerned.

For some churches, the radical Approach #1 may be the only way. For others, Approach #2 will offer a positive solution.

If you select Approach #2, use the following guidelines to change attitudes and behavior relating to the planning/decision-making structures in your church.

1. The congregation should define what it means when it says YOUTH. A high school junior and a first-year law student may both be classed as youth, but their contributions may vary considerably.

2. The purpose for youth involvement in the planning/decision-making structures of the congregation should be clearly defined so that a fair evaluation of the contributions can be made. A clear definition might indicate that youth will:
   a. contribute new insights.
   b. share content and experience known only to their generation.
   c. assume responsibility in accord with their ability and experience.

3. A process should be designed which will enable youth to participate. Participation or involvement is not automatic or inevitable. The process should be aimed at helping youth and adults deal with change. Change will be necessary because these persons have not worked together in democratic structures where their contributions are seen as equal. Just as a golfer learns a new way to hold his putter to improve his stroke, youth and adults will need to learn new ways of conducting themselves in work groups in order to enable positive relationships.

4. Training should be planned for the youth and adult members of the organization that will equip them to coexist in the planning/decision-making function. Such training would, for instance, equip the mature adult with new insights for:
   a. handling his viewpoint and contributions, based on the "years of experience" of the

younger person.

b. freeing himself to gain insights and new growth from the young person.

The benefits of training are not one-sided. Youth will be exposed to various models of adult behavior. These models will allow them to develop and test life-styles necessary to their becoming adults.

5. Adults should plan specific ways in which they can support youth's involvement in the planning/decision-making organization. A sponsor concept is a possibility. An adult sponsor would act as a guarantor for a youth member of the work group. Guarantor implies that he would demonstrate responsible participation in the work group and guarantee the right of the young person to move into that role.

6. The participation of youth should be placed in context for the youth participants. They should:

a. be briefed thoroughly on the past history of the congregation.

b. be briefed thoroughly on the current priorities and concerns of the congregation.

c. be briefed thoroughly on the anticipations of the congregation related to their involvement.

d. be given a chance to explore the issues facing the congregation on their (youth) terms, while being encouraged to seek consultation and resources from the whole congregation.

7. Consider the questions of youth-adult participation in the planning/decision-making process that may be unique to your specific congregation. For instance, in the case of churches that involve close family ties, what does it mean when you have a parent and child or child and a close friend of the parent on the planning/decision-making body?

8. Some personal considerations of certain qualities of life, such as depth of sincerity, patience, willingness to change, must be made by all concerned.

9. Each adult member of the planning/decision-making organization must ask himself/herself: How would I feel if I were the only adult on the high school student council? What if, after lengthy deliberation on an issue (an all-youth deliberation), one of the youth turned to you and said:

"What does our adult think?"

In some congregations the matter of youth participation in the planning/decision-making process may really be part of a wider question. Is there a clear understanding of the participation of youth in the congregation in general?

The answer to this question should embody a commitment to youth ministry on the part of the church. This is a commitment to persons and their faith development, not to the maintenance of a specific established program. (Program is that which develops in response to the "faith need" of the particular gathering of youth in a given congregation. Program will change as it becomes necessary to make new responses to the concerns of youth.)

Youth ministry is an ongoing process, never completed, and seldom reaching heights of great fulfillment.

It is a ministry specializing in change. Its major constituency (the youth) rarely stays in one position long enough to be photographed. The pain of yesterday becomes rather quickly the joy of tomorrow. Resiliency is the word!

The advocate hat is one that means:

Listen—to youth—to adults,
Care—for youth—for adults,
Interpret—to youth—to adults.

Try it on for size!

WE'RE NOT REALLY AGAINST THE CHURCH; WE JUST DON'T HAVE ENOUGH TIME FOR IT

by WALTER PULLIAM

This article is written by a pastor about his church and its attempt to "turn on" to a relevant ministry with youth. His guidelines can assist you in your ministry.

"What turns youth on to the church?" is a perpetual question for those engaged in youth ministry, a question that the church should keep asking —groping to answer. No two groups of youth are ever the same. None are ever exactly alike. Therefore, *those who work with youth will keep on*

> *asking,*
> *searching,*
> *designing,*
> *trying, and*
> *evaluating.*

BUT

back to the question, "What turns youth on to the church?" We asked some of the youth and adults in our church to answer that question. They talked about what's been happening to them in our church's ministry with youth. These are their answers to our question of what can turn youth on to the church.

TUNED OUT! Several negative things surfaced immediately. Youth resent being forced into a "religious mold" based on traditional views of pious behavior. They express a need for prayer and worship but not necessarily the kind of style that has emerged out of the nineteenth century. What was good for the church elders in their days of youth (and as present adults) may not be appropriate to the needs of today's youth. Force youth to conform to standards not their own, and you lose them.

Many youth question the church's dedication to itself. They accuse it of "serving itself," of being dedicated to "churchy" purposes and practices that have come out of the past and which are not open to serious study and questioning. When church elders go on the defensive, get red in the face, and fail to take seriously the questions of youth about the meaning and place of the church in today's world, youth drop out.

NOT REALLY AGAINST THE CHURCH—JUST NOT ENOUGH TIME FOR IT   Many youth are not "really" against the ideals, commitments, and aims of the church. They simply are not turned on by them and would rather be doing something else. They just do not have enough time for a church that's not "really with it."

WHY?

Youth seem to feel that the "going things" are happening outside the church. Only outside of the church school, worship service, and youth groups, do youth feel free to create, shape, and do the things important to them. The "real action," in the thinking of many youth, is in movements and groups that are not a part of the church's organization and tradition. While there is no active campaign against the church, there is the resistance to become or remain a part of it. *Why get hung up with another thing?* seems to be the prevailing attitude.

TURNING ON!   But what turns youth on to the church? Here are some of

116

the guidelines developed by our youth for an active, purposeful, "Christian" church. Rate your church.

"HEY, I AM ME!"

AN INDIVIDUALIZED APPROACH. A person is a person (created in God's image) and must be treated as such. This means "caring for people." It does not mean using people or trampling over the views and ideas of a few in order to keep the majority happy. It means listening equally well to all people regardless of age.

HERE'S MY SPOT!

A FEELING OF BELONGING. It is important "to have a place where I can come and play, rap, engage in various kinds of group and personal experiences," said one young person. "We need a place where personal relationships can be formed. Youth desire an atmosphere that exudes warmth and friendliness, not the cold, hard chairs of institutional grayness." A room that can contribute to youth's sense of belonging is an important room indeed. It will be a room that reflects the life, hope, expectation, and experience of the group living in it. It will have a "lived-in look" because living will be going on in it.

OVER AND UNDER 30

A SHARING ACROSS AGE LINES. One young person noted: "Different age groupings may have different sets of anxieties, but currents of interest can cut through age groups." Interaction across age lines can help people shape opinions and directions. As one young person put it: "We're not that certain about all that we're doing, and we can use some

help." Youth do not want to be boxed into an age group. A PERSON WHO IS HONEST, NATURAL, AND OPEN IS A PERSON WHO CAN RELATE TO PERSONS WITH SIMILAR CHARACTERISTICS IN ANY OTHER AGE GROUP.

NOT ALL ALIKE

VARIETY AND OPTIONS. All youth are not alike! Don't expect all of them to do the same thing at the same time. Alternatives and varieties are needed. Subjects should be of interest and should be life centered. They should deal with issues that are current and important to youth. "We would like the freedom to go, do, and talk about things we feel are important to us. For example, if a class is really involved and does not attend worship, no one should be disturbed."

I CARE!

A CARING AND HELPFUL PLACE. The church is unique because it cares for persons as tasks are being done. It's a "God-education place." The church is "an educational center for living. It can be a solid backdrop for us. We need that." Another person said, "In our church, ripples are not tidal waves, so we don't get washed around. People appreciate opposing ideas and interesting viewpoints." Tidal waves occur when a church is afraid of free thinking.

HONEST AND OPEN

THE CHURCH SHOULD BE A SUPPORTIVE COMMUNITY. By design and attitude it should be a friendly place and an open one. It should be a place where people honestly try to say what they mean straight. It needs to be a place for deep sharing, developing strong friendships, and meeting people you can trust.

NO FAMILY-NIGHT DISHES

REDEMPTIVE WORTH AND REDEEMING CHARACTER IN THE ACTION ENTHUSE THE YOUTH. In other words, many young people are interested in *doing* important things, not maintaining organizations. So rather than serve on a nominating committee, it may be more desirable to have youth relate to a youngster in a hospital, or give some tender loving care to an old man nearing the end of life, or alert a case worker to some intolerable living condition. These kinds of activities will be more important to some youth than rehearsing in a youth choir or cleaning up a church bus. They would rather spend time with youngsters at a day care center than wash dishes for a family-night dinner. dinner.

WANT TO RELATE

CONTINUING RELATIONSHIPS ARE DESIRABLE. Anything done, whether within the group or by the group, should contribute to continuing life. While there may well be a one-time meeting or the necessity to meet a single one-time need of some person, generally things that smack of the "Thanksgiving-do-gooder-basket" approach are put down. Young people seem to be looking for the deep meanings and mutual benefits attendant to continuing personal relationships.

GRASS ROOT IDEAS

IDEAS EMERGE FROM THE GRASS ROOTS. Young people really appreciate this approach as opposed to having it "laid on them." Persons like to be creative and appreciate settings in which they can work out ideas and approaches on their own.

IN CONCLUSION

Over the years we have tried to keep track of where we have gone in our youth ministries. Our growth has had some dramatic upsurges and some regressions, but our graph shows a growing number of young people and adults relating to what we term "ministry with youth." More important than the numbers is the fact that all of us have grown in our understanding of life, have matured somewhat in the faith, and have come to appreciate our differences and similarities as youth and adults.

Further, our experience has been that when people become related to persons in common experiences, looking at life together in common search for answers, we are able to share our deep faith in Jesus Christ and his meaning as Savior and Lord. We are able to move to the Bible as a basic resource, listen seriously to the views of others, and in so doing experience the Spirit of Christ among us.

It is our experience that most young people with whom we come into contact are not actually against the church; they just haven't time for another extracurricular activity. But when we can individually relate to youth and put into practice some of the foregoing statements and experiences, they do not find the church to be a "fifth wheel." In most of our situations, building the relationship is a slow, hard process.

PHILOSOPHY BITS FOR THE ADULT WORKER WITH YOUTH

by KEITH L. IGNATIUS

you're an adult who has become a "minister with youth."

do you feel? About your job, that is? Comfortable? Insecure? Ready to go? Been through it before?

The following article may be your kind of reading material. *If you're new* to the job of working with youth, the article will provide some pointers for getting started on the right foot. *If you are an old hand* at working with youth, use the article as an evaluation checklist. Measure your ideas, beliefs, and practices as an adult worker with youth against the philosophy bits presented here. Regardless of who you are, this article is only a starting point for your reading.

now to explore in detail the meanings and implications of working with youth.

YOUTH AND ISSUES

You can evaluate a group's discussion by the emotional involvement of its participants. When youth get hooked, the juices start to flow and feelings are expressed. It's a relevant discussion when intellectual gymnastics are crushed beneath the weight of personal feelings.

YOUTH LANGUAGE

Youth want adults to be adults. In other words, be yourself. Do not try to imitate youth language or dress. The youth language that most adults try to use is so far behind that it "turns kids off" instead of gaining their confidence.

PERFECT AGE

There is no "perfect age" for an adult worker with youth. Don't be boxed in by the stereotype that youth prefer a younger adult, someone closer to their own age. It's untrue. Some of the most uptight people are between twenty and thirty. Freer thinking, honesty, ability to listen, and openness are some of the preferred characteristics in an adult. Maturity is the key—not how old you are.

NOT ALL ALIKE

Youth are not all alike. They have different needs, interests, and abilities. Do not expect one thing, one activity, to satisfy all of them. Several small groups rather than one large group may be needed. Never try to place all youth into one mold! They will resent you and the church that places them there. BE ALERT to the fact that youth in grades 8-10 will generally participate in organized activities. Older youth tend to pull out of the organized scene during their late high school years.

TALKING AS A FORM OF RECREATION

Talking is an important part of youth living. Wherever they gather, spontaneous conver-

119

sation erupts—some of it superficial, some boisterous, some intimate and personal. What a youth talks about depends upon where *he is*—emotionally and physically—at the moment—and *who he's with*.

One nagging criticism that many youth have about the church is that its organized activities stifle serious conversation. They feel that the "planned event" is always deemed more important than the personal conversation of the participants. "No one usually bothers to check it out," youth criticize.

Talking is important to youth. Often it is a form of recreation for them. A church should provide a place and a time for this unique kind of recreational experience.

A PLACE TO TALK

Youth like to be comfortable, and they are most comfortable when in their own groups. The more adults around, the less comfortable youth are. They are as hesitant and uncomfortable in meeting new youth as adults are in meeting strange adults.

Most communities do not have a "talking place" for youth. But an interesting phenomenon of our time is the drive-in restaurant. There is usually at least one drive-in restaurant in every town that is the "meeting place" for youth.

Why? Because this one drive-in restaurant will tolerate a lot of cars and activities in its parking lot. Sit-down restaurants, bowling alleys, and such places will not tolerate mass gatherings. Their business is dependent on people buying, and many people won't buy when too many kids are around.

Survey your community. Do youth have a place to go during the evenings, a place where they can sit and talk? A place without too many adults? A place where they can stay for a while without having to spend a great deal of money?

ALL ORGANIZATIONS UNDER SCRUTINY

Youth have always questioned and criticized "the organization." (Even you did as a youth.)

Questioning the establishment is a part of growing up, of trying to discover who you are in relation to other people, of establishing your own system of values.

Do not be alarmed if your youth point to the negative aspects of school and church. But do take youth seriously. Also remember that many of our institutions have been guilty of social injustices. As an adult, defend only the right things in those institutions. Criticize the wrong, or the gap between you and your youth will grow rapidly.

YOUTH AND WORSHIP

Youth, in general, want to "experience religious feelings" rather than go through a religious ceremony. Most church youth TOLERATE rather than appreciate Sunday morning worship. No matter what adults say that youth should think about worship, the Sunday morning service for most youth is a religious ritual that has little meaning and validity for them.

Worship in most churches is adult oriented. The challenge to appreciate worship is a one-way challenge. It goes out only to youth—not adults. Youth are called on to work hard at finding meaning in a service that satisfies adults. Adults seldom have to work at finding meaning in worship forms that appeal to youth.

This is not to say that youth want extravagant or "way-out" worship services. Most youth would prefer a mixture of traditional and contemporary forms of worship. They would prefer, at times, using twentieth-century hymns and folk music to the religious music of the "Model-T Ford" era. Since youth are an integral part of the church congregation, some modifications would seem to be in order.

OFFICIAL YOUTH REPRESENTATIVES

Don't rely too often on youth representatives reflecting the feelings and attitudes of youth in general. We would like to think that one group of youth can speak for another, but this is not true. All of us are different and speak out of our own needs and interests. The elected representatives, especially youth officers in school, are often seen as being a part of the establishment by many youth.

DOING OLD THINGS IN NEW WAYS

A good motto to follow when working with youth is to "do old things in new ways." When you repeat the same thing too many times, people stop listening. Do the same thing too often, and people stop coming.

For example, always think of three different ways to sing a hymn, pray, read a Scripture, and then choose the most appropriate form.

AND FINALLY

In working with youth, do not assume that your traditional adult ideas are the best for your youth. Check it out with them. What may be important to you may not be very important to your youth. But don't go on the defensive! Talk out the problem with them and work out a mutually satisfying solution.

As an adult, you do not have to respect anyone because he is young. Nor should you show disrespect because he is young. Do take youth seriously and let them participate in serious decision makings. "One of the things I hate most about adults," said one youth, "is that they listen to me on unimportant things but turn me off on important issues and decisions."

Good luck
    and good living.

Pepsi Generation Resources

THE KIND OF RESOURCES YOU WANT DON'T EXIST

The ultimate dream of every youth worker is to have the "right kind of resources at the right time in the right place." Impossible dream! Why? Because every experience and every event demands its own special kind of resource. Who could review, store, and afford to buy the tons of materials needed for every "opportunity" in the existence of a youth leader.

Yet people try. We receive hundreds of letters each year from people asking for the "newest thing" available in youth ministry. People want to be informed about the latest mailing lists, know all of the "what," "how," and "where" of youth ministry resources.

And people buy
file
buy
file
WHY? ← (and forget where they put them) tons of youth ministry resources each year.

It is the perpetual search for new ideas, for the things that turn on the kids and turn off the adults (adults who criticize poorly attended youth meetings).

Another impossible dream! Resources play a very minor part in the turning on of kids to creative group living.

PURPOSE OF THIS ARTICLE
—an introduction to the Coke-Can-Concept of Resources

The purpose of this article is not to provide another listing of books, movies, records (although we will do a little of that at the end).

The purpose rather is to "tune you in on the know" about the how and why of resources. We will provide some new definitions of resources and introduce you to the *Coke-Can-Concept of Resources*.

BUT FIRST THIS MESSAGE . . .

> ### WARNING . . .
> Dependence on resources may be hazardous to the health of your group. Resources should be selected because they will help a group do what it needs to do. Determine the need of the group and then select the resources. To do it any other way may be "fatal"!

Now Back to Our Article

The *Coke-Can-Concept of Resources* is simply a "new way of seeing things," of sensing the infinite possibilities in common, ordinary things. It is the belief that a resource is anything, everything, and anybody. A resource is anything that will help us accomplish whatever purpose it is that we are working on. Everything around us has the potential of being very useful to us, if we can only see its ordinary and nonordinary possibilities.

A RESOURCE IS BASICALLY YOU and the way you look at and see things. It is a style of living, a way of looking at common ordinary things and making them work for you in uncommon and unordinary ways. It is CREATIVE SEEING.

For example. Put down the magazine. In the next few minutes, go outside and find some things which will illustrate the fact "that God is alive and doing well in the world." What did you bring back?

Try another "Creative Perception Test."

Place in front of you an empty coke can (or a coffee can or any other kind of can). Write all the ways this empty can could be creatively used.

Now write all the ways this same can could be used with a worship service.

USING A COKE CAN CREATIVELY

USING A COKE CAN IN WORSHIP

You may want to brainstorm the possibilities with other people, family, coworkers, etc. It is a fun experience, but it is the

FIRST STEP toward the creative use of resources—seeing all the possibilities in a given object.

The experience also reinforces the idea that anything and everything—films, chairs, books, empty cans—have a useful use, depending on your purposes and the needs of the group.

The person in the know about resources therefore, operates on the principle that a resource is anything and everything that will help him get his purpose accomplished. It can and often does mean doing some crazy (or creative) thing like:

USING A FILM RESOURCE by
—running the film backwards
—turning off the picture and listening to the sound track
—using only the picture without the sound
—letting the audience write their own sound track and etc.

LET'S CONCLUDE THIS ARTICLE

A resource is basically you and your way of seeing and doing things. (Remember that statement.) It is also your neighbor. A resource is your neighbor, your group member's way of seeing things, his way of working, his talents, ideas, concerns, and interests. It is him as person.

For a youth group to succeed (to really succeed) every member of your group needs to know and feel that he can contribute something special to the life of the group. Each person needs to feel that he has some special resources which at some time will be needed by the group. Help each member understand his uniqueness and importance as a "people resource." Your group will turn itself on—
—not by cute techniques and faddish gimmicks but through the process of people power (the CREATIVE GIVING AND RECEIVING OF HUMAN resources).

NOW, BACK TO THE "THINGS KINDS OF RESOURCES."

Books, movies, records, and things like that can help people turn on to themselves. For that reason we offer the following listing of Easter resources.

But First This Message . . .

WARNING . . .

Dependence on resources may be hazardous to the health of your group. Resources should be selected because they will help a group do what it needs to do. Determine the need of the group and then select the resources. To do it any other way may be "fatal"!

THE SWITCH TO STEREO

by KEITH L. IGNATIUS

The world is built on man's ability to talk and to listen—to communicate. Talking comes easily. Listening (good listening) is much more difficult, a feat that some people never quite accomplish. But they try. They try! And they try again! While telling you all the time how they're trying.

"Talk and listening go together
    like a horse and carriage,

and
    you can't have one without the other."

That's communication!

GOOD LISTENING! THAT'S THE CLUE TO EFFECTIVE COMMUNICATION.
AND THE FOLLOWING ARE SOME CLUES TO GOOD LISTENING.

THE SWITCH TO STEREO!

"Mono-listening" is a new word for poor listening, also called "selective listening." I only hear what I want to hear. I listen. But I blot out, distort, forget those things you're saying that don't really fit my belief pattern. "Mono-listening" selects only the beginning, the middle, and the end of a statement. I never listen to the things in between.

MORAL: Switch to the stereo-sound. Get his sound and add your own. It makes for "sweet music" and good communication.

PASS THE SALT!

I've got an idea that
    I want you to understand.
I've got a feeling that
    I want you to feel.
Are you listening?

Pass the salt!

Communication occurs at two levels: Functional: "Pass the salt"; and the relationship level: "I've an idea and a feeling that I want to share with you."

We need to be understood at both levels. If I ask for the salt, I don't want the pepper passed. Similarly, I want my idea or feeling understood—after a very difficult process.

GOOD LISTENING creates an atmosphere in which people feel free to speak about things as they are—as they see them.

What do people talk about when they are around you?

TUNED IN

A good listener is tuned in to the speaker. Both speaker and listener are on the same frequency. There's little static between them. The message is getting through loud and clear.

Why?

The listener is not preoccupied with his own thoughts. He is listening to feelings as well as the words of the speaker. He's got time to listen. He believes in the person. And so he listens. The speaker "hears his listening" and is able to reveal more of himself. Communication takes place!

CANNOT NOT COMMUNICATE

We cannot NOT communicate. There's no way to stop communicating. Every twitch, eye expression, and body movement is saying something about us. People read us like a book. Too often what we're saying with our body is not what we're saying with our words. The body speaks louder and more honestly than our mouths. A trained listener —or even an untrained one—catches the discrepancy.

What are you saying when you say, "Yes, I've got plenty of time to talk" and THEN FURTIVELY LOOK AT YOUR WATCH?

MORAL!

No unintelligible speeches, please! (See 1 Corinthians 14:6-20.)

GUIDELINES FOR FILM VIEWING

by KEITH L. IGNATIUS

Films are not an end in themselves and must never be used that way. To expect a film to carry the full load of teaching is to court disaster. A movie is not an easy exit from serious program/session planning. The person who chooses to use a film is responsible for seeing that the viewer understands what he has experienced via the film.

To present a teaching film without adequate follow-up discussion is almost always a "cop out" on

THE FILM HAS BEEN SEEN, BUT WHAT HAS BEEN LEARNED?

the part of the leader. The viewer has learned "something" from the film—but what? The message the viewer received as a result of watching the film may be altogether different from what the leader expected or wanted. Disaster!

Some films come with adequate discussion guides. Others do not. If you need assistance in helping a group understand what they've seen in a film, the following guidelines may be helpful. They can be used with commercial films shown in downtown theaters or with the ones presented in the youth room of your church.

GETTING READY FOR THE FILM

1. Plan for adequate space, live outlets, window blinds, and "air." A hot, stuffy room means "dull heads" and a dozing mentality after the film has ended.

2. Allow adequate time for BOTH the film and discussion. Don't wipe out the teaching possibilities of your film by failing to provide enough talking space. Thirty minutes is a minimum amount for an adequate discussion of the film. Remember, too, that it will take time for the audience to switch from a passive, inactive viewing role to an active, talking one. It takes a while for the "juices to get started," so plan for the inevitable blinking and yawning.

3. A film can be seen by hundreds of people but should be discussed in smaller groups of five or less people. Why? The more people there are, the less "air time" each person has to air his views and opinions. Some people are inhibited in large groups but talk freely in smaller ones. A large group discussion usually has a "mishmash" of ideas and thoughts but few basic conclusions. Therefore, if you are blessed with a hundred or so youth in your group, plan for small intimate groupings of about five.

4. Review the film before showing it. This is called "planning ahead." You may get some ideas that you didn't have. You will also be free to "watch the audience watch the film." Go on to the next section for the reasons "why" you should watch the audience.

VIEWING THE FILM

Introduce the film by giving its main themes, where it takes place, and why it was chosen for this particular session. Arguments rage as to whether the viewer should be instructed to look

126

for certain things in the film. One side says such instruction helps the viewer to grasp the main idea of the film because he is alerted to watch for certain things. The opposition argues that such an alert prejudices the viewer and he can end up missing other important elements. The conclusion is yours. Use your own judgment. The writer usually does not ask the viewer to look for things.

Discussion leaders should watch the audience as they view the film. Note their general reactions. Where did they get restless?

WATCH THE AUDIENCE WATCHING THE FILM	—At what point in the film did they utter a sigh of relief? —Where was the nervous laughter? —What kind of audience talking is there?

These reactions can be a starting point for the discussion or can be used to probe for a deeper response to the film. The leader can simply ask, "At this point in the film, there was a lot of nervous laughter. What was causing it?"

DISCUSSING THE FILM

Two discussion approaches are suggested here. One is a series of questions which can be asked by a leader in order to help viewers recall the impact of the film. The other is a questionnaire which is to be completed by the viewer. The choice is yours.

RECALLING THE FILM

It is important that the viewer try to recall the total film rather than isolated parts. By the time the group answers the following series of questions, they will have reviewed the film and at the same time gotten ideas of how others were affected by the film.

1. Discuss GENERAL REACTIONS and feelings. Invite a general free-for-all kind of discussion. After a few minutes the leader can interpret with these questions:
   a. What character affected you most? Why?
   b. What part of the film did you like best? Least?
   c. What were some of the moods in the film?

2. Let some FEELINGS that were aroused by the film be expressed.
   a. Recall some of your feelings during the film. Were you sad, bored, happy, etc.? At what points did you feel this way?
   b. Recall some of the audience's moods. Was there any nervous laughing, whispering, tenseness, etc.?
   c. Interpret some of the reasons for these reactions. Why did people laugh, get tense, etc.? (At this point, the leader can also give his views as a result of having watched the audience during the film.)

3. Have the GENERAL THEMES described.
   a. In a sentence or two tell what was the film trying to say.
   b. How should the church (yours included) be related to the theme(s) expressed in the film?
   c. Were there any biblical themes expressed?

d. If you could write a new ending to the film, what would you write?

The following "Media Rating Form" is to be answered by each person. Have one copy for each person.

MEDIA RATING FORM

by Ronald E. Schlosser

Following the viewing of a film or television program, complete this form to indicate the extent of your interest and reaction. In the multiple-choice sections, check all items which apply.

1. My initial reaction to the program or film:
   _____exceptionally well done
   _____very realistic
   _____held my interest
   _____nothing unusual
   _____mediocre
   _____boring
   _____stupid
   _____other (describe):

2. Did the program or film rely upon the visual for its impact, or was it mainly verbal?

3. The characters were:
   _____true-to-life
   _____appealing
   _____somewhat believable
   _____stereotyped
   _____shallow
   _____other (describe):

4. To which character were you drawn most of the time? Which one repelled you? Why?

5. My attitude or mood at the end of the program or film:
   _____angry   _____sad
   _____happy   _____excited
   _____irritated   _____depressed
   _____confused   _____thoughtful
   _____stunned   _____inspired
   _____relaxed   _____other (describe):

6. Which scene do you recall most vividly? Why?

7. Themes or values which were dealt with:
   _____love   _____pleasure
   _____hate   _____pride
   _____justice (or injustice)____self-discovery
   _____forgiveness   _____power
   _____ambition   _____prejudice
   _____guilt   _____sensuality
   _____freedom   _____greed
   _____redemption   _____human rights
   _____reconciliation   _____suffering
   _____loyalty   _____other (describe):
   _____truth (or deceit)

8. The issues or themes dealt with were:
   _____realistically treated____contrived or phony
   _____current concerns   _____ridiculous
   _____unrelated to life   _____other (describe):
   today

9. What values were evident in the life-styles of the main characters?

MANAGING BEHAVIOR PROBLEMS WITH YOUTH by GARY BARMORE

INTRODUCTION

The purpose of this article is to provide some directions for working with youth whose behavior disrupts and offends a group's activities.

There are no quick tips for handling behavior problems. Because each youth is unique, each situation is different. We present here a brief series of steps an adult worker with youth may want to put into practice.

This article is written by a pastor who has had experience in dealing with behavior problems.

THE SITUATION

I am the assistant pastor in a suburban church, and our story began when one of our seventh-grade teachers finally came to me. She was desperate. One boy was constantly disrupting her class. The final straw came when Clay began spitting at her and other members in the class.

I asked the teacher what happens in class with Clay, putting the process in behavior sequence. Here is what I found out. CLAY MISBEHAVES: getting out of his seat at the wrong times; interrupting loudly when others are trying to talk; hitting, pushing, and kicking others; spitting on others. The teacher and her assistant correctly figured that Clay was needing and seeking attention. So they would DIRECT THEIR ATTENTION TOWARD Clay when he misbehaved in order to give him recognition and let him know that they cared for him. (The misbehavior is a "sign" of his need, and they respond.) However, when the misbehavior became intolerable, the teachers would STRONGLY REBUKE Clay and sometimes even render mild punishment. My response to the teacher was that she was doing the right things, but the timing was wrong. Any person continues and increases behavior which is followed by reward. Teacher attention, even punishment, is no doubt rewarding for Clay. Therefore, he is developing poor behavior because that is precisely the thing which brings him reward (attention). I suggested rearranging the consequences so that Clay's misbehavior would be completely ignored (thus bringing no reward). At the same time his GOOD behavior, which previously was ignored by the teachers, would receive immediate reward by means of attention. For instance, whenever Clay listens to a story, participates in an activity, or relates acceptably to another student, then the teacher will go to him, use his name, touch him, show him that he is loved and appreciated. Teacher attention would follow good behavior rather than poor behavior.

REASONS WHY

The teacher and her assistant promptly put this program into effect and within a month reported to me that Clay was behaving acceptably in class. His attitude as well as that of the entire class toward teaching-learning had been vastly improved.

I was able to share with this teacher specific counsel to manage a behavioral problem because of my personal exposure to a field of psychology called "behavior-modification therapy." The key insight in this approach is that PERSONS LEARN BEHAVIOR ON THE BASIS OF POSITIVE REINFORCEMENT (REWARD). Behavior that is reinforced continues and increases, while behavior that receives no reinforcement fades away—undergoes the process of extinction. The most powerful reinforcers are those which are immediately consequent (following) a particular behavior.

A loving application of behavior-modification therapy, or "consequent management," can help us better understand the behavior of adults and youth and plan ways to help them change undesirable behavior, as well as to strengthen good behavior. This therapy takes for granted that we DO have values and behaviors we want youth to gain; we want them to behave with openness, honesty, integrity, and care for others. This kind of therapy does NOT require the services of a professional; rather, implementation is possible by a layman with some minimum training. In fact, "consequent management" has been used by parents ever since the first mother said, "As soon as you make up your bed, you can go play ball." All of us, whether we like it or not, are behavioral scientists with varying degrees of skill. The way we respond to the words and actions of others directly influences their future behavior, and the other person's response to us affects the further direction of our behavior.

This is not to say that all behavior problems are simply solved without the aid of professionals. WHAT IT DOES SAY IS THAT MANY BEHAVIOR PROBLEMS ARE THE RESULT OF IMPROPER LEARNING AND CAN BE CORRECTED BY PROPER RELEARNING. When quite serious disturbances are evident, naturally a professional needs to be consulted.

STEPS TO CONSIDER

Here are the steps which a caring teacher can take to help a young person with behavioral growth:

1. *Write a precise description of the ongoing behavior which is undesired, as well as a description of the desired behavior.* For example, if a particular student disrupts group discussion by leaving his seat and making noise around the room, then we would work with "noisy out-of-seat behavior."

2. *Record the frequency with which the behavior occurs.* Continuing with our example of "noisy out-of-seat behavior," the teacher would record the number of times per session the student leaves his seat and creates a disturbance.

3. *Look at the apparent consequences of both the behavior that is occurring as well as the behavior that is desired.* It may be that the consequence of "noisy out-of-seat behavior" is that the teacher says, "Johnny, please take your seat," at which time not only the teacher but all class members are attending to Johnny. On the other hand, when Johnny remains in his seat, he may get no attention whatever.

4. *Modify the consequences of the behavior so that good behavior is rewarded and poor behavior is ignored, and at the same time continue measuring the frequency with which the behavior occurs.* Using our example, the teacher might ignore Johnny

when he is out of his seat; but when he is in his seat and behaving in a way that does not disturb others, the teacher could respond positively to him, letting him know what a fine participant he is. The continuing record of his behavior is essential in order to determine if this consequent-management is helping, hurting, or is neutral regarding the problem.

A teacher can follow the same steps to help a quiet student learn to participate. The behavior to be extinguished is total silence, while the desired behavior is vocal participation. In arranging the consequences, the teacher would refrain from giving attention to the student after silence (e.g., asking why he is so quiet, won't he please talk); rather, the teacher would quickly respond and reinforce any vocal behavior that occurs.

CONCLUSION

Obviously, it is important to determine exactly what is reinforcing to a particular young person. I believe that concerned personal attention by a teacher—during or after class—remains the most powerful reinforcer available. Even this, however, can have an opposite effect if given in a condescending or gooey manner. Helpful teacher attention can take the form of eye contact, touch, words of understanding or humor, recognition of earnest participation, and praise.

Personal attention is a "social" reinforcer. "Nonsocial" reinforcers, such as candy, points toward a Disneyland trip, or assignment of privileged duties, can also be used but should always be yoked with social reinforcement so that the latter will eventually possess full reinforcing value in itself.

Of utmost importance is that the teacher maintain his or her focus upon the PERSON and his growth, not just the problem. With this in mind I am convinced that behavior-modification therapy provides a very helpful tool for parents, teachers, and pastors in order to facilitate behavioral maturing in the lives of persons with whom we minister.

THE ICEBREAKER

by KEITH L. IGNATIUS

INTRODUCTION

Leaders need to do everything possible to make the entry of a new person into an old group as easy as possible. If your new crop of youth is to survive the immediate test of "newness," "strangeness," and "cliques," the old and new must be mixed gently. Acceptance into a group can come slowly.

PURPOSE OF THIS SESSION

To help a group of new people be accepted into their new group.

This session can be used with youth or adults, or youth and adults together.

Let's go!

People coming into a new group usually have trouble mixing. Except for a few brave souls, youth will try to stick together, and the adults will find solace in each other.

YET

if a group is ever going to do anything meaningful, these cliques must be broken up. Time is always important so that the quicker people get together and past the superficial trivia, the more jobs the group will get done.

HOW?

Not the usual way

My name is _____.

I am sixteen.

I like to _____.

Try this instead—

Get people past the name-giving, hand-shaking stage by getting them:

- To move about in large groups
  small groups
  twos and threes
- To laugh at themselves
- To be slightly anxious
- To be slightly embarrassed
- To do things in such a way as to give them something to talk about:

(Silly little experiences they would never dream of doing by themselves.) People always want to put their best foot forward. Have them do some unexpected things and they "fall flat on their faces" in a pillow of feathers.

ICE SHATTERING

1. *People circulate,* looking at each other. No talking. Do this for a minute or two or three. Then have each one find a partner. Each team of two designates one of them as leader.

2. *Mirror-Mirror* (teams of two)
   a. No talking. The leader does any kind of antics. The follower follows. Roles are switched after one minute.
   b. Person introduces himself to his partner. Partner "mouths" the words, hand and face movements. Switch roles after one minute.
   c. Find a new partner. Designate leader.
   d. Leader introduces himself. Partner echoes (out loud) his words. Switch when leader calls.
   e. Put a couple of teams in the center of the group. They repeat their performance (1-2 minutes for each team).
   f. New partners.
   g. Gibberish (4 minutes).

      Partners talk (at the same time) about something that has happened to them during the month. When the leader calls "gibberish," they continue their story in unintelligible sounds. When the leader calls "talk," they resume talking. Leader does this several times.

h. Put a couple of "gibberish" couples in the center of the group (1-2 minutes for each team).

3. *Shoes and Sharing* of personal items (teams of two)

Shoes are removed and placed in the center of the floor. Partners describe shoes to each other. They find each other's shoes.

4. *Words and Thoughts*

Continue the getting acquainted:
—Stare at a new partner.
—Write down what you feel about him now (2-3 words).
—Write down three questions you'd like to ask him.
—Choose the most important one and ask it.

5. *People Movers*

Moving from two—to four—to eight (builds self-confidence and security).

Two people
can talk easier and share a lot and solidify vague personal ideas.

Four people
mean a wider variety of ideas—stimulation—self-confidence rises.

Eight people
sound and look more like an average group. Cause more intermeshing of ideas and negotiating. Demand more time for talking.

6. *Imaginary ball*

Ten to twenty minutes may be used for this activity. The group is broken into small groups of ten to fifteen people. They stand in a circle and in the center of the circle is an imaginary ball. A person volunteers to pick up the ball and begins tossing it back and forth to anybody he wants to in the circle. Each person is allowed to make the ball any size or shape, or pass it in any way he wants. It can be a balloon, marble, football, anything. The group plays for ten minutes, and the members spend ten minutes discussing how they felt about the experience.

7. *Quotations*

People are seated. Numbered slips of paper are handed to them. On each slip has been written a quotation from the Bible, newspaper, magazine, or a book. Then the leader instructs the person holding number one to rise, read the quote, and say anything about the quote that comes to mind. When he finishes, number two rises, and so on. The numbers should be scattered about the group so that people are not rising one after another down the line of chairs.

8. *Hands, Hands*

Using only hands, say "hello" and "how you are feeling."
Be angry with hands.
Make up.
Be joyful.
Talk.

9. *Names*

Ask for a volunteer to go to the chalkboard or a newsprint sheet and slowly, very slowly, write his full name, talking about it as he writes, saying whatever comes to his mind as he very, very slowly writes his name. Then, ask him questions about how he feels about his name, or how he felt as he wrote it. Next, ask him to say his full name. Then ask the group to say his name six times, speaking clearly and positively, giving a variety of inflections.

WHAT'S GOING ON?

by KEITH L. IGNATIUS

PURPOSE:

To help the group evaluate honestly a program session.

INTRODUCTION

Leaders, youth and adults, need to know what's going on inside the members of their group. They need to "keep in touch" with the realities of the situation. The evaluation chart for "What's Going On" can help put you and the group in touch with each other. Evaluate continuously. A hit-and-miss approach really won't help.

There is a twofold purpose in evaluation: (1) to get an honest evaluation or feedback on a particular session; (2) to help create an open atmosphere of honesty and trust in which the group members will feel free to express their opinions and feelings. To create such an atmosphere takes time. Continuous evaluation will move you toward that objective as people begin to realize that you are serious about wanting their personal views.

DIRECTIONS

- Duplicate a copy of the Evaluation Chart for each person or copy it on a large sheet of paper big enough for all to read.
- Each person silently answers each question. Some of the questions are yes and no. Others require one or more words.
- Divide the group into threes to discuss the answers. Then each group of three will share with the total group.
- On a chalkboard or large sheet of paper write the question WHAT HAVE WE LEARNED FROM THIS EXPERIENCE? List the responses of the group as to how the session could have been changed, modified, improved. Then ask WHERE DO WE GO FROM HERE? List the steps they suggest.

EVALUATION CHART

1. a. Were you satisfied with the group session today?   Yes___ No___
   b. How many of the group do you think found this session interesting? _____

2. a. Was the conversation/discussion dominated by a few persons?   Yes___ No___
   b. How many of the group will think the discussion was dominated by a few? _____

3. a. Was the conversation honest?   Yes___ No___
   b. How many people were being honest in their remarks? _____

4. a. Did you get to say everything you wanted to say?   Yes___ No___
   b. How many of the group will say they did not say everything they wanted to say? _____

5. a. What word would you use to describe your feelings right now? _____
   b. What word do you think most of the group will use as a description of their feelings? _____

6. What one specific thing did you learn as a result of this session?

7. What should have been done differently?

133

Section 5

RESOURCES

There is a flood of resources on the market today. Description of each resource would take more pages than are available here. A range of resources for groups with different interests and beliefs has been provided. You should preview resources before purchasing, when possible, to determine if they are appropriate for your group. The prices listed are subject to change.

Symbols

B: Book
F: Film
FS: Filmstrip
MM: Mixed Media
P: Picture or Photo
Ph: Pamphlet
R: Record
SG: Simulation
    Game
T: Tape

STUDY/ACTION RESOURCES

THE BIBLE

SOS (Switched-On Scripture) Series (T)

A series of cassette tapes which provide guidance and resources for group Bible study. By Dennis Benson. The six 60-minute tapes provide enough material for a six-session course. Includes leader's guide. Order from: Abingdon Press, 201 Eighth Ave. S., Nashville, TN 37202. Complete Set $39.95.

SOS 1: Acts
SOS 2: Acts
SOS 3: Jonah
SOS 4: First John
SOS 5: James
SOS 6: Psalm 23

To See, To Hear, To Choose

Cooperative Curriculum course on the meaning of the gospel for junior highs.

Teacher's Guide: 80 pages plus soundsheet, $1.95.

Pupil's Book: 32 pages, 75¢

Available at denominational bookstores.

The Way of the Wolf (MM)

Two record albums and a book which flesh out the gospel message.

Order from: The Seabury Press, Inc., 815 Second Ave., New York, NY 10017.

CAREER GUIDANCE

Church Vocations—A New Look (B)

By Murray J. S. Ford. Valley Forge, Pa.: Judson Press. $2.50.

Describes a wide variety of occupations related in some way to the church—both the institutional church and the church-in-the-world. Especially valuable for counselors who guide youth in choosing occupations.

Available in religious bookstores.

Life Careers (SG)

A simulation of certain features of the labor market, the education market, and the marriage market.

Sale $35.00 from The Bobbs-Merrill Co., Inc., 4300 W. 62nd St., Indianapolis, Indiana 46268.

Occupational Outlook Handbook (B)

Trends and information on occupations. Published every two years.

Order from: U. S. Government Printing Office, Washington, DC 20402. $2.25.

Vocation and Church Careers Kit (Ph)

Contains: *A Listing of Church Occupations*
College Majors and Careers in the Church
Resources on Vocation and Church Occupations
Student Financial Aid from Church Sources
What Is a Church Occupation?

Produced interdenominationally. Order from: Department of Ministry, National Council of Churches, 475 Riverside Drive, New York, NY 10027. $6.95.

Workforce

Bimonthly periodical with articles on social changes, efforts, and ideas for implementing social change through vocation. For information contact publisher: Vocations for Social Change, Inc., Box 13, Canyon, CA 94516.

What's Worth My Life? (MM)

A study unit for junior highs that focuses on the values, commitments, and goals that persons have determined as worth their lives. Folder with newspaper and variety of special resources, plus leader's guide.

Order from: Christian Board of Publication, Box 179, St. Louis, MO 63166. $3.50.

CHRISTIAN FAITH AND PERSONAL GROWTH

Disco-Teach Series

The Mission Singers perform popular songs, and accompanying leader's guides enable a group to discuss the message contained in the songs. All material is pretested in classroom situations before

recording. Six-album series.

Publishing by Abingdon Press, Nashville, TN 37200. $6.95. (Available in religious bookstores.)

Prayer—Who Needs It? (B)

By Annette Walters. Camden, N.J.: Thomas Nelson & Sons. $1.95. A contemporary look at prayer. Part of the Youth Forum series.

Sim-Soc (SG)

A simulation game that can be played for as long as a week, or as short as three rounds. Simulates society with participants seeking employment, earning currency, buying, traveling, hiring other people, etc. For 20 players or more.

Sale $3.95 per manual from: The Free Press, 366 Third Ave., New York, NY 10022.

Time Is My Own! (MM)

A study unit for junior highs on the stewardship of leisure time. Folder with newspaper and variety of special resources, plus leader's guide.

Order from: Christian Board of Publication, Box 179, St. Louis, MO 63166. $3.50.

The Two Faces of Faith (FS)

Explores the two ways in which Christians express their mission: through participation in the worship, nurture, and fellowship of the church and through their response to situations in daily life. Reading script and guide.

New York: Friendship Press. $7.50. (Available from denominational film distributors.)

The Value of Life (P)

Set of 22 black and white pictures, each about 18 inches square, by professional social worker and photographer, Daniel J. Ransohoff.

Order from: The Seabury Bookstore, 815 Second Avenue, New York, NY 10017. $5.00.

Values (SG)

A simulation game that explores what is important to each player and why. Clarifies feelings and provides for a dimension of encounter that helps players grow and change.

Comes complete with gameboard, spinner, tokens, instruction sheet, situation cards. For 3-6 players. New York: Friendship Press. $5.95. (Available in religious bookstores.)

COMMUNICATION

Cornell Candid Camera Collection (F)

Short film segments from Allen Funt's television series, "Candid Camera," are available for educational use. All are 16mm; running times vary. Some are b & w; others in color.

A few of these films might be useful in discussions of communication:

High School: Students are left alone in the principal's office with a letter supposedly criticizing their behavior on a school trip.

Good Samaritan: A Candid Camera staff member asks people for directions in New York, and at the same time drops garbage on the sidewalk.

Movie Price Changes: As people wait in line for movie tickets, the price is increased fifty cents.

All films are available *for purchase only.* Average price is $30.00. For catalog, write to: Du Art Film Laboratories, Inc., Cornell Candid Camera Collection, Du Art Film Building, 245 W. 55th St., New York, NY 10019.

Gold Is the Way I Feel (F)

Youth comment on their world as they talk about their own artwork. Useful for across-generation communication, as well as for stimulating creativity in youth.

16 mm, color; 9 min. Rental $10.00 from: American Baptist Films, Valley Forge, PA 19481.

Message to No One (F)

Portrays a "typical" suburban family situation where many talk and few listen. Recommended for local church parent-youth program.

16mm, color; 30 min. Rental $12.50 from: American Baptist Films, Valley Forge, PA 19481.

DRUGS, ALCOHOL, SMOKING

Drug Information Program (MM)

Four 16 mm documentaries in sound and color take on the appeals and hazards of drugs: *Scag*—heroin; *Weed*—marijuana; *Ups/Downs*—amphetamines and barbiturates; *Acid*—LSD. A drug identification chart, an instructor's handbook, and a student's handbook extend the impact of the films. For information, write to: Instructional Materials Division, Dept. 10A-10, Encyclopedia Britannica Educational Corporation, 425 North Michigan Ave., Chicago, IL 60611.

Drug Information Series (FS)

Straight, unadorned facts about drugs and drug abuse.

1. *Sedatives* ($26.00 with record)
2. *Stimulants* ($26.00 with record)
3. *Narcotics* ($26.00 with record)
4. *Psychedelics* ($26.00 with record)
5. *Marijuana: What Can You Believe?* ($48.50 —2 fs; 2 records)

Order from: Guidance Associates, 757 Third Ave., New York, N.Y. 10017

Family Life Filmstrips, Series I (FS)

An objective overview of vital, current health areas. For junior high up.

1. Tobacco and Your Health
2. Alcohol and Your Health
3. Venereal Disease and Your Health
4. Drug Misuse and Your Health

Each filmstrip with teacher's guide, $7.00. Set of 4 filmstrips, 2 records, 4 teacher's guides: $32.50. Order from: Family Life Publications, Inc., P.O. Box 427, Saluda, NC 28773.

Smoke (F)

A satirical film depicting the reasons people smoke. 16mm, b & w; 10 min. Rental $6.00 from: Cinema 16, 175 Lexington Avenue, New York, NY.

Young People and Drinking (B)

By Arthur H. Cain. New York: John Day Co. $4.75. A psychologist who specializes in treating alcoholics provides information on which youth can make wise decisions for themselves.

ECOLOGY

Earthcare Packet (MM)

Packet of materials on the various aspects of Christian concern for the environment, including a book, *New Ethic for a New Earth,* leader's guide, and resource pamphlets.

New York: Friendship Press. $3.95. (Available in religious bookstores.)

Ecology Probe-Planet Earth (F)

A serious environmental problem is dealt with by studying the problem through a science-fiction treatment. The film studies many aspects of ecology and strikes a final note that man must solve these problems.

Color; 10 min. From: Fordham Publishing Co., 2377 Hoffman Street, Bronx, NY 10458.

International Mission

Baldicer (SG)
A simulation game dealing with food production and distribution. Stresses the interrelated nature of world economy. For twenty players.

Guide on "India" for Adult and Youth Groups (B)
By Marilyn Hill. New York: Friendship Press. $1.35.

A study of *India: One-Sixth of the World's People* is a large undertaking, but the use of this interesting guide will help to give a group direction. Full of suggestions for some of the many ways to build a study into your church program, the Hill guide coordinates Friendship Press materials and outside resources into a workable study.

Listening In on India (R)
Indian music, languages, and worship patterns, interviews with Indians in various fields, and everyday experiences of an Indian child all help to make this a unique resource. Designed for use across the age groups, the record includes on one side material of particular interest to juniors, and on the other, material for youth and adults.

New York: Friendship Press. $3.95. (Available from religious bookstores.)

Mother India's Children (B)
By Edward Rice. New York: Friendship Press. $2.95.

Indian teenagers talk about themselves and their country, giving an intense and personal view of modern India. Among those the author talked with are a Brahman wife, married at fourteen, a teenage guru, Sikhs and Parsis, students and office workers. Highly illustrated with photographs by the author.

Photo Sutra: Pictures of India (P)
By Edward Rice. New York: Friendship Press. $1.50.

Eight black and white photos showing a cross section of Indian life. A well-known photojournalist, Rice gives insights into the real India through his pictures and also through his captions. These pictures are suitable for teaching. They also could be used for decoration—all eight at one time or rotating one at a time during a study.

Justice and Civil Liberties

Get Out There and Do Something About Injustice (B)
By Margaret E. Kuhn. New York: Friendship Press. $1.95.

A study-action manual to work toward doing faith and having justice, an alphabetic way of saying, "a guide for study, reflection, inquiry and action in response to what God is doing in the world." This is a book for action, but action backed up by a strong basis of knowledge and faith. There is extensive material for use in either traditional or experimental ways. Where the group using this manual "is" will direct the type of use.

Guide on "Faith and Justice" for Adult and Youth Groups (B)
By L. Wayne Bryan. New York: Friendship Press. $1.35.

Bright, creative, fresh ways of using the materials for a study of "Faith and Justice." Aids to study included here will stimulate interest in adults, youth, and young teenagers. Author shows how to use Friendship Press materials and resources you can discover and develop for yourself.

Up Against the Law: The Legal Rights of People Under 21 (B)
By Jean Strouse. New York: New American Library. $1.25.

Explanation of laws which are particularly relevant to youth, in such areas as: students' rights, marriage, drugs, sex, driving, the draft.

Peace

The Holy War (F)
A film of Cliff Robertson·reading the "Black Horse Prayer" written by Dr. Gorden Livingston. The message of the film is simple and clear: a Holy War can be fought in the name of all things save one—the name of God.

16mm, b & w, 8 min. Rental $10.00 from: SANE, 1411 Walnut St., Room 920, Philadelphia, PA 19102. *Rental within 24-hour bus service of Philadelphia only.*

The Selling of the Pentagon (F)
An original CBS production, this uncompromising documentary focuses on major areas of the Pentagon's public relations activities which reportedly cost from $30 million to $190 million. 16mm, color; 60 min. Rental $25.00 from: SANE, 1411 Walnut St., Room 920, Philadelphia, PA 19102. *Rental within 24-hour bus service of Philadelphia only.*

POVERTY

If I Were You (B)

By Barbara Smith. New York: Friendship Press. $1.75.

If I were you . . . what would my life be like in a situation of wealth . . . or want? A group project book for early teens to stimulate a deeper awareness of the injustices poverty often inflicts on its powerless victims.

Liberate the Captives (FS)

New York: Friendship Press. FS with script $7.50. FS with record $10.00. (Available from denominational film distributors.)

Shows how people of low economic status in a community can be brought together and organized to start working toward solutions of their own problems. Color filmstrip.

RACE RELATIONS

Black Resources Center (MM)

For information about current black resources contact: Black Resources Center, Department of Educational Development, Division of Christian Education, National Council of Churches of Christ in America, 475 Riverside Drive, Rm. 720, New York, NY 10027.

Bury My Heart at Wounded Knee (B)

By Dee Brown. New York: Holt, Rinehart & Winston, Inc. $10.95.

Describes the "plunder" of American Indians by the white man during the second half of the nineteenth century.

Christian Beliefs and Anti-Semitism (B)

By Charles Y. Glock and Rodney Stark. New York: Harper and Row, Publishers. $1.95.

A report about an empirical study of the churches and anti-Semitism. Asks: "Does the Christian faith currently have any effect on attitudes toward Jews?"

The Irishman (F)

A short TV spot on race relations. 16mm, color; 30 sec. Rental $5.00 from: Librarian, Division of Mass Media/The Board of National Missions of the United Presbyterian Church in the U.S.A., Rm. 1901, 475 Riverside Dr., New York, NY 10027.

SEX AND FAMILY LIFE

About Venereal Disease (FS)

A 24-frame filmstrip accompanied by 12″ LP 33 1/3 rpm record, produced by Audio-Visual and Health Education Sections of Los Angeles City Schools with the Los Angeles County Health Department.

Order from: Family Life Publications, Inc., Box 427, Saluda, NC 28773. $13.50.

Facts About Sex (B)

By Sol Gordon. New York: John Day Co. $1.90. A first book about sex for young people who do not like to read but want to know. Short, direct, concrete information well illustrated for sixth-grade reading level.

God, Sex and Youth (B)

By William E. Hulme. St. Louis: Concordia Publishing Co. $1.75.

Stresses Christian religion as a guide to sexuality values.

Growing Up Straight: What Every Thoughtful Parent Should Know About Homosexuality (B)

By Peter and Barbara Wyden. New York: Stein & Day Publishers, $6.95.

What all parents, teachers, and counselors should know about homosexuality.

Male/Female (B)

By Robert R. Hansel. New York: The Seabury Press, Inc. $1.75.

Contains leader's guidance and student's material for junior-high course in sex education.

Mates and Roommates: New Styles in Young Marriages (Ph)

By Eda J. LeShan. Public Affairs Pamphlet No. 468.

Discusses old and new life-styles and their expression in the institution of marriage.

Order from: Public Affairs Pamphlets, 381 Park Ave. South, New York, NY 10016. 35¢.

The Party (F)

A sensitive and probing portrayal of the sexual attitudes of six youth.

16mm, b & w; 28 min. Rental $11.95 from: American Baptist Films, Valley Forge, PA 19481.

WORSHIP/CELEBRATION

Alleluia
Songbook for inner-city parishes.
Order from: Cooperative Recreation Service, Inc., Delaware, Ohio.

Banners and Such (B)
A creative approach to banner making, written from actual workshop experiences.
Order from: Center for Contemporary Celebration, 1400 East 53rd. St., Chicago, IL 60615. $4.00.

Buttons
Three original designs on buttons which can be passed out during celebrations:
  1. Ankh: life symbol
  2. Whole Earth—Whole People
  3. Let Us Live
Order from: Center for Contemporary Celebration, 1400 East 53rd. Street, Chicago, IL 60615. 35¢ each.

Celebration (MM)
Worship resources, including two sound sheets of traditional and contemporary music.
Published by Graded Press, Nashville, TN $3.95.

Celebration for Modern Man (R)
A new concept in acoustical liturgy recorded by the Dukes of Ken jazz ensemble and the Voices of Celebration.
Order from: Center for Contemporary Celebration, 1400 East 53rd. St., Chicago, IL 60615. $5.35.

Change (MM)
A multimedia presentation with three reels of film (two are silent) to be run simultaneously on three 16mm film projectors and a wall large enough to project three images side by side, or three screens. Content covers the change in such areas as ecology, medicine, technology, and the concepts of God.
Rental $13.00 from: Division of Mass Media, Rm. 1901, 475 Riverside Dr., New York, NY 10027.

The Everybody Gap: A Folk-Rock Liturgy (MM)
A unique folk-rock service. Kit includes scripts, staging directions, color slides, and stereo album.
Order from: Contemporary Drama Service, Box 457, Downers Grove, IL 60515. $15.50.

Hymns Hot and Carols Cool
Singable tunes with words and faith.

Order from: Proclamation Productions, 7 Kingston Ave., Port Jervis, NY 12771. $1.00.

Let Us Break Bread Together (B)
By Carl Staplin and Dale Miller. St. Louis, Mo.: Bethany Press. $1.25.
Guide for a contemporary Communion service. Includes songs with guitar accompaniment.

A Time to Dance (B)
By Margaret Fisk Taylor. $2.95.
How to use symbolic movement or interpretive dancing in worship/celebration.

COMMUNITY MINISTRIES

The Coffee House Ministry (B)
By John D. Perry, Jr. Richmond, Va.: John Knox Press. $3.50.
Planning and building a coffee house and ministering through it.

Invest Yourself
Listing of involvement and action opportunities available to high school juniors and seniors and those over eighteen years of age. Approximately 26,000 specific openings in several hundred projects.
Order from: Commission on Volunteer Service and Action, 475 Riverside Drive, Room 830, New York, NY 10027. $1.00.

Issues and Action Packet (MM)
A multimedia packet to help a group explore why Christian action is a biblical mandate and to provide the group with skills for carrying out appropriate action.
  The Scene: 35mm slides illustrating major issues confronting American society. ($16.50)
  The Sound: 5½ min. record of sounds of American culture and counterculture. ($1.25)
  Multimedia Methodologies: How-to suggestions for using multimedia items in packet. ($1.05)
  Plumb Lines for Action: The meaning of ethical action. $1.05.
  The Draft—Decision, Issues, Actions: Suggestions for action in relation to the draft law. $1.05.
  Population: Controlled or Out of Control? Outline of the current population crisis. $1.05.
  The Environment and You: A primer on the crisis in the quality of our environment. $1.05.
  Hunger and Poverty: Dimensions of hunger and poverty in the United States. $1.05.

A Piece of the Action: 13-frame cartoon filmstrip indicating the need for organized action. $4.95.

Growing as a Group: Helpful techniques for enhancing group trust, cohesiveness, and processes of effective decision making. $1.05.

Action-Planning Workbook: A workbook to help the group devise concrete plans and strategies for action in relation to any problem the group wished to tackle. 80¢.

Celebrating in Action: Ideas for contemporary acts of worship in the midst of a world in change. $1.05.

Use Guide: Leader's guide. Order two or three for group leaders. 80¢.

Packet prepared by the Division of Christian Education of the United Church Board for Homeland Ministries, 1505 Race Street, Philadelphia, PA 19102. (Available in some religious bookstores.) $27.00 for packet. (Prices for individual pieces given above.)

Liberate the Captives (FS)

New York: Friendship Press. FS with record $10.00. FS with script $7.50. (Available from denominational film distributors.)

Shows how people of low economic status in a community can be brought together and organized to start working toward solutions of their own problems. Color filmstrip.

Way to Go, Baby!

By Eugene Langevin. Nashville: Abingdon Press. $2.95.

Describes a unique mission to street-corner youth.

LEADER DEVELOPMENT

Adventuring with Youth (B)

A loose-leaf notebook for the advanced adult worker with youth. Designed for "building a group in which each member is sensitive to needs, concerns, and feelings of the others."

Order from: Friends Central Offices, 101 Quaker Hill Drive, Richmond, IN 47374

Gaming (B)

By Dennis Benson. Nashville: Abingdon Press. $5.95.

Helps for leaders and groups who want to create their own learning games. Includes 2 records which serve as resources for games described in the book.

Learning Is Change (B)

By Martha Leypoldt. Valley Forge, Pa.: Judson Press. $2.95.

Designed to help leaders change so they can help their groups change.

Slide and Film Making Manual (B)

How to make slides and films without a camera. Order from: Griggs Educational Service, P.O. Box 362, Livermore, CA 94550. $3.00.

Television-Radio-Film for Churchmen (B)

Edited by B. F. Jackson, Jr.
Nashville: Abingdon Press. $6.50.
How to use television, radio, and film in the church.

Teaching and Learning: Grades 7-8 (F)

A color film which shows actual class sessions with junior highs and discusses the methods used. 16mm, color; 22 min. Rental $12.50 from: American Baptist Films, Valley Forge, PA 19481.

CATALOGS

Argus Communications

Tapes, posters, books, buttons.
Order from: Argus Communications, 3505 North Ashland Ave., Chicago, IL 60657.

Audio-Visual Resource Guide (B)

Over 1,800 listings of films, filmstrips, recordings, and slides, evaluated for religious education.
Order from: National Council of Churches, 475 Riverside Drive, New York, NY $3.95.

Contemporary Drama Service

Catalog of services. Includes drama playbits and entertainments.
Order from: Contemporary Drama Service, Box 457, Downers Grove, IL 60515.

Drug Abuse Catalog

Listing of materials related to drug abuse.
Order from: Presbyterian Distribution Service, 225 Varick St., New York, NY 10014. $1.00.

Full Circle

Interesting posters, books, films.
Order from: Full Circle, 218 East 72nd Street New York, NY 10021.

Guides to Educational Media (B)

By Margaret I. Rufsvold and Carolyn Guss. A list of media catalogs for: films (including free films), filmstrips, kinescopes, records, tapes, pro-

grammed instruction materials, slides, transparencies, and videotapes. Prepared for public school personnel, but helpful for religious educators also. Some catalogs are free.
Order from: American Library Association, 50 East Huron St., Chicago, IL 60611. $2.50.

Resources Galore (Ph)
Listing of fresh resources for creative educational ministries in the church.
Order from: Gramercy Plaza B-F, 130 East 18th St., New York, NY 10003. $1.00.

PERIODICALS
(TO KEEP UP WITH NEW RESOURCES)

Mass Media Newsletter
Biweekly newsletter reviewing new resources, especially films and TV programs.
Subscription $10.00 per year. Order from: Mass Media Ministries, 2116 North Charles St., Baltimore, MD 21218.

Media Mix
Up-to-date information on films, TV, print, recordings, and other media. Published eight times a year. Subscription: $9.00. Order from Claretian Publications, 221 West Madison St., Chicago, IL 60606.

Probe
Newsletter about new resources and creative approaches to church and community work.
Subscription $5.00 per year. Order from *Probe*, Christian Associates of Southwest Pennsylvania, 401 Wood St., 1800 Arrott Bldg., Pittsburgh, PA 15222. Published ten times a year.

Scan
Monthly newsletter which evaluates new resources. Subscription $6.00 from: P. O. Box 12811, Pittsburgh, PA 15241.

RESPOND

VOLUME 3
A RESOURCE BOOK
FOR YOUTH MINISTRY

Edited by MASON L. BROWN

RESPOND, VOLUME 3

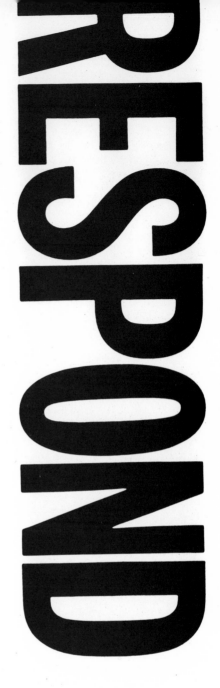

RESPOND

VOLUME 3
A RESOURCE BOOK
FOR YOUTH MINISTRY
Edited by MASON L. BROWN

JUDSON PRESS, ® Valley Forge

Library of Congress Cataloging in Publication Data
Main entry under title:
Respond; a resource book for youth ministry.
   Vol. 2 edited by J. M. Corbett; v. 3 by M. L. Brown.
   Includes bibliographies.
   1. Religious education—Text-books for young people—
Baptist. I. Ignatius, Keith L., ed. II. Corbett, Janice M.,
ed. III. Brown, Mason L., ed.
BX6225.R47   268'.4   77-159050
ISBN 0-8170-0600-1 (v. 3)

Photo credits: cover and p. 34, Heinz Fussle; p. 49, Richard
McPhee; p. 67, Wallowitch; p. 91, Bob Combs; p. 113, Rohn Engh.

What do I as an adult have to offer youth?
>   My whole self. All that I am and feel as a person.
>   The built-in maturity and love I have found in the midst of life,
>   which I can share.
>   Given not by the truckload but like daily vitamin pills.

What do I as an adult have to offer youth?
>   The opportunity to plan together and carry out significant
>   group experiences with the church.
>   Experiences which we can look forward to with hope and expectancy
>   and look back upon with meaning and joy.

What do I as an adult have to offer youth?
>   Freedom which they can handle.
>   Limits where they are needed.
>   Limits that are clarified and enforced with love, consistency,
>   and forgiveness.
>   Some of my wealth, being not a briber nor a skinflint.
>   All of my friendship, my love, my faith in God as known in
>   Jesus Christ and as biblically revealed.
>   Separation from adults, to be alone or with youth friends
>   when needed.
>   Hope when they are discouraged.
>   Meaning when life has fallen apart.
>   And a laugh now and then to break tension and
>   develop oneness across our age differences.

That is what I as an adult have to offer youth.

Mason L. Brown

Pick it up!
　　Hold it!
　　　　Love it!
　　See it as a beautiful example of a youth ministry resource and then—

We Suggest You Do This!

Browse through the book to see what's hidden behind its innocent look. Note the various sections. Read a couple of the plans. Get a feel of what's here and what may have some possibilities for your group. Discover the sensation of gripping an extensive compilation of action and study resources and leadership helps that have never been produced before. Realize, however, that—

It's Not the Gospel.

Respond is a book of suggestions. Don't be afraid to modify, tear out, change, or discard any of the material that is of no value to your group. (The editor will never know.) But don't throw away some stuff that you may use later—like twelve months from now.

Stay with It!

Browse through the book several times. Get to know it inside out. And when the moment comes that your group has an idea it wants to explore, but no resources, you can say, "Hey, I've got just the thing!" Flip to the appropriate page and surprise the "living daylights" out of them.

When Using the Suggested Articles:

1. *Read* through the session plans in order to get an idea of what the session is about.
2. *Reread* the target or purpose. Restate it in your own words. Then ask: Does it fit the group? How should it be changed? What other appropriate experiences does it enable you to recall?
3. *Reread* the procedures. How do they fit the needs of your group—size, temperament, amount of session time, setting, room size, equipment, leadership, etc.?
4. *Recheck* the preparation which will be needed. Do you have enough time to get ready for the session? Necessary resources? Leadership?
5. If you've got the answer to all those questions, get on with it and have a successful experience.

ONE FINAL COMMENT

Respond took a lot of hard work by a lot of people to produce. Our reasons for doing the book are:
1. It will make your work in youth ministry a little easier;
2. it will make you smile
　　more often
　　and not worry so much
　　about where you are in youth
　　ministry;
3. it will help your group and the gospel get together
　　more often and more intimately.

Good luck,
Good reading, and
A great ministry!

　　　　—From the people
　　　　of *Respond*

A NOTE ABOUT RESPOND, VOLUME 3

Respond 3, like *Respond 1* and *2* before it, incorporates the practical advice, down-to-earth ideas, and "meaty" study suggestions helpful in youth ministry. An index to *Respond,* volumes 1, 2, and 3, is provided at the back of the book. If you have a study topic in mind and need resources, check the index.

In some of the suggestions to the leader, use of a copy machine for advance preparation is one of the options. There is probably someone in your church who has access to a copy machine at a cost that is not prohibitive. You have permission to make extra copies of this material which would actually be used by your local church youth group.

CONTENTS

Section 2—Celebration Resources

CREATING YOUR OWN WORSHIP

WORSHIP/CELEBRATION PROGRAMS

SONGS AND READINGS FOR CELEBRATION

Section 3—Handles for Leaders—Youth and Adults

Section 4—Resources

Study/Action Resources

Section 5—Index to Volumes 1, 2, and 3

Section 1
RESOURCES FOR STUDY AND ACTION

CREATIVE BIBLICAL STUDY
by ROBERT F. WALK II

INTRODUCTION

Assuming that God's relationship to persons is creative and purposeful, how then can we turn to the text of the Bible and wrestle with it creatively? In the context of ministering with youth, use of the Bible becomes an area of crucial concern. How can we approach the source book of the Christian faith creatively, in such a way that its concerns will come alive? The Bible was the product of people walking the many roads of life and encountering the living God amidst the eternal issues of life and death. The Bible became, with God's help, a record of those personal experiences in words and with the feeling of faith. Taking a cue from the way the Bible was written we can approach the study of the Bible creatively.

PLANS

The first possibility is a group session on "Record Sounds and the Bible." One of the powerful forces which youth face is mass media. We all are bombarded with a continual flow of sights, sounds, and vibrations. Begin with the sounds of music. Study the themes of records as they relate to the themes of the Bible. Ask the group members to bring their favorite records or tape recordings. Then develop the session through the following steps:

1. Have a listening period—listen to the lyrics as well as to the music. Listen to the words, feelings, and themes presented.
2. Retain the thoughts and feelings of the record by listing them on newsprint, expressing them through a collage, the use of clay, or painting.
3. Have the group search the Scriptures for themes related to those of the records. For example, if the theme was "love," study 1 Corinthians 13.
4. Compare love as presented in the record and as it comes across in the Bible. Bible commentaries and a concordance will help in locating biblical themes. Alternate listening to a particular record with reading the biblical record.

A creative means of communicating the insights and learnings of records and the Bible might be a mass media approach. Divide responsibilities among group members. Have part of your group work on a self-styled 8mm movie that would capture the themes of both the Bible and the record. Check around. Someone in the church membership probably owns an 8mm camera which they will lend your group.

Another group could work on the script. As sound for the movie, tape the music of the records on one recorder and the words of Scripture on another. The simultaneous combination of messages ought to make more meaningful the truths of the Bible as they intersect with the concerns of life.

A second approach could be a group session on "Advertising Vibrations and the Bible." Another media force that penetrates young people deeply is the blurbs of the advertising industry. Have a creative Bible study on the themes of the Bible and the themes of advertising. An approach for developing the session might look like this:

1. Begin by having the young people cut ads out of newspapers and magazines. Paste these on newsprint.
2. Also urge the group to brainstorm about ads they remember from television and radio. Record these on newsprint or a chalkboard.
3. Have the group examine what the ads are saying, asking questions such as:
   - What do the ads say about people?
   - What do they reveal about human relationships?
   - Why are pretty girls used to sell so many products?
   - Does success in life really depend upon using a certain product?

13

- How do ads tend to control our minds and wills?
- What are the purposes of advertising?

4. Now have the group or groups open the Bible and wrestle with what it says about people, human relationships, and success in life. Utilize the following passages in your search:

Bibles Needed

- *Psalm 8*—To stimulate thinking about the purpose and meaning of man.
- *Matthew 25:31-46*—Ads sometimes give the impression you are not "in" and "accepted" unless you use the "right" product. What does the Scripture say about acceptance and human relationships?
- *Luke 12:22-31*—What does this say about our values and priorities? What ought they to be? How does our thirst for material possessions affect our life values?
- *Matthew 4:1-11*—What issues did Jesus struggle with in the temptations? Power? Wealth? Material versus spiritual? In what ways do ads tempt us with similar issues? How can we learn to be in charge of our minds and decisions?

A creative follow-up to the learning of this session might be to have the youth write up spot commercials on the meaning of God, faith, man, values, success, etc. These could be taped, written down, acted out in skit form, or painted on posters. The tapes or skits could be used as part of a church worship service. They could be shared with another age group or class during church school. Posters could be hung in church vestibules and/or maybe some store windows in town. In some areas the councils of churches are sponsoring spot commercials on radio. Maybe your group could explore the idea. The means and techniques of adver-

tising can be used to give greater depth to the meaning of life and to being human in the image of God.

A third method of creative Bible study is INNER LIFE FORCES AND THE BIBLE. This is not so much a group endeavor as an ongoing personal approach. As well as outside influences on the life-style and faith of young people, there are inner forces. With these in mind, encourage individuals in your group to begin keeping a daily or weekly written record of their personal activities, thoughts, feelings, dreams, hopes, disappointments, problems, relationships, and whatever else they feel is important to them. Relate these life experiences to the personal histories of such personalities as Abraham, Moses, Joseph, Ruth, Job, Isaiah, Jeremiah, Jesus, and Paul. As we read these personal histories in the Bible, we should keep in mind the following questions and relate them to our own lives:

- What were the main events of the lives of these biblical personalities?
- What were their strengths? Weaknesses?
- With what questions did they struggle?
- What part did faith in God play in their lives?
- What were their life goals?

In the light of these reflections we should be able to zero in more closely on where we are going in life and how to get there. Some group sessions could be based on the issues arising from these findings. Such a diary of life and Bible concerns is a means of shaping our growing life and faith.

The Word of God is creative. God's written word, the Bible, becomes the creative living Word in young people and adults as they are open and responsive to the leading of God's Spirit in their lives. In Christ the Word became flesh. May these approaches to life and the Bible cause the Word to become flesh in you, furthering your personal and group experiences in the abundant life.

14

HE TOLD THEM PARABLES

by CHARLES R. LANDON, JR.

TARGET

To understand the parable as a literary form and as a teaching tool and to study in depth one of Jesus' parables.

ADVANCE PLANNING

1. At your meeting immediately preceding this session, assign to members of your group the task of obtaining definitions (from dictionaries or grammar books) of these literary forms: allegory, parable, simile, analogy, riddle, metaphor, fable, myth, proverb.
2. Write each of the above literary form names on a separate piece of paper and tape the papers to the wall of your meeting place. When the definitions are given at the beginning of the session, have someone write them with magic markers on the appropriate papers.
3. Obtain from your pastor, church, community library, or some other source some commentaries on the Gospels or some one-volume Bible commentaries. Some suggestions: William Barclay's *Daily Study Bible,* the *Abingdon Bible Commentary,* the *New Bible Commentary Revised,* the *Wycliffe Bible Commentary.* Since these will be used for background information rather than for interpretation, you will not need technical commentaries nor older devotional books.

INTRODUCTION

The first three Gospels—Matthew, Mark, and Luke—devote considerable space to Jesus' most familiar form of teaching, his parables. There are about thirty-five of these parables. Though they appear simple and straightforward, their interpretation and understanding has been a major subject for debate among Bible scholars throughout the history of Christianity.

Biblical parables have been simplistically defined as "earthly stories with heavenly meanings," but this description belies their complexity. It also camouflages the sensationalism that has characterized much parable commentary through the centuries. In more recent years, Bible scholars have developed a set of guidelines to facilitate and standardize the interpretation and understanding of Jesus' parables.

Four of these guidelines are:

1. Each parable must be viewed from the perspective of the life situation in which it was told. Thus we must learn as much as we can about Palestinian Jewish customs and environment, since these factors constituted the life situation of Jesus' parables.
2. Generally speaking, each parable is designed to teach one central truth, though there may also be secondary teachings. The details of the parable are meant to reinforce this central truth, rather than to be interpreted individually or literally.
3. When Jesus provides introductory or explanatory remarks with the parable, the parable must be understood within the context of these remarks. The parable of the sower (Matthew 13:3-23) is an example of a parable with an explanation.
4. Each parable must also be understood within the context of the passage in which it is located.

For example, the parable of the good Samaritan (Luke 10:30-37) was told by Jesus in response to a lawyer's testing question.

This session will attempt to define and identify the parable as a literary form and then see how Jesus used one parable in his teaching.

PLANS

1. LITERARY FORMS

Have the people who researched the definitions of various literary forms write their definitions with magic markers on the appropriate papers taped on the walls. Note the distinctive nature of a parable. Share with the group, as informally as possible, the material on parables in the "Introduction" to this session. Then, on a chalkboard or large piece of newsprint, list as many of the parables as the group can name.

2. RESEARCH

Divide the group into three smaller groups. Each will study the parable of the mustard seed: Group 1 will study Matthew 13:31-32; Group 2, Mark 4:30-32; and Group 3, Luke 13:18-19. Allow members of each group to select copies of the commentaries you have collected to assist them. Then have each group answer these questions about this parable (make enough copies of this list for each group to have one):

• What is unique about the mustard seed/plant?
• Why would Jesus select this particular seed/plant for his parable?
• Is there some special meaning to the birds? To the branches? To the nests?

• What is meant by the "kingdom of Heaven"?
• What do you think is the central truth/teaching of this parable?

3. DISCUSSION

Have the groups reassemble into one group and compare answers to the questions. There will probably be general agreement that the central truth/teaching of the parable is that of growth of the kingdom of God, from tiny beginnings to vastness. To illustrate that this growth has indeed occurred, conclude the program with one or more of these activities:

a. Look at the beginnings of several of Paul's letters which suggest that the kingdom of God was spreading widely even in Paul's time. Compare Romans 1:8, Colossians 1:6, and 1 Thessalonians 1:8 to the tiny band of terrified disciples hiding in their "upper room" after the crucifixion of Christ.

b. Using a map of the world, illustrate the spread of the kingdom into all the world. Other resources include the various newsmagazines, denominational magazines, and other publications which carry reports of the "younger churches," such as Thailand or Zaire.

c. Read through with your group the words of the hymn "Jesus Shall Reign," which is a joyous affirmation of the truth of this parable.

d. Share a time of prayer, praising and thanking God for the extension of his Good News into all the world.

BRINGING THE PARABLES ALIVE

by CHARLES R. LANDON, JR.

TARGET

To sharpen our ability to understand biblical parables, especially their relevance to contemporary life.

PLANNING

1. Have on hand the commentaries, as well as several different translations and paraphrases of the New Testament.

Advance Preparation Is Needed Here

2. Try to read for yourself before the session Helmut Thielicke's two sermons on the "Parable of the Prodigal Son" in his book *The Waiting Father: Sermons on the Parables of Jesus* (New York: Harper & Row, Publishers, 1959).

3. If you used the program "He Told Them Parables," reflect on what happened in the group and in you during and as a result of this program.

INTRODUCTION

The two most familiar biblical parables, even to those who are otherwise biblically illiterate, are the parable of the good Samaritan (Luke 10:30-37), and the parable of the prodigal son (Luke 15:11-32). The latter has been the text for countless sermons to youth, normally with an emphasis on the folly of the younger son's ways and an exhortation to return to the Father and live as one

17

should. But is this really what Jesus was trying to illustrate; is this the central truth/teaching of this parable? Helmut Thielicke calls this the "Parable of the Prodigal Son." Other commentators have called it the "Parable of the Lost Son," since it is presented by Luke along with the parables of the lost sheep and the lost coin. This session is an attempt to understand this parable and then to translate it into contemporary terms.

PLANS

1. REVIEW

Go over with the group the first session's materials on parables in general, reiterating the four guidelines for interpretation and understanding. It would be wise to list these in abbreviated form on newsprint and tape to the wall as a visible reminder. An abbreviated form might be:
• Life situation
• One central teaching
• Jesus' remarks
• Bible context.

2. RESEARCH

Break the group into three or four small groups and have each of them use a different translation or paraphrase of the New Testament to study the passage (Luke 15:11-32) and then answer these questions (make enough copies of these questions for each group to have a copy and supply the groups with newsprint sheets and felt-tip pens to jot down their thoughts):
• What is the life situation pictured in this parable?

• Who are the primary characters? Secondary?
• Who do you think is the main character?
• With which of the characters do you identify most strongly or readily?
• What do you think is the central truth/teaching of this parable?

3. DISCUSSION

Reassemble the group and discuss the answers and opinions that have developed. It is important that you foster an atmosphere of openness rather than correctness, particularly as pertaining to identification with the characters. If you have not overdone this method in other programs, role-play the parable, assigning one person to each role. Or group role-play it with each character in the parable portrayed collectively by a small group. Allow time to discuss the feelings and dynamics that develop.

4. CREATIVE ACTIVITY

Have each person create a parable which communicates in modern terms what he believes to be the central truth/teaching of this parable. Or have small groups of two to four persons create such parables. Allow time for sharing the creations and for discussion. Be sure no one is put down or rejected through ridicule.

5. CLOSING WORSHIP

Read through the words of the hymn "There's a Wideness in God's Mercy," and share a time of quiet thanks to God for his mercy to us.

A Lenten-Easter program on the meaning of the crucifixion-resurrection event

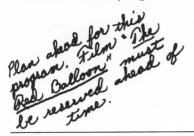

Plan ahead for this program. Film "The Red Balloon" must be reserved ahead of time.

UP, UP, AND AWAY!

by ROBERT A. NOBLETT

GETTING STARTED

At the outset of any conversation about the crucifixion-resurrection event in the life of Jesus Christ, there is a danger to be noted—the danger of being obsessed with mechanics to the exclusion of meanings. The community of faith should be concerned with the implications of the event for present existence.

If the resurrection had not occurred, there would be no Christian church. The story of the early church (Acts) and its subsequent development is ample testimony to the reality of the resurrection. This is the theme that Paul sounds in his first letter to the Corinthian Christians: "If there be no resurrection, then Christ was not raised; and if Christ was not raised, then our gospel is null and void, and so is your faith; and we turn out to be lying witnesses for God, because we bore witness that he raised Christ to life, whereas, if the dead are not raised, he did not raise him" (1 Corinthians 15:13-15, NEB). Think of the matter in these terms: I do not have to have a detailed understanding of aeronautics in order to allow a jet to carry me from Boston to Los Angeles; its power is of great service to me, even if I am a mechanical idiot! So also the resurrection. In order to be lifted by it, we need not know its metaphysics.

To break open a conversation about the crucifixion-resurrection event, the group should become familiar with the biblical material which reveals it. This goal can be accomplished by dividing into groups of four persons and having each group read one of the Gospel records regarding the trial-crucifixion-resurrection (Matthew 27–28:20; Mark 14:53–16:8; Luke 22:54–24; John 18:12–20:25). Following this, while still in small groups, ask for the various feeling responses the participants had while they read the material (or heard it read for them). Jot these responses down on a piece of newsprint. Share these feelings with the total group.

GETTING INTO IT

In order to understand fully the meaning of the crucifixion, it is important that we give it meaning in terms of present-day behavior. Ask the group to study the meanings of the word "crucifixion." Of course we do not hear of crucifixions in the sense of someone being nailed to a piece of wood, but we do nonetheless see evidence of crucifixion. The Random House Dictionary suggests as its last definition of crucify "to treat with gross injustice; persecute." That suggests some new ways in which to think of it. We can crucify people by spreading rumors about them, by denying them the staples of existence (food, financial well-being, etc.), by treating them unfairly, or merely by being indifferent to them. Have the participants relate contemporary examples of crucifixion in their families, their schools, their community, or the larger world.

Do likewise with the theme of resurrection. Ask the participants to give evidence of resurrection in everyday, common events. For example springtime, recovery from illness, reconciliation between people, and a new self-image, are all events which resemble the resurrection. Again turning to the Random House Dictionary, remind them that apart from the particular event we call "the resurrection," the word means "a rising again, as from decay, or disuse, etc.; revival."

1. THE HEART OF THE MATTER

But why does one willingly participate in self-giving even to the extent of death? Why does a soldier fling himself atop a grenade and save his comrades from destruction at the cost of his own life? Why would a parent quickly lay down his or her life for that of a son or daughter? Why did Jesus Christ tolerate the cross when he could have changed courses and lived? Though the word is overworked and often therefore trite, love is the answer to these questions. We give of ourselves

19

when we feel the object of our affection is indeed worthy of the sacrifice, is in fact dear enough to call forth such self-surrender. This is the biblical affirmation about God and us: "For God is love; and his love was disclosed to us in this, that he sent his only Son into the world to bring us life. The love I speak of is not our love for God, but the love he showed to us in sending his Son as the remedy for the defilement of our sins" (1 John 4:9-11, NEB). Furthermore, crucifixion—either our own or another's—is often the matrix out of which resurrection comes. When I enter into the misery of another, there is new life for both of us. When I am able to face my sickness, I have taken the first step in the recovery of health.

Have the group talk about motives for self-sacrifice and the results of such an action. Ask them to think of people they have known who have done this and what it led to. Ask them about occasions when they have seen something close to a crucifixion and have been moved to compassion, thereby experiencing something close to a resurrection. Or when they have been crucified, have forgiven, and have experienced resurrection.

2. FEELING THE MATTER

To communicate the idea of crucifixion-resurrection, you can portray it graphically and dramatically. One of the most effective ways in which this theme can be felt is to view a short, color film entitled *The Red Balloon*. This film is the story of a young boy in Paris who makes friends with a red balloon and his subsequent adventure in keeping the balloon safe from destruction. The absence of dialogue, coupled with the fact that the film has been widely acclaimed for its effectiveness, is ample evidence that the acting is superb. By means of music, body movement, and facial expres-

sion, the themes of suffering, crucifixion, and resurrection are richly and meaningfully presented. Check with local film libraries about its rental or with Brandon Films, Inc. (221 West 57th St., New York, N.Y. 10019). The film lasts 34 minutes.

Following its presentation, invite the group's response, especially in regard to the essence of resurrection. What does it mean to be resurrected NOW? When the Bible speaks of eternal life, it speaks of eternal life that can be realized at the present moment. The theme of our program is "Up, Up, and Away," and what we are suggesting is that the Christian person is one who realizes that he/she is free to participate in the spirit of Christ's resurrection and lives pro-life; he or she is free to develop to the utmost of his God-given potential. "Praise be to the God and Father of our Lord Jesus Christ, who in his great mercy gave us new birth into a living hope by the resurrection of Jesus Christ from the dead!" (1 Peter 1:3, NEB).

A feeling for resurrection could also be experienced by listening to the song "To Life" from the Broadway musical *Fiddler on the Roof*. The same follow-up would be encouraged.

3. COMING TO A CLOSE

To further the group's understanding of resurrection, try giving it tangible expression. If *The Red Balloon* is shown, distribute balloons, inflate them, and invite the group to put meaningful symbols on them with magic markers, and then bat them about. Perhaps someone in the group dances and could perform a dance that would be suggestive of new life, or the group could make collages that would present vibrancy and hope.

In any event, the program will be most useful when each one present is enabled to feel the power of resurrection.

RECYCLING: A PERSONAL REVOLUTION

by DAPHNE GILLISPIE

TARGET

To become more sensitive to what makes waste and to discover where the individual can help diminish that waste.

INTRODUCTION

How can one approach the question of ecology's destiny? Long after industry and government have drawn up plans to correct our wayward waste of resources, the individual still must act to correct these wasteful trends. So let us examine what the individual can do rather than sit back and wait for industry or government to do our "dirty" work for us.

PREPARATION

Supplies Needed

The person in charge of the meeting should gather together "disposables." (The term "disposaables" is misleading because it implies that plastic items can in fact be disposed of; on the contrary, most of these so-called "disposables" are not biodegradable and therefore are not disposed of at all. In other words, they do not decompose and break down into components that can reenter the natural cycle. Instead, these materials clog and clutter, forming permanent monuments to man's mindless wastefulness.)

The person in charge should place these "disposables" (plastic spoons, bottles, x-ray paper, pill containers, etc.) in the center of the room—enough should be brought for at least one per person expected. Any posters or flyers that can be collected or created can be hung on the walls.

21

PROCEDURE

1. USING DISPOSABLES

Each person should pick one of the items from the center of the room and should ponder possible uses for this item. Enough time should be allowed for creative and earnest thought. Try to think beyond the obvious or common suggestion.

After each person has had a chance to think through his item's uses and perhaps has recorded them, he should report to the total group, while a recorder records the suggestions on a flip chart or chalkboard. (Answers may range from household uses to art and craft possibilities. An interesting aside here is that a camp in New Hampshire is doing all of its arts and crafts from recycled items.)

When the suggestions are all listed, they should be sorted generally into categories of commonality: household, office, arts and crafts, etc. Divide the group into task forces by category for about fifteen or twenty minutes to discuss ways of implementing some of the ideas suggested. For example, if a person has picked a plastic pill container for his item and knows how to make a medallion by melting it in a hot oven, he might suggest that the church collect these for a camp project or for some other purpose.

Recycling can bring renewal in relationships. Also programs should instruct or enable a person to do something with the information learned. From this session your group might outline projects for the remainder of the year, involving many people outside your youth group as well.

2. REFLECTION

After a brainstorming session, spend some time reflecting upon what has happened. Some questions to help focus this pondering are these:

- What personal changes am I willing to make regarding recycling and consumption?
- How can I influence others to do some of the same? (The personal revolution involves you, but witnessing includes others.)
- What conclusions can be drawn from our emphasis on "throw-awayism"? (Specifically, what value is placed upon something that is created to be thrown away?)
- What more lofty achievements might man create so that his creations might be lasting "things of beauty"?

3. PONDER

Perhaps someone could read Psalm 84 aloud.

4. PRAYER

Help us, O God, to love and respect you and your creation enough to preserve it for posterity. We regret that our nation encourages "throw-awayism." We are tantalized by paper towels, plastic cups and spoons. We are encouraged to be efficient, get it done. Eat and dispose, clean and dispose. Save us from this false sense of efficiency and from our own ignorances. Restore to each of us a keen sense of responsibility for what we do and how we do it. Amen.

CHRISTIAN WITNESS
by RICHARD D. ORR

TARGET

To explore styles of witnessing in today's world.

INTRODUCTION

Is your life a true reflection of your faith? "Only let your manner of life be worthy of the gospel of Christ" (Philippians 1:27). *Every* Christian is a priest and prophet, a disciple, one who proclaims the Good News of God's love for all people. The teachings of Jesus are filled with instructions about sharing with the poor, about being concerned with the directions of society, about confronting the misuse of political or economic or religious power, about the need for justice and good relations.

Jesus' teachings are also filled with suggestions about an inner change and newness that exhibits itself in a self-awareness and appreciation, an "I-ness" that is deep enough and sure enough to invite the deepest, most "headed-toward-wholeness" self from other persons. "Love your neighbor as yourself" (Matthew 22:39) means paying attention to, remembering, discovering who *you* are and what *your* human situation means and also responding with sincere paying-attention and remembering and discovering about your fellowman. What is telling the "Good News"? What is the shape of the "invitation to wholeness"? How does one "share Christ"? Let's do some exploring together.

SESSION OPTIONS

1. ROLE-PLAYING

The situation is one in which four friends are gathered together for a reunion. These friends have been high school classmates and have since gone on to school or work and become adult members of the local church. Three of the persons, Penny, Ben, and Will, have continued in their hometown and in the same church. Rick left the old hometown and went off to find his vocation and values in a city faraway. Rick is home for vacation and is at a gathering with Penny, Ben, and Will. All of these three have particular ideas about what is most important to tell about their church and their faith.

In an initial conversation, let them each try to convince Rick that he should be involved in the church for the reason that each one holds as having the most importance. Some of the possible role ideas are:

PENNY loves the choir, the music, and the general feeling of "awe" that she gets from the worship service. She seeks to convince Rick that this is something that is missing from his life and that he ought to have.

BEN is very convinced that the educational mission of the church is at the heart of the Christian faith. He tells Rick of the "new models" they are developing in their church school and adult classes. He tries to convince Rick that he ought to be involved in this investigation and pilgrimage.

WILL is very enamored with the church as an institution in society and in particular its building. He tries to convince Rick that the church building has made a substantial contribution to the outreach of God in the community and that Rick ought to be involved with an institution that is making this contribution.

Step 1: The initial conversation in which each of the participants tries to "convince" Rick.

Step 2: Let each of the three (Penny, Ben, and Will) go back to a smaller group of participants and let this group tell their "star" in the role play what he/she should have said and how to proceed in the next conversation.

Step 3: A second conversation between the role players, in which Penny, Ben, and Will act on the instructions of their small group.

Step 4: Discuss what happened and the ideas that were brought to light. How did you feel about these ideas? How did they relate to the content of the Christian witness?

2. TELLING WHAT'S HAPPENED TO YOU

One possible definition of Christian witness is to tell your story, to tell those things that have meaning to you, those events that have revealed direction to you, and those beliefs that are most important to your understanding of how human lives interact with God's plan and Jesus' presence. The idea is that you can't speak for anyone else or you can't judge anyone else's story, but you can always tell what's happened to you as clearly and with as much concreteness as possible.

Step 1: Give everyone a large piece of newsprint and a felt pen or crayon.

Step 2: Ask each person to write the things that he honestly could say in telling what's happened to his/her life to influence understanding. One way to approach this might be to ask the members to break up these statements into categories:

- What are two or three of the things that you can honestly say you deeply believe with no hesitation, or how would you say the things you believe?
- What are two or three of the events in your life that have helped to shape it in the way that it is going?

- What do you see as being at the *heart* of the Christian message that you could tell about, based upon your experience and "what has happened to you"?

Step 3: Let each person share his or her witness in as direct and succinct a way as possible. Remember, this is not speaking for anyone else or implying that anyone else ought to have the same experience or the same beliefs as you. This is telling what has happened to you.

3. EXPLORING DIRECTIONS FROM THE BIBLE

Step 1: Assign each of the following texts to a person or a small group of persons for exploration:
Mark 10:17-22, The rich young man
Luke 19:1-10, The tax collector, Zacchaeus
Luke 7:36-50, The woman who was a sinner
Matthew 6:1-6, How to practice piety
Luke 18:9-14, The Pharisee and the publican
Luke 4:16-21, Instructions from Isaiah
Luke 10:29-37, A style of caring
Matthew 10:5-15, Sending out the Twelve
Matthew 5:20-26, Jesus and the law
Matthew 8:18-22, Witnessing and excuses

Step 2: Let the small group or person decide what has happened in the situation in the text. Identify as clearly as possible the setting and happening and who is seeking instruction about witnessing. What is the type and style of witnessing that is presented in the story or instruction? How would you put the instructions about witnessing that are presented here into your own words? Try to isolate two or three guidelines about Christian witness which seem to come from this text which you would be able to understand as instructions for you in this time.

Step 3: Let the individuals or groups share their understanding of the text and the guidelines they have discovered. Make a composite list on the chalkboard or newsprint of the guidelines emerging and discuss them together.

4. REFLECTING ABOUT WITNESS

Step 1: Place each of the following short sentences at the top of a piece of large newsprint around the room where you have your meeting. A copy machine would help with this preparation task.

Step 2: Let the persons who are participating walk around the room in ones or twos and make some reflective reaction to the statement they read at the top of the sheet.

Step 3: Ask them to put their remarks, comments, reactions, observations, and feelings in the blank space left on the newsprint sheet.

Step 4: Discuss the statements together with the reactions and try to come to some group consensus about which ideas seem to fit best with their feelings and beliefs.

Statements are as follows:

- The real battles of faith today are being fought in factories, shops, offices, farms, political parties, government agencies, in homes, in the press, and in the relationship of nations. The church should go into these spheres to work for the coming of the kingdom.

- The way Christians in the church ought to work at revealing God's love for the world is by regularly *planning opportunities* for praise and celebration of God's creation and the gifts he has given us.

- In a world that is torn by the divisions of generation differences, by the divisions of races, and by the divisions of countries at war, the primary witness of the Christian faith must be to work for understanding, for brotherhood, and the deepest of reconciliation.

- The major focus of the Christian message is a man's soul and his personal assurance that he is a citizen of heaven and one of God's chosen witnesses.

- In Christian witness, the appeal ought to be to the person's feelings and his understanding of letting Christ into his heart and not to his intellect or his work.

- Christ calls us, as members of the church, to be the leaven that leavens the world and the salt of the earth. Are we to accomplish this task by working with the major institutions of society or by working with individual persons and their goals?

- As Christian witnesses we have a product and we are called to sell it.
- Even when persons are not aware of their need, we have a responsibility to share our testimony and the Good News that we have experienced.
- The Christian witness is telling what's happened to you.
- The Christian testimony has to be a word of reassurance and answers.

5. EXPLORING DIRECTIONS

Divide the participants into three task groups and give them the following materials to work on for fifteen to twenty minutes. Again a copy machine will help with preparation.

Step 1: *Task Group #1*—With the material we have already investigated, through the Bible, the statements, and our own sharing of experiences, define together and make a list of some of the best ways that we, in this particular place and given the persons we are, might be able to give *personal individual* witness to our faith and experiences.

Task Group #2—With the material we have already discussed, decide and make a list of some of the best ways that we, in this place and given the persons that we are, might be able to *act as a group* or act within the groups and institutions already present in our community in a style of witnessing that is consistent with the instructions of the Bible and our understanding of the Christian faith.

Task Group #3—With the things we have already discussed, decide and make a list of the best ways that we will be able to suggest that *our church* may be able to enhance its style of witness and outreach.

Step 2: Discuss these various options together and decide which ones have major priority and begin making some assignments and time definitions about when we will start acting on them individually and together.

6. A MOMENT OF CELEBRATION AND DEDICATION

Step 1: Begin the celebration with the singing of songs that have special meaning to the group.

Step 2: Have readers read two or three of the texts that have been investigated in the earlier part of the sharing.

Step 3: A Litany of Intention: Invite as many persons as would like to do so to share their feelings in the following formula: "Because God is _____, (e.g., kind, inviting, loving, etc.). I will try to be _____ (your intentions).

Step 4: A Gathering of Voices for Closing: Let the leader say a phrase and the community repeat it in similar mood:

The time is alive for telling Good News.
Our lives can be messages.
Our minds can bring the gift of reason.
Our imaginations can be festive freshness.
Our spirits can sense needs.
Let strength come.
Let meaning be experienced.
Lord of life, be in us.
Lord of care, give us awareness.
Let us know and tell and live
          Good News!
Amen, yes, Amen.

GOOD NEWS!

by AL LUSTIE

TARGET

To begin to understand the relationship between what we do and what we are as sharers of Good News.

INTRODUCTION

"DON'T DO AS I DO! DO AS I SAY!" Has an adult ever told you that? Many parents seem to convey this message even if they do not use these words. Unfortunately, as moral instruction it is less than useless. What we are and what we do can influence others a thousand times more than what we say. The only time that what we say is influential is when *what we say* is consistent with *what we are* and *what we do*. Then our words may have tremendous power.

When we think about sharing good news with people, we discover that the best news we bring to most of our acquaintances is ourselves. When people are glad to see us when we walk into the room and they sense something about us that brings love, or respect, or order, or acceptance—that is good news. On the other hand, if our acquaintances cringe when they see us coming, no verbal messages about the love of God will come across as good news from us.

PLANS

BEGINNING WITH GOOD NEWS

After the group has come together, ask each person to introduce himself with his name and some good news he has for this evening. It could go something like: "I'm John Anderson, and my good news tonight is that my dad complimented me earlier today." Persons planning the meeting should be prepared to set an example. It is not necessary to "go around the circle," but as people from here and there share, everyone should have a chance to participate when he or she feels like it.

Then move to a brief discussion of people who share good news. How long has it been since someone in the group heard good news from a friend? Who was the friend? What kinds of good news would this group like to hear? Would it be good news for everybody, or would it be bad news for some? What kind of people seem to be able to share good news in ways that make it come across as GOOD news? What kind of people seem to share good news in ways that make it come across as BAD news?

BREAK INTO SMALL GROUPS

Pencil and Paper Needed

When groups of three or four persons are formed, ask each person to jot down on a piece of paper (not for sharing) a response to this statement: "the kind of good news I'd like in my life someday that I don't have now is. . . ."

After each person has had a chance to think and jot down a response, let the group discuss the phrase "evangelistic life-style." Explain that the word "evangel" has a basic meaning of good news. What would an evangelistic (Good News) life-style be like? What attitudes would a person see in such a life-style? What behaviors? Would a style of life, such as the one we are describing, "ring true" in this group?

After ten or fifteen minutes of discussion, come back into the larger group and report the ways each small group visualizes an evangelistic life-style. Spend a few minutes discussing any differences.

GETTING INVOLVED

Prepare in advance to share the characteristics of the following persons. Duplicates of this page could be made on a copy machine, or the material could be copied on 3″ x 5″ cards.

PETER: A humiliated, forgiven man. Impul-

Prepare in advance

27

sive, given to swearing, not above a little lying, sensitive, weeps when hurt, loves his friends, a bit loud-mouthed.

JIM: Bad-tempered, enjoys being important, comes across a little like an apple-polisher, curses people who don't like him, would like to crowd Peter out at times.

JOHNNIE: Jim's brother, almost as bad-tempered as his brother, is willing to team up with Jim to feel important. Also an apple-polisher, losing his temper easily, but capable of more loving acts than Jim.

Ask for three volunteers who will take the cards and begin acting as if the characteristics on the cards were their personal characteristics. For instance, the Jim cardholder could always try to act like the boss of the group, jump all over people who seem to resent this, etc. These three people will try to behave like Peter, Jim, and Johnnie for the next ten minutes.

Bibles Needed

During this time, encourage the group to read Acts 1:1-8. Point out that in verse 4 there is an order. In verses 5 and 8 there are promises ("you shall receive . . . " "you shall be . . . "). Discuss the relationship of the order ("you must wait . . .") and the three promises. What would all this have to do with an evangelistic life-style? Why should these people wait before rushing out to tell good news? What does the concept "spirit" mean to you? Can you relate it to a football game? A debate? Getting "psyched up" for job-hunting? Is this promise anything you know about personally? What would a person's life-style have to do with his "spirit"?

After ten minutes are over, have the persons behaving like Peter, Jim, and Johnnie end the role playing. Give them their real names back and be sure that they know, and you all know, that they are not in that role any longer. Now discuss for a few minutes: What would it take for these kinds of people (Johnnie, Jim, and Peter)

to be sharers of good news? Realizing that Peter, James, and John were disciples of Jesus (as we are, possibly), what relationship between their needs and Jesus' orders does this group see? In what ways are these relationships valid for us, today?

If there is time, read aloud Acts 2 from a modern translation of the New Testament. Does this sound like a crushed, cranky man? What has happened? Is this the only way to witness to good news?

AN ILLUSTRATION FOR CONCLUSION

"WHAT YOU DO SPEAKS SO LOUDLY THAT I CAN'T HEAR A WORD YOU ARE SAYING." And what you do tells me a lot about who you are. One man stands near the entrance of his church building each Sunday. As people enter to attend church school or the worship service, he confronts them with statements like: "Good morning. Do you know what they're doing now? They're trying to ruin our country. I don't know what the world is coming to! Why, when I was a boy they'd have been horsewhipped!" Total strangers and faithful members run into this tirade every Sunday.

Another man stands near the entrance of his church building. It is a large downtown church with many newcomers attending every Sunday. He has the gift of remembering names, and he greets people as they come in with a pleasant "Good morning" and calls them by name. If they are newcomers, he introduces himself, learns a bit about them, and welcomes them warmly. They will be surprised next week to be greeted by name.

Both men have a life-style. The second man has a good news life-style. The other man needs new power, a new focus, and (dare we say it?) a new spirit before he will ever come across as a bearer of good news.

28

AN EVANGELISTIC LIFE-STYLE

by AL LUSTIE

TARGET

To develop an awareness that an evangelistic life-style can be our life-style.

INTRODUCTION

Charlotte is a woman who spent many months wrestling with her feelings about her son. He was involved in the drug scene. During that time she continued to welcome him home, took homemade bread over to his "pad," and searched for non-coercive ways to love him and his friends. Over the months and years, evangelism was happening. While struggling with her feelings and her half-true ideas, repentance (change of attitude) began happening. At much the same time she recognized the full salvation that was hers in Jesus Christ. As she loved her son and his friends, there were many opportunities to proclaim (quietly) the mighty acts of God. She read of these in her Bible and saw them in the lives of her son's friends. At times she invited one or more of these new acquaintances to decide for Jesus Christ—and some of them did, including her own son. She regularly celebrated the presence of God with other people and was led into deeper and deeper commitments to this Savior-God in the midst of our world. For Charlotte, this effort involved sacrifice. She gave up working full time to work only part time; she has less time for her own projects because it takes time to be a part of God's love; she has let go of some ideas she had held that turned out to be less than true. As Charlotte looks back, she sees an evangelistic life-style emerging in her life that has some of the marks of those Christians mentioned in Acts 8 who never planned to be evangelists. They just lived the way Jesus had taught them to live when hit by their own disaster.

Without waiting for disaster, we are called to live an evangelistic life-style today. The story of Charlotte is true. What will be your story, I wonder?

PLANS

GETTING STARTED

With the whole group together, have someone read Acts 8:1-8 from a modern translation of the New Testament. Plan for a short pause between verses 4 and 5. Then have someone read Acts 11:19-21. Ask the group to respond to these incidents for five minutes or less.

Questions which may help the members focus their responses could include these: Where would you (or your family) go if you were being persecuted in this town for being Christians? Imagine yourselves fleeing to another place; what would you tell people about your reasons for coming? How would you respond to God if one of your family were imprisoned for being a believer and the rest of you were driven out of town? Would you tell your new acquaintances about your "jail-bird" relative? What would you tell them?

Now break into small groups of three or four persons each. Make extra copies of this page on a copy machine or have 3″ x 5″ cards prepared with one of the following definitions on each card:

1. Repentance: establishing a confessional mood which recognizes involvement in the sins of the world.
2. Affirmation: recognizing that there is salvation from these sins in affirming Jesus Christ as Savior and Lord.
3. Proclamation: recognizing that we must declare the mighty acts of God in every setting of life.
4. Invitation: recognizing that this sharing also involves calling others to decide for Jesus, so that they, too, may become what God intends for them as individuals, congregations, or institutions.
5. Celebration: recognizing that a sense of joy and gladness expresses God's transcendent gifts of life now and in the future.
6. Commitment: recognizing the necessity of shifting allegiance from our own self-deter-

Advance Preparation Is Needed Here

mined patterns of living to response to God's patterns of living which we learn through his Son. These patterns include involvement in the needs and oppressions of people in the world.

7. Sacrifice: recognizing the risks involved in living an evangelistic way of life; understanding that God's call is not easy, either personally or corporately. It involves standing with him in the hard places.

Have each group take one topic (or two if the total number of groups is limited). Explain that together these topics make seven characteristics of an evangelistic life-style. Ask each group to read its topic and to work with it awhile. The task is for all persons present to come to personal understandings of what the characteristic they are working with would look like in their lives.

Some questions that could help them might include: If I had this characteristic in my life this coming week, what would it involve? Who would it involve? What would I do differently? What attitudes in me might change? What are the arguments *for* having more of this characteristic in my life, and what are the arguments *against* having more of it in my life?

(It might help to have copies of these questions for each group to use as the members discuss the characteristic[s] they have.)

After about 15 minutes, regroup. Ask each group to share its card along with a few insights the group obtained from the discussion. Put these on newsprint or a chalkboard so that when every group has shared, all seven marks of an evangelistic style of life are before the total group.

OPTIONAL HAPPENING

At this point have two strangers dressed up as policemen or in Gestapo-like uniforms enter the room with clubs and order the group to line up against the wall. Have them read a list of charges against the group that center in its subversive faith and give them twenty-four hours to publicly come out against Christ or leave town. These men then

leave. Give the group about ten minutes to share its feelings about its predicament and ten minutes to discuss plans.

When the time is up, stop the discussion with a repeat reading of Acts 8:1-8. Have the group members reflect on how ready they are to begin living an evangelistic life-style. Then discuss the question: In what ways do we want to begin living an evangelistic life-style this week *without* being forced or persecuted?

Close with a circle in which each person turns to the person on his right and shares an affirmation with him, such as: "Jesus came to give us joy. I'm glad that includes you" or "God loves us all. I'm glad that includes you."

If the optional happening is not possible for your group, do one of the following:

1. Make a large poster-mural with the seven marks of an evangelistic style of life on it. This poster could include illustrations or art work. Plan to display it in your church.

2. Do a group drawing of your church, illustrating what your church would look like if all these marks were evident in your church life. For instance, how would your church people behave if they recognized their involvement in the sins of the world? Can that be drawn?

3. Do a group drawing of your youth group, illustrating what your group would look like if all these marks were evident in your youth group life.

4. Plan a project with a goal of sharing these seven marks of an evangelistic life-style with the whole church. The sharing might be at a morning service, a midweek service, via posters, cassettes, drama, etc. Plan the presentation and if there is time, begin working on it tonight. Carry out your plan.

When you close, form a circle, affirming the person on your right. This could include such phrases as: "Jesus came to bring joy into our lives, *(name)* _____. I'm glad that includes you. I'm glad it includes me."

WITNESS/INTERPRETER
by EUGENE TON

GOAL

To discover what it means to be a witness/interpreter of the Christian faith, especially in school.

INTRODUCTION

People seem to have many ideas about what is meant by the word "witnessing." What is witnessing? How does one witness? To what does one witness and why? Is witnessing simply telling someone something? What role does relationship play in witnessing? What is nonverbal witnessing? These and similar questions call attention to our difficulty to respond to the New Testament challenge to be witnesses.

Giving witness is not an option. We are always witnessing. The question is: To what do we witness? Christian witness is developing a style of life which reflects, declares, and experiences God's love. In the words of John's Gospel it is the "Word" becoming flesh. If this is so, then the life of a Christian becomes an interpretation of the gospel message. The way we respond to life situations, the words we speak, the attitudes we carry, the values by which we live all interpret the good news to that portion of the world with which we come in contact. The Christian is an interpretation and an interpreter.

One of the arenas of life open for Christian witness is the school. It is no doubt one of the most difficult, for it is truly the world of "our peers." As a Christian under the imperative to give witness, the challenge is there. But so is guilt, the guilt of failing to meet the challenge. Some of this guilt may come from ignorance.

This program attempts to deal with what witnessing is, particularly in a school setting. Three propositions are advanced for consideration. (Post these propositions in your meeting room.)

- Christian witnessing is an interpretation process. (Note: Interpretation is a two-way process, sending as well as receiving.)
- Christian witnessing involves personal relationships.
- Christian witnessing takes place in the context of life as it is being experienced at that moment.

PLANS

RUMOR GAME

Begin by playing the Rumor Game. The leader shares a rather complicated story of tense human relationships with the person next to him. That opinion is then whispered to the next person and so on until the last person hears it. At that time this person shares aloud what he has heard. Analyze what has happened in the transmission of the opinion and discuss the implications for Christian witnessing. What is implied about the interpretation process? What is needed to interpret adequately a message? Record your observations on newsprint or blackboard.

PROPOSITION STATEMENTS

Share the goal in such a way that each person has an idea of what could occur. Call attention to the proposition statements which have been posted prior to the meeting. Divide into three small groups, assigning one of the proposition statements to each group. The task of each group will be to discuss the statement, what it is saying, whether or not there is agreement and why. Each group can then introduce its statement and give a brief report of the discussion. Again, record observations on the same newsprint or chalkboard.

OPINION POLL

The following opinion poll should be duplicated or run on a copy machine in advance of the session. Give a copy and a pencil to each person. There are ten statements. Each one should be read and marked in one of the opinion categories.

OPINION POLL					
Statements	I Disagree	I Tend to Disagree	Undecided	I Tend to Agree	I Agree
I think Christian witnessing in school is:					
1. telling someone about the Christian faith.					
2. taking a stand on a school issue, such as busing, drugs, integration, etc.					
3. carrying and reading my Bible.					
4. inviting others to go to my church or youth group.					
5. becoming involved in school life helping to make my school a better school.					
6. affirming the "loners" and those shut out by others.					
7. calling attention to injustices and helping to right them.					
8. becoming a caring person about other persons.					
9. sharing the basis for one's values, principles, and actions in life's situations.					
10. handing out gospel tracts.					

DISCUSS

If your group is large, you may wish to divide into smaller groups to discuss the opinion poll. Taking each statement individually, ask those in the group to share what opinion they marked and why. In the process of discussion relate the opinion discussion to the observations already listed on newsprint or chalkboard.

WORSHIP

Read Acts 8:26-40 from a modern translation.

The passage might be read by asking two persons to take the parts of the Ethiopian and Philip. Another person could read the narrative portions of the selection.

Close with "Passing the Peace." The leader taking the hands of the person nearest to him could share in this manner: "I hope the Christian faith will mean _____ for you." He fills in the statement with what he hopes the faith will mean for the person he is addressing. That person then shares with the one next to him, and so on until the last one has received the peace.

WITNESS/EXCHANGING SELVES

by EUGENE TON

GOAL

To discover some of the dynamics of Christian witnessing and how this relates to witnessing in school.

INTRODUCTION

The charge to witness has long been associated with the Christian movement. New Testament Christians under the power and freshness of the Spirit of God shared their faith eagerly. The church began as a tiny seed and expanded under the impetus of sharing the faith. The missionary zeal and style of the apostle Paul set the stage and pattern by which the Christian church is covering the earth with its witness.

Against this kind of background, we today hear the challenge to witness. Often with guilt nudging us, we ask the question "How?" when the real question may be "What?" What is sharing the faith?

In this meeting we want to discover that witnessing is the exchanging of ourselves with others.

ADVANCE PREPARATION

If you have the S.O.S. Tape #1 *Experimental Study of Selections from the Book of Acts* (Abingdon Press) by Dennis Benson (available at religious bookstores), plan to use the section which gives an interview of a girl living in a commune tell-

33

ing of her rejection of her former life. Plan to use the blindfold exercise suggested on the tape and have a sufficient number of blindfolds on hand for the group.

PLANS

WRITTEN EXERCISE

After introducing the session and stating the goal, ask each person to make a list of all the ways that come to mind by which he or she is influenced by others. Opposite each form of influence he should indicate whether that influence is helpful or not helpful.

DISCUSSION

Ask each one to share his or her list with the leader and record the lists on newsprint or chalkboard. Be sure to ask whether each way of influence was helpful or unhelpful and why. Lead your group in a discussion of the relationship between the ways we are influenced and Christian witnessing, particularly in school. Some questions which may be used are: "How is one influenced?" "What takes place in the influencing process?" "What insight does this give us into Christian witnessing?" Record these insights on a separate newsprint headed: Insights into Christian Witnessing.

BLINDFOLD EXERCISE

At this time blindfold each person present indicating that you will be engaging in another exercise which may help in understanding what is involved in Christian witnessing. When all the blindfolds are in place, read Acts 9:10-19 (NEB). In silence allow each person to think about what has been read, trying to identify the feelings of blindness and someone coming to help. Talk about these feelings.

If you have the tape listed under "Advance Preparation," listen to the girl from a commune explain how she is trying to save her sanity. With the blindfolds still in place, lead your group in a discussion of the question: If this girl were a close friend of mine, what could I do for her? If you do not have this tape, use another illustration of a person searching for new values.

After all have had the opportunity to share their response, have a preselected girl go to each blindfolded person, take his or her hands in hers, and say with great emotion, "Help me!" Again have your group members discuss what they think could be done for the girl. It is hoped the responses in this discussion will be more personal and authentic because there has been an interchange of persons.

Blindfolds can now be removed. Discuss what insights have been gained about Christian witnessing through this experience. List these expressions under the heading "Insights into Christian Witnessing" on the newsprint where you have listed the forms of influence.

WORSHIP

The leader should sum up the insights. Read Acts 9:17 and 18. Like Paul you have been given sight. In a spirit of worship ask each person to write down what he or she has to give the school world tomorrow. In prayer and commitment these papers can be received as an offering to God.

THE MEANING OF PENTECOST
by ROBERT P. MEYE

TARGET

To understand better the meaning of the church's experience of Pentecost, especially as it is described for us in Acts 2.

PENTECOST

If, as is often said, there is great ignorance among Christians regarding the person and significance of the Holy Spirit (otherwise described as Holy Ghost, Spirit of God, or simply The Spirit), there is even greater ignorance regarding the meaning of Pentecost.

We need first of all to be aware of the meanings of the word "Pentecost" itself:

1. "Pentecost" is a word used to describe one of the three great "feasts" of the church calendar. It is celebrated seven weeks after Easter.
2. The word "Pentecost" literally means "fiftieth" in the Greek. Among early Christians (and others) who spoke Greek, it was used to describe the fiftieth day after the Passover (the time of Jesus' death).
3. For our purposes in this session, we need to take note of the adjective "pentecostal." Many Christians speak of a "pentecostal experience";

for many this term is used to describe a unique experience which is *like that* described in Acts 2.

If there are many Christians who have only a vague idea as to how to think of the Holy Spirit, there are also many scholars who are equally perplexed when they seek to understand what happened in Jerusalem to the disciples of Jesus after Easter on that first great day of Pentecost. We must be satisfied to seek only *some* ideas about Pentecost and its meaning.

PLANS

BIBLE STUDY

1. Have each person in the group imagine himself or herself to be one of Jesus' disciples after Easter. This was the greatest day in history for those disciples. Their wonderful friend had been killed and buried—and God raised him. He was not simply "back from the dead"—he was *the Living One!* He forgave them—they had betrayed him. He walked and talked and ate with them and spoke of the great future—the same Jesus with whom some of them had lived several years.

Imagine yourselves to be the disciples planning for the future. What would *you* do? What *could* you do?

2. Now, turn to Luke 24:44-49 and Acts 1:1-8 and read these passages aloud. Observe that Jesus instructed the disciples not to do anything until the Spirit should come. What do these texts teach about the Holy Spirit? Why do you feel that *power* is the key word describing the meaning of the Spirit for those earliest Christians (as in Acts 1:8)? Relate the meaning of power in Acts 1:8 to the many ways in which "power" is used today (student power, black power, people power). How do these kinds of power differ from mechanical power?

3. Now read Acts 2:1-16. What events or *phenomena* marked the coming of the Holy Spirit?

4. For discussion:
   • What do you think the disciples expected to happen?
   • How do you connect "speaking in tongues" (Acts 2:4, 6, 11) to the promise of Acts 1:8? What was "powerful" about *this* experience?
   • What was the immediate result of speaking in tongues? (Read Acts 2:41-47.)

A NOTE ON "TONGUES" (GLOSSOLALIA)

"Speaking in tongues" (glossolalia) is not unique to the book of Acts. Throughout the history of the church there have been instances of this phenomenon. Moreover, non-Christian religions and cultural groups also have had this experience.

There is apparently no one answer to the question "What is speaking in tongues?" To critics, tongues are "gibberish" or "ecstatic ejaculation" or "nonsense syllables." To those who experience them, tongues are a "second blessing" or a "powerful experience of God." Linguists have not found any resemblance to actual known languages. Suffice it to say that these strange speech sounds are for some Christians an expression of the (always powerful) presence and work of the Spirit emerging in a person's life.

A CONTEMPORARY PROBLEM

There are many Christians today who give testimony to the common experiences of "speaking in tongues." Often those who have this experience testify that it is one of the most wonderful things that ever happened to them and urge others to seek this same experience of the Holy Spirit. Other

Christians believe that speaking in tongues is not so important or that it belonged to the first century only, and they fear lest the chief effect of speaking in tongues today be the creation of division within the churches. How are we to live with the text of Acts and with the increasing debate in our own time?

Always remember the following observations, and they will help you answer the questions above:

1. Remember that Jesus himself was a man of the Spirit (read Mark 1:6-11), but the Gospels do not describe him as one who spoke in tongues.
2. Remember that God has special gifts for special times (read Acts 2:16-18).
3. Remember that the apostle Paul said that love should be our highest aim (read 1 Corinthians 14:1) and that speaking so as to be understood is more important than speaking in tongues (read 1 Corinthians 14:19).
4. Remember that the early Christians *did* receive the gift of speaking in tongues as the Holy Spirit was present in their lives (read from Acts 2; 1 Corinthians 12:10).
5. Remember that every gift of the Spirit has value only if it is accepted and used to build up the body of Christ (read Acts 2:41-42—the result

of the apostle's earlier speaking in tongues—and also 1 Corinthians 14:12).

SOLUTION

Remember all this from the Bible and be free to ask for God the Holy Spirit to work in you as he wills—and no one should criticize what you receive from the hand of God! The Bible teaches two things clearly—that the Holy Spirit works as he wills (John 3:8) and that we should not resist the Spirit (1 Thessalonians 5:19).

A PROJECT

Do you have any acquaintances who belong to a "pentecostal" church or group? You might ask them to share their understanding of Acts 2 and its meaning for them. Some people in all churches, including Roman Catholics, are involved in "speaking in tongues" nowadays.

DISCUSSION

In view of the five reminders above, can one be content to live as a Christian without speaking in tongues? How important is the pattern of Jesus' life for you?

38

THE HOLY SPIRIT

by ROBERT P. MEYE

TARGET

To understand better the meaning of Christian belief in the Holy Spirit.

INTRODUCTION

You have perhaps heard of the man who, when asked to describe God, said, "I knew very well who he was until you asked me." Unfortunately, many who confess belief in God carry around a very hazy conception of the Holy Spirit. (Right here we should note that there are also other ways of speaking of the Holy Spirit, such as, "Spirit of God," "the Spirit," "the Holy Ghost," "God's Spirit," "the Spirit of Christ.")

PLANS

Pencils and paper will be needed as the group responds to the following task.

Can you list five words which come to your mind when you think of the Holy Spirit—or which help you to describe to others how you understand the Holy Spirit? Don't be embarrassed about your words, no matter how strange or unlearned the list may seem. If you read in church history or even in the Bible, you will find that men who have been moved and blessed by the Spirit of God have often been ridiculed and misunderstood by others. The Old Testament prophets are a classic example of this fact; so was Jesus. And sometimes even Christians find it difficult to accept ways which other Christians attribute to the Holy Spirit.

THE HOLY SPIRIT AND THE APOSTLES' CREED

Even though they may not have a clear idea of the Holy Spirit, many Christians throughout the world regularly confess their belief in the Holy Spirit as they recite the Apostles' Creed together at worship each Sunday. Do you know the Apostles' Creed? Here is the so-called "Third Article" of the Creed which focuses on the Holy Spirit:

I believe in the Holy Spirit,

The holy Catholic Church
 [*reference is to church universal, not Roman Catholic*],
The communion of saints,
The forgiveness of sins,
The resurrection of the body,
And the life everlasting. Amen.

All these items are to be understood in special relation to the first line, which speaks of the Holy Spirit.

Now in a group of friends compare your answers to the question about your understanding of the Holy Spirit with the items in this creedal statement. Did you have even one of the items mentioned in the creed on your own list of words to be associated with the Holy Spirit? How were your lists different than the creedal list? Can you guess why this is so? (For example, is the creedal material more biblical in its orientation? Is it more concrete?)

The important lesson to be learned here is that we should not think about the Holy Spirit apart from those things which are important in our everyday life as Christians. Some of these, as suggested in the creed, are: the church of which we become a part when we believe in Christ; forgiveness of sins for which we pray daily; the fellowship of God's people which supports and nourishes us in the world; the resurrection and eternal life—the great experiences through which the Christian will enter some day into a whole new order of existence.

WHO IS THE HOLY SPIRIT?

The program leader may wish to use the following as an introduction to Bible study.

Jesus once told one of his disciples that seeing him was the same as seeing the Father. The same could be said of the relationship between Jesus and the Holy Spirit. The Holy Spirit is nothing less than God with us, Christ with us. Any understanding of the Holy Spirit that misses this point is not biblically informed.

39

The earliest Christians had many of the same experiences that we do, and they reported them to be a result of the Holy Spirit working in their lives. Their belief in the Holy Spirit was the means by which they understood the great and good things which were happening to them (as well as those things which they did).

- Do we have experiences in our lives that we can understand only as experiences of the presence of God? Read 2 Corinthians 1:21, 22, and Acts 2:38.

- Do we believe that God has worked in our lives for good? Read Galatians 5:15-25, especially verse 22.

- Do we believe that God has somehow bound us in a special way to other persons who have also trusted Christ? Read 1 Corinthians 12:13 and Romans 8:14-17.

In reading these texts and many others like them you can see how early Christians did not claim their common experiences for themselves but gratefully saw the work of the Spirit of God everywhere in their lives. That made them different!

THE HOLY SPIRIT TODAY

Pair off and share your faith with a friend in the following way.

Share what you think is the greatest thing that God has ever done in your life.

Then share one small quality change in your life which you have reason to believe is the result of someone else's help.

Once you have done this, regather as a larger group. Let each person share with the group that which is appropriate from what his companion shared with him or her. Share what you feel will be helpful to the total group and try not to embarrass your partner.

Now, recognize the fact that if you were a Christian in the first century, you would understand that these things were the result of the Holy Spirit working in your lives.

FURTHER REFLECTION ON THE WORK OF THE HOLY SPIRIT

As you have time, read and discuss either 1 Corinthians 12:7-11 (regarding the gifts of the Spirit) or Galatians 5:22-24 (regarding the fruit of the Spirit). You might even study both passages and ask how they relate to one another.

The leader now calls attention to sheets of newsprint scattered around the room. The following concerns should be written, one on each of the four pieces of newsprint: "Gifts of the Spirit we need are. . . ." "Fruits of the Spirit we need are . . . because. . . ." "I feel God's Spirit calls us to. . . ." "The mission of our youth fellowship, our church, should be to. . . ." A magic marker should be provided at each newsprint location.

Divide the total group into four groups. (If this makes the subgroups too small, adjust the plan.) Have groups move to each of the newsprint locations and react to the statement in writing. After five minutes have them choose one person to stay with the newsprint and the rest move on (counterclockwise) to the next location. The concern and the first group's response is then interpreted by the person who stayed at the newsprint. The new group responds to this and adds its own insights to the newsprint. At a signal from the leader a different person is chosen to remain behind. Another move is made, and the task is repeated. If time allows, this could be done one more time. When the program is over, an opportunity should be provided for all to look at all newsprints to see what happened after they left them.

CLOSING PRAYER

"Come, Holy Spirit, Come. Come, Lord, like a fire and burn; come, Lord, like the wind and cleanse. Convert, convince, consecrate us till we are wholly Thine. Amen."

40

WHY IS DISCIPLINE NECESSARY IN THE CHRISTIAN FAITH?

by DAVID E. CLOUD

PURPOSE

To see the significance of spiritual disciplines in the life of a maturing Christian. (Post on chalkboard or newsprint.)

GETTING THE PICTURE

Recruit three volunteer youth to stand in an informal cluster at the front of the room on the left side, and two adults to stand on the right side of the room.

TEEN 1: Discipline? Ugh! I hate it.

TEEN 2: Makes me think of my parents.

TEEN 3: Sounds like teachers. You can have them.

ADULT 1: Some young people experience discipline as punishment.

ADULT 2: True. And others see it as being required over and over again to do something they don't wish to do.

ADULT 1: I don't blame them for hating discipline.

ADULT 2: The problem is that negative experiences gang up on them and cut them off from potentially good and wholesome experiences with discipline.

ADULT 1: Well, at least they can see their inner doors beginning to open when they picture themselves as Christian.

TEEN 1: What does "inner door" mean? I don't get it!

ADULT 1: For me it is the door to personhood, the door to the center of self.

ADULT 2: I guess then they see the need for accepting one or more specific faith disciplines into their daily lives.

TEEN 2: What do you mean by "faith discipline"?

ADULT 2: Some examples of faith discipline would be prayer, Bible study, Christian social action, and practicing love.

ADULT 3: If the image of the Christian they want to be is being patterned after some Christian hero, such as a biblical or contemporary personality, their inner doors swing open more widely, and discipline is openly desired and joyfully practiced.

TEEN 3: Are you sure about that?

ADULT 1: I can see that cultivating the desire for a high self-image is a necessary, ongoing task if Christian disciplines are to be effective.

ALL THREE TEENS: Discipline? BAH!

PLANS

MATCHING GAME

Advance Preparation Needed

Divide the group into smaller search groups of four or five persons. Give each group a large (2 x 3 foot) newsprint and a felt marker. Divide each sheet with a line down the center. On the left side write the heading "I Can Teach," and on the right side write "I Want to Learn."

Allow up to ten minutes for everyone in each group to list one or two items in each column. Then ask one or more of the groups to make a list of what has made it possible for them to say they can teach someone something. The remaining groups are to discuss why they cannot do what they have said they want to learn.

After five minutes, call for each group's report. Keep a record of the number of times some aspect of discipline is mentioned and share the summary with the group. Look for an implied use of discipline.

STORY

Explain that the following story about the presence or lack of discipline in Doug's life has no conclusion. Writing a conclusion is the task of the group.

Doug was an excellent athlete in three sports,

41

having lettered two years in each so far. He wants to become a professional football player after college competition. During his senior year in high school he started running around with a fast crowd which enjoyed late night joy rides and drinking beer. He was arrested for driving under the influence, got his name in the newspaper, and had his driver's license suspended. His father is trying to use his influence to get the suspension revoked.

Have small subgroups prepare to act out a one-minute conclusion to the story, using one of the three questions as a guide.

The following persons might be portrayed: Doug, the coach, teammates, a Christian friend, Doug's father and mother.

- What do you think the coach said when he found out?
- What did the team do?
- How might a Christian boy relate to Doug's special need?

Applaud each one-minute "production" at its conclusion in support of those who risked coming before the total group.

DISCUSSION

How realistic were the roles being played? Were the solutions practical, helpful, unreal, or destructive? How did you feel playing the role assigned? What has this role play taught us about Christian disciplines? How might one or more of the Christian disciplines (prayer, worship, Bible study, giving of self in love to others) have helped Doug? Be specific.

QUESTIONNAIRE

Why discipline? (Place the following questionnaire on newsprint or use an overhead projector, or

use it as a litany in this session and for reference in the following sessions on discipline.)

Ask for a show of hands on each of the ten items by saying, "How many believe that number _____ is a valid reason for having discipline in the Christian faith?" Write the number with a felt marker on the line provided. After individuals have responded to the ten questions, their scores will be recorded.

1. _____ To develop trust in others.
2. _____ To gain self-control.
3. _____ To accomplish personal goals.
4. _____ To have happiness.
5. _____ To find life's lasting values.
6. _____ To be a responsible citizen.
7. _____ To be ready in a crisis.
8. _____ To reach maturity.
9. _____ To become fully human with others.
10. _____ To know and obey God's will.

Advance Preparation Needed Here

Encourage discussion about any differences in the number of votes for the various items. Allow freedom for variances of opinion.

WORSHIP

Read Matthew 6:25-33.

Use the list above as a closing prayer (litany). The whole group begins with "Lord, help me to develop trust in others." Then use "Thank you, God" as a response after each phrase.

ASSIGNMENT (a challenge to use discipline)

Everyone select one area of life where faith discipline is needed and practice that discipline for a whole week. See what God does with you. Give him thanks.

WHAT FAITH DISCIPLINES
SHOULD THE CHRISTIAN PRACTICE?
by DAVID E. CLOUD

PURPOSE

To explore what it means to be a Christian and which faith disciplines are needed to be effective. (Post this on newsprint or chalkboard.)

GETTING THE PICTURE

Ask: What does it mean to be an apprentice worker on a job? (A person who learns the skills of a trade while helping with or while doing the work.) Those who accept Jesus Christ as their Savior at a young age have a lifelong vocation of becoming like him, the master teacher. To be an apprentice to Jesus is not easy.

Write the following emphasized words on the chalkboard as you use them in giving this background material: Jesus *demonstrated* the values of such an *in-service training program* for us today. Recall his selection of twelve men and the informal and formal training he arranged for them. For example, they asked, "Master, teach us to *pray*." And he did. Jesus' own *worship* habits, patterns of *Scripture study,* and the *giving* of *himself* to meet the *needs* of others built a solid foundation for ac-

cepting, believing, and obeying his verbal teaching.

They saw and later experienced the reserves of *power, wisdom,* and *courage* which came from keeping in constant touch with the Father, God. Jesus said that his followers would do even greater things than he. That group includes young people and adults today.

PLUNGING INTO THE SESSION *Advance Preparation Needed Here*
COLLAGE

Here is one way to get at what the group understands a Christian to be and what he does. Have a sheet of newsprint for each grouping of four or five persons. Also provide a supply of magazines, scissors, glue, crayons, and watercolor paints. Ask the members to use any one or all of the materials on the table to describe on the newsprint sheet what they see as the ideal Christian—what he is like as a person, what he does.

After fifteen or twenty minutes have the groups share their "portrait of a Christian." What do the collages say Christians do? Are faith disciplines noted? Why or why not?

Acrostic

(This is a way to determine the group's familiarity with faith disciplines and their application.)

Write the letters D-I-S-C-I-P-L-I-N-E-S under each other along the left side of the chalkboard. Ask members to suggest rapidly words which they feel are related to the various faith disciplines, one or more for each letter. The resulting acrostic may be used in a closing worship service.

Here is a sample acrostic, with added explanation:

D *oubting doubts* (challenge them in order to strengthen one's faith in God)

I *nspiration* through *worship* services (gives one the motivation to serve God with joy)

S *cripture reading and study* (being open to God's truth)

C *onfession of sin* (humility before God, readiness to serve)

I *nspiration*—private *meditation* (thinking God-thoughts)

P *rayer* for self and others (keeping the power line open)

L *iving for others* (responsible action, including suffering)

I *nspiration* (seeing God's truth wherever it may be found)

N *eed to witness* (at all times and places, by life and word)

E *nabling* personal *resources* to be used for God's purposes, in church and the community (time, talent, treasure)

S *tudy* and *search* and *question* in the quest for harmony in God's plan (resources other than the Bible)

Discussion

Which faith disciplines do the words refer to? Which are the most useful, practical? Which are easy and which are hard? What are the benefits?

Use of Discipline

Have the group look over the acrostic for ways to get soul food and count the number of faith disciplines with which they have had experience. Ask them to hold up the number of fingers which corresponds to the number they have experienced. Record the numbers on the target as in the diagram. If two have experienced one or two, write 2 on the first band around the target.

Then ask, "How many of them do you want to experience?" Again, take a count and record on the target.

44

Discuss what is the relationship between the HAVES and the WANTS. Are they alike or are they widely different on any band? If there are quite a number who want more experience, ask them to share what they feel is keeping them from the experience now. Offer any help you can.

WORSHIP

Ask one or more students to read the specified Bible passages at the appropriate time during the devotional talk. Have them stand or sit at different places around the room.

Share: To be a Christian is to live a certain way of life—the life which is pleasing to God (John 8:28-29). The foundation for that life is a person (Jesus, Luke 6:47-49). Christians cannot grow unless they eat of God's Word daily. How strong, healthy, and energetic would we be if we only ate one meal a week on Sundays?

So it is with that part of us which is created in God's image, our spiritual natures. "Slavery to God," said St. Augustine, "is perfect freedom" (John 8:31-32, 36). Bible study, prayer, worship, meditation, and giving of our resources to meet the needs of persons are some of the ways we are given the perfect freedom to become the mature selves God created us to be.

Accepting faith disciplines may cause the Christian to experience some unpleasantness (Romans 8:17). Dave Wilkerson of Teen Challenge says, "Enough of this frivolous joy-pop feeling for Jesus.

. . . Jesus has to be a way of dying before He can become a way of living."[1]

Close in a friendship circle with a period of silent meditation, interrupted every fifteen or twenty seconds with a short question for thought: "How satisfied am I with my Christian faith? After this time together, will my life be any different? Am I willing to go further on the journey into my soul? If not, what will I do?" Close with a short prayer and everyone singing "Amazing Grace."

EVALUATION

After the meeting, but before anyone leaves, post or call attention to the following questions, which have been prepared ahead of time. Encourage everyone to respond. Explain that you will use the information to plan further meetings on this subject and that you will be available to anyone who wishes to discuss what he or she wrote.

1. Write one spiritual success you have had in your lifetime.
2. Write one of your spiritual disappointments.
3. Has this meeting helped clarify any questions you have had about faith disciplines? How? (Be specific.)
4. What would you like more help with in your spiritual life?
5. From whom would you like to receive help?

[1] David Wilkerson, *The Jesus Restoration* (Old Tappan, New Jersey: Fleming H. Revell Company, 1972), p. 8.

SHOULD FAITH DISCIPLINE BE EXTERNAL OR INTERNAL?

by DAVID E. CLOUD

PURPOSE

To clarify the source of one's faith discipline. (Post this on newsprint or chalkboard.)

PHYSICAL WARM-UP

Have outdoor or indoor games, or do some stretches, bends, and jumps together as a group. Laugh and enjoy the loosening up.

GETTING THE PICTURE

IMAGINATION GAME

(The leader should practice the game before trying to lead it in order to get the feel of how to time the suggestions and questions.)

In a low-pitched, calm, and very relaxed voice give these instructions: Have everyone either sit or lie on the floor in a very relaxed position, away from each other. Darken the room somewhat so the bright lights do not distract. Have all persons close their eyes. Suggest that they listen and feel their own breathing—allow one minute. Ask them to imagine that they are rocks. Every fifteen or twenty seconds ask a question to encourage them to clarify their mental picture: What is it like to be a rock? How heavy a rock are you? What color are you? What can you do as a rock? What would you like to do? What does it feel like to be a rock?

Suggest that they begin to come back to reality, still with their eyes closed. Allow silence between the instructions: Listen again to your own breathing. Can you feel the breath moving in your lungs? You may want to reach out to touch the floor (or the seat you are sitting in). After thirty seconds,

turn on the lights gradually, maybe a light from another room first.

DISCUSSION

Ask: How did you feel? Allow all those who volunteer to share their feelings. What decisions did you make in your imaginary experience? What caused you to make them (an outside force, or from within)? List the suggested causes on the chalkboard or newsprint under these headings:

MOTIVATING FORCES	
OUTSIDE	WITHIN

How did you feel about each motivating force? Place a "G" beside those they feel *good* about, and an "S" beside those which are rated *so-so,* and an "R" beside those rated *rotten.*

What do their feelings say about whom they want to make decisions in their lives? Others or self, mostly? A balance? Suggestions from others and the final decision by the self?

ROLE PLAY

Ask for three or four persons to volunteer to be in a role-play situation dealing with making a decision about the use or nonuse of a faith discipline—offering to lead the mealtime prayer at home.

Characters needed:

MR. CROWN (father)—He runs the home with a stern hand, does not appear to have deep religious beliefs, though he attends worship fairly regularly and the Men's Bible Class to be with his friends.

MRS. CROWN (mother)—A warm, open person, appears religious.

DEE (daughter)—Junior high age, attends church, withholds her feelings and beliefs.

PAUL (son)—Senior high, very active at church, has learned to pray there.

SETTING—Sunday noon dinner. The whole family went to church earlier. Mr. Crown asks one of the children to give the mealtime prayer. What happens next?

DISCUSSION

What decisions were made? (List them on the chalkboard by the name of the family member who made them.) How did each decision affect the others around the table? How did the players feel toward the other play members? Which decisions helped? Which ones hurt?

Ask the observing members to give the players various suggestions as to new behavior which they feel would improve relationships in the Crown home. List these on the newsprint. Ask the players how they feel about the suggestions. *Role-play* the same situation with the players adopting any new behavior which they feel will contribute to better family relations.

Then discuss what helped the family. What slowed down or stopped progress in decision-making? Place the group's ideas on the chalkboard:

Helped	Slowed Down/Stopped

Ask the players who tried out new behavior to share how they feel about it.

APPLICATION

What do the findings on decision-making which were discovered during this session tell us about where our discipline in the Christian faith should come from? External or internal, or both? Look around the room at our newsprint lists and thoughtfully consider your answer.

Whatever your decision, you have to live with it, but not alone. How can we be supportive of one another at school, home, work, church, play, in our decision-making as maturing Christians?

MEDITATION AND FOLLOW THROUGH

Read 1 John 2:3-6. Ask yourself: If I took this Scripture passage seriously, what would I do this week that I haven't done before in the area of faith discipline? Put your name on your paper. Write down your thoughts. Be specific. We'll mail the paper back to you in a week so you can check out your behavior. You may want to continue making some alterations in the weeks ahead. (Collect the sheets.)

Everyone stand, cross arms, and join hands in a friendship circle. Place the papers in the center of the circle on the floor. Focus attention on the papers while singing the song "You've Got a Friend." Each time the word "friend" is sung, let your eyes move to join the eyes of a friend in the circle. Flash a short, unspoken prayer for him or her, especially in regard to the special need expressed on the sheet of paper which is lying on the floor.

CHRISTIAN BELIEF AND THE OCCULT
by ROGER C. PALMS

TARGET

To understand why the occult is so attractive to people and to help Christians think through what they know about it.

INTRODUCTION

Have you ever knocked on wood? Have you had a hunch that turned out to be true? Have you seen amazing truth in your horoscope? Every time you cross your fingers, say a prayer, or read your "stars" in the paper, you express your belief in some kind of supernatural power. The crux of the issue is whether or not the supernatural power of God can be separated from the powers of the occult.

If you ask some occult believers why they have gone into the occult as a religious belief, their answers will sound almost Christian.

"It is a way to experience miracles!"

"Prayer is important to me, and prayer is really mental telepathy."

"When I contact the spirit world, I'm doing what Jesus did when he talked with Moses and Elijah on the Mount of Transfiguration."

"Witches' covens are a warm fellowship."

"Ouija boards are a type of divine revelation."

People are flocking to the many types of occult religious practices because they say that these help them to find God. And some of these people claim to be Christians.

But people who have left the occult to become Christians teach that the occult is Satan's way of drawing people to himself while letting them think that they are discovering God. People in the occult are always seeking God, but seldom turn to him by way of Jesus Christ.

This program will deal with the Christian's reaction to the occult and help him discover Christian resources for teaching others about the occult.

PLANS

GETTING INVOLVED

"What's wrong with having a seance?" a Christian mother asked her son and daughter who seemed so alarmed over the proposed plans for their younger sister's overnight camping trip.

"Saturday night they are going to have a seance at the campfire. It's just for fun; they'll enjoy themselves."

FACING THE ISSUE

As the group sits on the floor or in chairs in a circle, talk about the younger sister's planned seance with her friends. What is your first reaction? As the group begins to wrestle with this story (and it's a true story), the different information and feelings that each person has about the occult will become apparent. Don't argue with each other, but listen to what each person says.

DISCUSSION

What would you do if this were your sister? Would you care that she is going to get involved in a seance? What would you say to her? What would you say to your mother about the seance?

MIND BENDERS

Passing out Bibles, let each person look up one or more of the references listed. These references should be made available in advance. The Scriptures tell of Satan's power, demonism, and who Jesus is.

Leviticus 19:31
Deuteronomy 18:10-13 *Advance Preparation Needed*
Matthew 13:19
Acts 8:18-24
Ephesians 6:10-13
Philippians 2:6-11 *Bibles Needed*
Colossians 1:11-20
James 4:7-8
1 Peter 5:8-10
1 John 3:8
1 John 5:18-19
Revelation 12:9

When each person is equipped with a passage of Scripture, all may serve as prompters while two people dialogue the following three encounter experiences with the younger sister.

1. The sister comes home from the camping trip and announces that the seance was a success. They had indeed contacted the spirit world, and she is happy about some wonderful directions given to her by departed spirits. They told her how she could better prepare for her future.

Her brother (or sister) must respond to her. What should that response be? The brother (or sister) can dialogue with the "younger sister" as long as he or she feels qualified and then yield to someone else in the group who can dialogue, using Scripture as a reference point. This person responds until someone else takes his or her place.

Whoever plays the role of the little sister should not be silly or an arguer. Let her simply be convinced of her position.

2. The younger sister comes home and announces that the seance was a failure. She says that there is nothing to this occult business and that anyone who says that he can contact the spirit world must be stupid. She denies that there is any reality to occult belief.

Again, one at a time, people play the role of the older brother or sister, each one speaking as he or she feels qualified.

3. The sister comes home and announces that although the seance didn't work, she is certain that contacting the departed spirits in the spirit world is like prayer, only greater. Instead of just talking to God, she believes that she can talk to many people in heaven to get their views on things. She intends to try it often to "improve my Christian life."

Each of these three encounter situations will require listening, understanding, and responding lovingly (not arguing, ridiculing, or criticizing). The experience will show how attractive the occult can be, how difficult it is to pinpoint the problems in it, and will create an awareness of the spectrum of Scripture that relates directly or indirectly to the occult.

DISCOVERY

Dividing into buzz groups, let each group discuss one of the following questions:
1. Where do you think casual dabbling in the occult leads?
2. How does the word "supernatural" make you feel? What first comes to mind? Do you react positively or negatively?
3. Is there a force in today's world we can call Satan?
4. Do you believe Satan manipulates people by means of a seance?
5. If persons contact the spirit world once, do you feel they will want to do it again?
6. Do you think a person who tries a seance also would want to try other forms of occult religion, like visiting mediums, following astrology charts, practicing spells in witchcraft, or even making a pact with Satan if it will give him "power" or "guidance"?
7. Do you believe a person could discover Jesus through the occult?

Ask each group to bring back its answers to the larger group, sharing the consensus of opinions given in the buzz group.

WRAP-UP

Unrolling a long piece of shelf paper on a table or the floor and passing out pencils or crayons, let each person take one section of the paper for his work space (single sheets will do, but there is value in working closely together). On his section of the paper, each person should list every reason he or she can think of why Christians might be tempted to try one of the occult practices.

When everyone is finished, each person can read his reasons out loud to the whole group. When all of the reasons have been shared, one person can ask the whole group: "Does anyone have a reason on his paper that Jesus Christ cannot satisfy or answer if people would trust him instead?" Several people may think that they do have a reason that Jesus cannot satisfy or answer; if so let the group members discuss it and draw their own conclusions.

WORSHIP

Forming a circle, pray for each other. Mention the person on your right by name asking that he will stay close to Jesus Christ for the guidance and direction he needs in his life.

THERE IS NO HERE AND THERE
by RUSSELL E. BROWN

TARGET

To understand that the nature of the gospel involves us in the whole world and that today there are many avenues for youth in world involvement.

INTRODUCTION

"God so loved *the world.* . . ." There cannot be peace in the U.S.A. while war is raging in any other part of the world. Any Good News from God in this country has to be Good News for all mankind. If it is for one continent or one race or one nation only, it is not from God. As we intensify our proclamation of Christ as Lord in our own communities, will we also honor and proclaim him as Lord of the whole world?

PLANS

PLAN FOR THE UNIT

This session is the first of three programs dealing with the present situation in the world mission of the Christian church. The first session deals with personal involvement. The second session will consider how we can be supportive of others, both American missionaries and national church leaders of other nations, in the work they are doing. The third session will discuss how the gospel relates to the developing nations and the meeting of the physical needs of people.

If you want to use these programs as a unit, you will want to plan ahead. A film or filmstrip would be helpful for either the second or third session in this series. The following are possible sources for audio-visuals:
1. Consult your denomination's listing of films and filmstrips on missions.
2. Persuade your church to purchase the filmstrip entitled *Crusade Against Hunger,* from Agricultural Missions, Inc., 475 Riverside Drive, New York, NY 10027. $5.00.
3. Write to Japan International Christian University Foundation for materials on the work of that institution (475 Riverside Drive, New York, NY 10027).
4. Filmstrips on missions may be available in your community, from church audio-visual libraries, or ecumenical agencies.

PREPARING FOR THIS MEETING

1. Have any adults in your church worked overseas for a private firm? If so, perhaps you could invite them to tell of any opportunities they found for Christian fellowship and service overseas.
2. If you have men in your church who in military service overseas found opportunity for Christian fellowship or worship, ask them to tell about it.
3. Look for reports from students who have been in a Junior Year Abroad program or who have traveled abroad. Invite foreign students to speak to your group.
4. Do some research about influences—religious and otherwise—that the United States is currently experiencing from Asia, Africa, or Latin America. For example: The Bahai Movement, Yoga or various forms of Hindu meditation, the Krishna Consciousness Cult, Zen Buddhism, Soka Gakkai.
5. Ask your pastor about the "Laymen Abroad" program, or Union Churches Overseas, or write for information about this to Committee on Laymen Abroad, Division of Overseas Ministries, 475 Riverside Drive, New York, NY 10027.
6. Check your denominational publications for articles on missions.

MEETING OUTLINE

THOUGHT STIMULATORS

Have a display table with materials or pictures on any of the above movements from overseas that

51

are influencing the U.S.A., or on your church's mission program overseas, on students abroad, or laymen abroad programs. Ask the young people as individuals or in small groups to look over materials for about ten minutes and report back.

BRAINSTORMING

1. You have probably heard people say:

"We have enough problems here at home without getting involved with the rest of the world."

"We need to clean up our own backyard before we can set out to save the rest of the world."

The fact is that there is no "here" nor "there" in this world. We are constantly affecting each other around the world. For example:

When there was a dock strike in New York City, within a day or two the Volkswagen factory in Germany had to shut down.

To stop traffic in heroin in the U.S.A., agents must stop the sources in Southeast Asia.

Because of the need for doctors and nurses in the U.S.A. there is a large immigration of doctors from India and nurses from the Philippines each year.

2. Describe some of the following and tell why they have become popular today in the U.S.A.: Karate, Yoga, the signs of the Zodiac, the Bahai faith, Krishna Consciousness. Are these indications of the impact of Asian ideas on the U.S.A.?

3. With airplanes traveling all over the world, what means are used to prevent epidemics of disease from spreading through air travel?

4. Some people say: "Trying to spread Christianity is interfering in other people's lives."

With world trade, international business, and travel on the increase, should Christianity be quarantined in the U.S.A.? Does the American leave his Christianity at home on the shelf when he goes overseas? Or is carrying the gospel everyone's task?

REPORTS

Laymen Abroad Program. This program seeks to provide orientation for Christians who will be living overseas, to help them understand the culture and relate to the people with a positive Christian witness.

English-speaking churches overseas. Many large cities of the world have an American union church or an English language church which provides fellowship and ministry to Americans working in that culture.

Junior Year Abroad programs of American colleges.

Work camps or other special work and service opportunities for youth overseas.

EXAMPLE: A Presbyterian layman, an engineer, had the opportunity to put in a bid for his firm for a sewage system for the city of Bangkok, Thailand. His firm got the job, and he was able to save the city several million dollars over what other firms would have charged. When the job was done, the mayor of Bangkok, a Buddhist, called in the American engineer and asked him why he was willing to help save the city several million dollars in their installation costs. Can you imagine what this Christian engineer replied? After he had given his witness to honesty in business, the mayor replied, "Then let us give thanks to the Christian God for your coming to help us."[1]

EXAMPLE: Recently Miss Bethene Trexel, a college girl from Gilmore City, Iowa, took her junior year from Sioux Falls College to travel to Japan and study at International Christian University. As she returned she shared with us a few snatches of reflection about her year and the new horizons she experienced:

. . . I think I subconsciously began to accept that people

[1] Incident reported by Secretary for Southeast Asia, United Presbyterian Church.

were going to do far more for me than I could for them, and so all I could do was be me and live and love. . . . I had a great year because of good relationships. . . . Really it's not to ignore differences but to go deeper that is truly satisfying. . . . Hiking club and teaching English were my main activities, in time involvement and satisfaction. . . . I hadn't planned to teach English . . . but there was such a demand for native English speakers. . . . Nearly anyplace someone might come up to me and ask, "May I please speak English with you?" I'd usually agree and met some interesting people that way. . . . I also did some work with the campus bilingual newspaper, belonged to Japan-United States Student Congress, was a member of the ICU Church Mission Committee, and attended a seminar on Becoming Human in the Modern World. . . . I really think getting to know people well and letting them really know me was both my most valuable contribution and most creative activity.

. . . From the example of Japanese students, being asked for my opinion many times, study, getting closer to the action, and knowing many nationalities including more concerned Americans, I have become much more aware of world affairs. . . . I believe in missions which say "I have been blessed and need to share." The institutional Christian Church . . . has the resources to do great good. I have seen it and been proud in Japan, Taiwan, and Hong Kong, where concerned people show it, usually through secular teaching. . . . I saw mission work and knew missionaries, I worshipped with Christians of other races, I saw longing for good and physical need. . . . Christ has made a difference in my response to life. People matter most. Positive living, rather than "do not's" or theory, is important. . . . I cannot lead a middle-class existence of becoming settled, acquiring things, being satisfied; I must be worthwhile.

. . . Really, nothing can prepare one for experiences abroad; just people with the right attitude must be sent.[2]

CONSIDER OTHER INVOLVEMENTS OF PEOPLE OVERSEAS:

1. Christian servicemen among the Seabees in Okinawa constructed a chapel in their spare time, for Okinawan worship.
2. The Union (English language) Church in

[2] From Junior Year Abroad report by Bethene Trexel, quoted by permission.

Tokyo, Japan, financed a telephone ministry to help Japanese people in emergency needs.
3. California Youth Caravan joined Japanese students to build a chapel for a youth camp in northern Japan, with the cost of the chapel met by funds raised in the U.S.A. and Japan.
4. An American doctor and his family paid their way to go to Thailand to spend their vacation with the doctor serving as physician at a small hospital-clinic in the hills so that the missionary doctor there could get away for a three-month furlough.
5. An American engineer went at his own expense to Africa to put in a water pumping system for a mission compound and hospital.
6. Peace Corps young people in the Philippines gave Christian witness as they took part in the Philippine churches.

SUMMARY

What are the values in direct involvement in mission overseas which are possible to youth and laymen today?

What dangers or limitations are there in this program?

Just as we hope as laymen to make a Christian contribution overseas, are there ways in which Asian and African Christians can or do make a contribution to us as they visit the United States?

WORSHIP SUGGESTIONS

Bible verses to ponder:
   Romans 1:16—not ashamed of the gospel
   2 Timothy 1:6—stir up the gift of God in you
   Acts 17:26—He made from one every nation
See the poem "Discovery," in *Songs of the Slums*, a book of poems by Toyohiko Kagawa (Abingdon Press).
Look up prayers from around the world, *The World at One in Prayer*, by Daniel Fleming (Harper & Row, Publishers).

THE THIRD-WORLD CHURCH
by RUSSELL E. BROWN

TARGET

To recognize that we can't all go overseas, that some of the biggest tasks in mission cannot be "do-it-yourself" projects in which we are directly involved, but that we need also to give backing and support to the national churches of the developing countries and their indigenous leadership.

INTRODUCTION

Personal experiences in another country can add much to our understanding and make us more committed Christians and church members. But there are also limitations in this direct involvement. For example, on a short visit overseas we usually lack the understanding of language and culture that would make possible a deep level of communication. We are usually limited to the contribution we can make through a specific task, plus the witness of our life.

So if we are to help with a deep and lasting contribution to the spread of Christianity, we must be ready to help support the national churches of those countries and their leaders and the career missionaries who are able to work with them at a depth level.

You might want to show a film or filmstrip in this session illustrating the work your denomination is doing overseas. Or you might want to have a Third-World guest present who could report on the situation of the Christian church in his country.

PLANS

BRAINSTORMING

What do we mean by the terms "the third world" or "the developing nations"?

These terms are attempts to get away from the formerly used term "the underdeveloped nations." This term seemed to be derogatory or judgmental, so someone changed it to "the developing nations." However, this term still seems to be a "put-down," suggesting that we are developed and they are not, or that the basis of deciding the status of a nation is the degree of its use of machinery and Western technology. So the new term for the developing nations and peoples is "third world," with the understanding that the first world would be Europe—North America and the second would be the Soviet bloc countries. Also the Black population within the U.S.A. may refer to themselves as a third-world people.

DISCUSS

A church in New Jersey has provided scholarship funds to help bring third-world Christian leaders for theological studies in the United States. This has brought to the church personal contact with Asian and African churchmen who return to become leaders in their nation. The vestibule of the church, lined with portrait pictures of these leaders, is a wonderful and constant reminder of the world contacts of this church. Could your church find similar contact with third-world church leaders?

Advance preparation is needed here

54

Other possibilities: Look about in your community to see if there are immigrants from third-world nations living in your midst. Or your church might hold a foreign students' weekend, bringing several overseas students from a nearby city to be guests with you for the weekend.

One church in Michigan had a fine group of Indonesians in their rural community one weekend —all of them in church Sunday morning, even though their own faith was Moslem. They enjoyed a rich experience of international and interfaith sharing. Other churches have developed correspondence with a church in the third world and exchanged pictures and greetings.

Can you think of other ways to make your church's supportive relationship to third-world churches and leaders more vivid?

REPORT

Meet a third-world Christian leader—*Thra Benny Gyaw, of Thailand ("Thra" means teacher or leader).*

When the Thai government began to take an interest in the long neglected mountain people, they hired anthropologists from the West to investigate the life and customs of each tribal group.

Thus, Peter Kunstadter, Ph.D., anthropologist of the University of Washington, arrived in Maesariang, Northern Thailand, assigned by the Thai government to study the Karen people. He is Jewish by race but agnostic in thinking. His wife is a believing, practicing Catholic. He knows both the Jewish and the Christian religious heritage better than most believers.

Because he did not know the Karen language, he sought out a Karen who knew English as his interpreter and found Thra Benny Gyaw. Thra Benny has been a lifelong Christian. Brought up in the church in Burma, he graduated from Judson College in Rangoon and held responsible positions in Burman life until the exigencies of post-war political turmoil landed him in Thailand.

He is an enthusiastic Christian. He and his wife, La Say, manage a boarding house, acting as parents to a family of fifty Karen mountain children who have come down to the town of Maesariang to attend school. Besides this, he is a competent linguist, now engaged in translating the New Testament into the Karen dialect spoken by the mountain people· in Thailand. He is a leader of the Karen church, making many evangelistic trips with missionaries and pastors to the isolated villages of his non-Christian brethren.

Anthropologist Peter Kunstadter and Thra Benny quickly developed high mutual regard and personal friendship. They lived in non-Christian Karen villages for weeks at a time while Dr. Kunstadter filled notebooks with his analyses of the life situation of the people. Thra Benny was quick to catch on to the vast value of anthropological analysis, but remained a winsome and caring Christian person. Soon men were gathering for his teaching and prayer meeting early in the morning, while it was

still dark, before they left for the day's work in the mountainside fields.

Of course Benny did not waken Dr. Kunstadter to attend these informal conversations and prayers. When Dr. Kunstadter realized what was happening, he was quite put out with his interpreter and friend because he was not included. Benny said: "You don't want to get up in the night for religious talk and prayer. You don't believe in God. You wouldn't want to come." To which Dr. Kunstadter replied: "What do you mean, I wouldn't want to come? How can I understand these people if I don't know what they are praying about? What these people are praying about could be the most important thing in this village." And so he came, asking Benny to translate the prayers of these new seeking Christians, word for word.

The February, 1972, issue of the *National Geographic* magazine carries the feature story of Dr. Kunstadter's study of the Karens. He describes life in the village of Laykawkey in typical secular-anthropological spirit. He points out the problems as the twentieth-century world presses on this village: population crowding, lack of adequate food supply, the debilitating effects of poor nutrition, primitive agricultural methods, and opium smoking. The anthropologist *can only describe*. But Thra Benny and the Christian church of Thailand *can prescribe*.

From the Christian hospital in Maesariang public health workers are teaching family planning. Christian agriculturalists are introducing better crops and methods. A school is opening. And today the village of Laykawkey has become a Christian village.[1]

SUMMARY

Thra Benny and his fellow Christians have manpower and zeal. They believe that the Christian faith opens the minds of villagers to new ideas, and that linked to Christianity is the hope for better health, better agriculture, and a chance to help Thailand villages to survive. But for this program financial help is needed beyond what the Christians of Thailand can provide, and also medical and agricultural personnel from the American mission group in Thailand is needed to work along with Thai fellow workers. Part of our involvement in world mission can be to give the backing of prayer and financial support to programs of this nature around the world.

WORSHIP

Romans 10:14-15 ". . . unless they are sent."
Ephesians 2:13-18 ". . . he came and preached peace to you who were far off."

[1] Account described by Thra Benny Gyaw to an American Missions Executive.

"If a man does not keep pace with his companions, perhaps it is because he hears a different drummer. Let him step to the music which he hears, however measured or far away."

—Henry David Thoreau

HE HEARS A DIFFERENT DRUMMER
by JEAN YOST MAYER

TARGET

To give positive feelings about loners as individuals with offerings to make.

INTRODUCTION

In our culture, where grouping and crowds are given such importance, many tend to have negative thoughts about those who choose to stand apart. When dealing with youth, it is important to remember that the most voices present at any given time may not express the best direction for the program to go. I have seen examples where a youth prefers to teach in the church school rather than participate in a youth group that, to that person, seemed cliquish and superficial. These people may feel they have an offering which is greater than that to which the group will say OK.[1]

In the age of busy-ness that we now live in, it may be necessary to face the division of time problem. Some "loners" (from your perspective) may be busy in other groups such as school, sports, or volunteer work. Such things hold a higher priority for that person. They may also be very worthwhile activities. Mention of accomplishments in outside endeavors in the youth paper or church bulletin might say to that person that he is accepted.

Another possibility is the youth who feels too insecure. "What I am is not good enough." A group can help here, but "rushing" the person with false smiles and handshakes will not do the job. Sincere efforts by sensitive adults and youth will find offerings this person has that make him OK as

[1] This is a reference to Thomas A. Harris' book entitled *I'm OK—You're OK*, published by Harper and Row. It is recommended reading for anyone interested in relationships among people.

he is right now. *It is important not to make a loner feel that change on his part is necessary before the group will "accept" him.*

PLAN

The program is designed to let those in the group, both adult and youth, feel like or identify with one who is alone or seems to stand apart. Preparation consists of reserving a room large enough so that those participating can get away from each other. Newsprint and markers or a blackboard and chalk are also needed.

EXERCISE

1. Tell each person in the group to find a place where he or she can be alone and not look at anyone else. Suggest that they face a wall or corner.
2. Some biblical figures were loners. Abraham obeyed God when asked to leave his home and sojourn in a land of promise. Jacob was alone when he met God and dreamed of a ladder. Moses was alone when he met God at a burning bush. Elijah was alone when he met God as a still small voice. Read about him in 1 Kings 19:10-14. As we are together, yet alone, let us listen to words of others who knew the meaning of being alone: Psalm 69:16-20; Ecclesiastes 4:7-12; and John 16:31-35. Jesus was alone in temptation. He felt alone upon the cross.
3. Ask the group to think of a very lonely moment in each of their lives when they felt like crying or did cry because "nobody cared." (2 minutes)
4. Ask the group to turn to one other person and in twos discuss each person's moment. Be sure

to listen as you expect the other person to listen to you. (8 minutes)

5. Separate yourselves again and think of a time when being alone brought you joy or pleasure, such as listening to a record or tape or walking barefoot in the rain. (2 minutes)

6. Again in twos, tell each other about that experience. (8 minutes)

7. Gather the group around the newsprint or blackboard. If the group numbers more than sixteen, consider two groups with two leaders. Eight to ten is an ideal size. The remainder of this program should take at least thirty minutes. It can continue to the end of your meeting time or as long as feelings and ideas keep coming from the group.

8. Make two columns on the newsprint or blackboard and ask for good and bad feelings about being alone. Notice how the group comes forth with answers. Are good or bad feelings mentioned first? Are people discussing how they *felt* or simply relating facts? "My Mother was late picking me up at the airport (fact), and I was scared (feeling)!" "I spent the day reading in my room (fact) and it was so relaxing (feeling)." Do you feel that people in the group are beginning to look at some good factors in being alone as well as bad ones?

9. Ask the group to share what or who "brought them out" of bad "alone" situations. Does this give any hints as to needs of youth in your church who "don't seem to fit in"? What actions might be taken? After determining action steps, be sure that plans are made to delegate action. (The plans should be discussed only if the "loners" are not present.) Some might include:
   a. Ask the pastor for a program spot at a church dinner or other appropriate time where a loner poet might read some original poetry and/or someone who plays a guitar or other instrument may perform. Why not ask whoever plans these programs regularly to invite the loner to participate?
   b. Check with the church school superintendent to see if any young loners might be suited for work in the church school. Make sure they are included in teachers' meetings and not considered "only helpers who don't have time to come to meetings."
   c. Does your church tape the sermon for shut-ins? Could your "electronics loner" do this?
   d. Could going to a state or national conference be a help to "open up" the youth who needs a broader scope to relate to?
   e. Does your church need someone to build or repair so the kid with the hammer-and-saw-love has something to do?

The most important factor is a sincere appreciation of what the loner feels about his or her situation. The adults' attitude of acceptance or a feeling that the youth is OK is most important. The "Why don't you join us on Sunday night?" as you pass in the hall or on the street does not give the loner a chance to tell you what he or she is all about. The telephone committee can be your worst enemy. It can be impersonal and allows a person to say "no" too easily. Are your callers dedicated to bringing more young people to realization of individual worth? Is the group using the fact that "everybody got a call" to exclude some who are harder to get to know?

Another factor is that some people never "join." This situation calls for a different kind of ministry —the one-to-one conversation where you listen and assure the individual that he or she is OK.

YOU CAN MAKE A DIFFERENCE
by ROBERT B. WALLACE

PURPOSE

This is the first of two meetings designed to help your youth group develop a sense of responsibility for the community in which you live and to develop skills for helping to bring about change. The first session will help you focus on a particular concern, and the second will give you an opportunity to try your skills in making a difference in your town.

Jesus represents the crossing point of man and God, and he reminds us that God is to be met at the place where we take human need seriously; but we can best serve others when we look at their needs in the light of Christ.

Remember your chemistry? A "catalyst" is an element which enables a reaction to take place. The Christian is called to be a catalyst. That means he is not to get the spotlight and draw attention to himself (and his youth group) but is to be the one who gets things started, brings the right people together, asks the big question, and then moves into the background. Another term is "change agent." The Christian needs to know that he can help catalyze change. He or she can make a difference!

PREPARATION

advance preparation

Have a small planning group prepare the first meeting which will attempt to pinpoint: (1) What are the major social problems in your town? (2) Which of these can youth best speak to? (3) Which one of these do you feel is most crucial at this time?

supplies needed

Arrange for several persons to serve on a panel. Invite one or two political leaders in your community, two youth from another church (remember you don't want to do this alone if you are really concerned about others), and select one of your group to moderate.

Have newsprint on the wall with markers and small cards and pencils ready.

PROGRAM

1. Open with a brief worship experience in which you list the changes that Jesus helped bring about in his world. Portray him as a "change agent." Show how he was a catalyst to change in Zacchaeus (Luke 19:1-10) and the woman at the well (John 4:7-42). Introduce the program by explaining that the goal is to help us decide our responsibility as Christians for our town.

2. Have each person in the group write on a card the major problems in your town. If help is needed for this task, you might mention the following areas of concern: political life, how decisions are made, who has the power (who does not), recreation opportunities, crime control, use of public land and property, pollution control, needs of the poor, and street repair.

3. Collect the cards and write the problems on the newsprint.

4. Ask the panel to respond to the listing and discuss:
   - What do they think are the major problems?
   - Which of these problems can youth be most effective in solving?

5. Ask the total group to choose one area of concern for your focus. Use this formula to decide which is the right one for you.

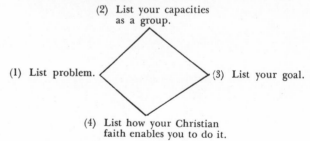

(2) List your capacities as a group.

(1) List problem.　　　(3) List your goal.

(4) List how your Christian faith enables you to do it.

Some diamonds will look like this because they are long on problem but short on goal. Another will look like this because the group simply doesn't have the capacity to handle it. If this is the case with you, then focus on a problem where you have more capacity. But be careful. Don't underrate yourselves!

6. Ask for volunteers to work on developing a strategy for your task.

STRATEGIES FOR CHANGE
by ROBERT B. WALLACE

PURPOSE

To help the group see that, no matter how small, it can be a catalyst or change agent. To be effective as a change agent you need:

1. A support community. You can't do the job alone, and someone needs to keep giving you courage and Christian perspective.

2. To have a clear objective and strategy (specific steps), so as not to be victimized by all the temptations to compromise.

3. To enable others to do the job and take responsibility.

Possibly you will want to put these points on the board for the meeting.

PREPARATION

A task force should meet at least once to list objectives along with negative forces (that will work against your goal) and positive forces (help you can count on). The task force should also decide some strategy (how we'll provide a support group and who are possible allies in working on the problem).

Have someone else plan the actual meeting (the task force will have enough to do).

PROGRAM

1. Have the task group report and give its list of objectives and strategies.

2. Play a game in which everyone in the group (except the task force) acts out a scene portraying one or more persons who have decided to be change agents attempting to bring about change. For example: If the problem is the quality of movies, stage a meeting of the Chamber of Commerce. Have someone be a chamber member with whom the youth have spoken and another be a young person who is attending the meeting. Have the remaining people represent the negative forces you have listed. Role-play a discussion.

   Ask the task force to be critics who will watch for:
   • What kind of support was given to those who sought to bring about change?
   • Were the objectives clear?
   • Did the change agent enable people or did he seek to do it himself?

3. Ask for group response and review how you will go about actively influencing change. Select persons to be the change agents in your group and ask the task force to monitor the project and report back in three weeks.

4. Close with prayer for those who will be your change agents.

VANDALISM
by JOHN ANDRE

INTRODUCTION

Recently, in a small midwestern town, two boys walked up to a parking meter during the day and began shaking it until it came loose from the ground. Later, a car was bombarded with eggs. Vandalism!

Why do people commit acts of vandalism? Is it a form of rebellion? Are they just mean? Why do they want to damage another person's property? Is it actually an attempt to hurt the person through their property?

Many times the real motivation is suppressed hostility towards a world that has demanded conformity. This is one way in which the person is able to release his hostility.

We all experience suppression in our lives from outside forces. We must find ways of releasing the negative feelings which come from being suppressed. Acts of vandalism are the result of misdirected hostility.

The youth group of a church can be helpful by discussing ways of releasing hostile feelings. Helping youth find constructive ways of releasing their hostile feelings can be more beneficial than moralizing on the "no-nos" of acts of vandalism. While destruction of property cannot be condoned, we must ultimately help each other find more constructive ways of releasing feelings.

PROCESS

DEFINITIONS AND FINGER PAINTING

Introduce the topic for the meeting by having the group members write a definition of vandalism. They should then be given finger painting supplies and put in groups of two or three. Each group is to work together to make a painting that illustrates their feelings about vandalism. Give them approximately twenty minutes to finish.

As a total group share the meanings of the paintings and discuss the following questions: What constitutes an act of vandalism? Share your experience from any time you have felt like doing an act of vandalism. What did you do with your feelings? This is primarily an opportunity to gather data, not an opportunity to moralize.

DRAMA

If you prefer, drama can be used to discover the feelings of the vandal and the victim. Divide the group in half. One group is to play the role of vandals and discuss how they felt breaking the windows of a homeowner. The other group should select a couple to play the role of the homeowners, and the rest of that group would play their neighbors. In the second role play, have a homeowner discuss with his neighbors how he felt when he found his home vandalized.

DISCUSSION

Following either option, a discussion should follow of ways in which hostility can be released in constructive ways. Examples of hostility being released constructively are: beating a pillow until exhausted, playing tennis, etc.

Discuss ways to identify the real sources of hostility in the lives of youth and help them design ways to resolve their hostility at the source. Perhaps through a meaningful dialogue the feelings of hostility can be resolved constructively.

WORSHIP

Have someone in the group read 1 Corinthians 13 and conclude by having the group share any feelings they now have. Finally, sing or listen to the record "Bridge over Troubled Waters."

POSITIVE STEPS TO NARROW THE GENERATION CHASM
by SHARON BALLENGER and KATHLEEN SPENCER

TARGET

To come to a realistic understanding of my role in the family and to explore some new ways of relating to family members.

LEADER'S PREPARATION

Bring paper and pencils, felt-tip pens, crayons; a 2' x 4' piece of wood; a 3-D or small jigsaw puzzle; Bibles.

Read the program and Bible verses before the meeting. *Adapt* the activities to your own group and facilities. *Relax,* have fun, let the group do the talking.

INTRODUCTION

Attention! Sit up straight, chin up, shoulders back, minds alert. Surprise! We're going to participate in a program relating to families. Probably never in the history of the whole world have there been so many articles, TV shows, books, sermons, institutes, symposiums, class sessions, and town meetings dealing in, around, and about the *family.* We've run the gamut from wringing our hands wondering if Dad really should be the head of the family or the opposite end! All of this concern addresses itself to the disturbing question, "Should families as we know them today even exist?" My, that is a frightening thought!

Well, relax. Studies show that most people still believe in the family structure, and homes, and real live LOVE. Therefore, this program deals with YOU as a family member—how you fit in with Mom, Dad, brothers, sisters—how you see conflicts in the home—and explores more effective ways of BEING a family member.

PLANS

PART ONE

The following ideas are designed to encourage discussion within your youth group. Choose one or two that seem the most suited to your group members and go on from there.

In Scripture

Have a member structure a model of his family using other group members. Show how each person in the family relates to the others. EXAMPLE: Mom and Dad are close so they stand close together. But brother "A" and Dad don't get along, so brother "A" stands by mother far away from father. But I am closest of all of the kids to my Mom, so I stand between my Mom and brother "A". Any group member who wishes to share his family structure in this FAMILY SCULPT should do so; the group should ask questions and make observations.

In Quiet Words

Depending on the closeness of your group, take time to share and relate the following:
- A time you felt close to Mom/Dad.
- Describe a big fight you've had with a family member and how it was resolved.
- Describe one parent as if he or she were not related to you, i.e., as an individual, a person, and not a parent.

DISCUSS FEELINGS

Have group members mill about the room. At the signal "back to back" they are to select a partner and stand back to back with that person. If there is an extra person the leader participates. When all have partners, the first topic below is stated. At the signal "face to face," couples turn around and discuss the given topic for three minutes. After the time is over, the leader announces "back to back." New groups of twos are formed standing back to back. The second topic for discussion is given, and at the command "face to face" the second topic is discussed. All four topics are to be used in this way. An opportunity should be provided for the whole group to share insights from the discussions. Here are the topics to be used:
- This is how I get my way (in my family).
- This is one way I share feelings.

- This is how I fight.
- This is one way I show love.

PART TWO

These activities give the group a chance to experience and examine emotions that are felt in the family group. Do as many as possible.

On Trust

Have the group divide into twos and alternate leading each other blindfolded around the room. Discuss trusting relationships. How am I accepted in my family? In what way do I show acceptance of other family members? Whom do I trust most in my family?

On Fear

Have each member walk blindfolded (or with eyes closed) on the edge of a 2′ x 4′ piece of wood. Discuss fear of the unknown, fear of things which you don't understand. What are my fears? Is my family aware of my fears? What fears do I see expressed by Mom/Dad? Can I help alleviate any of these?

On Pressure

Have each member try to assemble a puzzle (3-D or jigsaw) in thirty seconds. Discuss experiencing pressures in the family. Is there pressure to compete or conform in my family? How do pressures on me from my school and my friends cause conflicts in the family?

Creative Expression and Worship

THINK TANK

In the next few minutes, based on the discoveries you've made regarding your present role in your family, brainstorm with other group members some possible new ways of relating to family members in the coming weeks. Be inventive. Don't criticize anyone's idea. Jot down those ideas you may be able to use. Try for positive, refreshing, *loving,* communicative means for relating to family members. Determine to try at least one realistic method. Perhaps a follow-up meeting could be used so that group members can share their experiences.

Some ideas that may bob up are: "I will try to ask for and listen to my parents' opinions." "I will urge my folks to share their feelings with me." "I will try to see my family as a group of individuals who love each other."

Read, then paraphrase, these Bible passages relating them to your family experiences:

James 3:1-5

Luke 2:41-49

Luke 15:20

REMEMBER: A generation chasm is as painful for parents as it is for you. But only your desire to change the conditions with others will reverse or alter the status quo.

WRAP UP

Have each member express his thoughts about the hour with crayons, felt-tip pens, or even words. Here's a sample thought which may help to provoke expressions on what has happened in the group:

After we talked about trust, I felt creepy. I realized my Mom doesn't want to talk to me because I never talk to her anymore, or I yell, if I say anything at all. I don't know why I do it. But I can see now I feel put down when Mom disagrees with my ideas. I bet she doesn't realize how much she hurts me. This discussion has told me that if I talk more with Mom she may come to understand me better, and therefore she wouldn't disagree with me so much. I'm scared to try, but I don't like all the fighting I've experienced.

SOME NEW EXPRESSIONS OF SOME OLD WORDS: "I DO!"

by ROBERT A. NOBLETT

INTRODUCTION

If you have been reading the daily papers or the weekly news magazines lately, you've undoubtedly noticed that more and more attention is being focused on the new marriage styles. People are asking whether marriage, as presently constituted, is as meaningful and viable as it is meant to be. In short, is it working?

When speaking of the causes that have given rise to the new styles of marriage, it might be helpful to think in terms of an old law of physical science: For every action, there is an opposite and equal reaction. Further, when we think of action and reaction, we think of extremes. And that is precisely the reason why many new forms of marriage have emerged. There has been, in many cases, justifiable dissatisfaction with marriage as it has been "normally" constituted. Extreme cases of insensitivity and unfairness have caused some to throw out the baby with the bath water and in turn, embrace forms of married life that are a far cry from those originally practiced.

Before going a step further, we ought to say what we mean by new marriage styles! They refer to a whole cluster of new arrangements which vary significantly from marriage as it is commonly viewed and practiced in American culture and which include the following forms: (1) role reversals, where husband and wife may exchange culturally accepted and expected roles (the wife may become the breadwinner and the husband the homemaker); (2) trial marriages and contractual arrangements, whereby a couple agree to live together for a specific period of time, at the end of which they decide whether or not to continue; (3) communes, where many families live together and share "family" responsibilities, such as food preparation and child care, forming what is called an "extended" family; (4) single parent families; and (5) trio or larger group marriages.

PLANS

EXPRESSING FEELINGS

To break open the conversation about the present disenchantment with the "typical" marriage, have the group reveal the kinds of feelings they have about contemporary marriage. What is good about it? What may be lacking in it?

While the group members will not have experienced marriage firsthand, they do live in families and daily observe their parents. Moreover, they have exposure to other married couples through school, church, and family friends.

Record these feelings on newsprint. As a way of getting people moving, the leader might refer to two TV "families" that represent opposite extremes and ask for a critical evaluation of both. This approach would enable the conversation to begin on common ground and also pave the way for the introduction of more personal feelings. No one is apt to jump in right away and spill deep feelings about the marriage of people close to him or her.

The feelings will obviously reflect the experience and perceptions of the group members. Some will feel marriage to be exciting, fulfilling, and meaningful, and others will feel it to be inhibitive, intolerable, dull, and dehumanizing. Those who have embraced the new marriage styles, of course, fall into the latter camp. But negative feelings do not just occur. There are reasons for them. Have the group members then focus their attention on the reasons why people have negative feelings which have led to the creation of the variant styles.

As a way of introducing some affirmative input in the midst of a critical debate on marriage, the group might enjoy some readings from Lois Wyse, who has written several books of poems for married people. (Check your local library.) Her books are most insightful and offer a glimpse of married life in full bloom.

EVALUATION

Now evaluate, from the perspective of the Christian faith, the new marriage styles. It would be counterproductive to simply criticize, so think of those tenets of the new marriage styles that would enhance the Christian understanding of marriage.

BIBLE STUDY

The prior question, of course, is what is the Christian understanding of marriage? The roots of the Christian position are to be found in biblical faith, where the rightness and honor of the institution are strongly affirmed. The picture we receive is that marriage is natural and healthy and to be encouraged. ". . . a man shall leave his father and mother, and be made one with his wife; and the two shall become one flesh" (Mark 10:7, NEB). Moreover, it is an intimate relationship and one which the Bible uses to define God's relationship with us. It was created by God for the fulfillment of men and women. Through the marriage relationship, a man and a woman are able to experience life's deepest meaning and significance. Marriage affords two people the experience of understanding what it means to create and to nurture and to grow in affection.

COMPARISON

Recall now your discussions about new marriage styles and list those practices in the new styles which you feel would enhance the Christian understanding of marriage.

In an attempt to test out your conclusions about the new marriage styles, consider inviting three or four couples from your church who would be willing to discuss, openly and against the backdrop of their marriages, the new styles. Or, invite persons practicing these new styles of marriage. Ask them how they view their marriages in light of religious faith and what contributions they feel the new marital variations could make to Christian marriage. In fairness to both the couples and the program, these people should be contacted far enough in advance so that they can prepare adequately.

WRITING A MARRIAGE CONTRACT

As an alternative or a further feature of this meeting, have the participants draft their own marriage ceremonies, keeping in mind the many issues that have been raised since the beginning of their conversations about the new styles in marriage. Have them pay particular attention to the content of the vows they would make to their "unknown" husband/wife. Again, the wider parish might be interested in your conclusions, and those conclusions could be presented via these written ceremonies which could be published in the church newsletter.

Whatever conclusions you may reach, always keep in mind that marriage at its best is a relationship which is meant to make it possible for a man and a woman to walk, as Peter Marshall termed them, "the halls of highest human happiness!"

66

IS MARRIAGE A SOMETIMES THING?

by ROBERT A. NOBLETT

INTRODUCTION

We would be remiss if we assumed that those who have advocated the new marriage styles were in toto a group of malcontents who had nothing better to do other than raise havoc with a perfectly good institution. The fact that one marriage in four ends in divorce is a sobering statistic. The question before us then is this: What can we learn from the debate? Or, what are the legitimate issues that deserve a hearing?

PLAN

COMMITTEE RESEARCH

Ask the group to think of themselves as a committee appointed to investigate and then report back on new marriage styles. There has been much conversation in the community about this matter, and community leaders are concerned that the public debate be harnessed and used for constructive ends. This committee, then, will divide itself up into smaller groupings, each of which will research one of the questions that is going to be the subject of debate. After meeting separately, the group will return and in round-table fashion will give its report on the question it researched. Its "report" may take any form desired. Perhaps it will be verbal; perhaps it will be a role-playing situation; an art form could be used—music, a drawing, a collage.

Write each of the questions and the material under it on separate sheets of paper and give one to each of the small groups.

Here are the questions:

1. What Are We to Make of Mama?

Whenever we read of new marriage styles, we soon hear of the feminist movement. Women's liberation has had much to say about what marriage ought and ought not mean for women.

In the late fifties, there was a weekly television program entitled "I Remember Mama." Mama was a placid person, almost part of the home furnishings. But she has come a long way since then! Reacting to the continual rebuffs of male chauvinism and affirming her rightful place in the scheme of things, the American mother has experienced a revolution in her role. Now the talk is of day-care centers, women's rightful place in the business community, and female participation in the political process.

The tragedy of the situation is that those at opposite poles of opinion have unproductively attacked each other. Those who choose to remain housewives are deemed victims of male dominance, and those who choose careers and children are deemed irresponsible parents.

The question now is: What value can be derived from both stances, and is it possible that in sifting from both, a "new woman" can emerge? Bat this one about. What would you say constitutes the "new married womanhood"? Is it children and vocation, or is it children versus vocation? What is her "wifely" role? What of her community role? Keep in mind that you are to give a report which highlights the values of the debate.

Study of and reaction to the following Scripture passages may be helpful: Proverbs 31:10-31; 1 Timothy 2:8-15; 2 Timothy 3:16.

2. Is Marriage a Sometimes Thing?

Another theme that can be heard in the debate over new marriage styles is that of marital success and failure. There are those that advocate a trial period in a marriage that will allow the participants time to see if a marriage in fact can be created. While some may find the tactic questionable, there can surely be no one who can find the intent objectionable. More should pursue their marriages with seriousness and intentionality! Here is where the crunch comes: Is it possible for a deep marriage to develop within a context where every marital act is carried out under the banner of temporariness, or is it apt to do the very thing it is trying to avoid—provide a rationale for holding back the gut commitment that is indispensable to the growth of a marriage? In other words, if the whole thing is a kind of adult version of "playing house," might the participants be prone to hold back their total inner selves either out of laxity or the fear that the partner may get frustrated (as indeed everyone gets frustrated in marriage) and use the trial arrangement as a way of easing out of his or her responsibility? These are some of the issues this group should raise.

3. How About Papa?

The conversation and activity about women's liberation has automatically forced us to rethink the role of the male in marriage and the family as well. What about Papa? Traditionally he has been breadwinner and monarch of his home. But now people are asking if both man and wife have been robbed of the fullness of familial experience by being "assigned" to traditional roles.

Since the wife/mother is being discussed in another group, let us zero in on Dad and raise the following questions: For practical reasons (Mother is home more than Dad and is usually more versed in culinary arts) women usually assume greater responsibility for the rearing of children, but could it be that this is even a greater reason for Dad, when he is home, to spend time with and share responsibility for his children? The fact of the matter is, the loss is his, should he neglect to do so. Moreover, might Dad understand more fully his wife's role and perhaps free her for other equally important undertakings (community involvement, reading, etc.), if on frequent occasions he assumed some of the domestic chores such as cleaning, cooking, and food shopping? Further, will it not enhance the solidarity of the family if husband and wife (and, when appropriate, children) share together in decisions (financial, social, recreational) which affect the entire family?

In one recently publicized situation, the husband was in a position to free himself from one day of work per week, and assume full domestic responsibility. While this would not be possible in a majority of cases, should the father and husband see his family responsibilities extending far beyond the workaday world?

Study of and reaction to the following Scripture passage may be helpful: Ephesians 5:21-33. Consider the significance of Jesus' name for God, "Father."

4. How Extended Should the Family Be?

The term "extended family" means a situation where a family of mother, father, and children has ties beyond itself. These may be with relatives or friends. This idea has been the driving force behind the establishment of many communes which bring together people of more than one family unit.

The American experience in the recent past has largely been with the nuclear family. This has especially been the case since the era of widespread mobility during which families have spread across the land, or for that matter, the globe. But now people are asking if there is not benefit, especially for children, in having family relationships with people across the age span.

Consider these issues: Can the nuclear family become too ingrown? What can this lead to? Further, what steps can a family take to make their children, and even mother and father, feel more at home in the world?

Study the following Scripture passages and react to them: Genesis 2:24; Matthew 19:5-6; 2 Timothy 1:5; 3:14-15.

REPORTS

When the tasks have been completed in the subgroups, gather as a total group to hear the reports. This should lead to a general discussion of the issues involved.

WORSHIP SUGGESTIONS

Stand in a circle and join hands. Ask one person to lead in prayer, pausing after each sentence so that the group has time for silent reflection and prayer.

Prayer suggestion: Let us thank God for all the ways in which he has blessed us. (Pause.) Let us thank God for our homes, the love of parents, and others in the home. (Pause.) Let us thank God for our Christian faith and for its meaning. (Pause.) Help us, O God, to develop as whole persons today so that we will have a meaningful marriage tomorrow. (Pause.) Help us to be wise in our dating relationships today that they might be a good basis for a marriage relationship in the future. (Pause.) In Jesus' name. Amen.

SO WHAT'S NEW?

by HAROLD D. MOORE

PURPOSE

To discover how the roles of ministers today are changing and to learn what is new and challenging about those changes.

INTRODUCTION

A minister who was about to retire after a long and effective ministry was recently heard to say, "The ministry has changed more in the last five years than it did in all the other years of my work."

The roles of ministers are changing. Changes are largely dictated by the rapid acceleration of change that we all experience in our culture. The minister who tries to respond to the needs of the people must constantly adjust his or her way of working in order to have an effective ministry.

The minister has long been identified with certain roles in the life of the church and community. Preaching, leading in worship, officiating at weddings or funerals, offering prayer on public occasions are the more visible roles of the minister. Changes in these roles are rather easily seen when they occur.

Ministers experience the greatest change in the less visible roles. The stress which people are experiencing puts increasing demands on the minister for greater skills and services. Personal and family difficulties require the minister to be an effective counselor. Skills in resolving conflict are needed more and more. As institutions grow more complex and experience greater stress, the need for understanding how organizations develop and function becomes more important.

Most ministers find they need skill in the areas of interpersonal relationships and group work. These are the areas for which they feel least equipped by their formal training. Many ministers engage in continuing education as a means of upgrading their skills and effectiveness.

An important part of any ministry is the relationship between the minister and the people he or she serves. One of the real factors in the changing role of the minister is the difference in the ideas of ministers and lay people. Many congregations experience differences in theology, social issues, the mission of the church, or the way it should conduct its worship. Ways of dealing creatively with these tensions often result in changing roles for the minister.

One of the best ways to understand the changing role of the minister is to ask some ministers what their experience is. Our plans for this meeting suggest three ways of doing that. Choose the plan that seems most appropriate for your group.

PLAN ONE

Invite two ministers to come as guests to your meeting, one minister who is near retirement age and another who has just started in the ministry.

Instead of having them speak to the topic of changes in the ministry, arrange the program so you can find out from them what you want to know.

One way to do this is to arrange the format like a TV "Meet the Press" interview. (If you have videotape equipment or movie equipment, you may want to film the "show" in advance.) Select three or four youth to be the interviewing panel and have them ask questions of the guest ministers. The focus of the questions should be something like this:

1. How do they see the role of the minister today?
2. How has the older minister experienced changes in the work of ministry over the years?
3. How does the younger minister anticipate the role of ministers to change in the years to come?

After the simulated TV discussion has been concluded, ask the entire group to sum up what they heard. Ask what things seem promising, hopeful, and even exciting about the changes that are taking place in the ministry.

PLAN TWO

Sometimes ministers are not available at a specific time. If that is the case, have one person interview an older minister and another person interview a younger minister. Have their interviews take the same focus as the interviews in Plan One. Then have the two interviewers play the role of the younger minister and the older minister, following the same format of Plan One.

PLAN THREE

A third option is to show the 15-minute movie *Making a Difference*. This is a film of three ministers talking about their work. (This movie may be available from your denominational film library. If they do not have it, they can probably tell you where you may obtain it.)

The effective use of a film requires a great deal of preparation on the part of the presenter. A guide for the use of the film accompanies it.

WORSHIP

Scripture: Luke 4:1-15
Meditation

A brief meditation might point out how the temptations of Jesus presented three distinct roles for ministry. Verses 3 and 4 present the temptation to meet only the physical needs of people. Verses 5 and 6 present the temptation to minister to the needs of people through political power. Verses 9 to 11 present the temptation to leave the responsibility of ministry up to God. Jesus rejected all of these roles and accepted the role of a servant.
Scripture: Philippians 2:5-11
Prayer

WHO, ME?

by HAROLD D. MOORE

PURPOSE

To help the group members think about the Christian ministry and consider it as a viable choice for their life and work.

INTRODUCTION

One of the most important choices you will ever make is the choice of a life work. Some people allow themselves to simply drift into an occupation. Others take time to make a thoughtful choice about how they will invest their lives.

The world of work holds up a bewildering array of occupational possibilities for the young person. Literally thousands of occupations are available from which to choose. The Christian ministry is but one choice among these countless others. Not everyone can or should be a minister. It is an option, however, that deserves our careful consideration.

There was a time when the word "ministry" would bring to mind only the thought of a pastor in a local church and the activities which made up his or her work. It is not unusual today to think of a number of other kinds of ministry. Ministers serve as chaplains in hospitals, penal institutions, and the armed forces. They serve as college and university pastors. They work as ministers of music and education. Urban ministries, counseling ministries, administrative ministries, and a number of others could be added to this list.

A wide variety of professional people also find a ministry in church-related occupations. Serving as non-ordained, sometimes commissioned personnel, these persons render invaluable service to the Christian cause. Doctors, nurses, social workers, business administrators, and many others are a vital part of the professional leadership ranks of the church.

If you like to work with people in a service profession and want to do so as part of the work of the church, some form of Christian ministry may be for you. Strength of character, dedication, and a willingness to prepare oneself for service are all essential qualities for the consideration of a church-related occupation.

The basic educational requirements for serving as an ordained minister are a four-year college degree and a three-year seminary degree. In addition to this, certain specialized training may be necessary. For those who work in the non-ordained professions, the basic requirements of their profession must be met, plus some seminary training.

Many people in church-related ministries find great satisfaction in their work through being able to respond to the needs of people. To be able to do that, in the name of Christ, is a great privilege.

PREPARATION

You will need a chalkboard or some newsprint and marking pens for this session. Be sure to have these ready to go before the time of your meeting. You will need to ask one or two people to help you as described in the process below.

THE PROCESS

1. Begin the meeting by asking the members of the group to report aloud what word first comes to mind when you say the word "ministry." Have one or two people ready to write these words on the chalkboard or newsprint just as quickly as words are suggested. Allow this to go for as long as words are being suggested. Words like "preach," "help," "serve," will probably be among those listed.

2. When the responses of the group have been recorded, state the purpose of the session and share some or all of the introductory material. You may want to talk to your minister in advance of the session and add some of his or her thoughts about the ministry.

3. Divide into groups of three or four persons to discuss these questions:

• What do you find personally appealing about the ministry?

• What would you find personally difficult about the ministry?

Allow ample time for the members of the groups to engage each other at a serious level.

4. Reconvene the group for a report-back of what was significant in the small-group discussions. You might want to put these on the chalkboard or newsprint for further discussion.

WORSHIP

Opening: A letterhead of one of the major denominations carries the sentence, "Where a line representing my talent crosses a line representing the world's need . . . there is God's call for me."

Hymn: "Take My Life and Let It Be"

Scripture Reading: Matthew 25:31-40

Prayer: Ask for God's guidance in the choice of a life work.

Hymn: "O Master, Let Me Walk with Thee"

Resource Suggestion: You may wish to write your denominational headquarters for material on church occupations. "A Listing of Church Occupations" is a valuable summary description of fifty church-related occupations and the educational requirements for each. This listing is available from The Department of Ministry, National Council of Churches of Christ in the U.S.A., 475 Riverside Drive, New York, New York 10027.

WHAT'S A PERSON TO DO?

by DONALD R. RASMUSSEN

INTRODUCTION

A most crucial decision that youth have to make is their choice of a vocation.

Since the Reformation, attitudes about the relationship between faith and work have been somewhat disordered. We spoke of "full-time Christian service," meaning church related occupations, thereby implying that faith is somehow compartmentalized. More recently, however, the trend has been to emphasize that every Christian is in "full-time Christian service" no matter what his job may be.

With this in mind, it is particularly important that the church aid students in the important decision about their life work, and here's how to do it!

PLANS

A good way to introduce the subject to your youth might be to use a film or develop a "happening" that will get them thinking about the world of work. A particularly useful film is *Revelation Now* (Family Films) which is free of "talk" but yet gets youth to think about and be able to identify some feelings of anticipation, confusion, frustration, etc.

After the film, have the youth list their feelings and talk about how they empathize with the young man in the film. Writing these feelings down will help them to be seen as positive forces in decision-making as the program progresses.

SCRIPTURE INPUT

Have the group check out such passages as Genesis 1:28; Hebrews 11:8; Ephesians 4:1; 1 Corinthians 7:17. A study of these will lead to a discussion of what is meant by "call."

There is more to choosing a career than sitting around and hoping that lightning will strike or a voice will speak. Even when it seems as though the "light dawns suddenly," analysis often shows that there has been considerable discovering, praying, planning, and exploring beforehand. Normally the "call" comes quietly, when we have discovered all that we can by use of the mind God has given.

TWO GUIDES

Most of the preceding may sound quite ethereal to youth and not really down to the nuts and bolts of the matter. The question they have is: "How can I discover what I should do in life?" Of course there is no simple answer; if there were, guidance counselors would be out of business. But there are guides that a young person can use to find his way through the maze of occupational choice—guides that can make the discovery process less rough and threatening. Discuss these guides with your group.

1. Discover the Needs of the World

If there is anything that Jesus tried to impress on his followers, it was that they were to be about ministry to the world. In the parable of the good Samaritan, Jesus applauds the unhesitating service given by the Samaritan. Again in Matthew 25 the righteous are inheritors of the kingdom because they fed the hungry, gave drink to the thirsty, welcomed the strangers, clothed the naked, and visited the sick and those in prison. So we find that the needs of our fellow humans become a part of God's "call."

At this point it may be helpful to have the youth list (on chalkboard or newsprint) as many of the world's needs as they can. Such conditions as physical and mental illness, poverty, nutritional starvation, illiteracy, and the need to spread the gospel may be mentioned. This exercise will help youth to begin thinking in terms of a healthy Christian activism about their vocational choice.

2. Discover Yourself

If a Christian is ever to be of help in and to the world he must first know himself. It is more diffi-

75

cult to know one's self. The needs of the world are readily apparent, but knowing one's gifts requires definition and evaluation.

Have the youth divide up into triads (groups of three) and assume the following roles: speaker, responder, and observer. The speaker tells the responder the positive things he sees in the responder's personality and the types of employment in which he or she can envision the responder. The responder may ask questions only for clarification of what the speaker has said. At the end of three minutes the observer takes a few seconds to report what he feels has been going on, and then chairs and roles are switched until all have had an opportunity to understand their personalities as perceived by others.

Advance Preparation Needed

GUEST COUNSELOR

Most school guidance departments are happy and anxious to cooperate with a church in a program such as this and are willing to send a guidance counselor to participate. At this time, the counselor can help the youth understand the following terms and how an analysis of them can be helpful in determining occupational choice: personality; interests; aptitude; ability; achievement. The counselor should point out the standardized tests which evaluate those categories and give some clue as to how these instruments can aid the student in a vocational choice. The counselor should be careful to point out that tests are not foolproof and are to be used only as guides.

Your guest school guidance counselor should have access to a variety of good books and other resources which would be helpful.

Following are some areas of concern you may want to ask your guest leader to deal with: How valid is the "Protestant work ethic" which claims that all legitimate work has dignity? What are occupation trends today? What occupations are now overcrowded? What occupations are anticipated to be overcrowded? There are 40,000 different jobs available in the U.S. today. How can I become familiar with more of them? What is the relationship between life-style and occupational choice? In our changing society how can I prepare so I can be vocationally flexible?

NOTE

Youth advisors are aware that this is one "program" that will continue for several years, and they should make an effort to be supportive as young people struggle through their questions and concerns relating to vocational choice.

RESOURCES

FILMS

Adventures of an * —a ten-minute, color animation—tells the story of life and opens the way for a discussion on the workaday routine.

Mr. Gray —this ten-minute color film illustrates how the day by day routine can imprison unless there is a deeper meaning in life.

Revelation Now —twelve minutes, color—helps youth confront the trauma of growing up as they make decisions and search for meaning.

FILMSTRIPS

If you are unable to get a guidance counselor to come as a guest, quite often your school guidance department will be happy to give you some resources to help you do the job.

Testing, Testing, Testing Part II—a fifteen-minute sound, color filmstrip useful in understanding the place of standardized tests (published by Guidance Associates).

BOOKS

Occupational Literature by Gertrude Forrester— lists places youth can write to get inexpensive or free literature on almost any occupation. Probably available from any public and/or school guidance library.

Occupational Outlook Handbook —a U.S. Government publication which gives growth and trend information for occupational groups telling the nature of the work, employment outlook, etc.

You and Your Lifework—A Christian Choice for Youth by Science Research Associates, Inc. —a way to help youth plan for their careers on the basis of faith.

The Dictionary of Occupational Titles —would be especially helpful for juniors and seniors.

Encyclopedia of Careers —a two-volume set on careers and occupational guidance covering 71 major career fields and 650 occupations (Chicago: J. G. Ferguson Publishing Co.).

The California Occupational Preference Survey — a useful vocational interest inventory.

CREATIONS AND CREATORS

by GEORGE A. LAWSON and RHODA LAWSON BARBER

PURPOSE

To prompt individual reflection through group discussion of literature and poetry.

SETTING

This meeting should take place in comfortable surroundings, such as a living room or church lounge. Seating should be circular. On the wall post art prints and short quotations that illustrate life experiences, such as prints you've selected from the art department of the public library and large-print quotes you've copied from the Bible, from *Speakers' Resources from Contemporary Literature* by Charles L. Wallis, or from other sources. Examples:

1. An excerpt from the creation story in Genesis 1 and 2.
2. From Sinclair Lewis' *Babbitt:* "Thus it came to him merely to run away was folly, because he could never run away from himself."[1]

Obtain copies of the poem "We Are Transmitters" from the book *The Complete Poems of D. H. Lawrence,* edited by Vivian de Sola Pinto and F. Warren Roberts (New York: The Viking Press, Inc., 1964). One copy will do, but several copies would be helpful.

[1] Sinclair Lewis, *Babbitt,* Signet Classic Edition (New York: Harcourt Brace Jovanovich, Inc., 1922, renewed 1950), p. 242. © by Sinclair Lewis. Reprinted by permission of the publisher.

INTRODUCTION

This meeting should begin with a few statements about religion and the arts. Here are some ideas:

When the Bible tells us that man was made in the image of God, it means that, like God, we are also creators. Animals make nests and dams as necessities of life, but man, like God, can create spontaneously and joyously. The arts are creations of man. They tell us something about the man or woman who created them, something about all human beings, and something about God, who is the supreme Creator.

PROCESS

ART WALK

Ask the group to walk around the room, looking at the art prints and quotations. Tell them that meaningful art is art that speaks to you, that enables you to see life and your faith more clearly. More important than knowing exactly what the artist is trying to say is your response to the art.

Which of these prints on the wall says something to you or addresses your life? What other paintings have done that?

POEM DISCUSSION

The purpose of this discussion is to let the poem "We Are Transmitters" illuminate facts about the lives of the group members and their relationship to Christianity. Your role is that of a good question-asker and a good listener. If you think of better questions than these, keeping in mind the purpose of grounding the poem in the youth's experience, ask them.

Be prepared to phrase each question in alternate ways, in case a youth asks, "Can you say that another way? I'm not sure I understand."

Begin by reading aloud Mark 4:24: ". . . the measure you give will be the measure you get, and still more will be given you."

Pass out a copy of the poem to each person. Ask one youth to read the poem aloud all the way through. (You may want to give him advance notice.)

Then ask someone to read the first two lines aloud and ask: What do you see when you hear the word "transmitter"? What does a transmitter do? What does "transmitting life" mean to you? What other words would you use (creating humanness, giving vitality)? Whom do you know who transmits life? How? Whom do you remember from a movie or book who failed to transmit life and through whom life failed to flow? How? When have you transmitted life? When have you failed to transmit life?

Ask another youth to read the next two lines aloud; then ask: What emotion do you feel when you hear those lines? Embarrassment? Anger? What does the "mystery of sex" symbolize? What does this mean: "Sexless people transmit nothing"?

Ask someone to read the next three lines aloud. What is it like to transmit life into our work?

When have you worked (perhaps on a school project) with enthusiasm and creativity and felt rewarded by more enthusiasm and creative possibilities?

Ask another to read the next five lines aloud. Can we transmit life only if we are artists or professional persons or straight-A students? Into what situations can we put our whole being? Name some other situations with the potential for "life transfusions." Into what situation this week would you like to pour some life?

Ask someone to read the next four lines aloud. Does transmitting life mean giving people whatever they want? Where have you witnessed someone giving what he thought was help to a person who needed something different or needed to discover his own solution? Who are the "living dead"? When do they "eat you up"? (When you let them take advantage of you?) Jesus gave of himself constantly, but when did he refuse to give people what they wanted? (Overturning tables in the temple, Matthew 21:12-13; refusing to be the political hero, Matthew 4:8-10, John 6:15.)

Ask another to read the last two lines aloud. Where did Jesus "kindle the life quality"? Where have you "kindled the life quality"? Do you see an opportunity for "kindling the life quality" this week or in the near future? What is the one thing the author has said to you?

WORSHIP

Close with prayer that the lives of your group may be rekindled in faith.

A FAITH LOOK AT BABBITT

by GEORGE A. LAWSON and RHODA LAWSON BARBER

PREPARATION

Everyone participating should read the novel *Babbitt* by Sinclair Lewis before arriving at the meeting. It is imperative that the leader read the novel. Round up copies from branches of the public library or order paperbacks from a bookstore well in advance of the meeting. Pass out the copies of *Babbitt* at least two weeks before the discussion date and ask the youth to read it "with their theological glasses on." You may wish to pass out a list of questions to stimulate thinking as they read, such as: Where do you see compassion? boredom? hope? hypocrisy? Christian behavior? unchristian behavior?

This meeting should be held in a comfortable room where youth can sit on the floor or sprawl on lounge furniture.

The method of discussion used for this meeting hits several levels. First, let the youth respond with impressions they remember from the book. Then ask more reflective questions. Finally, encourage them to relate the book to their lives theologically by asking in several ways, "What does that have to do with you?" It is important not to confuse the three levels by jumping from one back to another. The discussion will be most effective if you keep the conversation on the topic at hand and discourage rambling. Don't ask too many questions and don't let the length of the discussion exceed the interest span of the youth.

PROCESS

This method of discussion can be used for any art form. It is especially helpful after a group has seen a film together. Below are some sample questions; don't announce the topical names, as these are guidelines for you.

1. IMPRESSIONISTIC QUESTIONS

What exterior (outdoor) scenes do you remember? (Zenith, fishing in Maine) What interior scenes do you recall? (Babbitt's house, office) What sounds do you remember? What minor character sticks out in your mind? What lines of dialogue struck you? What objects do you recall?

Paul Tillich has defined a symbol as anything representative of a deeper reality. What symbols were used in *Babbitt*? (car, cigar, cigar lighter)

2. REFLECTIVE QUESTIONS

Whom did you like? dislike? With whom did you identify? Were you surprised? What was the role of women in the book?

Read:

"They're getting so they don't have a single bit of respect for you. The old-fashioned coon was a fine old cuss—he knew his place—but these young dinges don't want to be porters or cotton-pickers. Oh, no! They got to be lawyers and professors and Lord knows what all! I tell you, it's becoming a pretty serious problem. We ought to get together and show the black man, yes, and the yellow man, his place. Now, I haven't got one particle of race-prejudice. I'm the first to be glad when a nigger succeeds—so long as he stays where he belongs and doesn't try to usurp the rightful authority and business ability of the white man."[1]

Whom do you know who talks like that?

Read:

"What is not generally understood is that this whole industrial matter isn't a question of economics. It's essentially and only a matter of Love, and of the practical application of the Christian religion! Imagine a factory—instead of committees of workmen alienating the boss,

[1] Sinclair Lewis, *Babbitt,* Signet Classic Edition (New York: Harcourt Brace Jovanovich, Inc. 1922, 1950), p. 120. Reprinted by permission of the publisher. © by Sinclair Lewis.

the boss goes among them smiling, and they smile back, the elder brother and the younger. Brothers, that's what they must be, loving brothers, and then strikes would be as inconceivable as hatred in the home!"[2]

This excerpt portrays one image of the church in Babbitt's day. What other images of the church do you recall? (Zillah's Pentecostalism)

What emotions were expressed in the book? Where did you see emotion? What emotions did you experience as you read, and where?

Where were you shocked? What music would you have played for a certain scene? What was your mood at the end of the book?

Where were feelings and opinions expressed honestly? Where were they repressed or distorted? Where did you notice pride or refusal to consider another's opinion? Where did you see inconsistency or hypocrisy? Where did people compromise their beliefs?

Where did you notice a change in a character other than Babbitt? What was Babbitt's goal in life at the beginning of the book?

Read:

Just as he was an Elk, a Booster, and a member of the Chamber of Commerce, just as the priests of the Presbyterian Church determined his every religious belief and the senators who controlled the Republican Party decided in little smoky rooms in Washington what he should think about disarmament, tariff, and Germany, so did the large national advertisers fix the surface of his life, fix what he believed to be his individuality.[3]

What does that show about Babbitt's style? When did Babbitt seem most human to you? When did

[2] *Ibid.,* pp. 251-252.
[3] *Ibid.,* pp. 80-81.

he fail? When did you feel the most pity for Babbitt?

Three quotes reveal changes in Babbitt's life:

He was haunted by the ancient thought that somewhere must exist the not impossible she who would understand him, value him, and make him happy.[4]

Thus it came to him merely to run away was folly, because he could never run away from himself.[5]

". . . I've never done a single thing I've wanted to in my whole life! I don't know's I've accomplished anything except just get along. I figure out I've made about a quarter of an inch out of a possible hundred rods. . . . Well, maybe you'll carry things on further, I don't know. But I do get a kind of sneaking pleasure out of the fact that you knew what you wanted to do and did it. . . . Don't be scared of the family. No, nor all of Zenith. Nor of yourself, the way I've been. Go ahead, old man! The world is yours."[6]

In which case did Babbitt see his situation most clearly?

What was Babbitt's problem or struggle? How did he deal with it?

Does Babbitt remind you of anyone you know? Where do you see yourself in Babbitt? That is, where do you see his problems in your life?

Briefly, what is the book about?

3. THEOLOGICAL QUESTIONS

When were Babbitt's illusions destroyed? When did he realize his finiteness and know he couldn't ultimately plan and control his life? We can call this the activity of God.

[4] *Ibid.,* p. 236.
[5] *Ibid.,* p. 242.
[6] *Ibid.,* p. 319.

Paul Tillich speaks of sin as separation from God, self, and others. Where does this separation occur in the book?

Read: "Whatever the misery, he could not regain contentment with a world which, once doubted, became absurd."[7] Have you ever experienced anything similar? When do you think Babbitt was free? When was he not free?

Read:

"Ought to be ashamed, bullying her. Maybe there is her side to things. Maybe she hasn't had such a bloomin' hectic time herself. But I don't care! Good for her to get waked up a little. And I'm going to keep free. Of her and Tanis and the fellows at the club and everybody. I'm going to run my own life!"[8]

How does this compare with Christ's message of love? Can a Christian really run his own life? When did Babbitt live some aspect of Christ's lifestyle? When did he seek to do the right thing, rather than seek the approval of man? (Refused the Good Citizen's League)

How did Christ's rebellion against status quo (Matthew 23) differ from Babbitt's? How else do Christ and Babbitt differ?

Read:

Instantly all the indignations which had been dominating him and the spiritual dramas through which he had struggled became pallid and absurd before the ancient and overwhelming realities, the standard and traditional realities, of sickness and menacing death, the long night, and the thousand steadfast implications of married life. He crept back to her. As she drowsed away in the tropic languor of morphia, he sat on the edge of

her bed, holding her hand, and for the first time in many weeks her hand abode trustfully in his.[9]

When has an important event made your worries and complaints seem trivial or forced you to re-evaluate your situation?

What statements about life does this story suggest?

How is *Babbitt* similar to other stories you have read or seen portrayed on the screen?

4. CLOSING

In conclusion, read the author's note to *The Web and the Rock* by Thomas Wolfe:

This novel is about one man's discovery of life and the world . . . through fantasy and illusion, through falsehood and his own foolishness, through being . . . egotistical and aspiring and hopeful and believing and confused, and pretty much what every one of us is, and goes through . . . and becomes.[10]

Then, read a segment of Joan of Arc's trial from *The Lark* by Jean Anouilh:

CAUCHON: You are saying . . . that the real miracle of God . . . is man. Man, who is naught but sin and error, impotent against his own wickedness—

JOAN: And man is also strength and courage and splendor in his most desperate minutes. I know man because I have seen him. He is a miracle.[11]

Let the quotes sink in silence, without your trying to moralize with them.

[7] *Ibid.*, p. 236.
[8] *Ibid.*, p. 295.

[9] *Ibid.*, p. 305.
[10] Thomas Wolfe, *The Web and the Rock* from Charles L. Wallis, ed., *Speaker's Resources from Contemporary Literature* (New York: Harper & Row, Publishers, 1965), page 183.
[11] Jean Anouilh, *The Lark*, translated and adapted by Jean Anouilh (New York: Random House, 1956), page 171.

HOW DO YOU FEEL?

by WAYNE MAJORS

PURPOSE

To understand what emotions are and how to handle them.

INTRODUCTION

Joe—"How do you feel about Sue?"

Bill—"Sue? I think Sue is a . . ."

There is a great difference in what you think and what you feel. You think with your mind, but your feelings are more physical than that. Your emotions often express themselves right in the "pit of your stomach." It's the difference between what goes through your mind and what happens within you when you almost have a head-on collision on the highway. Your mind says, "I'm going to die or be hurt." Your stomach knots up and adrenaline is pumped into your system and you feel *fear*. Fear is the emotion. *I'm going to die* is the thought.

In the two-sentence conversation at the beginning of this lesson, Joe asked for Bill's emotion, and Bill replied with his thought. Bill's best response might have been, "I'm very angry with Sue." That would have been a simple statement of his feeling or emotion.

We find it difficult to speak about emotions. To reveal our emotions is to let another person know what's inside of us, and we usually guard our inner feelings like a secret treasure. Keeping our emotions a secret can be dangerous in several ways. It can keep us at a distance from other people. We never let them know us completely; we only let them know what we think. Also, doctors have known for years that holding emotions inside can make a person physically or mentally ill. If you are angry, for example, and you keep your anger in you, it can give you an upset stomach or even ulcers. A poster slogan that expresses this says, "When I repress my emotions, my stomach keeps score."

In this session, we will try to learn what emotions are and how to handle them in ways that will be harmless to ourselves and others.

PLANS

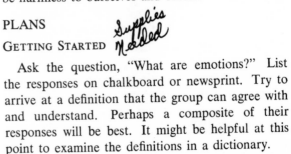

GETTING STARTED

Ask the question, "What are emotions?" List the responses on chalkboard or newsprint. Try to arrive at a definition that the group can agree with and understand. Perhaps a composite of their responses will be best. It might be helpful at this point to examine the definitions in a dictionary.

Next, make a list of emotions on chalkboard or newsprint with each person in the group helping to make the list. Edit the list, marking out feelings expressed in general terms, such as "good," "bad," "nice," "rotten." Try to make it a list of specific emotions. When the group is satisfied that the list is complete, they may want to share examples of the times when they have felt each of the emotions on the list.

In case the group fails to come up with a list of emotions, here are some to work with: confident, excited, loved, accepted, appreciated, needed, embarrassed, hurt, ambivalent, shocked, aghast, overwhelmed, resentful, angry, furious, hateful, revengeful, guilty, anxious, afraid, annoyed, irritated, rattled, confused, nervous, neglected, shut out, ignored, misunderstood, unappreciated, belittled, and put down.

DISCUSSION

At this point you may want to discuss some or all of the following questions:

- Are some emotions good and some bad?
- Which are good?
- Which are bad?
- What makes us say that one is good and another is bad? (If we do.)

- Would it be better to say that some emotions are "comfortable" and some are "uncomfortable" instead of good and bad? Why or why not?
- Can you fake an emotion?

ROLE PLAY

CHARACTERS

SAM: A newspaper delivery boy who must deliver papers each day or he will lose his route. This job is very important because Sam's family is poor and they need the money. Sam has an old bike that he rides on his paper route. The bike is Sam's most prized possession and almost his only one.

SAM'S FATHER: He works for the city street department and worries constantly about making enough money to take care of his family. Sam's paper route is important to him too; it is the only way Sam can have clothes and books for school.

PETE: Sam's best friend who lives in the house behind Sam.

DIRECTIONS

Write out the description of each of the characters on cards or paper and make name tags for each character. Ask for volunteers to do the role play. Read Part I and role-play it, continuing the role play past the point where the bike is discovered. Then stop and discuss what happened:
- What emotions did Sam feel?
- How did he express them?
- What emotions did his father feel?
- How did he express them?
- How did Sam and his father respond to each other's emotions?

Part I: Sam had a newspaper route, and he had an old bicycle that he rode each morning to deliver his papers. This morning he picked up his papers from his front porch, rolled each one carefully, and filled *his bag. He carried it outside to his bike in the backyard. When he turned the corner of the house, there was his bike—fenders smashed, spokes kicked in, and the basket torn off. Someone had destroyed it during the night. Sam's father comes outside and sees Sam and the bike.*

Part II: Pete is eating breakfast when he hears Sam and his father in the next yard. He goes over and sees the bike. He offers Sam his bike to use on the paper route.

After acting out Part II, discuss it, using these questions:
- How did Pete feel when he saw the bike?
- How did he express his emotion?
- How did Sam feel when Pete offered to let him use his bike?
- How did he express it?
- What other ways could Sam, his father, and Pete have expressed their feelings?

LOOKING AT SCRIPTURE

Read the following Scripture passages and discuss:

Matthew 21:10-13   What were Jesus' emotions? How did he express them?

John 12:1-8   What feelings were probably present in this story? Mary's feelings? Jesus' feelings? Judas' feelings? How did they express them?

Matthew 22:37-40   Is Jesus talking about emotions? How do we express these kinds of emotions?

Ask: How can we best express our emotions? Is talking about them enough? Should we act them out? If so, how? If not, why not? What must be taken into consideration when we decide to act out our emotions?

Close with prayer.

83

Section 2
CELEBRATION RESOURCES

Creating Your Own Worship
Worship/Celebration Programs
Songs and Readings for Celebration

PLANNING WORSHIP/CELEBRATION

by ROBERT T. HOWARD

"When I see a stately tree or a delicate flower or a beautiful sunset, I worship," one person told me. He was explaining why he didn't attend the church any longer. "I don't need all that activity or those people to help me worship. It's personal between God and me."

Another expressed it this way: "Everything is too formal and dry in the church's worship. It's like an act everyone is putting on, but nobody really believes it, they've done it so many times. It doesn't touch *today's* needs."

There are others who offer the complaint that modern trends in worship are ruining its meaning. "Bringing guitars and banners into the church, using common language and informal dress is giving up the dignity God deserves," one stated.

"How can it be genuine worship when everything is so carefully planned?" asked still another. "I can't believe God moves according to the instructions of an order of worship prepared by some preacher or committee. Worship ought to be free and open, so real feelings can flow."

Together, these voices raise a valid concern about worship: how can it be *personal, contemporary, traditional,* and *spontaneous* at the same time? Anyone given the task of planning worship is faced with this multiple dilemma. Given the variety of expectation found among most congregations, planning for worship is perhaps more difficult than ever before.

However, there is a way to meet this apparently impossible demand. Worship planners do not have to give in to the loudest voices or those with the strongest urges. In fact, a responsible committee can often help a congregation or a youth group widen its experience through a serious attempt to make worship personal, contemporary, traditional, and spontaneous.

No worship format or single worship service will meet the varied needs in a congregation. Where there is freedom for change in worship patterns, the needs of more persons will be met.

THE COMMITTEE'S TASK

The committee responsible for planning worship should first carefully recognize its purpose. Planning worship is not a matter of deciding what will be done and said, by whom and when, in order *to make worship happen.* Genuine worship cannot be forced or required; it must be released by those who worship. The task of the planning committee, then, is to determine what actions, moods, and music, in what sequence, will help release the experience of worship for persons in the congregation.

Essential to this task is the admission that the planning doesn't make worship occur. The work of the committee still leaves room for the unexpected, the spontaneous, the personal event to appear in worship. There may be "open" places in the format—for instance, a brief period of silence or a call for personal response to a reading —or simply an implied openness to hymns and other congregational actions. The worshipers, not the plan, make the experience.

This approach obviously requires a keen sensitivity by the committee members. In their planning, they must be aware of the basic concerns and experiences of the people who form the congregation. Some helpful survey questions at this point are: "What events (victories, losses) have affected some of these people recently?" "What happenings do several people hold in common as part of their relationship?" "How will these events and happenings be included in the worship potential?" The committee's main purpose is to provide a setting in which the lives of the people may be opened, touched, and reaffirmed by the claims of the gospel of God.

COMMUNITY IN CELEBRATION

Another key to the committee's work is an understanding of the purpose of worship. The primary reason a group assembles for worship is to achieve some goal of the whole group; it is a community experience. While on a given day the group's need may be the sharing of grief at the death of some beloved member, the continuing objective of worship is preparation for being the "salt of the earth," active participants in God's continuing creation of the world.

This preparation includes accepting the past week's events—their losses as well as victories—and finding strength from them. It includes reaffirming each person's belonging in the community of faith. It includes renewal of concern for and commitment to the work of the gospel in the world. In summary, in worship people are celebrating the fact that "God is at work among us."

The committee, then, sees the worship experience as an opportunity to strengthen the life of the community of faith, and encourage the lives of individual members for their service in the world. The ideal worship experience will conclude with the people eager to "go back to work" with a renewal of commitment to affect the world with the gospel.

GUIDELINES FOR PLANNING WORSHIP

Here are some general helps for a committee to follow in determining the most likely "openings" through which expression of life and faith can be made by a specific congregation.

HARMONY OF MOOD

Regardless of other interests carried by participants in worship, the experience must give high priority to a conscious recognition of God's role in the "dialogue." To include this concern in the planning, there are several moods which need to be allowed in the worship. These moods emerge from the meaning of the Christian faith. Whatever they may be called, they include such expressions as praise, thanksgiving, confession, forgiveness, intercession, inspiration, dedication, response, and commitment.

Whether in various combinations or in a different order, these moods should be part of the worship experience. Through such openings the central features of the faith are given opportunity to touch lives. It is also through the inclusion of these moods that the genuine traditions of earlier generations are maintained, thus not only strengthening a dependence on God, but keeping worship in a historical perspective.

Important to this guideline is the achievement of harmony in these moods. Overdrawn or inappropriate emphasis at any point can weaken the depth of worship. The shifting from one mood to another should be clear but not too abrupt. They should build toward a peak at the conclusion of worship, usually ending with response or dedication.

Conscious expression of these moods is essential to the celebration of a faithful people.

BALANCE OF TONE

Another guideline for planning worship recognizes the keen balance needed in congregational participation. Each person brings attitudes, feelings, experiences, needs, hopes, and expectations when he arrives for worship. Opportunities for expressing these should be made a part of the worship. At the same time, members of the congregation need to reaffirm the shared experience of the community.

The committee can seek to give each of these tones a means of expression. By various actions and elements of involvement, the worshiping community can see itself accepting the "offerings" of its members for joint celebration and thus give recognition both to the personal and corporate significance of worship.

Achievement of balance between these two tones depends upon knowledge of the congregation. Not only is the readiness of the congregation for sharing its community life important, but the elements of expression acceptable to the worshipers must be evaluated and used wisely.

FLOW OF ENERGY

The planning committee should also give concern to the "life" of worship. Unless there is authentic involvement and enthusiasm, worship is cold. There also must be a pattern to the flow of energy to prevent an incomplete experience.

For instance, the attention of the worshipers on personal needs is valid, but should not receive the heaviest emphasis of energy. An opportunity for the community to hear and respond to the revelation of God is also necessary to the celebration. This subjective-objective flow is another key to help the committee.

To design a worship format which encourages energetic involvement is important. Helping worshipers to become responsible for the achievement of worship is not an easy task but is necessary to insure a complete experience. This includes an active "listening" by the congregation and permits the faith dialogue necessary to Christian worship.

PUTTING IT TOGETHER

Using these guidelines, the planning committee may select elements which help achieve their potential. There is a wide variety of resources available.

Hymns, prayers, responsive readings, litanies, anthems, special music, Scripture readings, unison statements, the sermon, the offering, and other more common elements become instruments in the enabling of worship.

One of the secondary responsibilities of the planning committee is to become familiar with newer actions to include in worship. These should be introduced to the congregation whenever there are opportunities, because worship should always be contemporary, not just on those occasions when a special format is followed. Thoughtful preparation and sensitive concern for the growing edge of the congregation can make such discovery a continuing experience.

Resources available to the committee may be found in several service books. Many more recently published books offer suggestions about newer elements, including use of multimedia. Some books which a committee will find helpful are:

Multi-Media Worship: A Model and Nine Viewpoints, Myron B. Bloy, Jr., ed. New York: The Seabury Press, Inc., 1969.

Ways of Worship for New Forms of Mission, Scott Francis Brenner. New York: Friendship Press, 1968.

Contemporary Worship Services, James L. Christensen. Old Tappan, New Jersey: Fleming H. Revell Company, 1971.

There is no single "secret" to effective celebration. Planning helps to eliminate unnecessary barriers and encourage the free expression of life—both the life of the community and the life God will provide—through Christian worship.

CELEBRATING OUR TOGETHERNESS

by GEORGE A. LAWSON

PURPOSE

This worship experience should emphasize the intentional, decisional, serving nature of Christianity and encourage a sense of group corporateness rather than individualism.

CONTEXT

This service could be used to conclude a retreat or celebrate a completed project or graduation.

THE ROOM

The room should contain various elements which will suggest the theme. Art prints (in various styles) of the Lord's Supper and those expressing the brokenness of life (e.g., Picasso's *Guernica*) and the unity of life (e.g., Picasso's *Mother and Child*) may be used.

On a poster, place this quote from Eugene O'Neill's *The Great God Brown*:[1] "BROWN: Man is

[1] Eugene O'Neill, *The Great God Brown* from Charles L. Wallis, ed., *Speaker's Resources from Contemporary Literature,* (New York: Harper & Row, Publishers, 1965), p. 115. Used with permission of Random House, Inc.

born broken. He lives by mending. The grace of God is glue!"

Use a rectangular table or a number of tables arranged in a square or rectangle. In the center (on an additional small table if you follow the latter plan) arrange some objects that will draw attention to the worship theme (Christian symbols, broken objects, a chalice, sculpture, a candle). Place a loaf of French bread at the leader's place and a small cup of juice at each place. If some of the "broken things" were broken because of some event in the life of the group, they could have a special meaning and significance.

THE SERVICE

The leader may be a youth, an advisor, or the minister. He or she leads the group in singing a few songs. Suggestions: (1) hymn "For All the Saints," stopping between verses to call out names of great humanitarians and churchmen, e.g., Martin Luther King, Jr., Albert Schweitzer, or a member of the group; (2) Psalm 117 (as it appears in the *Songbook of the Ecumenical Institute,* Chicago); (3) words the group has composed to sing

to popular tunes like "Amazing Grace." Encourage free body movement such as foot stomping, hand clapping, swaying, and tapping on chairs and tables to begin the worship with an enthusiastic, celebrative quality.

When everyone is seated, the leader asks: "What does it mean to worship God in the midst of the twentieth century's scientific and cultural revolutions? Worship should include full participation by everyone; it should be a rehearsal of the way life is; it should enable us to be totally obedient to God and live a life of involvement, of giving ourselves to others."

A youth leads the group in an antiphonal psalm reading.

The leader then leads a five-minute conversation asking the group to respond to these questions: What are some objects used in the Communion service? When has Communion been meaningful for you? What does Communion symbolize for you today as a modern Christian?

A youth reads 1 Corinthians 11:23b-26.

The leader breaks the loaf and points out that a meaning of the Communion bread is that it repre-

sents the brokenness of life. (Life never seems to turn out the way we expect it to.) He pours juice into his glass from a container and says that it symbolizes the "spilled-outness" of life, our capacity to give of ourselves in the midst of the brokenness.

The leader passes the loaf around the table. Each person breaks off a piece, eats it, and drinks the juice. The leader announces that sentence prayers for church and world problems may be offered. (They are begun by a couple of youth who have been asked in advance.) As each person concludes his sentence with "Amen," the group responds with "Amen" or the chorus of the spiritual "Amen," thus affirming that the prayer is not only that of an individual but of the group.

The group sings a concluding song, such as "They'll Know We Are Christians by Our Love."

Group Benediction: Go forth into the world in peace; be of good courage; hold fast to that which is good; render to no man evil for evil; strengthen the faint-hearted; support the weak; help the afflicted; honor all men; love and serve the Lord, rejoicing in the power of the Holy Spirit. Amen.

MEANING IN A FIRE

by JERRY L. BELDEN

MATERIALS NEEDED

1. A well-built campfire that will burn approximately two hours
2. Cassette tape player
3. Cassette tape of selected Christian folk music
4. Books—*God Is Beautiful, Man* and *God Is for Real, Man,* both by Carl F. Burke (Association Press, New York)

SETTING

Out of doors around campfire or indoors around fireplace. Only light is that of the fire.

PERSONS NEEDED TO LEAD SERVICE

One person can lead the worship service, but the service will have much more meaning if more than one person leads it. For example, one person with a guitar could lead the singing; another person could read the Scripture; and another person lead the group conversation.

THE SERVICE

TAPED MUSIC

Christian folk music

GROUP SINGING

Sing songs informally. Use songs which the group knows. Some suggestions are: "He's Got the Whole World in His Hands," "Jacob's Ladder," "Let Us Break Bread Together," "Lord, I Want to Be a Christian."

SCRIPTURE

1. "When a Man Gets Pulled Out" (John 3:1-21) from *God Is for Real, Man* by Carl F. Burke.
2. "Getting Sins Fixed Up" (Acts 10:34) from *God Is Beautiful, Man* by Carl F. Burke.

GROUP SINGING

Sing some more songs informally or have someone sing a solo, perhaps with guitar accompaniment.

GROUP CONVERSATION

Using tongs or two long sticks, remove several coals of varying sizes from the fire, each coal being left several inches apart from any other coal. Allow the group to watch the separated coals for three or four minutes, noticing that the glow of the coals by themselves gets dimmer by the moment. Then put the coals into the fire to burn once again.

Encourage the group members to talk about their thoughts as they watch the coals losing their glow.

Then ask: If we are Christians, can we be on fire? How? How can we keep our fire going and our life aglow?

CLOSING

Ask the members of the worshiping congregation to join hands in friendship in a circle. Then tell them that following a closing prayer, each person should affirm the other members of the worshiping congregation with a handshake, a "God bless you," an embrace, or some other meaningful expression. Pray a simple, meaningful, brief prayer, expressing what has happened in the worship service.

Use of cameras, records, art, live music, and the spoken word to create worship in a new format

REJOICE IN THE LORD: A CELEBRATION
by PATSY C. PETERSON

INTRODUCTION

Describing in words a worship/celebration like the one suggested in these pages is very difficult. The full dimension of meaningfulness can be captured only through active participation in the service. The reader should keep in mind that the accurate "translation" results when the ideas set forth here are adapted and used in his or her own local setting.

This celebration is based upon the words of Psalm 118:24 and Philippians 4:4. The most authentic worship/celebration events come through a group process of shared experience. We have many gifted youth in our midst today, and this service is designed for a group of youth to dedicate their time and talents to God and praise him in a service of joyfulness.

The following pattern of suggestions is only a guide for directing youth to express, on a high, affirmative note through visual images, music, and spoken word that Christians truly have something to CELEBRATE. The pattern set forth in these pages is of a multimedia nature, since there are so many ways in which youth of today can utilize their God-given talents in proclaiming their faith through the various forms of media.

MEDIA

The media suggested for use are:

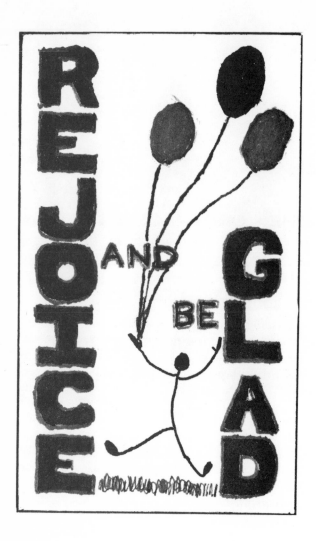

CAMERAS

Whether simple Instamatic or sophisticated 35mm or super-8mm (movie), cameras are accessible to and used by many youth. Also, the projectors necessary for showing slides and movies are now owned by these same youth or their parents. Photography can be a welcome means for the less verbally oriented person to make significant theological statements.

RECORDS AND TAPE RECORDINGS

These provide another means of meaningful expression of faith. Some contemporary records are especially good for church use. Youth can also make their own tapes of music, sound collages, etc., in creating a worship event.

ART

This has been somewhat neglected in the recent past by the church. Artistically gifted youth can contribute to celebration and church art through designing and making banners. Two simple designs for banners which could be utilized in this celebration are shown at the beginning of this chapter.

LIVE MUSIC

This has had a long and important role in communicating the faith. In addition to vocal music, guitar, trumpet, and organ are suggested for use in the service outlined in these pages. These instruments mentioned are intended to serve only as indicators of how various musical instruments can be an integral part of celebration. Instrumentalists are a great enhancement to a celebrative event.

WORDS

The verbal aspect is not to be neglected, as it is a vital means of communication. Encourage youth gifted in writing to prepare poetic and prose materials to be used at appropriate points of the service.

OUTLINE

A basic outline for "Rejoice in the Lord":
BECOME
Preparing

Greeting
Questioning
Replying
Affirming
REJOICE
Proclaiming through song
Proclaiming words and visual images
Affirming through song
BEGIN
Challenging
Dedicating and giving
Taking form

THE EVENT

A good starting point for implementing this outline is to select a core group of youth and one or two adult facilitators who will be responsible for preparing the worship event. With the aid of the more detailed information below, this core group can develop an event for its own local setting and needs.

BECOME

As participants begin to gather for the celebration, they can be given some orientation for the overall mood of the event by having recorded music playing before the first formal greeting. Some selections that can be used for this are: selections from the album *Switched-On Bach* (Columbia); "Classical Gas" from the album *Mason Williams Phonograph Record* (Warner Brothers-Seven Arts); "Joy" (Mega—45 r.p.m.); and "Popcorn" (Musicor—45 r.p.m.).

The initial moments of the celebration are important for the development of a spirit of community. A brief, informal, responsive call to worship is an excellent first step. Youth gifted in verbalizing can contribute at this point. The greeting should incorporate Scripture passages mentioned in the Introduction.

With the mention of rejoicing and gladness in the greeting, a rather natural question might arise with respect to how it can be possible to rejoice and be glad. A predetermined person can raise this question. Here again, a verbally gifted person could prepare a "script." Headlines could be used

in a creative manner to suggest the context of life and worship.

The reply to the question can then move into the audio-visual element of the celebration. The use of the recording "Lean on Me" by Bill Withers (Sussex—45 r.p.m.) and accompanying slides which complement visually the words of the song can be effective. A challenging presentation results if slides are projected with two projectors. One projector could contain slides depicting struggles of mankind. This projector should be started at the same time as the record. The second projector could contain slides of Christ symbols, i.e., pictures of Christ, crosses, and other Christian symbols. (The pictures of Christ can be obtained by taking a photograph of large pictures found in most churches.) The other slides could be handmade by methods described in "How to Make Slides" in *Respond, Volume 2*. The second projector should not be started until the line of the song lyric, "Lean on me when you're not strong." The first projector should be turned off with the conclusion of the music, but the second projector showing Christian symbols should continue to flash slides on the screen for several seconds during a period of silence following the end of the record. Thus the emphasis is placed upon the importance of a Christ-centered life.

A time of corporate sharing following the record and slides can be developed through spontaneous responses to the statement: "To be a Christian is like. . . ." This method of sharing will further facilitate the community aspect of worship. (One person might give a brief explanation of how simile is used as a creative litany. Through this method each person is provided opportunity to make his own affirmation of faith. Some may choose to remain silent, and it must be understood that for some silence is a more meaningful participation than open participation.)

REJOICE

When the affirmations of faith have been made, the stage is set for active rejoicing. Philippians 4:4 set to music in round form can be the invitation to rejoice.

Re - joice in the Lord al - ways, and a-

gain I say re - joice. Re - joice! Re-

joice, and a - gain I say re-joice.

When first group starts second line, the second
group starts first line; when second group starts
second line, the third group starts first line; etc.;
etc.

Banners can be brought into the place of worship and put in appropriate positions as the congregation is singing the round.

Additional songs which can be used to follow the singing of the round and the placing of the banners are: "All You Peoples, Clap Your Hands" by Ray Repp, "Clap Your Hands" by Paul Quinlan, and "To Be Alive" by Ray Repp from *Hymnal for Young Christians, Volume 2* (Chicago: F.E.L. Publications, Ltd., 1969); verses 1 and 2 of "This Is the Day" by Cyril A. Reilly and Roger Nachtwey from *Hymns for Now II* (St. Louis: Concordia Publishing House, 1969). Guitar accompaniment is especially good for all of the above songs. In addition to the hymnals mentioned previously, *Songbook for Saints and Sinners* by Carlton R. Young (Carol Stream, Ill.: agápe, 1971) is a good collection of hymns of contemporary nature and is helpful when a search is being made for songs for contemporary celebration.

For a change of pace, further proclamation can be made with the use of a super-8mm movie planned and prepared by youth. The film should show local scenes depicting: (1) life struggles, (2) life in Christ, (3) life as Christian celebration. The sound track of the movie can be composed of readings of creative writing of young people or taped music or a sound collage reflecting the moods of the visual images appearing on the screen.

Affirmation of the celebrative ending of the movie can be the community singing of the carol "Joy to the World." Singing this carol at times other than the Christmas season can be very significant.

BEGIN

Celebration truly begins when one accepts the challenge for Christian involvement in the humdrum of the everydayness in the world. Typical everyday-type needs and situations can be reviewed and a challenge made to meet these in the strength of Christ. This segment of the event provides another opportunity for the spoken word prepared for the community by those gifted with verbalizing.

At the conclusion of the challenge, each person can be requested to write on a slip of paper one specific time during the coming week that he will dedicate to assist someone with a specific, known need. These offerings can be brought forward to a designated place. If physical surroundings permit, a rustic cross can be in view at all times during the service, and the offerings can be placed at the base of the cross. As people move forward and then return to their places, "Joyful, Joyful We Adore Thee" can be played by organ and trumpet. A trumpet descant makes for a more interesting offertory. One descant that can be used is:

Trumpet in D   by David Barger

A time of silence is recommended following the offering. Then one of the worship leaders can quote the words to "Christ Takes Form" by Kent Schneider. (The words and music to "Christ Takes Form" can be obtained by writing to The Center for Contemporary Celebration, 1400 East 53rd Street, Chicago, IL 60615.) The leader can then invite the community to participate in singing this benediction. An effective way to do this is to have the community sing the hymn two or three times and then, continuing to sing, move into the world.

NOTE

This worship/celebration entails planning and participation on the part of many people. The most rewarding facet of a service like this is that encounter with God becomes reality as individuals come together in shared experiences of "being in Christ."

REJOICE IN THE LORD!
AND
AGAIN I SAY REJOICE!

WE ARE THE CHURCH

by JERRY L. BELDEN

MATERIALS NEEDED

1. Number of chairs, placed in a circle, equaling the number of persons present
2. Record player
3. Recording of *Jesus Christ Superstar*
4. Book: Carl F. Burke, *Treat Me Cool, Lord* (New York: Association Press, 1968)
5. Songbook, *Hymns for Now* (Concordia Publishing House)
6. Paper cups, one for every four members of the worshiping congregation
7. *New English Bible*

SETTING

The place of worship can be anywhere the worshiping congregation can come together in a flexible circle, sitting on the floor or on chairs.

LEADERSHIP

One person can lead this worship experience, but if more than one person leads, it will be more meaningful. For example, if one person leads in the call to worship, the prayer, and the benediction, another person with a guitar could lead the singing, and a third person could then lead the action experience.

ORDER OF SERVICE

MUSIC

Play selections from *Jesus Christ Superstar*.

CALL TO WORSHIP

"Let each of us share what we believe the world needs most, in one word, as our call to worship."

The members of the worshiping congregation will then respond by saying many things like "Love," "Peace," or "Jesus."

PRAYER

"Everybody's Got the Same Father," pages 84 and 85 of *Treat Me Cool, Lord* by Carl F. Burke.

SONG

"They'll Know We Are Christians"

EXPERIENCE

1. Divide the worshiping congregation into groups of fours (quads).

98

2. Give a paper cup to each quad.

3. The person given the cup is to hold it until the following instructions are given; then that person will begin the action.

- The cup is the church. First person is to do to the cup what he would like to do to the church, nonverbally.

- Then the second person receives the cup (the church) in whatever shape the first person leaves it. He then does to the church (the cup) what he feels needs to be done under the circumstances, without saying a word. After the second person finishes, he passes it on to number three who does what he thinks needs to be done and passes it to number four. Number four then continues to do what he feels needs to be done to the church under the circumstances that he finds it and passes it back to number one.

- Then the quads pass the cup around again, with each person telling what he did to the cup and why.

- After the quads are finished, the number one person will share what happened in his quad with the total worshiping congregation.

4. The leader should then summarize the experience, bringing out the importance of the church in our lives, even though for all of us the church is not perfect and there are many things we would like to change about it.

SCRIPTURE

1 Corinthians 12:12-27 (NEB).

SONG

"Sons of God," page 23 of *Hymns for Now*

BENEDICTION

In closing, the leader asks each one in the group to share how "we are the church" by putting his thoughts into one sentence. In response to this, the leader leads the group in singing a chorus of "Amen," page 11 of *Hymns for Now*.

MUSIC

Selected portions of *Jesus Christ Superstar*

A SUMMONS TO CELEBRATION!

by ROBERT A. NOBLETT

FOR OPENERS

Do you ever get the feeling that we live in an era of gloominess? No question about it, there are many realities that make us feel their crippling tragedy (and indeed as Christians we ought to feel tragedy and do something about it); but we are something less than effective if we bring to such situations only more gloom! Let us suppose that we go out of our home on a cold winter day only to find our car's battery stone dead. So we call the garage for help. But what happens if we find that the battery in the tow truck is just as dead? If we are going to be of significant assistance to other people, we will want to approach with our batteries in tip-top shape and fully energized. Let us think about worship as a reenergizing process and suggest some steps in planning a worship experience around the theme of celebration.

WHAT WE'RE ABOUT

The invitation to worship is not unlike the invitation that is extended to us by any body of water as we stand on its shores. It conveys a certain magnetism and draws us near. We wade in, become familiar with it, and soon find ourselves enjoying it to the hilt. We feel supported and buoyant as we rest on its surface and we feel warm and relaxed as the sun shines down in its fullness. To extend our analogy further, when we come to worship we are attracted by its message of hope, and trust that during our experience of it we are rendered buoyant by our fellow worshipers. Together we break open once again the good news of the gospel and take the nourishment it offers us.

SOME STRUCTURE

THE SUMMONS

Worship is an intentional act which has a beginning and an ending. It opens with a statement of affirmation. Since our theme is to be celebration, have a participant draft a summons to worship which incorporates a sense of gladness and hope. For example:

Serve the Lord with gladness!
  Come into his presence with singing! . . .
Enter his gates with thanksgiving,
  and his courts with praise!
  Give thanks to him, bless his name!
For the Lord is good;
  his steadfast love endures for ever,
  and his faithfulness to all generations (Psalm 100:2-5).

That's a traditional one. It would doubtless be more meaningful if a person could write a summons that comes out of personal experience. Something like this may be more authentic and meaningful: "The pace of our lives is often so great that we feel like we are on a merry-go-round that not only goes round and round but up and down as well. I invite you, therefore, to participate in an act of worship through which we will hear once more the good news that God holds us in deepest affection and wants for each of his children happiness and wholeness."

The summons could be delivered by the reading of poetry, or the viewing of a poster, or the playing of music. In ancient Israel, the day of worship began with the blast of a trumpet!

DEVELOPING THE THEME

The theme can be simply declared: "It is our purpose to talk together about celebration." Have the participants list and then share together those things which make them happy and celebrative. Background music played while they are writing could be encouraging. Select music which draws out the theme, such as "My Favorite Things" from *The Sound of Music* or the song "Joy Is Like the Rain" from the album of the same name (Avant Garde, stereo AVS-101).

100

Another method would be to contact the participants some time before the day the worship is to be experienced and have them bring in various media which would express sources of joy—pictures, slides, home movies, cassette recordings, art prints, etc. In either case (you may want to do both), allow for a time of individual elaboration and explanation.

CREATING A COMPOSITE

Another vital element in worship is the proclamation of the Word. This portion is usually referred to as the homily or sermon, and its purpose is to bring the wishes of God—as we understand them from biblical faith and present personal experience—to bear on the lives of the worshipers.

We know today, moreover, that there is a great deal of power in a group of people—an infinite amount of understanding, of insight, of energy—and so why not use it in the development of a corporate sermon—a composite of the thoughts and feelings of the group regarding the nature of celebration?

Your church library or your pastor has a biblical concordance, so secure it and find the list of biblical references under the heading "joy." Divide them up among the participants and have them feed back to the group what the various references seem to be suggesting about the essence of joy.

Jot these thoughts down on newsprint. Then have the group think together about what stands behind, what allows for, those happy moments they have spoken of earlier. For example, one person may have written down a family picnic as something which affords deep delight. Why is that? Could it have something to do with the fact that the family cares for each other, listens to each other, supports each other?

Through this process, the worshipers should be able to create a composite sermon on joy or celebration. It would be helpful to summarize and list on newsprint the conclusions. The result might be something like this: Christians celebrate because God loves them; this love has been most deeply expressed in the event of Jesus Christ; and whenever Christians behaviorally reflect the wish of God that his children live together in peace and mutual respect and understanding, they are providing for that moment when happiness and celebration will be decidedly felt.

WRAPPING THINGS UP

Worship calls forth resolve. When we leave the experience, we ought to be different from when we began. Worship is an act of reaffirmation. There should be some sort of commitment made on the part of the participants to give daily embodiment to feelings of celebration and joy. This might be expressed by having the group join hands and sing a favorite hymn or song ("Joyful, Joyful, We Adore Thee" or a popular song which tells of happiness) or engage in unison prayer or simply repeat together the summary of thoughts developed in the composite. At the conclusion of worship, the participants should feel they are in closer touch with themselves, their friends, and God. When this happens, we know worship to be authentic.

JOY!

Suzi Grizzard

© Suzi Grizzard, used by permission.

NEW REALITY

Donald Nelson

Donald Nelson

(Based on the story of the paralytic at the temple gate)

( ) Chords in parentheses are for low voice or for use with capo.

2. And then they came and glanced my way.
Peter and John their names they say.
Not a cent have we to give,
But we can help to make you live.

3. And then they took my trembling hand.
They lifted me and made me stand.
Imagine me a-walkin' 'round,
My happy tears washed the ground.

4. O praise to God for what he's done.
I'm free again—my battle won.
Lord, take my hand and guide my way,
Help me to live my faith each day.

FREEDOM

Debbie New

Bill England

High in the sky the ea-gle soars. My spir-it breaks loose and yearns to go with him. To-geth-er we drive—down, down, down. Sud-den-ly he wheels and climbs, Leav-ing my spir-it to plum-met to the earth be-low, As the ea-gle soars in the free-dom of the heav'ns a-bove.

HOW TO LOVE GOD

Connie Ketter

How can you say you love God? How can you say you love God when you don't e-ven love your broth-er? How can you say you love Christ? How can you say you love Christ when you hav-en't giv-en him your life?——— Praise the Lord with all your heart. Praise the Lord with all your soul. Praise the Lord with all your mind. Praise the Lord; then you can say you love God, then you can say you love God, but on-ly if you've giv-en him your life.

A JOINING OF VOICES

by Richard Orr

(Shouts and exclamations to be used at the beginning of a joyful moment)

We're alive.

Thank you, Lord. Your hand has touched
our dust.
You gave us breathing air and
breathing space.

We thank you, Lord, for the sight and sense
to see the flowers,
to hear the wind,
to feel the waters in our hand,
to sleep with the night and wake with the sun,
to sing praises to you,
to hear your voice in our happenings.

Our hearts are stirred with each new sight and
sound. Like a stream, the whole world pours into
our eyes,
our hands,
and fills our souls with living gladness.

O Lord, our God, continue to surprise us with
joy!

A-A-A men!

HANDLES FOR LEADERS—YOUTH AND ADULTS

GUIDELINES FOR RAISING MONEY
by ROGER W. PRICE

A project to raise money inevitably involves time, effort, and sometimes a preliminary expense. When is a work project a good expenditure of your and your youth group's energy and when is it not? This question sooner or later must be faced.

Very few groups have to earn money to pay for basic youth ministry resources. The great majority of churches consider it their responsibility to provide church school materials and supplies as well as other resources, such as the *Respond* books.

If money must be raised for basic program expense, a lot of time that should be spent in study, fellowship, and worship will be lost. Churches should consider basic resource materials as necessary, such as pews, hymnals, lights, water, and other such items.

Most groups, however, have to seek financial support for special projects, e.g., mission trips, work projects, retreats, camps, special conferences, or for contributing to a special cause.

More and more churches are taking the responsibility of caring for all of the advisors' expenses, especially so on special trips, conferences, or projects. Most adult workers with youth spend a considerable amount of money as it is, on snacks when youth come over, babysitting while they are with the youth group, books, etc. Plan ahead and you may be able to get a special item included in the church budget if a trip or conference is especially expensive to the adults who work with youth.

SHOULD YOU GO THE PROJECT ROUTE?

Many factors need to be considered in evaluating the benefits to be received from a project against the expenditure of time and energy that will be needed. The board of finance or the board of trustees in many churches has rules that regulate the timing and kind of money-raising projects that can be carried out by church groups. You should check your situation to find out whether there are such rules before planning your project.

While there is no clear, objective way to measure the worthwhileness of a project, there are some general guidelines that need to be considered and questions that should be asked.

1. When can planning be accomplished, and can the youth carry out much of the responsibility? Use as little time as possible from your regular activities so that the project doesn't become all-consuming.

2. Are you sure it's worth the effort? It's always possible that work projects are a way of avoiding serious struggles in theology, the Christian life, group cooperation, or another important area of a group's life. Consider those who will benefit and how they will be aided. The comparison between time and effort and probable return must be considered. Some projects take a lot of preparation and work with relatively little financial return.

109

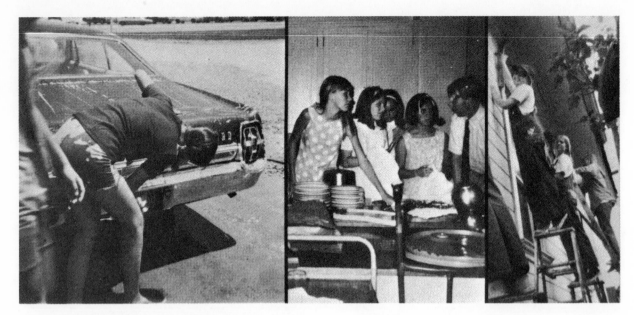

3. Will this particular project be disruptive of time in study, worship, or other areas of group life? Not everyone responds to everything in the same way. Be sure that a young person is not excluded because he can't work on a project or go on a trip.

4. Can you do what you say you will in a project, and can you do it well? It's better to have a smaller project and do it well than fail or do a sloppy job in a larger undertaking. Remember you may want to do another project in the future and that success or failure may be judged on how well you do now.

5. Have enough safety precautions been taken? While something can go wrong anytime and someone may be injured, there are some work projects which by their very nature have more risk of injury than another activity. Who is responsible for medical bills if someone should be injured? Some groups have blanket accident insurance, or insurance may be purchased at a low cost for each activity. Check with an insurance representative in your church to discover if your group is covered or can be covered by a policy.

6. Do you need any special equipment or special skills? If you are going to have a car wash, you need hoses, vacuum cleaners, etc. You also need to decide, for instance, who is going to drive the cars through a car wash, if this is necessary. Other projects call for their own special equipment.

7. Look ahead to potential problems. Think of various alternatives to problem situations, e.g., rain might affect your project. Include information on the alternate plans in your publicity.

CHOOSING A PROJECT

The number and kind of youth projects to raise money is almost endless. The following activities have all been used in the past with people either paying a set price or making a donation for the service given:

- garage or rummage sale
- bake sale
- car wash
- ice cream social
- Sunday morning breakfast for the whole church
- dramatic play or talent night
- fine arts festival
- hobby show
- chili supper
- sending out mailings (for businesses or other organizations at particular times in the year)
- slave day (Youth are auctioned off for a day to the highest bidder. This event can have the side benefit of providing good youth-adult dialogue.)
- collect bottles, cans, newspapers, etc.
- sell various items, e.g., Christmas cards, candles, candy, etc.
- spook house at Halloween

- dinner at church annual meeting or other special occasion
- decorate a float for a parade, e.g., the Tournament of Roses Parade on New Year's Day in Pasadena, Calif.

Look around. You will find some particular need or interest in your community or church that your group could fulfill.

GETTING THE WORD AROUND

A good job on publicity is desirable for several different reasons. The church needs to know what the youth groups are doing. Many adults who are not in contact with kids seem to develop negative attitudes toward youth from much of what they see and hear in the newspapers and on TV. If you are doing something good, let others know about it. We need more good news.

The congregation will certainly be more willing to support a group's work projects when they know that the receipts are going for a good cause. Publicity may also bring specific donations from some very unexpected sources. Individuals you never thought of before may make a generous contribution because a project is of particular interest to them or they like what the group is doing.

At times, after careful consideration, you might choose to approach a particular individual and ask him or her to make a contribution. Individuals are often most willing to make a special contribution, particularly if it can be arranged so that the

money goes to pay the way of someone who otherwise might not be able to share in a particular event. Some care should be taken so that a young person who has financial problems, whose way is paid, is not embarrassed by having others know about this arrangement. The more privately this can be arranged, the better.

If you do choose to approach individuals or groups (e.g., adult church school classes) to make a contribution to your project, be sure you don't overwork a good thing.

ADVANTAGES OF PROJECTS

Two possible advantages to projects have not yet been mentioned. Work projects have a way of increasing a sense of fellowship in a group as the youth 'work together on a common task. This factor can often be of great importance.

A work project may also give the adult youth worker an opportunity to work alongside, and informally talk with, a young person who may be quite shy and seemingly unresponsive in a regular group meeting. At times it seems easier to talk while working together on a task than just individual to individual.

Work projects are neither bad or good in and of themselves. How they are used and the way they are carried out determine their value. They can be a very useful tool in accomplishing a particular goal.

111

GUIDELINES FOR SERVICE PROJECTS

by DUANE L. SISSON

THE PLACE TO START

Someone in the youth group feels the group should become involved in a meaningful service project. Now how do you go about it?

At the outset the whole group should get on board. Something like this usually starts with one or two individuals, but the commitment of the group is important if it is to be successful. The group needs to respond in its own way. Groups are like persons. They each have their own personality and interests, their own individual characteristics. What works one place will not work in another. What is true for one group often is not true for another.

The first answer to the question of how the group is to get involved is to discover who you are as a group. Is there real interest in Christian service? Is a service project the task that has top priority for your group at this time or are there other things that must be completed and put together before the group is spiritually ready and mature enough to undertake service for others beyond itself? What kinds of skills do you have to offer? What service is needed in your community? What blocks of time are involved in a specific opportunity for service? Are the members of the group available at the time needed? How about the problems related to regular transportation?

Manufacturing service projects is probably the one thing we should never do. Service is a two-way street. The very fact you feel that your group needs to do something indicates that service is for the group as well as others. We "do" to meet our need as well as the needs of others.

If service is to meet the need of your group, then the leader's responsibility is to help the group define its need for itself. Listening is very important in accomplishing this task. In group life, concerns are voiced in many ways. We need to be aware of what is being said and aid the group in listening to each other. Rather than dumping on the group the idea that they need to do a project, we can support that voice within the group calling for service.

CHOOSING A PROJECT

When a group wants to give to itself, then its members are ready, as a group, to choose a service project. Certainly a criterion for choosing a project is that it must meet a real need. Nothing kills service more than doing something that was manufactured to meet our need and not really to accomplish a task for someone else. A group needs to

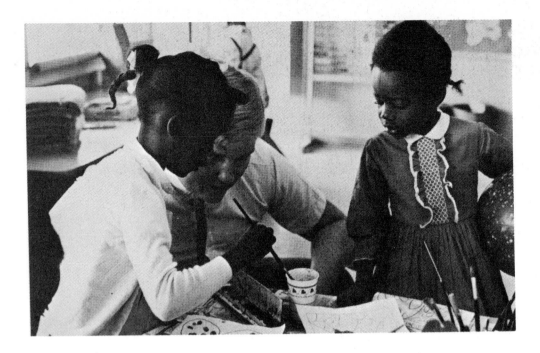

subordinate its own desire to the goal of fulfilling the needs of the other. This method is not always convenient, but service, real service, as in the good Samaritan story, is seldom convenient.

The group must have an understanding of what it can do, including the time it can give a project. Another thing that can successfully kill the spirit of service is the inability to finish a project.

It is good at the outset to set a time limit on the group's service commitment. Example: "We will agree to provide eight tutors for one-to-one teaching at the community center each Tuesday afternoon from 4:00-6:00 P.M. for eight weeks starting the first of the month." This kind of contract can be completed by the group. If a group starts a task with no ending point in mind, the time of ending is likely to be frustrating and divisive to the group. If the time period in the original contract is fulfilled and the group continues to be enthusiastic, the time can be extended, but a new agreed-upon ending date needs to be clearly established. If there is no sense of completion, even in an ongoing project, a group can develop a real sense of frustration and failure. "We did it!" is not just an expression of pride. It reflects completion of a commitment and offers a revealing sense that God can work through you, and service does accomplish something in us and for others.

In order to find projects which the group can do, a group should develop a list of needs around them in the church, the neighborhood, the community, the country, and the world. Developing a possible project list is not manufacturing service projects but becoming aware of real needs. And there are real needs all around us. As the group makes a list, they will discover some projects they cannot do. Others they may be able to do may not be as glamorous. The very act of choosing a project which they feel needs to be done may develop a real sense of the purpose and mission of this project. Becoming aware of the potential value of the project is an important step in having it become a fulfilling experience for the group.

EVALUATION

In carrying out a project for and with others, a group should communicate to the recipients of the project that what the group is doing is aiding the group as well as the recipients. Thus, those receiving the aid of the project are involved in giving also. When the project itself is seen as a two-way experience for both parties, then we get away from the paternalistic attitude which sometimes curtails or sours a service project experience.

It is great to give. In God's economy, giving is always receiving. Capitalizing upon the interest of youth to give and guiding them into meeting real needs on both parts is a beautiful and rewarding responsibility for you as a youth worker.

THE PLAY'S THE THING – FOR LOOSENING UP,
FOR GROUP-BUILDING,
FOR COMMUNICATING
by LUCINDA C. RAY

Drama in youth ministry has traditionally been viewed as a vehicle for examining significant issues. This use of drama continues to be important. Drama is also helpful in loosening up a group and in building a sense of togetherness within the group.

If your church youth group is typical, its members include some who are interested, some who are indifferent, and some who are painfully self-conscious about participating in drama. The process of giving these people sheets of paper with lines for them to read or memorize may not result in the production for which you had hoped. Before your group members plunge into the structure of a specific play or role-playing situation, they may need loosening up and freeing up.

Theater games are group exercises which are remarkable in their ability to loosen and free people, as individuals and as a group, for creative activity. A series of these exercises is suggested here. You may be able to think of others. However, the general progression from simple to more involved is important to follow.

THEATER GAMES

LOOSENING UP AND BODY AWARENESS *(10 minutes)*

Rationale

Most people are self-conscious and tense if asked to perform, but they are frequently powerless to locate or relax this tension.

Exercise

1. Have everyone lie on the floor. Tell them that they all have wonderful, useful, fancy bodies, but much energy is expended when they are nervous. Help them experience relaxation in contrast with tension.

2. Ask the participants to tighten up every muscle in their bodies: fingers, ankles, stomach, throat, calves, ears. Name the parts. Keep reminding them by naming body parts.

3. After about one minute, say, "Now relax." Then point out how much work it takes to be tense.

4. Next, help them relax more specifically by asking them to tighten and then relax individual

muscles, beginning with toes, insteps, ankles, heels, etc. Be as specific as possible. Even teeth can be a source of tension! (Remember, concentrating tension on a specific body part, such as a tense neck, can also be a great key to creating a character in a script.)

5. After you have helped them to become aware of every muscle and have helped them to relax, gradually get them to sit up. Take this exercise slowly. Some people are completely relaxed only when they're sleeping!

6. As an extension of this exercise, try doing it standing up, or while the group walks around the room.

BODY MOVEMENT *(5 minutes)*

Rationale

Faced with a performance, many people become physically immobilized. For many the range of acceptable body movements is *very* small. Bodies can do many things that we normally don't allow them to do—think of all the fun we miss!

Exercise

1. You, the leader, can help to free the group by contorting your own body as grotesquely as possible. The more absurd *you* look, the less uncomfortable *they* will feel about their own bodies.

2. Ask the group members to move their bodies in as many different ways as they can think of. Suggest things like: putting head between legs, heel behind ear, jumping, stomping, walk holding ankles. Have everyone move at the same time, so that no one is on display. Continue for 3–5 minutes.

3. Keep reminding them that "it's OK to experiment," "give your body a holiday," "think of how bored your body usually is." The more encouragement you give, the more creative and experimental your group will become.

NOISES *(2–3 minutes)*

Rationale

Same as Body Movement.

Exercise

Point out how few noises people are allowed to make: speaking, singing, whistling, and sometimes crying or shouting. Help them by making a few weird beeps, blats, honks, rasps. Then ask everybody to experiment with noises *at the same time,*

so no one is listening to anyone else. Most groups find this exhilarating.

MACHINES *(10 minutes)*

Rationale

Let the group see that the exercises used so far can be given some meaning. Have fun.

Exercise

1. Ask each person to select one movement and one sound which he or she can repeat easily and rhythmically. (For example, flexing arms and saying Blug-Blug-Blug-Wheeeeee.)

2. Start with one person in the center doing his movement and sound. One at a time, each person then physically connects to the previous person with his own movement and sound.

3. When all are connected, it should be a moving, bobbing, noisy, humming machine. Try commanding it to speed up, slow down, or break down.

4. If your group is large enough, divide into two groups (8–10 each) so each can see the other machine. Every machine will always be different.

5. An extension of this exercise might be to try message machines: a happy machine, an angry machine, a lonely machine. Using words and sounds, try a litter machine (throwing cans and wrappers), a begging machine, an ecology machine, an advertising machine, an assembly line.

6. Your group members will be more creative in these ideas if you have given them a chance to explore a range of movement and sound first. You may need to take a break part-way through and loosen them up again.

GIVING FACES *(5–10 minutes)*

Rationale

This exercise is like Noises and Movement, except it increases contact between members of the group.

Exercise

1. Ask the group to sit on the floor in a tight circle.

2. The leader starts, explaining that he or she will "give" a face to the next person. That person will try to duplicate the face until the giver is satisfied. Then the "mirror" modifies the face into a new one and gives that new face to the next person.

3. Make the original face as weird as possible, so that people will be willing to try anything.

4. Go around the circle several times.

5. As an extension of this exercise, you might want to try having the first person *mold* the second person's face with his hands, like clay, creating a new face. The person whose face has been molded finds out what he or she looks like by having the third person mirror the face with his own. The second person then molds the third person's face, and so on. [Warning, some people may find the molding too threatening.]

GIVING MOVEMENT AND SOUND *(10 minutes)*

Rationale

Same as faces.

Exercise

1. Group should form large circle, standing.

2. Leader stands in the center and then creates a movement and sound—perhaps squatting, quacking like a duck, and flapping wings.

3. The leader waddles up to someone in the circle. The chosen person moves into the circle with the leader, duplicating the leader's movement and sound. When the leader is satisfied, he moves out.

4. The new leader then modifies the duck routine into something of his own choice, picks someone else, and the game continues.

MASKS *(10–15 minutes)*

Rationale

To help group members create dialogue and character in a non-threatening way.

Exercise

1. Provide the group with cut-out face masks made from poster board with cartoon-type faces drawn on in magic marker: old people, children, villains, hippies, beauty queens, football players, animals—anything which suggests a character.

2. Each group member selects a mask and creates a voice and body position for the character.

3. Pair up the people and give everyone the same simple conflict situation (i.e., one tries to beg money from the other; one person in a hurry to buy something while the other is taking his time selling; one person sitting in a seat assigned to the other at a play or sporting event, etc.).

4. The pairs hold a dialogue for 1–2 minutes. Then ask everyone to switch partners. Continue

four or five times. Since the whole group is talking at once, there is no audience. Remind the group to let the created character do the talking.

These exercises should help your group members become more comfortable with each other and with their own capabilities to create. (In fact, they may be helpful exercises to warm up for any type of program.) I frequently end such a program by handing out copies of James Thurber's *The Last Flower* (or "The Owl Who Was God," "The Unicorn in the Garden") and let the whole group act out the story while one member reads it. Again, no one is responsible for memorizing lines, and all can be free to move and interpret the story.

Parables from the New Testament; readings from the Old Testament such as Job, Psalms, or Proverbs; poetry; news stories from newspapers or magazines would also be effective. This is your chance as a leader to direct their creative energy toward an issue or idea.

Here are some of Jesus' Parables which make good drama material:

	Matthew
Pearl of great price	13:45-46
Unforgiving servant	18:21-35
Wicked husbandmen in vineyard	21:33-41
Guests declining an invitation to a feast	22:1-14
Strain gnat: swallow camel	23:24
Ten virgins	25:1-13
Sheep and goats	25:31-46

	Luke
Two debtors	7:40-49
Good Samaritan	10:25-37
Friend at midnight	11:5-13
Prodigal son	15:11-24
Elder brother	15:25-32
Rich man and Lazarus	16:19-31
Two prayers	18:9-14

Following a session using Theater Games, your group may move comfortably into role playing, simulation games, play reading, or even play production. But don't forget that the whole concept of exploration of the body as a way of communication, and of assuming another character as demanded by role playing or play production, is really a very difficult process. Adolescents are already unsure of who they are, and adults may have a great deal invested in maintaining their self-image. It may be well to use exercises such as these frequently for warm-up exercises before going on to a script or role.

116

VALUES OF DRAMA

A major benefit which drama can offer to your youth group is involvement and group-building. If you can get them turned on to a script and involved in rehearsals and preparations like costumes, scenery, publicity, lighting, props, you will have a ready-made series of programs, regularly attended by a committed, enthusiastic group of youth. You will learn about and from each other, rely on each other, and become a cohesive group in a way not often experienced in a Sunday evening program series. What is more, you may end up with a production which will help others in your church and community "see what the young people are up to."

CHOOSING PLAYS

A word here about choice of material is in order. Much of what is available in play catalogues under the heading "religious drama" is poor material. Use a good play which has something important to say and then help the group to identify the relationships between the play and their understanding of the Christian faith. After all, the aesthetic taste of today's young people is highly refined, due to the mass media, and material written only for use in churches is not likely to meet the standards we use even in TV viewing. Below are some suggestions for material.

If you're a novice director, start with easy material and work up. A short one-act play, done well and enjoyed by all, is a far better experience than a long, agonizing, poorly-done classic.

An excellent comprehensive resource for the beginner is *Drama Resource*: Resources for Youth Ministry; Volume 2, Number 1, Winter 1970; The Lutheran Church Missouri Synod. (Check to see if this is available in your nearest religious bookstore.)

Most of the plays listed below can be located in your local community or school library. Those marked with a star are available in religious bookstores.

ONE-ACT PLAYS	Cast Size	Issues
Two in a Trap by Arlene Hale*	2 women	poverty/wealth
Hello Out There by William Saroyan	2 men, 1 woman	self-discovery
Wandering by Sanford Wilson	2 men, 1 woman	adolescent looks at life
Infancy by Thornton Wilder	3 men, 2 women	education
Aria da Capo by Edna St. Vincent Millay	4	war and peace
Santa Claus by e.e. cummings	10+	giving
Impromptu by Tad Mosel	2 men, 2 women	communication
Dino by Reginald Rose	10+	juvenile delinquency
Spoon River Anthology by E. L. Masters	any number	people
Three New Dramatic Works and 19 Other Very Short Plays by William Saroyan	any number	short sketches on many subjects

LONGER PLAYS		
Inherit the Wind by Lawrence and Lee	40+	truth (Scopes trial)
J. B. by Archibald MacLeish	20+	based on book of Job
For Heaven's Sake by Kromer and Silver*	10	musical satire on the church
Godspell by Stephen Schwartz	10	musical review based on book of Matthew

ADDITIONAL RESOURCES FOR THE DIRECTOR

The Stage Manager's Handbook by Bert Gruver
(New York: The Drama Book Shop, 1953)

Playmaking with Children from Kindergarten Through Junior High School by Winifred Ward
(New York: Appleton-Century-Crofts, 1957)

RESOURCES

All three volumes of *Respond* contain different listings of resources. If the resource you are looking for is not listed here, try *Respond, Volume 1 or 2.*

No attempt is made to evaluate the resources, but brief descriptions give pertinent information about subject matter, type of media, price, source.

When possible, resources should be previewed before purchasing to determine if they are appropriate for your group.

SYMBOLS

B: Book
F: Film
FS: Filmstrip
MM: Mixed Media
P: Picture or Photo
Ph: Pamphlet
R: Record
SG: Simulation Game
T: Tape

STUDY/ACTION RESOURCES

THE BIBLE

Gospel Game (SG)
Simulates the writing of contemporary gospels of the New Testament under the conditions of New Testament times. Order from: John Washburn, P.O. Box 6855, Santa Rosa, CA 95406. $3.00.

The Last Times (SG)
This game allows you to experience first-century Palestine. The focus is on political and religious events which climax in Passion Week. Rental, $5.00; Sale $10.00. Order from Brite Games, Box 371, Moline, IL 61265.

People Are Talking (R)
Jesus spots originally prepared for radio broadcast. (Available for in-church use only.) Rental $1.00 from: Librarian, Division of Mass Media, The Board of National Missions of the United Presbyterian Church in the U.S.A., Rm. 1901, 475 Riverside Drive, New York, NY 10027.

Simulation Exercises on the Sayings of Jesus (SG)
Experiential activities which help students get "inside" the parables and teachings of Jesus. Order from: John Washburn, P.O. Box 6855, Santa Rosa, CA 95406. $5.00.

Using Biblical Simulations (B)
By Donald Miller, Graydon Snyder, and Robert Neff. Tells how to use simulation and role play to study the Bible. Judson Press. $4.95.

CAREER GUIDANCE

Church Vocations—A New Look (B)
By Murray J. S. Ford. Describes a wide variety of occupations related in some way to the church. Judson Press. $2.50.

First Things First (FS)
Demonstrates the importance of making a vocational decision early in life with a clear Christian motivation or a goal in mind. For junior high up. 80-frame filmstrip, color. Leader's Guide and Reading Record. Order from: Abingdon Audiographics, Nashville, TN 37202.

Life Careers (SG)
A simulation of certain features of the labor market, the education market, and the marriage market. Rental $4.50 from: Simulation, Church Center for the United Nations, 777 United Nations Plaza, Room 10E, New York, NY 10017.

Listen, Listen (F)
Each man must do his own choosing about his life's work and then act accordingly. Order from: Educational Affairs Department, Ford Motor Company, American Road, Dearborn, MI. Free.

CHRISTIAN FAITH AND PERSONAL GROWTH

An Andrew Webber and Tim Rice Interview (T)
A 60-minute cassette tape on which the authors of *Jesus Christ Superstar* discuss how they put the show together, their own views, etc. Discussion guide included. Order from Lutheran Church Supply Store, 2900 Queen Lane, Philadelphia, PA 19129. $5.95.

Is It Always Right to Be Right? (F)
A parable in which a country reaches a crisis because, when differences arose among the people, each side stood firm in its rightness. Animated cartoon; winner of Academy Award for best animated short subject. 16mm film; color; 8 min. Rental $25.00 from: Steven Bosustow Productions, 20548 Pacific Coast Highway, Malibu, CA 90265.

For Man's Sake (B)
By John Faulstich. A 64-page booklet described as a "do-it-yourself" book on theology for high-school-age and older youth. United Church Press. 50¢ at religious bookstores.

The Lesson (R)
A modern parable, originally prepared for radio broadcast. (Available for in-church use only.) Rental $1.00 from: Librarian, Division of Mass Media/The Board of National Missions of the United Presbyterian Church in the U.S.A., Rm. 1901, 475 Riverside Dr., New York, NY 10027.

Let Faith Be Your Camera (MM)
By Wilbur Patterson. Flip chart, 11″ x 17″, designed to illustrate the idea that "faith to the Christian is a continuing dialogue between being and doing." $2.50.

The Doodle Film (F)
The story of a compulsive doodler. Illustrates growing trend away from conformity. 16mm, color, 10 min. Rental $15.00 from Learning Corporation of America, 711 Fifth Ave., New York, NY 10022.

Normal Adolescence (B)
Group for the Advancement of Psychiatry offers insights and helpful information on adolescence. Order from: Family Life Publications, P.O. Box 427, Saluda, NC 28773. $1.65.

Raw Love (RAP 5) (T)
Part of the RAP tape series by Dennis Benson. A six-session study on "the hard, cold truth about a little-understood fact of life." Published by Abingdon Press. Available at religious bookstores. $7.95.

Science and Faith—Twin Mysteries (B)
By William G. Pollard. The Christian looks at similarities and differences in science and faith. Part of the Youth Forum series. Thomas Nelson Inc. $1.95.

Tension (RAP 1) (T)
Part of the RAP tape series by Dennis Benson. Guides a group in understanding and dealing with tension. Published by Abingdon Press. Available in religious bookstores. $7.95.

A Time to Seek (B)
By Lee Fisher. Deals with the issues of life and faith which confront young people today. Abingdon Press. $1.95.

Up the Establishment (RAP 6) (T)
Part of the RAP tape series by Dennis Benson. Subtitled "How to Sell the Body for the Daily Bread While Keeping the Soul Pure and Unmortgaged." Abingdon Press. $7.95 at religious bookstores.

The Value Game (SG)
Helps groups understand how values change and are changed by events and situations. People try to make honest decisions as they judge the actions of others. 10-20 situations occur. 5-35 people. Time: 1-2 hours. Herder & Herder. $7.95 at religious bookstores.

What Makes Service Christian (B)
By Boyd Nelson. Christ came to us in service that we might learn from his example. Biblical values remind followers of Christ that their vocation is of necessity one of service. Friendship Press. 65¢ at religious bookstores.

Why Man Creates (F)
The many aspects of human creativity are well thought-out in this excellent production. Color. 25 minutes. Free from Modern Talking Pictures, 1212 Avenue of the Americas, New York, NY 10036.

Youth Considers Doubt and Frustration (B)
By Paul Holmer. Helps youth deal with adolescent doubts and frustrations. Thomas Nelson Inc. $1.50 at religious bookstores.

Youth Considers Personal Moods (B)
By Reuel Howe. Helps youth understand and deal with the "moods" they experience during adolescence. Thomas Nelson Inc. $1.95 at religious bookstores.

Youth—Where the Action Is (B)
A Through-the-Week resource for youth which relates home and school issues, such as science, history, and problems facing the nation and world. Cooperative Press. Leader's Guide, $3.45; Student's Book, $1.75 at religious bookstores.

COMMUNICATION

Communicating with Junior Highs (B)
By Robert Browning. How to listen to, learn from, and engage in dialogue with younger teens. Abingdon Press. $1.95 at religious bookstores.

Generation Gap (SG)
The game simulates the interaction between a youth and his parent. Certain issues are set up which must be reconciled. Conflict is present. Parents and teens do not compete against each other but against other teens and parents playing the game. 4-10 players. ½-1 hour. Western Publishing Co., Inc. $15.00 at religious bookstores.

High Wall? Low Wall? No Wall? (B)
By Ruth Cheney. A look at the walls that separate parts of our lives; between friends; youth and their parents; black and white; rich and poor. Especially for junior highs. Friendship Press. $1.75 at religious bookstores.

Parent-Adolescent Communication Inventory, Form A (Ph)
Assessment of parent-teen relations for both counseling and teaching. Provides clues to communication difficulties, promotes understanding. Order from Family Life Publications, Inc., Box 427, Saluda, NC 28773. Specimen set, 35¢.

Youth Considers Parents as People (B)
By Randolph C. Miller. Attacks the communication gap between parents and youth. Thomas Nelson Inc. $1.50 at religious bookstores.

DRUGS, ALCOHOL, SMOKING

Barney Butt (F)
Animated film cartoon dealing with smoking and the heart. 16mm, color, 12 min. Contact your local Heart Association for rental.

Drugs (RAP 4) (T)
Part of the RAP tape series by Dennis Benson. Helps a group study the implications of drug abuse. Published by Abingdon Press. $7.95 at religious bookstores.

The Drug Game (F)
A short TV spot on drug abuse. 16mm, color, 60 sec. Rental $5.00 from: Librarian, Division of Mass Media/The Board of National Missions of the United Presbyterian Church in the U.S.A., Room 1901, 475 Riverside Drive, New York, NY 10027.

Family Life Filmstrips, Series I (FS)
An objective overview of vital, current health areas. For junior high up.
   1. Tobacco and Your Health
   2. Alcohol and Your Health
   3. Venereal Disease and Your Health
   4. Drug Misuse and Your Health
Each filmstrip with Teacher's Guide, $7.00. Set of four filmstrips, 2 records, 4 teacher's guides: $32.50. Order from: Family Life Publications, Inc., P.O. Box 427, Saluda, NC 28773.

The Long Trip (F)
A short TV spot on drug abuse. 16mm, color, 60 sec. Rental, $5.00 from: Librarian, Division of Mass Media/The Board of National Missions of the United Presbyterian Church in the U.S.A., Room 1901, 475 Riverside Drive, New York, NY 10027.

99 Plus Films on Drugs
Evaluation of films on drugs and drug abuse. Order from: Educational Film Library Association, 17 West 60th Street, New York, NY 10023. $3.00.

Pot Is Rot and Other Horrible Facts About Bad Things (B)
By Jean C. Vermes. Facts youth need to know about health dangers in cigarettes, alcohol, drugs, and VD. Association Press. $1.75.

Smoke (F)
A satirical film depicting the reasons people smoke. 16mm, b&w, 10 min. Rental: $6.00, from Cinema 16, 175 Lexington Avenue, New York, NY 10016.

What About Drinking? (F)
A discussion of the problems of drinking. 16mm, b&w, 10 min. Order from: The Methodist Service Department, 100 Maryland Avenue, N.E., Washington, D.C. 20002.

Young People and Drinking (B)
By Arthur H. Cain. A psychologist specializing in treating alcoholics provides information from which youth can make wise decisions for themselves. John Day Company, 1968. $3.40.

ECOLOGY

Cry of the Marsh (F)
This film documents vividly the destructive processes to wild life and natural resources when a prairie marsh is drained and burned. Color, 12 min. Rental, $14.00 from: Bill Snyder Films, Box 2784, Fargo, ND 51802.

Earthcare Packet (MM)
Packet of materials on the various aspects of Christian concern for the environment, including a book, *New Ethic for a New Earth,* leader's guide and resource pamphlets. Friendship Press. $3.95 at religious bookstores.

124

Ecology Probe—Planet Earth (F)
A serious environmental problem is dealt with by studying the problem through a science fiction treatment. 16mm, color, 10 min. Order from: Fordham Publishing Company, 2377 Hoffman Street, Bronx, NY 10458.

The Environment and You (B)
By Richard A. Baer, Jr. Booklet from Issue and Action Packet. Published by United Church Press. Total packet, $24.95. Booklet, 95¢ at religious bookstores.

Environmental Action: Recycling Resources
A junior high course on environmental problems and solutions. Teacher's manual, student's book, two filmstrips, record, simulation game. $12.50. Order from: Office of Environmental Affairs, Continental Can Company, 633 Third Avenue, New York, NY 10017.

Population (RAP 3) (T)
Part of the RAP tape series by Dennis Benson. Helps a group study the problems of the environment. Published by Abingdon Press. $7.95 at religious bookstores.

INTERNATIONAL MISSION

Conflict (SG)
A game which simulates a futuristic model of a disarmed world based on a nation-state system. Designed to enable learners to consider imaginative alternative structures for the future. For 24-36 players. Rental, $12.50 from: Simulation, Church Center for the United Nations, 777 United Nations Plaza, Room 10E, New York, NY 10017.

Crisis (SG)
Participants become members of six nations and try to resolve a tense situation in a mining area of enormous importance to the entire world. For 18-

36 players. Order from: Western Behavioral Sciences Institute, P.O. Box 1023, La Jolla, CA 92037. $25.00.

The Cross Is Lifted (B)
By Chandran Devanesen. A small volume of poems about India and her people, planned for personal or group use. Sensitive drawings by Frank Wesley illustrate the book, expressing the truths of the Christian faith through the symbols of Indian Art. Friendship Press. $1.25 at religious bookstores.

Mandate for Mission (B)
By Eugene L. Smith. The big, complex world is all around us. What does this constantly changing situation mean to the church? Friendship Press. $1.75 at religious bookstores.

Dangerous Parallel (SG)
A simulation of international negotiation and decision-making in which the participants are divided into six teams representing the cabinets of six nations involved in a world crisis. For 18-36 players. Rental $7.50 from: Simulation, Church Center for the United Nations, 777 United Nations Plaza, Room 10E, New York, NY 10017. Sale $60.00 from Scott Foresman and Company, 1900 East Lake Avenue, Glenview, IL 60025.

End of the Dialogue (F)
A documentary study of apartheid in South Africa. The harsh reality of enforced racial separation and oppression of black Africans by a small white minority is portrayed. Housing, employment, education, recreation, and police surveillance are some of the areas covered. Color, 42 min. Cokesbury. Rental, $15.00 from Mass Media Associates, 2116 North Charles Street, Baltimore, MD 21218.

Fun and Festival from India, Pakistan, Ceylon and Nepal (B)
By Irene Wells and Jean Bothwell. An updating of

this perennial favorite. Contains games, recipes, songs, readings, dress, and many program ideas. A useful book for all ages, both in groups and for solo reading. Friendship Press. 95¢ at religious bookstores.

Future-Maker in India: The Story of Sarah Chakko (B)
By Mary Louise Slater. A gifted teacher gave her students a great legacy: her ideal of poise as a sense of proportion, of appreciation of relative values, both material and spiritual. Miss Chakko, a born leader, was a president of the World Council of Churches. Friendship Press. 95¢ at religious bookstores.

Journey into Nigeria (F)
A film giving a well-rounded view of life in one of the newly independent countries. Presents the situation of the Christian church there and attitude of the church toward missionaries. Color, 35 min. Cokesbury. Rental, $10.00 from Mass Media Associates, 2116 North Charles Street, Baltimore, MD 21218.

Mission with Integrity in India (B)
By Renuka Mukerji Somasekhar. Equally at home in India and the West, the author speaks the truth in love about both churches and mission boards and about their often uneasy relationships in these days of change. She has extensive experience within the Indian church. Friendship Press. $1.25 at religious bookstores.

Sing the Glory of Africa (FS)
The glories of Africa, past and present, are celebrated in this full-color filmstrip. Side 1 of recording contains narrative of script. Side 2 includes music and folktales from Africa. Color. 33⅓ rpm record. Sale, $10.00 from: The Service Center, 7820 Reading Road, Cincinnati, OH 45237.

Tauw (F)
A typical day in the life of a 20-year-old African man points up problems of social change; the generation gap, the breakdown of family life. Filmed in Dakar by the Senegalese producer Ousmane Sambene, whose sensitive work has won him world recognition. Color, 26 minutes. Cokesbury. Rental, $12.00 from Mass Media Associates, or your local film depository.

Walk the Distant Hills: The Story of Longri Ao (B)
By Richard G. Beers. This Christian leader of India played a reconciling role when India was being separated from British rule and had to cope with tribal divisiveness. As a strong man of peace, he walked the Naga hills in behalf of unity. Friendship Press. 95¢ at religious bookstores.

JUSTICE AND CIVIL LIBERTIES

Confronted! (B)
By Myra Scovel, et al. Discussion Starters on Faith and Justice and on India. Walk-on dramas requiring no props or memorization of parts. Groups will find many hours of good discussion flowing from the use of these brief dramas. Friendship Press. $1.35 at religious bookstores.

Don't Church Me In (R)
By Allan E. Sloane. The old struggle between the established church and its newer, more aggressive leaders is dramatized in a witty yet provocative manner. Recording 33⅓ rpm. Friendship Press. $5.00 at religious bookstores.

Get out There and Do Something About Injustice (B)
By Margaret E. Kuhn. A study-action manual to work toward doing faith and having justice. Friendship Press. $1.95 at religious bookstores.

Guide on "Faith and Justice" for Adult and Youth Groups (B)
By Wayne Bryan. Bright, creative, fresh ways of using study materials on Faith and Justice. Friendship Press. $1.25 at religious bookstores.

Good News, Anyone? (B)
By Jean Louise Smith. A group process book helps junior and middle highs analyze ways in which contemporary artists, musicians, and writers may be helping us relate the tenets of the Christian faith to the injustices in modern society. Friendship Press. $2.75 at religious bookstores.

Grace at Point Zero (B)
By Loren E. Halvorson. Writing in the form of an imaginary script of the future, the author takes a hard look at what he calls "an unhealthy separation of Christian faith and social justice." Friendship Press. $1.75 at religious bookstores.

Handbook of Everyday Law (B)
By Martin J. Ross. A home legal encyclopedia which is easy to understand. Harper & Row, Publishers. 95¢ at most bookstores.

Look Back and Dream: Great Moments in Mission (R)
By Warren Mild. Dramatic episodes in the lives of Christians of other generations who sought to relate faith and justice in meaningful ways. Included are Walter Rauschenbusch, early exponent of Christian social action; Dorothea Dix, who campaigned energetically for reform in mental hospitals; William Carey, Robert Raikes. 33⅓ rpm record. Friendship Press. $5.00 at religious bookstores.

See It! Do It! Your Faith in Action (B)
By David Ng. Yes, you *can* do something about injustice—and here is a book to help young people see it and then act to correct it. You will walk through ancient Bethel with the prophet Amos and visit modern Chinatown, San Francisco. You can discover social justice in the arts, learn how to start an underground newspaper, work at renovating a town. And finally, with the help of a list of possibilities, you can plan actions to promote justice in your own town. Friendship Press. $2.50 at religious bookstores.

To Set Things Right: The Bible Speaks on Faith and Justice (B)
By Justin Vander Kolk. Is today's demand among Christians for greater concern for social justice scriptural? Yes, by all means, says the author as he probes the deep biblical roots of the demand for social justice. Here is a Bible study piece for individual or group use that will undergird our understanding of the whole thrust of the "Faith and Justice" issue. Friendship Press. $1.25 at religious bookstores.

Up Against the Law: The Legal Rights of People Under 21 (B)
By Jean Strouse. Explanation of laws which are particularly relevant to youth, in such areas as: students' rights, marriage, drugs, sex, driving, the draft. New American Library Inc. 95¢ at religious bookstores.

Voices of Protest and Hope (B)
Compiled by Elisabeth D. Dodds. The world, through contemporary writers, speaks to the church in no uncertain terms about justice as they see it and seek it. Friendship Press. $1.95 at religious bookstores.

NATIONAL MISSION

Change (RAP 2) (T)
Part of the RAP tape series by Dennis Benson. Helps a group deal with change in society. Published by Abingdon Press. $7.95 at religious bookstores.

127

The Church Resources Game (SG)
A simulation about the mission of the church: what that mission should be, what resources are required, and how existing resources can best be used. The game forces the players to think about mission in the concrete terms of resources and situations. Cost: $9.95. Available for purchase directly from Urbandyne, 5659 S. Woodlawn Ave., Chicago, IL 60637 or Urbandyne, P.O. Box 741, Saratoga, CA 95070.

PEACE

The Draft—Decisions, Issues, Actions
By Russell G. Claussen. Booklet from Issues and Action Packet. Published by United Church of Christ. Packet, $24.95. Booklet, 95¢ at religious bookstores.

Hiroshima & Nagasaki (F)
Filmed by Japanese photographers immediately after the bombings, this is by far the most poignant statement of the horror of nuclear war ever produced. 16mm, b&w; 15 min. Rental, $15.00 from SANE, 1307 Sansom Street, Philadelphia, PA 19107. *Rental within 24-hour bus service of Philadelphia only.*

Interviews with My-Lai Veterans (F)
1971 Academy Award winner for best documentary short. Interview with five American soldiers who were at My-Lai are compressed into a candid recollection. 16mm, color; 22 min. Rental $25.00 from SANE, 1307 Sansom Street, Philadelphia, PA 19107. *Rental within 24-hour bus service of Philadelphia only.*

POVERTY

The Food Crisis (F)
Areas of the world in which starvation is a way of life are contrasted with those of abundance. 16mm, b&w; 60 min. Rental $10.00 from: Mass Media Ministries, 2116 North Charles Street, Baltimore, MD 21218.

Hunger and Poverty (B)
By Tilford E. Dudley. Booklet from Issues and Action Packet. Published by United Church of Christ. Packet, $24.95. Booklet, 95¢ at religious bookstores.

If I Were You (B)
By Barbara Smith. A group project book for early teens to stimulate a deeper awareness of the injustices poverty often inflicts on its powerless victims. Friendship Press. $1.75 at religious bookstores.

Liberate the Captives (FS)
Shows how people of low economic status in a community can be brought together and organized to start working toward solutions of their own problems. Color filmstrip. Filmstrip with script $7.50. Filmstrip with record $10.00. Available at religious bookstores.

Starpower (SG)
Players assume roles as members of groups in a class society. Identifies abuses of power, characteristics of social organization, and communication skills. For 20-40 players. Complete kit, rental, $3.00 from: Simulation, Church Center for the United Nations, 777 United Nations Plaza, Room 10E, New York, NY 10017. Sale: instructions only, $3.00; complete kit, $35.00 from: Western Behavioral Sciences Institute, P.O. Box 1023, La Jolla, CA 92037.

Whenever People Hurt (FS)
The problem of hunger through the eyes of American youth. Sale, $3.50 from: National Council of Churches, 475 Riverside Drive, New York, NY 10027.

POWER

Disarmament (SG)
A simulation which involves two groups in the problems of conflict, trust, and negotiation. For 8-30 players. Instructions and discussion guide available from: Simulation, Church Center for the United Nations, 777 United Nations Plaza, Room 10E, New York, NY 10017.

Napoli (SG)
A simulation in which the participants serve as members of a legislature and attempt to be re-elected at the end of a term. Valuable ethical reflection may come from considering the sources and power of influences on their election. For about 40 players. Rental, $4.50 from: Simulation, Church Center for the United Nations, 777 United Nations Plaza, Room 10E, New York, NY 10017.

The Money Game (SG)
Simulates some of the economic interactions between developed (rich) and developing (poor) nations. For 18 players. 25¢ per copy. Order from *Concern* magazine, 475 Riverside Drive, Room 401, New York, NY 10027.

Plans (SG)
Participants are members of interest groups using their influence to produce change in American society. For 12-36 players. Rental, $4.50 from: Simulation, Church Center for the United Nations, 777 United Nations Plaza, Room 10E, New York, 10017.

Politics Is People (MM)
A study unit for junior highs which deals with political responsibility and encourages action. $3.50. Order from: Christian Board of Publication, Box 179, St. Louis, MO 63166.

Powerplay (SG)
Five teams begin with equal amounts of power. As they interact, the power is redistributed unevenly. For 20-50 players. Instructions available from: Simulation, Church Center for the United Nations, 777 United Nations Plaza, Room 10E, New York, NY 10017.

The Road Game (SG)
A study of competition. Teams (red, blue, green, yellow) attempt to build roads across each other's areas. Permission must be negotiated. Team with most roads wins. 8-35 people. Can be used with youth, children, adults. Time: 45 minutes to two hours. Herder & Herder. $7.95 at religious bookstores.

RACE RELATIONS

A Bibliography of Negro History and Culture for Young Readers (B)
By Miles M. Jackson Jr. Where to find materials on Negro history. University of Pittsburgh Press. $2.50 at most bookstores.

Black-American History and Culture (R)
A "stereo history" of black America. Order from: Scholastic Records, 906 Sylvan Avenue, Englewood Cliffs, NJ 07632.

Black Resources Center (MM)
For information about current black resources, contact: Black Resources Center, Department of Educational Development, Division of Christian Education, National Council of Churches, 475 Riverside Drive, Room 720, New York, NY 10027.

Bury My Heart at Wounded Knee (B)
By Dee Brown. Describes the "plunder" of American Indians by the white man during the second half of the nineteenth century. Holt, Rinehart & Winston. $10.95 at most bookstores.

Christian Beliefs and Anti-Semitism (B)
By Charles Y. Glock and Rodney Stark. Asks: "Does the Christian faith currently have any effect on attitudes toward Jews?" Harper & Row, Publishers. $1.95 at religious bookstores.

The Ebony Book of Black Achievement (B)
By Margaret Peters. A resource for black history. Gives biographies of outstanding black men and women. Johnson Publishing Company. $4.95 at religious bookstores.

Freedomways, A Quarterly Review of the Freedom Movement (P)
Freedomways Associates, Inc., 799 Broadway, NY 10003. $3.50 a year.

The Jesus Bag (B)
By William H. Grier and Price M. Cobbs. Case histories and commentary on the black experience in religion. McGraw-Hill. $6.95 at most bookstores.

Let's Face Racism (B)
By Nathan Wright, Jr. The Christian looks at racism. Part of the Youth Forum Series. Thomas Nelson Inc. $1.95 at religious bookstores.

Life and Times of Frederick Douglass (B)
Edited by Genevieve S. Gray. Biography of the runaway slave who became an advisor to Abraham Lincoln. Grossett & Dunlap. $4.50 at most bookstores.

The Mechanical Man (F)
A short TV spot on race relations. 16mm, color. 30 sec. Rental $5.00 from: Librarian, Division of Mass Media, The Board of National Missions of the United Presbyterian Church in the U.S.A., Room 1901, 475 Riverside Drive, New York, NY 10027.

The Negro in America, A Bibliography (B)
Compiled by Elizabeth W. Miller and Mary L.

Fisher. Cambridge, MA: Harvard University Press. $10.00 at most bookstores.

Today's Negro Voices by Beatrice M. Murphy (B)
Poems of black youth from 13 to 20. Simon and Schuster. $2.95 at most bookstores.

We Will Suffer and Die If We Have To (D)
By Colin Hodgetts. A folk play about the polarization of blacks torn between the nonviolent and violent movements. Judson Press. $1.95 at religious bookstores.

SEX AND FAMILY LIFE

Between Parent and Teenager (B)
By Haim G. Ginott. Specific communication advice, constructively given. The Macmillan Company. $5.95 at most bookstores.

Christian View of Sex Education (B)
By Martin F. Wessler. Opportunities for sex education by pastors, teachers, youth workers. Offers approaches and programs. Concordia. $2.25 at religious bookstores.

Dating Problems Checklist (Ph)
Enables high school and college students to register their problems and talk freely with counselors and group leaders. Order from: Family Life Publications, Inc., Box 427, Saluda, NC 28773. Specimen set 35¢.

Facts About Sex (B)
By Sol Gordon. A first book about sex for young people who do not like to read but want to know. John Day. $3.95; paper, $1.90 at most bookstores.

Facts You Should Know About VD (B)
By Andre Blanzaco, et al. Gives young people information they should have. Lothrop, Lee and Shepherd. $3.95 at most bookstores.

Family Life Filmstrips, Series 2 (FS)
Deals with problems faced by youth and attempts to instill a healthy respect for the consequences of undisciplined reaction and experimentation. Titles:
Running Away
Venereal Disease
Unplanned Parenthood
Suicide
Order from: Family Life Publications, Inc., P.O. Box 427, Saluda, NC 28773. Each filmstrip with teacher's guide: $8.00. Set of four filmstrips, 2 records, 4 guides: $38.00.

The First Nine Months of Life (B)
By Geraldine Flanagan. Development of a baby from fertilized egg to birth. Illustrated and detailed. Simon and Schuster. $4.95 at most bookstores.

The Human Reproductive System (B)
By Morris Krieger and Alan Guttmacher. Details and explains human reproduction in simple language. Thoroughly illustrated. Basic biology in color. Sterling Publishing Co. $4.95 at most bookstores.

Life Can Be Sexual (B)
By Elmer N. Witt. Shows how sex, sexuality, and Christianity interrelate. For ages 15 and over. Concordia Publishing Co. $2.25 at religious bookstores.

Lucy (F)
The story of an unwed, pregnant teenager in a Puerto Rican family. Unusual insight into the feelings of the girl, her boyfriend, her family. 16mm, color, 13 min. Order from: Pictura Films Distribution Corp., 43 W. 16th Street, New York, NY 10011. Rental, $25.00.

Male/Female (B)
Contains leader's guidance and student's material for junior high course in sex education. The Seabury Press, Inc. $1.75 at religious bookstores.

Resource Guide in Sex Education for the Mentally Retarded (B)
Resources for specialized instruction in sex education. Order from SIECUS Publications Office, 1855 Broadway, New York, NY 10023. $2.00.

Sex Before Twenty (B)
By Helen Southard. Help in making constructive decisions about dating and sex behavior for junior high and above. J. P. Dutton. $3.50 at most bookstores.

Sex Knowledge Inventory—Form Y (Ph)
Explores information and misinformation about sexuality. A good opener for a sex education program, if used wisely. Order from: Family Life Publications, Inc., Box 427, Saluda, NC 28773. Specimen set 35¢.

SIECUS Study Guides (B)
Study guides for various aspects of sex education and family life education:

#G01 Sex Education
#G02 Homosexuality
#G03 Masturbation
#G04 Characteristics of Male and Female Sexual Responses
#G05 Premarital Sexual Standards
#G11 Sexual Encounters Between Adults and Children
#G13 Concerns of Parents about Sex Education
#G14 Teenage Pregnancy: Prevention and Treatment

Order from: SIECUS Publications Office, 1855 Broadway, New York, NY 10023. 50¢ each.

Teenage Sex Counselor (B)
A book for youth reluctant to seek or receive per-

131

son to person guidance. Sympathetic, warmly human help for directing all aspects of maturing toward a well-adjusted adulthood. Barron's Educational Series. $1.50 at most bookstores.

To Be a Woman (F)
A film showing girls and young women speaking for themselves, about their attitudes, self-images, and their basic convictions. Discussion oriented. 16mm, color; 13 min. Order from Billy Budd Films, Inc., 235 E. 57th St., Room 8D, New York, NY 10022. Rental, $17.50.

Understanding Sex (B)
By Alan F. Guttmacher. A frank and commonsense book mainly for youth but also of great help to teachers, counselors, and parents. New American Library. $4.95 at most bookstores.

When You Marry (B)
By Evelyn Duvall and Reuben Hill. A most constructive book for older teens with serious thoughts about marriage. Association Press. $5.95 at most bookstores.

Why Wait Till Marriage (B)
By Evelyn Mills Duvall. A book to help youth understand the reasons for sexual moral standards. Association Press. 75¢ (paper) at most bookstores.

Your Dating Days (B)
By Paul Landis. Helps youth understand the opposite sex, decide when to marry, and know how to select a mate. McGraw-Hill. $3.25 at most bookstores.

Youth Considers Marriage (B)
By David R. Mace. Helps youth look at the problems and fulfillments of marriage. Part of the Youth Forum series. Thomas Nelson Inc. $1.50 at religious bookstores.

WORSHIP/CELEBRATION

Alleluia (B)
Songbook for inner-city parishes. From Cooperative Recreation Service, Inc., Delaware, OH 43105.

Banners and Such (B)
A creative approach to banner-making, written from actual workshop experiences. $4.00. Order from: Center for Contemporary Celebration, 1400 East 53rd Street, Chicago, IL 60615.

Buttons
Three original designs on buttons which can be passed out during celebrations:
1. Ankh: life symbol
2. Whole Earth—Whole People
3. Let Us Live
35¢ each. Order from: Center for Contemporary Celebration, 1400 East 53rd Street, Chicago, IL 60615.

Celebrate Life (R)
A youth-oriented record with "journey kit" (booklet which contains song lyrics and line drawings). Songs by Paul Hansen. Cover unfolds to make a 12″ x 24″ poster. Order from: Youth Ministry, 2900 Queen Lane, Philadelphia, PA 19129. $6.50.

Celebration for Modern Man (R)
A new concept in acoustical liturgy recorded by the Dukes of Kent jazz ensemble and the Voices of Celebration. $5.25 at religious bookstores.

Celebration Now (F)
The words and music for three contemporary Christian songs provide an audio "backdrop" for scenes of Christian acceptance. 16mm, color, 12 min.; produced by Family Films. Rental $14.00 from religious film libraries.

Change (MM)
A multimedia presentation with three reels of film (two are silent) to be run simultaneously on three 16mm film projectors and a wall large enough to project three images side by side, on three screens. Content covers the change in such areas as ecology, medicine, technology, and the concepts of God. Rental $13.00 from: Division of Mass Media, Room 1901, 475 Riverside Drive, New York, NY 10027.

Don't Turn Me Off, Lord: And Other Jailhouse Meditations (B)
By Carl F. Burke. A new collection of meditations and prayers originally prepared for use in the chapel of the jail where the author has been chaplain since 1963. Association Press. Cloth, $3.50; paper, $1.75 at religious bookstores.

The Dust and Ashes Songbook (B)
By Jim Moore and Tom Page. Songs for the Christian to use both inside and outside the church. Abingdon Press. Book, $1.50; record, $4.98 at religious bookstores.

The Holy Family (FS)
Displays and interprets nativity paintings by artists from Asia and Africa. Color filmstrip and record. Sale, $5.00 from National Council of Churches, 475 Riverside Drive, New York, NY 10027.

Hymns Hot and Carols Cool (B)
Singable tunes with words of faith. Proclamation Productions. $1.00 at religious bookstores.

Let Us Break Bread Together (B)
By Carl Staplin and Dale Miller. Guide for a contemporary communion service. Includes songs with guitar accompaniment. Bethany Press. $1.25 at religious bookstores.

Multi-Media Box (MM)
Hand-painted slides, material for making film loops, a tape of original music and sound, plus directions for creating media for use in a celebration (or in a teaching-learning experience). Order from: Synesthetics, Inc., 5933 16th St., N.W., Washington, D.C. 20011. $27.50.

Now Songs (B)
A collection of contemporary gospel songs. Abingdon Press. $2.50 at religious bookstores.

Revelation Now (F)
Three contemporary Christian songs from the well-known "Hymns for Now" collection provide a musical background for integrated visuals which show a typical nineteen- or twenty-year-old boy facing the trauma of growing up. Produced by Family Films. Rental $14.00 from religious film libraries.

Raise a Jubilee: Music in Youth Ministry (MM)
Resource for youth and adults. Discusses ways music is integrated into youth ministry. Includes two soundsheets. Published by Graded Press, Nashville, TN 37202. $4.25.

Songs for Celebration (B)
A hymnal for the church wherever it's happening! Order from: Center for Contemporary Celebration, 1400 East 53rd St., Chicago, IL 60615. $2.75.

Teaching and Celebrating Advent in Home and Church (Ph)
Packet of eight pamphlets on Advent. Order from Griggs Educational Service, 1033 Via Madrid, Livermore, CA 94550. $3.00.

Time Being (MM)
A variety of materials for preparing a celebration "happening" of up to three hours, for groups of ten to thirty. Contains weather balloons, equip-

ment for a light show, sheet of plastic, instructions for using taste and smell in meditation, how-to instructions for celebration. Order from: John and Mary Harrell, Box 9006, Berkeley, CA 94709. $17.00.

A Time to Dance (B)
By Margaret Fisk Taylor. How to use symbolic movement or interpretive dancing in worship/celebration. United Church Press. $1.95 at religious bookstores.

Ventures in Worship (B)
A loose-leaf collection of tested models and forms of contemporary worship. Order from: Dr. D. J. Randolph, 1908 Grand Avenue, Nashville, TN 37203. $1.50.

Ventures in Worship #2 (MM)
A packet of worship materials. Abingdon Press. $2.50 at religious bookstores.

COMMUNITY MINISTRIES

God's Turf (B)
By Bob Combs. Describes the ministry of Teen Challenge to street youth and addicts. Old Tappan, NJ: Fleming H. Revell Co. $2.50 at religious bookstores.

It's Happening with Youth (B)
By Janice M. Corbett and Curtis L. Johnson. Description of youth ministries that have developed in response to community needs. Harper & Row, Publishers. $4.95 at religious bookstores.

CAMPING

Backpacking (B)
By R. C. Rethmel. Specific information on just how the backpacker keeps down the weight of his

pack is the primary purpose of this book. Burgess. 95¢ at most bookstores.

Cameron Daycamp Manual (B)
A manual for training teenage-volunteer leadership for an inner-city daycamp. Order from: Griggs Educational Service, 1033 Via Madrid, Livermore, CA 94550. $3.00.

The Fun in Winter Camping (B)
How-to-do-it suggestions for winter experiences in the out-of-doors. Association Press. $1.00 at religious bookstores.

Let the Bible Speak Outdoors (B)
By Mary Elizabeth Mason. Insight, inspiration, and practical help for leaders in outdoor experiences. National Council of Churches. 70¢ at religious bookstores.

Recreation for Retarded Teenagers and Young Adults (B)
By Bernice Carlson and David R. Ginglend. Especially valuable for the camp leader. Abingdon Press. $4.95 at religious bookstores.

Try the World Out (MM)
Camping resources for early teens. Emphasizes relationships between campers and their physical environment. Leader's book, filmstrip, 2 records, student's book. Abingdon Press. $7.50 at religious bookstores.

Voices for the Wilderness (B)
Edited by William Schwartz. Leading ecology spokesmen explain their concern for the preservation of the wilderness. Ballantine. $1.25 at most bookstores.

LEADER DEVELOPMENT

Basic Bible Study for Teachers (MM)
A self-instructional filmstrip kit which trains teach-

ers to identify key persons of the Old Testament, as well as to use basic Bible reference books. Filmstrip, cassette tape recording, leader's manual, participant's worksheets. Order from: Griggs Educational Service, P.O. Box 363, Livermore, CA 94550. $12.00.

Christian Education for Socially Handicapped Children and Youth (B)
By Eleanor Ebersole. A manual for chaplains and teachers of persons under custody. United Church Press. $1.25 at religious bookstores.

Communicating the Gospel Today (MM)
A book in a box which examines the contemporary situation and describes a method for drawing theological implications. Includes directions for a workshop in non-verbal activity, art cards, sounds, incense, light. Order from John and Mary Harrell, Box 9006, Berkeley, CA 94709. $14.00.

Education and Ecstasy (B)
By G. B. Leonard. Describes a concept of learning which applies to all living things. Dell Publishing Co. $2.25 at most bookstores.

Film and Slide Making Kit (MM)
Contains everything you need for a class to create their own 16mm film and sets of slides without cameras. Order from Griggs Educational Service, 1033 Via Madrid, Livermore, CA 94550. $20.00.

40 Ways to Teach in Groups (B)
By Martha Leypoldt. A variety of group methods for learning, plus the resources to use with each method. Judson Press. $2.50 at religious bookstores.

Gaming (B)
By Dennis Benson. Helps for leaders and groups who want to create their own learning games. Includes two records which serve as resources for games described in the book. Abingdon Press. $4.95 at religious bookstores.

Growing as a Group (B)
By Robert R. Hansel. Booklet from Issues and Action Packet. United Church Press. Packet, $24.95. Booklet, 95¢ at religious bookstores.

A Handbook of Structured Experiences for Human Relations Training, Vol. III (B)
This book, plus volumes I and II, contain a wide variety of experiences that can be utilized in human relations training. Order from: University Press Associates, P.O. Box 615, Iowa City, IA 52240. $3.00.

Resources Galore (Ph)
Listings of fresh resources for creative educational ministries in the church. Order from: Gramercy Plaza, B-F, 130 East 18th Street, New York, NY 10005. $1.00.

Slide and Film Making Manual (B)
How to make slides and films without a camera. Order from: Griggs Educational Service, 1033 Via Madrid, Livermore, CA 94550. $2.00.

Teaching and Celebrating Lent—Easter (Ph)
A packet of eight pamphlets designed for teachers to use as resources in the recognition and celebration of the season of Lent and Easter. Titles: "Some Questions of Concern"; "Days to Remember and Celebrate"; "Children's Creative Writing"; "An Easter Story"; "Biblical Resources"; "Teaching Activities"; "Family Activities"; "Bibliography." Order from: Griggs Educational Service, P.O. Box 362, Livermore, CA 94550. $3.00 plus postage.

Teaching and Learning (F)
Shows actual class sessions with junior highs and discusses the methods used. 16mm, color; 22 min. Rental $12.50, from film libraries.

Teaching Early Adolescents Creatively (B)
By Edward D. Seely. A manual for church school teachers. The Westminster Press. $2.95 at religious bookstores.

Young People and Their Culture (B)
By Ross Snyder. Ways of creating a meaningful youth culture, with specific resource suggestions. Abingdon Press. $4.50 at most bookstores.

Youth, World, and Church (B)
By Sara Little. Shows how youth, who are full members of the congregation, can become involved in the church's mission. John Knox Press. $1.95 at religious bookstores.

Catalogs

Argus Communications
Tapes, posters, books, buttons. Order from: Argus Communications, 3505 North Ashland Ave., Chicago, IL 60657.

Audio-Visual Resource Guide (B)
Over 1,800 listings of films, filmstrips, recordings, and slides, evaluated for religious education. $3.95. Order from: National Council of Churches, 475 Riverside Drive, New York, NY 10027.

Council Press Catalogue (B)
Catalog of resources available through the National Council of Churches in the area of Christian education, mission, overseas ministries, etc. Order from National Council of Churches, 475 Riverside Drive, New York, NY 10027.

A Catalog of Plays for Church Use
Order from: Baker's Plays, 100 Summer St., Boston, MA 02110.

Contemporary Drama Service
Catalog of services. Includes drama, playbits, and entertainments. Order from: Contemporary Drama Service, Box 68, Downers Grove, IL 60515.

Drug Abuse Catalog
Listing of materials related to drug abuse. $1.00. Order from: Presbyterian Distribution Service, 225 Varick Street, New York, NY 10014.

F.E.L. Church Publications
Catalog of music, recordings, and folk hymns. Order from: F.E.L. Church Publications, 22 East Huron Street, Chicago, IL 60611.

Full Circle
Interesting posters, books, films. Order from: Full Circle, 218 East 72nd Street, New York, NY 10021.

Guidance Catalog
Materials on drug education, motivational guidance, career/vocational guidance, etc. Order from: Guidance Associates of Pleasantville, NY 10570.

Guide to Educational Media (B)
By Margaret I. Rufsvold and Carolyn Guss. A list of media catalogs for films (including free films), filmstrips, kinescopes, records, tapes, programmed instruction materials, slides, public school personnel, but helpful for religious educators also. Some catalogs are free. $2.50 from American Library Association, 50 East Huron St., Chicago, IL 60611.

Kairos
Worship resources, films. Order from: Kairos, Box 24056, Minneapolis, MN 55424.

Media for Christian Formation: A Guide to Audio-Visual Resources (B)
By William A. Dalglish. Comprehensive listing of audio-visual resources that can be used in a local church. $7.50 at religious bookstores.

Reigner Recording Library Catalog
Lending library of sound recordings and sound

motion pictures, especially of well-known ministers and public speakers. Includes worship services, radio programs, television programs. Order from: Union Theological Seminary in Virginia, Richmond, VA.

PERIODICALS

Christian Art
Especially recommended for those utilizing the creative arts. Subscription $6.00. Order from: *Christian Art,* 1801 West Greenleaf Ave., Chicago, IL 60626.

Cultural Information Service
Capsulizing of the cultural scene in seven areas: Americana, Art, Drama, Film, Literature, Rock Music, Television. Subscription $6.00. Order from: Youth Ministry, 2900 Queen Lane, Philadelphia, PA 19129.

Going to College Handbook
An annual in periodical format which contains articles helpful to youth who are anticipating going to college. Order from: Outlook Publishers, 512 East Main St., Richmond, VA 23219. $1.00.

Mass Media Ministries
Bi-weekly newsletter reviewing new resources, especially films and TV programs. Subscription $10.00 per year. Order from: Mass Media Ministries, 2116 North Charles St., Baltimore, MD 21218.

Medialog
A monthly publication of the Teacher Learning Center, 1942 Virginia Street, Berkeley, CA 94709. $5.00 per ten issues.

Media Mix
Up-to-date information on films, TV, print, recordings, and other media. Subscription $5.00. Order from: George A. Pflaum, Publisher, 38 W. Fifth Street, Dayton, Ohio 45402.

Modern Media Teacher
For media people. Subscription $5.00. Order from George A. Pflaum, Publisher, 38 W. Fifth Street, Dayton, Ohio 45402.

Probe
Newsletter about new resources and creative approaches to church and community work. Subscription, $5.00 per year. Order from: *Probe,* Christian Associates of Southwest Pennsylvania, 220 Grant Street, Pittsburgh, PA 15219.

Scan
Monthly newsletter which evaluates new resources. Subscription, $6.00 from: *Scan,* P.O. Box 12811, Pittsburgh, PA 15241.

Simulation Sharing Service
An ecumenical service to provide the use of simulation gaming in the church's ministry. Subscription: $5.00 from: Simulation Sharing Service, Box 1176, Richmond, VA 23209.

Spectrum
Feature articles, media section with survey of films, filmstrips, and recordings. Subscription, $5.00. Order from: Division of Christian Education, National Council of Churches, 475 Riverside Drive, New York, NY 10027.

INDEX TO VOLUMES 1, 2, and 3 of RESPOND